Discovering the Riches of the Word

Intersections

INTERDISCIPLINARY STUDIES IN EARLY MODERN CULTURE

VOLUME 38 – 2015

The titles published in this series are listed at *brill.com/inte*

Discovering the Riches of the Word

Religious Reading in Late Medieval and Early Modern Europe

Edited by

Sabrina Corbellini
Margriet Hoogvliet
Bart Ramakers

BRILL

LEIDEN | BOSTON

Cover illustration: "Dat boeck vanden leven ons liefs heren Jhesu Christi" (Zwolle, Peter Os van Breda: 20 november 1495). Groningen, University Library, INC 131 A.

Library of Congress Cataloging-in-Publication Data

Discovering the riches of the word : religious reading in late medieval and early modern Europe / edited by Sabrina Corbellini, Margriet Hoogvliet and Bart Ramakers.
     pages cm. — (Intersections : interdisciplinary studies in early modern culture, ISSN 1568-1181 ; volume 38)
     Includes bibliographical references and index.
     ISBN 978-90-04-29038-9 (hardback : alk. paper) — ISBN 978-90-04-29039-6 (e-book) 1. Christian literature—History and criticism. 2. Christians—Books and reading. 3. Christianity and literature. I. Corbellini, Sabrina, 1969– editor.

BR117.D57 2015
809'.93527405—dc23

2014048902

This publication has been typeset in the multilingual 'Brill' typeface. With over 5,100 characters covering Latin, IPA, Greek, and Cyrillic, this typeface is especially suitable for use in the humanities. For more information, please see brill.com/brill-typeface.

ISSN 1568-1181
ISBN 978-90-04-29038-9 (hardback)
ISBN 978-90-04-29039-6 (e-book)

Contents

Notes on the Editors

Sabrina Corbellini
is Rosalind Franklin Fellow at the University of Groningen (department of Medieval History). Her current research is concerned with the reconstruction of the readership of religious texts in late medieval Europe. From 2008 to 2013, she was Principal Investigator of the ERC-Starting Grant project "Holy Writ and Lay Readers".

Margriet Hoogvliet
is a lecturer and researcher at the University of Groningen and Leeds. Her current research is concerned with readers of biblical and religious texts in French during the fifteenth and early sixteenth centuries. She has also published extensively on text-image relations, political communication in the period of Catherine de Médicis, and the history of cartography (*Pictura et scriptura: textes, images et herméneutique des mappae mundi (XIIIᵉ–XVIᵉ s.)*, Turnhout: 2007).

Bart Ramakers
is Professor of Historical Dutch Literature at the University of Groningen. He specialises in medieval and sixteenth-century drama and has a particular interest in the intersections between performative and visual culture. He is an editor of the *Netherlands Yearbook for History of Art* (NKJ).

Notes on the Contributors

Élise Boillet
is a researcher at the Centre d'Études Supérieures de la Renaissance (Université François-Rabelais, Tours). Her research interests centre on early modern Italian religious literature. At the CNRS, she coordinates the research theme, *Profane et sacré dans la culture européenne des XIVᵉ–XVIIᵉ siècles.*

Suzan Folkerts
is a postdoctoral researcher at the University of Groningen with a NWO Veni grant for her project "From monastery to market place. Towards a new history of New Testament translations and urban religious culture in the Low Countries (c. 1450–1540)". In 2010, she earned her PhD with a dissertation on the manuscript transmission of medieval saints' lives.

Éléonore Fournié
is an independent Scholar. She received her PhD in Medieval history from the École des Hautes Etudes en Sciences Sociales in Paris and graduated from the École du Louvre in Paris. She is the author of *L'iconographie de la Bible historiale* (Turnhout, 2012).

Wim François
is Research Professor of the Special Research Fund of the KU Leuven. He focusses on the place of vernacular Bible reading in the early modern period, as well as on Bible commentaries edited by Louvain and Douai theologians during the Golden Age of Catholic biblical scholarship (1550–1650).

Ian Johnson
is Reader in English and a member of the Institute of Mediaeval Studies at the University of St Andrews. He is founding General Editor of *The Mediaeval Journal* and was for many years General Editor of *Forum for Modern Language Studies*. Among his latest books is *The Middle English Life of Christ: Academic Discourse, Translation and Vernacular Theology* (Turnhout, 2013).

Hubert Meeus
is Professor of Dutch Renaissance Literature and Theatre History at the University of Antwerp. His subjects of research are literature and theatre in the Low Countries during the sixteenth and seventeenth centuries and the history of the printed book from its invention until 1800.

Matti Peikola

is Professor of English at the University of Turku. His research interests include Middle and Early Modern English language, discourse and textual scholarship, codicology and bibliography, Wycliffite studies, and writing literacy in early colonial New England. He is currently working on a critical edition of *Wyclif's Wycket* as well as exploring patterns of production and transmission of the Wycliffite Bible in later medieval England.

Elisabeth Salter

is currently Professor of English and Head of the Department of English at the University of Hull. She is developing her research on popular reading in late medieval and early modern England by extending her work on popular religious reading and creativity, with a particular focus on works of religious instruction including catechetical texts.

Lucy Wooding

is Senior Lecturer in Early Modern History at King's College London. Her research interests centre on late medieval and Reformation England, with a particular interest in the intersections between visual and print culture. She is the author of *Rethinking Catholicism in Reformation England* (Oxford, 2000) and *Henry VIII* (2008).

Federico Zuliani

is a PhD student at The Warburg Institute, University of London. He studied at the Universities of Milan, Copenhagen and Geneva. His subjects of research are religious minorities in the sixteenth and seventeenth centuries, especially in Denmark and Italy, and the history of biblical exegesis.

List of Illustrations

Introduction: Discovering the Riches of the Word

Sabrina Corbellini, Margriet Hoogvliet, Bart Ramakers

Religious learning involves reading. More than that, it is largely constituted by reading [...] Religious reading requires and fosters a particular
set of attitudes to what is read, as well as reading practices that comport
well with those attitudes; and it implies an epistemology, a set of views
about what knowledge is and about the relations between reading and
the acquisition and retention of knowledge.[1]

With these words, the theologian Paul Griffiths describes the fundamental relationship between the act of reading and the practice of religion, and
emphasizes the extent to which religious reading is strictly connected to the
development of specific attitudes and relations between the reader and the
religious text, relations that are 'at once attitudinal, cognitive, and moral, and
that therefore imply an ontology, an epistemology, and an ethic'.[2] This pecu-
liarity, which characterizes the intensity of the religious reading experience
and the personal engagement required of the reader, is based on two central
features of the religious reading experience, which are only in apparent contradiction with each other: on the one hand the essential stability of the religious text, and on the other the ever-continuous and ever-repeated character
of the religious reading act. As Griffiths so poetically puts it, religious texts are
'understood as a stable and vastly rich resource, one that yields meaning, suggestions (or imperatives) for action, matter for aesthetic wonder, and much
else'. They are often considered as 'a treasure-house, an ocean, a mine: the
deeper religious readers dig, the more ardently they fish, the more mindedly
they seek gold, the greater will be their reward'.[3] The religious text has to be
'uncovered, retrieved and opened up' in the conviction that 'what is there to be

---

1 Griffiths P.J., *Religious Reading: The Place of Reading in the Practice of Religion* (Oxford:
   1999) 40.
2 Griffiths, *Religious Reading* 41.
3 Griffiths, *Religious Reading* 41. This terminology is for example very often used in prologues
   to medieval and early modern Bible translations, in which the readers are invited to experience the salvific message through the direct access to the vernacular texts. For a recent
   overview of medieval vernacular Bible translations and their readers, see Corbellini S. – Van
   Duijn M. – Folkerts S. – Hoogvliet M., "Challenging the Paradigms. Holy Writ and Lay Readers
   in Late Medieval Europe", *Church History and Religious Culture* 93 (2013) 169–186.

© KONINKLIJKE BRILL NV, LEIDEN, 2015 | DOI 10.1163/9789004290396_002

read always precedes, exceeds, and in the end supersedes its readers'. As a consequence of the intrinsic power of religious texts, however, the reading process is not limited to a single event or a unique experience. There is no and there cannot be a 'final act of reading in which everything is uncovered, in which the mine of gold has yielded all its treasure or the fish pool has been emptied of fish. Reading, for religious readers, ends only with death, and perhaps not then: it is a continuous, ever-repeated act'.[4]

As will become clear from this short discussion of various aspects of religious reading practices in late medieval and early modern Europe, the continuous process of uncovering and retrieval and the continual search for the riches of the Word in religious texts are far from passive, and they involve the readers in a process that requires specific habits, techniques, attitudes and devices as well as a level of mental and physical engagement that goes far beyond the occasional meeting between the 'world of the reader' and the 'world of the text'.[5] One of the most evident features of this engagement is the stress on the process of 'internalization' of religious texts through a practice that first involves the use of mnemotechnical devices, then the transformation of the text into 'food for the soul' and finally the capability to 'ruminate', to recall the text even in the absence of the material and physical presence of the book. Likewise, religious texts from this period often incite their readers to follow the example of St Cecilia who, having memorized the Gospels, always wore them in her heart as a bundle of myrrh, her body thus becoming a book (see also the article by Ian Johnson in this volume).

The importance of these reading techniques aiming at internalizing reading material is testified to by their relevant position in Hugh of St Victor's (1096–1141) *Didascalicon*, probably the first treatise dedicated to reading and reading techniques. In the third book of the *Didascalicon*, Hugh describes the importance of memory:

> We ought, therefore, in all that we learn, to gather brief and dependable abstracts to be stored in the little chest of memory, so that later on, when need arises, we can derive everything else from them. These one must often turn over in the mind and regurgitate from the stomach of one's memory to taste them, lest by long inattention to them, they disappear.

---

4 Griffiths, *Religious Reading* 41.

5 The terms 'world of the reader' and 'world of the text' have been used by Paul Ricoeur in the third volume of his work *Temps et récit* (*Le temps raconté*). The terms are cited by Cavallo G. – Chartier R., "Introduction", in Cavallo G. – Chartier R. (eds.), *A History of Reading in the West* (Cambridge: 1999) 1–36, here 2.

I charge you, then, my student, not to rejoice a great deal because you may have read many things, but because you have been able to retain them. Otherwise there is no profit in having read or understood much.[6]

This process of 'mastication of the word', an intensive and slow reading style, contributes to the assimilation of the content of religious works and to transform the reading text into 'lecturature', an activity that 'is typically not passive, not done with the principal goal of amassing information [...]. It is done, instead, for the purpose of altering the course of the readers' cognitive, affective, and active lives by the ingestion, digestion, rumination, and restatement of what has been read'.[7] Far from being merely a characteristic of historical periods characterized by a scarcity of books, such as early medieval Europe, religious reading is a particularly intensive, physical and emotional approach to textuality that has the power to transform a daily activity into a spiritual experience. It engages the readers, moreover, in a process of self-fashioning and moral transformation, which accompanies them during their private and public lives.

The description of religious reading as a daily activity in which large strata of the late medieval and early modern population were engaged might sound strange in the light of traditional views that emphasize the inaccessibility of (religious) texts, in particular for lay readers. However, recent scholarship has stressed the relevance and impact of literacy in medieval towns as well as the massive presence of religious literature in the urban landscape, and the varied possibilities for large groups of readers to approach religious textuality.[8] The accessibility of religious texts, the impact of religious readership and the investigation of the diverse modes of religious readership in late medieval and early modern Europe are at the very heart of the contributions to this volume, which attempts at crossing disciplinary and chronological boundaries to present a wide-ranging overview of approaches to the study of religious readership

---

6 The text is cited from the English translation by Taylor J., *The Didascalicon of Hugh of St. Victor: A Medieval Guide to the Arts* (New York – London: 1961) 94. On Hugh of St Victor and his reading techniques, see also Hamesse J., "The Scholastic Model of Reading", in Cavallo G. – Chartier R. (eds.), *A History of Reading in the West* (Cambridge: 1999) 102–119.

7 Griffiths, *Religious Reading* 55; Hamesse "The Scholastic Model of Reading" 104. The term 'lecturature' has been coined by Dagenais J., *The Ethics of Reading in Manuscript Culture: Glossing the Libro de Buen Amor* (Princeton: 1994) 24.

8 Mostert M. – Adamska A. (eds.), *Uses of the Written Word in Medieval Towns*, Medieval Urban Literacy II (Turnhout: 2014); Corbellini S. (ed.), *Cultures of Religious Reading in the Late Middle Ages: Instructing the Soul, Feeding the Spirit, and Awakening the Passion* (Turnhout: 2013).

in the period from the fourteenth to the seventeenth century and over a broad geographical area, from England to the Italian Peninsula. They thus challenge the traditional paradigms that distinguish between late medieval religious traditions and early modern Protestant and Catholic Reformation innovations, between Northern and Southern Europe, between exclusion from and participation in religious readership and between the scarcities of diffusion in the manuscript era and its abundance after the 'printing revolution'.[9]

The long period covered by this book—from the fourteenth to the seventeenth century—might seem surprising, because the contents apparently neglect developments that are generally perceived as irreversible turning points in history and, most importantly for this book, as marking profound changes in religious reading practices: the Protestant Reformation and the reactions of the Roman Catholic Church. Taken together, the contributions to this book make clear that in spite of the deep confessional divide, numerous similar reading practices continued to exist among medieval and early modern readers, as well as among Catholics and Protestants, and that the latter two groups in certain cases even shared the same religious texts.

It is still necessary to argue that religious reading during the period from the fourteenth to the seventeenth century should also be described in terms of continuity, because according to commonly accepted historical knowledge Protestantism, in opposition to the Roman Catholic Church, would have required that laypeople learn to read the Bible, thus enabling for the first time in history the emergence of religious reading practices among the laity. For instance, as recently as 2007, Sascha Becker and Ludger Wößman published a re-evaluation of Max Weber's thesis concerning the relation between Protestant ethics and the emergence of capitalism. They argued that differences in wealth between Protestants and Catholics in nineteenth-century Prussia can be explained by differences in schooling, because Luther 'explicitly favoured the advancement of universal schooling, for the simple reason that people had to be literate in order to be able to read God's Word, the Bible', and that 'Protestants acquired more schooling than Catholics for religious reasons'.[10]

---

9   The contributions to this volume are the results of two scientific meetings organized in the years 2011 in Leeds, UK (International Medieval Congress) and 2012 in Groningen, NL. The scientific meetings have been organized as part of the activities of the ERC-Starting Grant research project "Holy Writ and Lay Readers. A Social History of Vernacular Bible Translations in the Late Middle Ages", funded by the European Research Council (2008–2013).

10   Becker S.O. – Wößmann L., "Was Weber Wrong? A Human Capital Theory of Protestant Economic History", *Munich Discussion Paper* 2007–7; online http://epub.ub.uni-muenchen.de/1366/1–59, here 8, 10.

While it is true that Christianity has an intrinsic tension between the Evangelical call 'to spread the Word' (as in *Mark* 15:15–16) and the necessity to protect the *inscrutabilia Dei* from unqualified readers who might come up with unorthodox interpretations, this does not mark a simple dichotomy between the categories 'Protestant' and 'Catholic'. On the contrary, this tension applies to both the Middle Ages and the early modern period, and to Protestants and Catholics alike.[11] Several contributions in this book show that evangelization and religious instruction were taken very seriously during the Middle Ages and that even the illiterate, the very poor and children can be identified as readers targeted by these texts.

The reconstruction of this essential process is approached from several angles, using sources from a broad European area, and it is reconstructed through the use of various methodologies. Through a materialist philological approach to manuscript MS Harley 6333, Matti Peikola shows how the paratextual apparatus of the English vernacular Gospel harmony *Oon of Foure*, copied together with Biblical books in the Later Version of the Wycliffite translation, reveals a concern to communicate the weekly Gospel readings during Sunday's Mass as faithfully as possible to laypeople, even if the original was in fact not suited for this goal. The scribe, whose work testifies to an active engagement with the biblical text, has added lists of liturgical Pericopes, adapted to the specific wording of *Oon of Foure*, together with reading instructions most likely with a lay audience in mind, so that the reader could read the Pericopes 'as [they are read] in the Church'.

In her essay Elisabeth Salter explores popular reading practices and experiences through an innovative use of anthropological approaches. Departing from a case study of two different English rhyming versions of the Ten Commandments in Lambeth Palace Library MS 853, she shows how acculturation may occur through familiarity with a text. The same two poems also serve as the basis for a reader-centred approach that 'explores the possibility that a text such as the Ten Commandments as found in rhyme in Lambeth MS 853 might be open to, or stimulate, a range of interpretations that include potentially heretical understandings'.

Close reading of medieval book lists and inventories, in combination with prologues and reading instructions, confirms that lay men and women did actually have access to the vernacular Bibles and religious treatises, as is demonstrated in the contributions by Suzan Folkerts (focusing on the Netherlands) and Sabrina Corbellini (based on Italian sources). In her contribution Suzan Folkerts discusses methodological issues of approaches to lay Bible reading

---

11   See also the contributions to Lutton R. – Salter E. (eds.), *Pieties in Transition: Religious Practices and Experiences, c. 1400–1640* (Aldershot: 2005).

during the later Middle Ages in the Low Countries, for which she proposes a complementary approach, combining evidence from medieval book lists with codicological and textual sources. This enables her to demonstrate that the vernacular Bible was available to laypeople in the Low Countries and that lay reading of Sacred Scripture was actually encouraged.

The contribution by Sabrina Corbellini shows, moreover, to what extent the reading of religious texts can be connected to the formation of late medieval mentalities and to the creation of professional ethics, even outside the strict application in the development of a specific lay religiosity. Although this process is most clearly visible in the late Middle Ages, this 'ethical reading' of the sacred texts in lay writing can be traced back at least to the early thirteenth century, when non-professional users of the Holy Writ, such as the *causidicus* Albertanus of Brescia, authored treatises in which they re-interpreted biblical pericopes in lay and practical perspective.[12]

The early start of this process is confirmed by Margriet Hoogvliet's contribution. She demonstrates how catechetical texts in French addressing laypeople circulated as early as the thirteenth century. Moreover, she stresses the growing impact of these texts, as the numbers of copies of religious texts in French in the late fifteenth and early sixteenth centuries must have been particularly high. These texts often contain explicit instructions to laypeople for frequent re-reading and for memorizing, but also for collective reading sessions in order to share religious knowledge with other laypeople.

On the other hand, there is ample evidence that even after the Council of Trent the Roman Catholic Church continued to take religious instruction of the laity very seriously. Likewise, religious reading was an important practice of the Catholic laity during the sixteenth and seventeenth centuries that was warmly encouraged. The religious texts laypeople had at their disposal were often medieval works in a linguistically updated form, or recently written works. Certain texts were even shared by both confessions, the Bible and Thomas à Kempis's *Imitatio Christi* being the two most important examples. This continuity of reading practices, from orthodox to dissenting audiences, from the Middle Ages to the early modern period, is addressed by Elisabeth Salter in her article.

In his contribution, Wim François demonstrates how in the sixteenth century, although ecclesiastical officials pleaded for measures to be taken,

---

12   For a discussion of the connection between biblical reading and ethical values, see
      Corbellini, S., "Looking in the Mirror of the Scriptures. Reading the Bible in medieval
      Italy", in François W. – Den Hollander A. (eds.), *"Wading Lambs and Swimming Elephants":
      The Bible for the Laity and Theologians in the Late Medieval and Early Modern Era* (Louvain:
      2012) 21–40.

Catholic authorities in the Low Countries did not ban the printing and reading of vernacular Bibles. As long as translations followed the Vulgate and their reading and interpretation remained connected and subordinate to the liturgy, preaching and teaching of the Church, ordinary believers could freely use a vernacular Bible. However, Church officials, not in the least theologians from the University of Leuven, remained concerned about laymen transgressing the aforementioned limits. Therefore, they sought to censure popular and influential authors like Erasmus—who openly pleaded for vernacular Bible reading—and instead promoted the comprehensive and unequivocal prohibition of the vernacular Bible. Although the Index of Trent of 1564 eventually forbade vernacular Bible reading and vernacular Bible printing came to a halt after the Iconoclastic Fury two years later (in the southern, Catholic, Low Countries at least), New Testaments kept being printed—and obviously read. Religious reading could even be considered as a medicine for laypeople against the 'pestilent' teachings of the Protestants, as Margriet Hoogvliet concludes from the study of several little known sixteenth-century religious texts in French.

The continuous attention to the translation and distribution of religious texts—the Psalms in particular—in the sixteenth century is demonstrated and investigated by Élise Boillet in her contribution. Through a detailed analysis of paratextual elements, in particular page titles and prologues in printed Psalm translations in a period ranging from the second half of the fifteenth to the end of the sixteenth century, Boillet describes how authors of Italian printed texts in the sixteenth century wished to enable the readers to grasp the richness and the depth of the biblical text rather than remaining on the surface and gaining a mere superficial knowledge of it. In this process two seminal transformations are acknowledged: in first instance, the will of the translators to extend the readership of the Psalms from a 'specific' to an 'universal' readership, and secondly the growing attention of authors, editors and printers to the 'new needs in terms of religious knowledge' (such as a stress on the truth of sources and doctrine) and of linguistic and literary qualities (in particular on the choice of an up-to-date vernacular).

As already stated, catechisms and catechetical literature in general represented another favourite genre of religious reading. Authors on both sides of the religious divide suggested and implemented diverse means to lure their—mostly adolescent—readers into reading these books. In his contribution Hubert Meeus demonstrates how such means aimed to stimulate not just independent reading, but also 'reading aloud, rereading, memorization, recitation and discussion'. He provides us with some fascinating examples from 'Jesuit-made' materials printed in Counter-Reformation Antwerp. Apart from detailed reading instructions, authors used a plethora of compositional and editorial devices to win the hearts and minds of their readership: question-and-answer formats, songs, illustrations, emblems, even cut-out wheels of fortune. Some even chose titles that were slight variations of names of ethically loathsome but popular books to attract juvenile readers' attention. Judging from the many printed collections, songs were considered very effective. So-called *contrafacta* had the additional advantage of counteracting the bad influence of the immoral worldly songs from which some of their melodies were taken.

The increased output of printed texts from the 1470s onwards did not put an end to the relevance of medieval texts, quite the opposite.[13] Éléonore Fournié shows in her article that the printed versions of the medieval *Bible historiale* continued to find audiences well into the seventeenth century. In taking such a 'long term perspective', slight changes and transformations can, however, be detected in readers' responses to this 'old' translation (the text is described as a 'manifestly medieval work'). Owners in the sixteenth century were mostly lay and male, and the information they added was particularly unspecific. As the author notes, 'the *Bible Historiale* is a work situated "in-between": not precious enough for being the object of sumptuous dedications, but sufficiently important to be personalized'. Inscriptions tend to become longer and more articulated in the seventeenth century, and they reveal a growing interest from the clerical side (both individuals and institutions), as well as from female religious. Next to possibilities for the reconstruction of ownership patterns, the research results show evidence of an active use of the text, often within the framework of the performance of religious activities by individuals and groups, lay and religious alike. The printed *Bible historiale* was 'a heritage Bible, a family Bible, a Bible of laypeople and clerics'.

The evidence of the massive circulation of medieval religious literature itself can even be studied in order to better understand sixteenth-century transformations, as Federico Zuliani demonstrates. His contribution centres on the question of the relative failure of Calvin's appeal to the Reformed and the philo-Reformed (the so-called Nicodemites) in Italy to change their way of life. The reason could be found in the analysis of sources at the disposal of Italian readers, in which Nicodemus is presented as 'a very positive example of a true

---

13   This is a hotly debated subject and the literature is still burgeoning. One of the most relevant publications for the present book is: D'Avray D.L., "Printing, Mass Communication, and Religious Reformation: The Middle Ages and After", in Crick J.C. – Walsham A. (eds.), *The Uses of Script and Print, 1300–1700* (Cambridge: 2004) 50–70. More generally, see also: Pleij H., "Printing as a Long Term Revolution", in Wijsman H. (ed.), *Books in Transition at the Time of Philip the Fair. Manuscripts and Printed Books in the Late Fifteenth and Early Sixteenth Century Low Countries* (Turnhout: 2009) 287–307; Pettegree A., *The Book in the Renaissance* (New Haven: 2010).

believer in Christ'. As the author stresses, these texts 'may have given a positive rather than a negative idea to those who took, or were accused of having taken, him as a role-model'. These medieval sources, which were widely available in sixteenth-century Italy and still formed the backbone of theological formation at Italian universities, propagated a positive image of Nicodemo, whose spiritual growth is stressed, for example, by Nicholas of Lyra and Anselm of Laon, as well as in a later phase by Tommaso de Vio and Erasmus. This positive interpretation, interestingly enough, did not change in philo-Reformed works, such as those by Ochino and Brucioli.

The *Meditationes vitae Christi* (early fourteenth century) is counted among the most widespread texts throughout Western Europe with a remarkably long-lasting relevance. Ian Johnson addresses three vernacular English versions—the first being Nicholas Love's *Mirror of the Blessed Life of Jesus Christ* (c. 1410)—spanning the early fifteenth to the seventeenth century and testifying to the continuing relevance of this text for devotional practices. The changing paratexts, meanwhile, reflect the transforming religious and political contexts that its Roman Catholic readers had to face. Specific changes in attitude that can be detected from the preface of the 1606 Douai version include an emphasis on Christ as a primarily moral example for the reader, replacing the centrality of Christ incarnate in Love's original text. Another new element is the increased distance perceived between lay readers and readers with an advanced religious knowledge. The prefatory epistle of John Heigham's 1622 revision of Love's original borrows ideas from Jesuit learning, and in the new context of exile and marginalization the author uses terms of protection and hospitality in order to advertise the merits of his work.

Even if the idea of a distinctive disruption separating the Middle Ages from the early modern period was challenged as early as 1927 by Charles Homer Haskins—who argued that the innovations in philology, philosophy, natural sciences and theology actually started with the renaissance of the twelfth century—the debate is still on-going and has even regained prominence during recent years.[14] Jacques Le Goff has very recently renewed his argument in favour of historical continuity, and proposes to define the Middle Ages as

---

14   Haskins C.H., *The Renaissance of the Twelfth Century* (Cambridge, MA: 1927). Jack Goody and Peter Burke have challenged traditional Burckhardtian representations of the Italian Renaissance in favour of an inclusive European and even global approach: Goody J., *Renaissances: the one or the many?* (Cambridge: 2010); Burke P., *The European Renaissance: Centres and Peripheries* (Oxford: 1998). See also the contributions to: Lee A. – Péporté K. (eds.), *Renaissance? Perceptions of continuity and discontinuity in Europe, c. 1300–c. 1550* (Leiden: 2010).

a long period continuing well into the eighteenth century.[15] The idea of historical continuity from the twelfth century even until the present day is also central to the arguments of Constantin Fasolt, who has stressed how important it is for modern European societies to acknowledge that their identities are rooted in innovations and developments that originate in the twelfth century.[16] The centrality of historical continuity is also an important support for the relevance of the contributions to this book: they do not address irrational reading practices from a remote past, but issues of continuity, exchange and inclusion, which still resound in our own times. Likewise, in an inspiring essay, Paul Zumthor has suggested that modern readers who read texts from the past and make them accessible to others become participants in the reception of the texts concerned as well, and that the modern engagement with texts from the past reflects modern rather than historical identities.[17]

Religious readership by all means implied active readership, not only in the sense of believers (religious as well as lay) collecting, buying, borrowing, copying and excerpting texts, but also in the sense of reading them in a performative manner. The kind of habits, techniques, attitudes and devices referred to above, as well as the mental and physical engagement involved in reading religious texts, amounted to a primarily bodily experience that went much further than the purely intellectual or cerebral process we normally think of when talking about reading. In a particular sense even illiterate persons could 'read', through perceiving and interpreting illustrations or by being prompted by rubrics and incipits they recognized to remember and recite, tacitly or vocally, the complete versions of formulaic texts they had learned by heart through oral transmission, like prayers. Songs had that effect, too, as we can gauge from the contribution by Hubert Meeus.

There is every reason, therefore, to expand the scope of religious reading, by literate and illiterate alike, to dealings with books that do not even involve the looking at and understanding of word sequences written or printed on parchment or paper. Whereas most text-oriented research is geared towards traditional hermeneutics in the sense of establishing a coherent explanation on a meaning-level—virtually ignoring historical readers and their dealings

---

15   Le Goff J., *Faut-il vraiment découper l'histoire en tranches?* (Paris: 2014). See also: Summit J. – Wallace D., "Rethinking Periodization", *Journal of Medieval and Early Modern Studies* 37/3 (2007) 447–451.

16   Fasolt C., "Hegel's Ghost: Europe, the Reformation, and the Middle Ages", *Viator* 39 (2008) 345–386. See also Raedts P.G.J.M., *De ontdekking van de Middeleeuwen: Geschiedenis van een illusie* (Amsterdam: 2011).

17   Zumthor P., *Performance, réception, lecture* (Longueuil, Québec: 1990) 99–120.

with the text—performance-oriented research seeks to analyse how texts involved their readers and stimulated in them a number of responses during and after the act of reading.[18] They responded to what they read, to the extent that they mentally re-lived or re-experienced what was described in the text or, in the case of dialogic or dramatic discourse, assumed the role of one of the interlocutors and thus co-acted in the dialogue and action. Images, either created in words (through description) or in lines and colors (through miniatures or woodcuts), stimulated their imagination and memory.

This (re)enactment of text and image took place predominantly on a mental level, but could affect their bodily functions as well, leading to emotional responses, as well as to imitative behavior, thus creating habits of both mind and body.[19] Given the importance of the various circumstances (mindset, background, time, location, position) under which reading took place—circumstances sometimes explicitly described or alluded to—both the textual tradition (manuscript or print; one-text or miscellany) and context of use (individual, familial, social) of these texts have to be taken into account. Books can demonstrate a number of features as regards content, style, narrative, and spatial organization that invited users to read them performatively, that is, to mentally and/or bodily (re)enact them.[20] Through their performativity these genres and modes—prime examples are allegories and dialogues—increased especially laypeople's access to areas of knowledge, both intellectual and practical, and enhanced their ability to achieve a higher level of religious acculturation. Recent studies have reconstructed readers' responses to a combination of text and image, in combination with rubrics and layout.[21] Such analyses

18   Johnson W.A., "Toward a Sociology of Reading in Classical Antiquity", *American Journal of Philology* 121 (2000) 593–627; Morris D.B., "Reading is Always Biocultural", *New Literary History* 37 (2006) 539–561.

19   Dinzelbacher P., "Über die Körperlichkeit in der mittelalterlichen Frömmigkeit", in: Dinzelbacher P., *Körper und Frömmigkeit in der mittelalterlichen Mentalitätsgeschichte* (Paderborn: 2007) 11–49; Stevenson J., *Performance, Cognitive Theory, and Devotional Culture: Sensual Piety in Late Medieval York* (New York: 2010).

20   Jardine L. – Grafton A., "'Studied for Action': How Gabriel Harvey Read His Livy", *Past & Present* 129 (1990) 30–78; Schechner R., *Performance Studies: An Introduction* (New York – London: 2006); Fischer-Lichte E., *The Transformative Power of Performance: A New Aesthetics* (London – New York: 2008); Gertsman E. (ed.), *Visualizing Medieval Performance: Perspectives, Histories, Contexts* (Aldershot: 2008); Sutherland A., "Performing the Penitential Psalms in the Middle Ages", in Gargnolati M. – Suerbaum A. (eds.), *Aspects of the Performative in Medieval Culture* (Berlin – New York: 2010) 15–37.

21   McGrady D., *Controlling Readers: Guillaume de Machaut and His Late Medieval Audience* (Toronto: 2006); Brantley J., *Reading in the Wilderness: Private Devotion and Public*

may be supported by traces of use, user notes, contextual evidence concerning book ownership and use, as well as insights drawn from four areas that informed and conditioned performative reading: the visual arts, preaching, theater and rhetoric.[22]

In his contribution Bart Ramakers discusses three closely related forms of reading competence involving performativity: 'performative literacy', 'performative reading' and 'performance literacy'. He illustrates these with the help of two so-called table plays by Cornelis Everaert, a sixteenth-century playwright from Bruges. They demonstrate Everaert's performative literacy, in the sense that they were informed by his reading experience of devotional treatises and by his ability to visualize this experience through writing, in this case through the composition of these two plays. Furthermore, these treatises—prayer books on the rosary and on the seven blood-sheddings of Christ—called for a performative reading, inviting their users to mentally reenact the Passion. Finally, the plays stimulated the audience's performance literacy; that is, they demonstrated how to encounter and deal with an object's material actuality, through showing how to handle and use particular objects, which were gifts that were presented to the regaled officials in whose honour the plays were performed. Thus, drama in general and Everaert's table plays in particular, provide important clues not just on the subject matter of popular religious reading, but also on its methods and effects.

As already stated, reading could involve more than text alone and in a sense stood open to the illiterate as well. It brings us to the subject of looking at pictures as a viable alternative to reading books, or indeed to the former as a form of reading, especially in the fields of religion and devotion. In her contribution Lucy Wooding explores the extent of, and responses to, such reading of images in Tudor England, thus testing the idea that the Reformation replaced images with words. Again it turns out that particular genres and reading habits continued beyond the religious divide, albeit in altered form, and that critical evaluations of image use were being formulated before and after—by orthodox and

---

Performance in Late Medieval England (Chicago – London: 2007); Kramer B., *Een leken-boek in woord en beeld. De Spegel der minschliken zalicheid* (Hilversum: 2013).

22 Amsler M., *Affective Literacies: Writing and Multilingualism in the Late Middle Ages* (Turnhout: 2011); Kienzle B.M., "Medieval Sermons and their Performance: Theory and Record", in Muessig C. (ed.), *Preacher, Sermon and Audience in the Middle Ages* (Leiden – Boston: 2002) 89–124; Berardini V., "Discovering Performance Indicators in Late Medieval Sermons", *Medieval Sermon Studies* 54 (2010) 75–86; Otter M., "Vultus adest (the face helps). Performance, expressivity and interiority", in Carruthers M. (ed.), *Rhetoric beyond Words: Delight and Persuasion in the Arts of the Middle Ages* (Cambridge: 2010) 151–172.

reformists alike. Reading images, treating them as texts that referred to, or were about, the religious or devotional content depicted, prevented believers from identifying them with that content, thus avoiding idolatry. A combined reading of texts and images was an even better way to reach this goal—images that by the way could be material but also mental or spiritual, called for or evoked by texts. Wooding demonstrates this with examples from the veneration of the Passion, and the crucifixion in particular, Passion narratives, sermons and especially poetry kept on stimulating their readers' or listeners' imaginations, even after the Reformation. In Wooding' words: 'The crucifixion was still, therefore, something which required the eye of the beholder'.

As several contributions in the volume demonstrate (e.g. Corbellini, Hoogvliet, Peikola), religious material was not only made accessible to the readers, but the same readers were instructed on how to approach religious texts in order to fully enjoy the process of uncovering and discovering the riches of the Word. Through paratextual elements, such as glosses and prologues, the readers were coached towards a growing self-awareness of their own religious potential and of their possibilities for participating in the religious experience and performance (Ramakers, Johnson, Peikola). Moreover, they were challenged to develop their own interpretation (with a stress on the social, ethical and moral content of religious reading) and to transform themselves into agents in the dissemination of religious knowledge. One of the most important manifestations of the agency of religious readers is the application of principles of selective readership, which implies the use of navigation tools and the active selection of reading materials. As Griffiths so eloquently states, 'religious readers are in search of flowers. They find them, naturally enough, in the works they read, the gardens they work: these gardens are full of fragrant blooms to be culled, carefully pruned, and rearranged into new bouquets'.[23] This continuous search for texts, interpretations and combination and re-combination of religious texts demonstrates to what extent religious reading, an activity that is traditionally linked to authoritative and normative institutions and their efforts of 'encapsulating' textualities within a well-defined set of norms, could somehow grant to the readers space for personal and private experiences and performances.

The possibility for religious readers to be granted space in the construction of their identities does not, however, imply that religious reading finds its unique fulfilment in solitude and isolation. On the contrary, real and

---

23   Griffiths, *Religious Reading* 97. The circulation of religious works with titles such *Garden of Oration* (e.g. in the contribution by Corbellini) enhance the importance of this metaphor for the description of religious readership.

imagined textual communities contributed to the increase of religious literacy and its practice, to the provision of reading material and to creation of networks for the distribution and exchange of religious texts.[24] Although the contributions in this volume stress the importance of these shared practices in Western Europe, the relevance of communal reading activities in the transmission of (religious) knowledge cannot be overestimated. In the study of ancient literacies, as well as in the exploration of the social and cultural history of reading practices in medieval Arabic lands, the opening of research perspectives taking into consideration groups and networks instead of mere individual readers offers a new and richer picture of how knowledge could be transmitted and assimilated.[25]

In conclusion, the contributions in this volume are a first attempt at studying religious reading in a long-term perspective, covering the period from the thirteenth to the seventeenth century, with a specific focus on the fifteenth and the sixteenth century. The choice for these 'long fifteenth and sixteenth centuries', a period of profound transformation on a social, cultural and foremost religious level, and the stress on continuities and endurances is not intended to erase divides and boundaries, but rather to reassess evidence and sources in order to hopefully present a new and well-balanced evaluation of the relevance of religious reading for the study of late medieval and early modern cultures.

Bibliography

Amsler M., *Affective Literacies: Writing and Multilingualism in the Late Middle Ages* (Turnhout: 2011).

Becker S.O. – Wößmann L., "Was Weber Wrong? A Human Capital Theory of Protestant Economic History", *Munich Discussion Paper* 2007-7; online http://epub.ub.uni-muenchen.de/1366/1–59.

---

24 Scase W., "Reading Communities", in Treharne E. – Walker G., *The Oxford Handbook of Medieval Literature in English* (Oxford: 2010) 557–573; Hoogvliet M. *"Pour faire laies personnes entendre les hystoires des escriptures anciennes*. Theoretical Approaches to a Social History of Religious Reading in the French Vernaculars During the Late Middle Ages", in Corbellini, *Cultures of Religious Reading* 261–267.

25 Hirschler K., *The Written Word in the Medieval Arabic Lands. A Social and Cultural History of Reading Practices* (Edinburgh: 2012); Johnson W.A., "Constructing Elite Reading Communities in the High Empire", in Johnson W.A. – Parker H.N., *Ancient Literacies: The Culture of Reading in Greece and Rome* (Oxford: 2009) 320–330.

Berardini V., "Discovering Performance Indicators in Late Medieval Sermons", *Medieval Sermon Studies* 54 (2010) 75–86.

Brantley J., *Reading in the Wilderness: Private Devotion and Public Performance in Late Medieval England* (Chicago – London: 2007).

Burke P., *The European Renaissance: Centres and Peripheries* (Oxford: 1998).

Cavallo G. – Chartier R., "Introduction", in Cavallo G. – Chartier R. (eds.), *A History of Reading in the West* (Cambridge: 1999) 1–36.

Corbellini S., "Looking in the Mirror of the Scriptures. Reading the Bible in medieval Italy", in François W. – Den Hollander A. (eds.), *"Wading Lambs and Swimming Elephants": The Bible for the Laity and Theologians in the Late Medieval and Early Modern Era* (Leuven: 2012) 21–40.

——— (ed.), *Cultures of Religious Reading in the Late Middle Ages: Instructing the Soul, Feeding the Spirit, and Awakening the Passion* (Turnhout: 2013).

Corbellini S. – Van Duijn M. – Folkerts S. – Hoogvliet M., "Challenging the Paradigms. Holy Writ and Lay Readers in Late Medieval Europe", *Church History and Religious Culture* 93 (2013) 169–186.

Dagenais J., *The Ethics of Reading in Manuscript Culture: Glossing the Libro de Buen Amor* (Princeton: 1994).

D'Avray D.L., "Printing, Mass Communication, and Religious Reformation: The Middle Ages and After", in Crick J.C. – Walsham A. (eds.), *The Uses of Script and Print, 1300–1700* (Cambridge: 2004) 50–70.

Dinzelbacher P., "Über die Körperlichkeit in der mittelalterlichen Frömmigkeit", in: Dinzelbacher P., *Körper und Frömmigkeit in der mittelalterlichen Mentalitätsgeschichte* (Paderborn: 2007) 11–49.

Fasolt C., "Hegel's Ghost: Europe, the Reformation, and the Middle Ages", *Viator* 39 (2008) 345–386.

Fischer-Lichte E., *The Transformative Power of Performance: A New Aesthetics* (London – New York: 2008).

Gertsman E. (ed.), *Visualizing Medieval Performance: Perspectives, Histories, Contexts* (Aldershot: 2008).

Goody J., *Renaissances: the one or the many?* (Cambridge: 2010).

Griffiths P.J., *Religious Reading: The Place of Reading in the Practice of Religion* (Oxford: 1999).

Hamesse J., "The Scholastic Model of Reading", in Cavallo G. – Chartier R. (eds.), *A History of Reading in the West* (Cambridge: 1999) 102–119.

Haskins C.H., *The Renaissance of the Twelfth Century* (Cambridge, MA: 1927).

Hirschler K., *The Written Word in the Medieval Arabic Lands: A Social and Cultural History of Reading Practices* (Edinburgh: 2012).

Hoogvliet M., "*Pour faire laies personnes entendre les hystoires des escriptures anciennes*. Theoretical Approaches to a Social History of Religious Reading in the French

Vernaculars During the Late Middle Ages", in Corbellini, *Cultures of Religious Reading* 261–267.

Jardine L. – Grafton A., "'Studied for Action': How Gabriel Harvey Read His Livy", *Past & Present* 129 (1990) 30–78.

Johnson W.A., "Toward a Sociology of Reading in Classical Antiquity", *American Journal of Philology* 121 (2000) 593–627.

———— "Constructing Elite Reading Communities in the High Empire", in Johnson W.A. – Parker H.N., *Ancient Literacies: The Culture of Reading in Greece and Rome* (Oxford: 2009) 320–330.

Kienzle B.M., "Medieval Sermons and their Performance: Theory and Record", in Muessig C. (ed.), *Preacher, Sermon and Audience in the Middle Ages* (Leiden – Boston: 2002) 89–124.

Kramer B., *Een lekenboek in woord en beeld. De Spegel der minschliken zalicheid* (Hilversum: 2013).

Lee A. – Péporté K. (eds.), *Renaissance? Perceptions of continuity and discontinuity in Europe, c. 1300–c. 1550* (Leiden: 2010).

Le Goff J., *Faut-il vraiment découper l'histoire en tranches?* (Paris: 2014).

Lutton R. – Salter E. (eds.), *Pieties in Transition: Religious Practices and Experiences, c. 1400–1640* (Aldershot: 2005).

McGrady D., *Controlling Readers: Guillaume de Machaut and His Late Medieval Audience* (Toronto: 2006).

Morris D.B., "Reading is Always Biocultural", *New Literary History* 37 (2006) 539–561.

Mostert M. – Adamska A. (eds.), *Uses of the Written Word in Medieval Towns*, Medieval Urban Literacy II (Turnhout: 2014).

Otter M., "Vultus adest (the face helps). Performance, expressivity and interiority", in Carruthers M. (ed.), *Rhetoric beyond Words: Delight and Persuasion in the Arts of the Middle Ages* (Cambridge: 2010) 151–172.

Pettegree A., *The Book in the Renaissance* (New Haven: 2010).

Pleij H., "Printing as a Long Term Revolution", in Wijsman H. (ed.), *Books in Transition at the Time of Philip the Fair. Manuscripts and Printed Books in the Late Fifteenth and Early Sixteenth Century Low Countries* (Turnhout: 2009) 287–307.

Raedts P.G.J.M., *De ontdekking van de Middeleeuwen: Geschiedenis van een illusie* (Amsterdam: 2011).

Scase W., "Reading Communities", in Treharne E. – Walker G., *The Oxford Handbook of Medieval Literature in English* (Oxford: 2010) 557–573.

Stevenson J., *Performance, Cognitive Theory, and Devotional Culture: Sensual Piety in Late Medieval York* (New York: 2010).

Summit J. – Wallace D., "Rethinking Periodization", *Journal of Medieval and Early Modern Studies* 37/3 (2007) 447–451.

Sutherland A., "Performing the Penitential Psalms in the Middle Ages", in Gargnolati M. – Suerbaum A. (eds.), *Aspects of the Performative in Medieval Culture* (Berlin – New York: 2010) 15–37.

Taylor J., *The Didascalicon of Hugh of St. Victor: A Medieval Guide to the Arts* (New York – London: 1961).

Zumthor P., *Performance, réception, lecture* (Longueuil, Québec: 1990).

CHAPTER 1

Approaching Lay Readership of Middle Dutch Bibles: On the Uses of Archival Sources and Bible Manuscripts

Suzan Folkerts

Napoleon De Pauw (1835–1922) was a lawyer of the city of Ghent, who, like a Renaissance man, in his spare time edited many medieval literary and archival sources. In 1879 he published an article on medieval book owners in Ghent.[1] After introducing some book lists from monastic and aristocratic circles, he presented some newly found book inventories of Ghent citizens. Out of an astonishing total of about 42,500 fourteenth-century deeds from the archives of Ghent, which describe the estates of the deceased citizens, De Pauw had found five inventories in which books were mentioned, four of them regarding lay citizens and vernacular books, the fifth a Dominican preacher and Latin books. Three of the four lay citizens that were mentioned in the deeds owned or inherited a Middle Dutch Bible, which is of interest for this contribution on lay readership of vernacular Bibles. Although these inventories are well known and have been cited often—especially after their edition in the catalogue of medieval book lists from Belgium by Albert Derolez and Benjamin Victor—one problem De Pauw dealt with has not been touched upon by later investigators of the inventories.[2] However, this problem, concerning the supposed

---

* This article is a fruit of the ERC Starting Grant project "Holy Writ and Lay Readers. A Social History of Vernacular Bible Translations in the Later Middle Ages" of Sabrina Corbellini. I wish to thank her and Margriet Hoogvliet for our inspirational conversations, their support and their comments on my work. I also would like to thank Renée Gabriël for her helpful comments on an earlier version of this article. This article was partly made possible by NWO.

1 De Pauw N., "Middeleeuwsche boekerijen in Vlaanderen van priesters, heeren en poorters", *Nederlandsch Museum. Tijdschrift voor Letteren, Wetenschap en Kunst* 6,2 (1879) 131–176.

2 Derolez A. – Victor B., *Corpus catalogorum Belgii: The medieval booklists of the Southern Low Countries vol. III: Counts of Flanders; Provinces of East Flanders, Antwerp and Limburg* (Brussels: 1999) 116–120, nos. 24–28. For example, these book inventories were cited in a study on the readers of the work of Jacob of Maerlant: Oostrom F.P. van, "Maerlant voor stad en burgerij" in Pleij H. et al., *Op belofte van profijt. Stadsliteratuur en burgermoraal in de Nederlandse letterkunde van de middeleeuwen* (Amsterdam: 1991) 52–68, here 61–62.

medieval prohibitions of vernacular Bibles and Bible reading by laypersons, is very relevant to the current research theme of religious reading. Since the article was published a long time ago and only in Dutch, De Pauw's main argument regarding this problem will be repeated here.

One of the deeds comes from the *Wezenboek* of 1335–1354 and concerns a young boy, Louis De Beere, who inherited five books from the marital fund of his parents after the death of his mother in 1353. *Wezenboeken* ('orphans' books') describe the estates of deceased citizens who left underage children, for whose care the city council was responsible as chief guardian.[3] Louis's father was John De Beere, a glove-maker, and his mother was named Margareth of Wachtbeke. He was placed partly under the supervision of the priest John of Wachtbeke, probably his uncle, who took care that he received an income and an education. The deed states that, besides a quantity of money and food, Louis would receive 'a book called *Bestiary*, an *Elucidarium*, a *Martin*, a vernacular *Of the Landlord*, and the Gospels in Flemish'.[4] Some years later, in 1359, for unknown reasons Louis's father John was deprived of his guardianship. Curiously, the five books were mentioned in the accompanying deed again: they were to be placed under the surveillance of the chief guardian of the orphans John of Woelputte.[5] Thus the boy was not able to make free use of them anymore without the consent of his chief guardian. The story grows even more suspenseful. When a new guardian was appointed in 1360 and the goods were handed over,

---

3   Boone M., "De Gentse staten van goed als bron voor de kennis van de materiële cultuur: mogelijkheden en beperkingen (Late middeleeuwen-vroege moderne tijden)", in Daelemans F. (ed.), *Bronnen voor de geschiedenis van de materiële cultuur: Staten van goed en testamenten/ Sources pour l'histoire de la culture materielle: Inventaires après décès et testaments. Handelingen van de studiedag te Bussel/ Actes de la journée d'étude de Bruxelles 24-10-1986, Archives et bibliothèques de Belgique/ Archief- en bibliotheekwezen in België: Numéro special/ Extranummer* 25, 2 (Brussels: 1988) 51–73, here 51–52.

4   'eenen bouc die men het (sic) *Bestiaris*, eenen *Lucidaris*, eenen *Martin*, een diechs (sic) *van den Landheren* ende de *Ewangelien* in vlaems'. De Pauw, "Middeleeuwsche boekerijen" 147–148. The vernacular titles *Bestiaris* and *Lucidaris* suggest that these were Middle Dutch books, not their Latin equivalents. This is confirmed by a later deed, which speaks of four vernacular books ('iiij dietsche bouke'. See below, n. 6). De Pauw identifies the *Martin* as Jacob of Maerlant's *Wapene Martijn*. See also Derolez – Victor, *Corpus catalogorum vol. III* 116–117, nos. 24–25.

5   'ende oec van eenen bouke die heet *Bestiaris* en i *Lucidaris*, eenen *Martijn*, eenen dietsche *van den Lantheeren* en den *Ewangelien in vlaemsch*, mids dat Jan de Beere vors. de zelve bouke gheloofde te legghene onder den her Janne van Woelputte'. De Pauw, "Middeleeuwsche boekerijen" 152.

only *four* books were mentioned.[6] De Pauw suggests that the fifth, unspecified missing book concerns the vernacular Gospels. Bearing in mind the problems that Jacob of Maerlant met publishing his rhymed translation of the biblical *Historia Scholastica*, he supposes that the vernacular Gospels were considered 'dangerous' for laypeople by the clergy.[7] Since John of Wachtbeke, the previous guardian of Louis, was a priest, De Pauw assumes that John did not consider the Gospels an appropriate book for the young son of a glove-maker and therefore did not return it.[8]

De Pauw's ideas were formed by the current opinion in the late nineteenth century that vernacular translations of the Bible were forbidden by Roman Catholic authorities and, therefore, must have been rare.[9] This opinion, shared by Protestant and Catholic researchers alike, is still persistent, although it has been disproved by Andrew Gow, who speaks of the 'Protestant paradigm'.[10] In reality, the vernacular Bible was never generally forbidden, but Bible translators repeatedly testified in their prologues of the opposition of the clergy, even if they were respected clergymen or monks themselves. The translator of the Middle Dutch History Bible of Herne (1359–1361), presumably a Carthusian monk, wrote a similar complaint to Jacob of Maerlant's, stating that some of the clergy disapproved of the secrets of the Holy Writ being explained to

---

6   'It. de vocht heeft onder hem iiij dietsche bouke'. De Pauw, "Middeleeuwsche boekerijen" 154. This line is, by the way, a later addition to the deed. This proves once more that the books were an essential part of the goods, because, next to the arrangements regarding guardianship, they were explicitly mentioned.

7   Van Maerlant wrote in his prologue that he had experienced much resistance from clerics when he translated the biblical material of Peter Comestor's *Historia Scholastica* in the vernacular. See Moolenbroek J. van, "Maerlants *Scolastica* of *Rijmbijbel*: een waagstuk?", in Moolenbroek J. van – Mulder M. (eds.), *Scolastica willic ontbinden: Over de Rijmbijbel van Jacob van Maerlant*, Middeleeuwse Studies en Bronnen 25 (Hilversum: 1991) 13–34, here 14.

8   De Pauw, "Middeleeuwsche boekerijen" 152–153 and 155.

9   De Pauw literally wrote that the vernacular Bible was forbidden: 'boeken (. . .), waaronder er zich een bevond door de Katholieke Kerk verboden!' De Pauw, "Middeleeuwsche boekerijen" 153.

10   Gow A.C., "Challenging the Protestant Paradigm: Bible Reading in Lay and Urban Contexts of the Later Middle Ages", in Heffernan Th.J. – Burman Th.E. (eds.), *Scripture and Pluralism: Reading the Bible in the Religiously Plural Worlds of the Middle Ages and Renaissance*, Studies in the History of Christian Traditions 123 (Leiden – Boston: 2005) 161–192. For a history of this 'paradigm', see Gow A.C., "The Contested History of a Book: The German Bible of the Later Middle Ages and Reformation in Legend, Ideology, and Scholarship", *The Journal of Hebrew Scriptures* 9 (2009) 1–37.

common laypeople.[11] The view that vernacular Bibles were forbidden and rare was nourished by these prologues and other clerical sources, such as papal bulls and letters.[12] For example, the letter *Cum ex injuncto* of Pope Innocent III to the bishop of Metz in 1199, in which he forbade the secret gathering of laypeople discussing Bible translations in order to prevent heresy, has often been interpreted as a general prohibition of vernacular Bibles.[13] Although De Pauw could be right in assuming that the guardian disapproved of the boy Louis De Beere using a vernacular Gospel book and therefore withheld it from him, medieval practice contradicts the assumption that vernacular Bibles were rare or nonexistent. This leaves us with the question of lay ownership and readership of vernacular Bibles. In this article we will, on the basis of archival sources and the Bible manuscripts themselves, investigate what evidence these sources provide for lay ownership and readership of Middle Dutch Bibles in the period to circa 1522. First, we will collect and present archival material that bears witness to lay ownership and readership of Middle Dutch Bibles. Second, we will discuss methodological issues concerning these archival sources. Third, we will complement our findings with data provided by Middle Dutch Bible manuscripts and some literary sources. As we will see, in the Low Countries the vernacular Bible was not only available, but lay reading of the Bible was even stimulated by some prominent clergymen. Finally, we will plead for a complementary approach, combining archival, manuscript and literary sources.

Until very recently, the study of Middle Dutch Bible translations was concentrated on the origin of the translations, the authors, and their intentions. This was caused partly by the rich variety of translations and adaptations.

---

11   Kors M. – Claassens G.H.M. (eds.), *De Bijbel voor leken. Studies over Petrus Naghel en de Historiebijbel van 1361* (Turnhout – Leuven: 2007) 26–27.

12   For more examples, such as the correspondence of Pope Calixtus III and Lambert Le Begue and the work of Guibert of Tournai, see: Simons W., " 'Staining the Speech of Things Divine': The Uses of Literacy in Medieval Beguine Communities", in Hemptinne Th. De – Góngora M.E. (ed.), *The Voice of Silence: Women's Literacy in a Men's Church*, Medieval Church Studies 9 (Turnhout: 2004) 86–110, here 87–92.

13   Deanesly M., *The Lollard Bible and other medieval biblical versions, Cambridge Studies in Medieval Life and thought* (London etc.: 1920, 1966²) 33–34. She characterises Innocent's letter as hostile to vernacular translations and argues that contemporaries already interpreted the letter as a prohibition of laypeople reading the vernacular Bibles. For criticism of this view, see Boyle L.E., "Innocent III and vernacular versions of Scripture", in Walsh K. – Wood D. (eds.), *The Bible in the medieval world: Essays in memory of Beryl Smalley, Studies in Church History: Subsidia* 4 (Oxford: 1985) 97–107, here 105. See also Van Moolenbroek, "Maerlants *Scolastica*" 16–17, here 17, n. 15.

It simply takes a lot of time to identify a text, and to contextualise a particular Bible translation.[14] The focus on the authors was also caused by the interests of and the choices made by the researchers involved. For example, the identification of the translator of the Middle Dutch History Bible of Herne of 1359–1361 took many years and many studies, whereas the reception history has only just begun to be investigated.[15] Although the study of Middle Dutch Bible translations seems to move slowly towards new approaches, the field of Middle Dutch literature in general has already shifted towards a focus on the reception (contexts) of texts. This is a consequence of succeeding methodological renewals, such as the introduction of cultural-historical perspectives in the 1960s and 1970s, and the *überlieferungsgeschichtliche Methode* and the 'Material Philology' or the return to the manuscripts in the 1980s and 1990s.[16] The project 'Holy Writ and Lay Readers: A Social History of Vernacular Bible Translations in the Late Middle Ages', executed at the University of Groningen (2009–2013), has speeded up the process of moving from context of origin to context of reception of vernacular Bibles.

Lay Readership of Middle Dutch Bibles: Archival Sources

As stated above, of the five book inventories from Ghent that De Pauw found, no less than three mention Middle Dutch Bibles owned by lay citizens. Besides

14   This approach was also chosen in a recently published dissertation on a Southern Dutch lectionary: Jonker E., *Het Amsterdams Perikopenboek. Volkstalige vroomheid in veertiende-eeuws Vlaanderen* (Leiden: 2010).

15   See Kors – Claassens, *De Bijbel voor leken* 17–29. Kors identified the translator as Petrus Naghel, a Carthusian monk from Herne, but this identification is debated. In a new history of Dutch Bible translations Claassens calls this identification very plausible, yet uncertain. Claassens, G. "De Hernse Bijbel (ca. 1350–ca. 1400)", in Gillaerts P. et al. (eds.), *Bijbelvertalingen in de Lage Landen. Elf eeuwen van vertalen* (Heerenveen: forthcoming 2015). The manuscript transmission of the History Bible of Herne has been studied at the Catholic University of Leuven (KULeuven) as part of an as yet unfinished PhD project.

16   See Brinkman H., "Oude en nieuwe filologie bij Herman Pleij", *Neerlandistiek.nl* 09.01c (May 2009) 1–10, http://www.neerlandistiek.nl (consulted on 09-1-2012); Janssens J., "Begrijpen en begrijpen is twee . . . Een halve eeuw medioneerlandistiek", *Queeste: Journal of Medieval Literature in the Low Countries* 19,1 (2012) 1–19; Brinkman, "Oude en nieuwe" 5–6 and Janssens, "Begrijpen" 4, n. 18 deny the direct influence of the New or Material Philology on Middle Dutch literary studies. Instead, the appreciation of the material carriers of the texts, especially in the series *Middeleeuwse Verzamelhandschriften uit de Nederlanden* (Medieval Miscellanies from the Low Countries), was inspired by projects on *Überlieferungsgeschichte* of Kurt Ruh's research group in Würzburg.

the glove-maker's son Louis De Beere, a Bible was owned by a young man named Reinkin, son of Master (presumably a physician) Simon Elyaes, as well as the brewer John Wasselins.[17] According to a document that was included in the *Wezenboek* of 1375–1376, after Master Simon Elyaes and his wife had died their son Reinkin received, amongst other things, a chest and three books (a chest was a typical place to store books). The books include the *Legend of Barlaam and Josaphat*, a 'Small Mirror', and 'one part of the Bible'.[18] This Bible was possibly the History Bible of Herne, which was available by then and was composed as a two-volume book and usually also copied as such. It could also have been a set of Gospels and other New Testament Bible books, which were already circulating in Southern Dutch translations from the late thirteenth and early fourteenth centuries onwards. The third case concerning Bible possession is the inventory of the goods of the deceased citizen John Wasselins in the *Wezenboek* of 1388–1398.[19] Thanks to the investigations of Dirk Kinable we know that Wasselins was a brewer.[20] The deed mentions that one of his heirs, Wasselkin Maes, went on a journey and never returned, and that the goods were to be given to his other heir John Boene, but with some provisions in the case of Wasselkin's return. The estate contained no less than 30 books, including a Flemish Bible ('een Bibele in vlaemsche'), and some devotional, instructive, moral, historical, scientific, and literary writings.[21] Again, this Bible could be the History Bible of Herne as well as a Gospel manuscript or a New Testament, although Gospels or a New Testament would have typically been indicated as such.

How should the figures mentioned above—five book lists in a corpus of 42,500 acts, among which three vernacular Bibles in the possession of laypeople—be interpreted or contextualised? Is this not too small of a sample to be meaningful? Mikel Kors, who was interested in the Bibles that probably

---

17   The other case, which is not treated here, concerns a *Spieghel historiael* by Jacob of Maerlant in two volumes, which were, according to the *Wezenboek* of 1364–1365, bequeathed by the rich cloth cutter and alderman William Van Den Pitte to his daughters Willekine and Merkine Van Den Pitte. De Pauw, "Middeleeuwsche boekerijen" 156–161.

18   'Item, i coffer en iij bouke, j Barlam, j Cleennen Spieghel, ende j deel van der Biblen'. De Pauw, "Middeleeuwsche boekerijen" 162. See also Derolez – Victor, *Corpus catalogorum vol. III* 118, no 27.

19   De Pauw, "Middeleeuwsche boekerijen" 165–171.

20   Kinable D., *Facetten van Boendale. Literair-historische verkenningen van Jans Teesteye en de Lekenspiegel* (Leiden: 1997) 30.

21   De Pauw, "Middeleeuwsche boekerijen" 168–169 (edition of the book list in the deed) and 171–174 (description and identification of the book titles). See also Derolez – Victor, *Corpus catalogorum vol. III* 119–120, no 28.

concerned the History Bible of Herne, was pessimistic about these figures. On the basis of three surviving manuscripts before 1400, De Pauw's findings of the Bibles of John Wasselins and Simon Elyaes, and the catalogue of Derolez and Victor, he stated that the History Bible was copied very rarely in the fourteenth century, and even more rarely for private persons.[22] He explains this by referring to the existence of heretic movements and a decree of 17 June 1369 by the Roman emperor Charles IV in which he called for the search for heretic writings in the empire and the prohibition of certain books discussing the Bible.[23] By suggesting that prohibitions of the vernacular Bible accounted for the small number of circulating copies, Kors actually stands in the tradition that Gow described as the 'Protestant (and Catholic) paradigm', believing in a firm resistance of the clergy towards the reading of the vernacular Bible by laypeople.[24] De Pauw, although himself convinced of the existence of an ecclesiastical prohibition of the vernacular Bible, was not pessimistic. His explanation runs as follows. Only when ownership of (inherited) goods was disputed, was documentation needed. The small number of five deeds with book lists does not mean that books were rare, but rather that disputes over them were.

This can also be argued on the basis of an article by Linda Guzzetti, who studied inheritance rules and the position of widows in Flanders.[25] Testaments came into existence for religious purposes, in order to regulate donations and remembrances. Only through a testament could a person donate goods to persons other than family members after his or her death.[26] Normally family members, male and female alike, were considered the legitimate heirs. This applies to Teutonic common law in general: Folkert Bakker wrote the same in his study of books in archival sources from Groningen.[27] In Flanders widows

---

22   Kors – Claassens, *De Bijbel voor leken* 113.

23   Kors – Claassens, *De Bijbel voor leken* 113–114 and 144.

24   See above, n. 10. To my view, Kors's arguments are not very convincing. To which fourteenth-century heresies is he referring, and does this situation apply to the Low Countries? Furthermore, did a decree by the Holy Roman emperor have any influence in the Low Countries? One can seriously doubt that, since the cities and territories of the Low Countries were still quite autonomous in the fourteenth century.

25   Guzzetti L., "Women's Inheritance and Testamentary Practices in Late Fourteenth- and Early Fifteenth-Century Venice and Ghent", in Kittell E.E. – Suydam M.A. (eds.), *The Texture of Society. Medieval Women in the Southern Low Countries* (New York: 2004) 79–108.

26   Guzzetti, "Women's Inheritance" 87.

27   Bakker F., "Handschriften en boeken in Groningse archiefstukken tot 1597 (II)", *Driemaandelijkse bladen voor taal en volksleven in het oosten van Nederland* 40,1–2 (1988) 1–26, here 2. Bakker, "Handschriften" 2, 17 provides another finding of a vernacular(?) Gospel book. It was given by the prioress Hisse of Ewsum to her natural brother Wigbold

inherited the marital fund and acted as administrator themselves, without a tutor. De Pauw's fifth case—not mentioned above because it regards only Latin books—concerns, in all probability, just such a widow. In 1349, the mother of the deceased Dominican monk John of Coudenhove inherited his Latin books, including a Bible.[28] The Dominicans claimed John's books, but the aldermen of Ghent ruled in favour of his mother. We assume the books were his personal belongings, as were the clothes, which were also mentioned in the document. There is no mention of a testament, and with the lack of a will John's mother was the legitimate heir. She defended her legal claim to her son's books, and therefore we know of their existence. Finally, there is another issue at stake here. Although books are rarely mentioned in archival sources such as inventories of estates and wills, if they are, the chances that a Bible is among those books listed are very high. This is visible when one consults the catalogue of book lists by Derolez and Victor, which is considered as the basis for investigations into book ownership in the Southern Low Countries.[29]

In what follows, we will argue that there is no need to be pessimistic about lay readership of vernacular Bibles in the Low Countries. On the contrary, the sources indicate a large readership. The explanation for Kors' pessimistic view—aside from the Protestant paradigm—can be found in his scope of interest: he only searched for fourteenth-century material. When the (long) fifteenth century is taken into account, figures are much higher. In this contribution, fifteenth-century book lists and inventories are included in the research. Derolez and Victor's catalogue of book lists from the Southern Low Countries has been consulted as well as other secondary literature, mainly concerning the Northern Low Countries. This resulted in a preliminary number of 57 Middle Dutch Bibles or Gospels found in deeds, wills and inventories.[30] None of them can with certainty be identified as one of the surviving manuscripts, which

---

of Ewsum ('vor ene cleyne groete welke evangelien, al is dat ghave cleyn myn gunst is groet').

28 De Pauw, "Middeleeuwsche boekerijen" 141–143.

29 See Folkerts S. – Gabriël R. (eds.), *A Bunch of Books. Book Collections in the Medieval Low Countries*, thematic issue of *Queeste. Journal of Medieval Literature in the Low Countries* 20,2 (2013).

30 This number is based on my own findings in secondary literature. Compare with the figure of around 69 Italian Gospels and New Testaments found in inventories from Italy. See Corbellini S., "Instructing the Soul, Feeding the Spirit and Awakening the Passion: Holy Writ and Lay Readers in Late Medieval Europe" in Gordon B. – McLean M. (eds.), *Shaping the Bible in the Reformation: Books, Scholars and Their Readers in the Sixteenth Century* (Leiden: 2012) 15–39, here 35, n. 62.

form a corpus of 433 Bibles, Bible books or large biblical excerpts.[31] Given the
fact that goods and books were registered only rarely, we can only guess how
many Bible manuscripts must have been present in the houses of inhabitants
of towns beyond the examples that are mentioned here. We should note here
that in late fifteenth-century deeds and book lists it is not always clear if an
item such as 'bibel' (Bible) or 'ewangelie' (Gospel) refers to a manuscript or to
a printed book. From 1477 on, the Old Testament and the Epistle and Gospel
lessons were printed in Middle Dutch. Overall, the introduction of the printing
press resulted in even higher numbers of lay owners of Bibles than the manuscripts were able to provide. The total number of editions of Middle Dutch
Bibles (mainly Psalters and lectionaries of Epistle and Gospel lessons) in the
period between 1477 and 1522 is circa 65. The number of preserved copies of
these editions is around 300.[32] The percentage of lay owners is not known for
all of these editions, but Mart van Duijn found that around 80% of the 61 surviving copies of the Delft Bible of 1477 belonged to laypeople, beguines and lay
brothers of religious communities.[33]

Ghent turns out to be an excellent provider of sources. It is not our intention to write a case study on Ghent here, but we start our investigation in
this Flemish city. This city was the stage of intense writing and reading
activities, not least of which those with a devotional and religious character.
Already around 1400 we find several professional scribes who bought, rented
and copied books. They owned or rented houses for their workshops, which
were centred near the alderman's house.[34] Herman Brinkman, who studied
these workshops, also found more descriptions of estates with books in the
archives of Ghent. One of the cases he mentions concerns the biblical book
of Psalms: in 1396, Margareth De Luede left a Psalter and a Book of Hours to
her child and a priest, presumably the child's guardian.[35] John De Clerc, one
of the scribes who owned a workshop in Ghent, bought around 30 books from
Sister Margareth sVrients from a hospital in Ypres in 1402, which he rented to

---

31   Folkerts S., "Te 'duncker' voor leken? Middelnederlandse bijbelvertalingen vanuit het per-
        spectief van de gebruikers", *Jaarboek voor Nederlandse Boekgeschiedenis* 18 (2011) 155–170,
        here 159–160; Folkerts S., "Reading the Bible Lessons at Home: Holy Writ and Lay Readers
        in the Low Countries", *Church History and Religious Culture* 93,2 (2013) 217–237, here 228.

32   Figures are based on the *Biblia Sacra* database http://www.bibliasacra.nl; and the
        Incunabula Short Title Catalogue http://www.bl.uk/catalogues/istc.

33   Duijn M. van, "Tussen vorm en betekenis. Delftse Bijbels in handen van lezers en gebrui-
        kers", *Madoc* 25 (2011) 206–216, here 209.

34   Brinkman H., "Het Comburgse handschrift en de Gentse boekproductie omstreeks 1400",
        Queeste: Journal of Medieval Literature in the Low Countries 5,2 (1998) 98–113.

35   Brinkman, "Het Comburgse handschrift" 104, n. 32.

fellow citizens for money.[36] Some of these books are mentioned in a later act as histories and *gesta*,[37] but a collection from a hospital presumably contained liturgical and devotional books as well, with the most likely possessions being a Psalter or a lectionary.[38] We can, hypothetically, imagine a vernacular Bible being rented by Ghent citizens to be read or copied. This example shows that archival sources not only sum up book titles, but also make visible how books were used or spread.

Leaping a hundred years forward in time, to 1500, we find another book list from Ghent. It is part of the estate of Elisabeth De Grutere, the widow of Simon Borluut, a rich Ghent citizen.[39] After the death of her husband, Elisabeth moved to live with the beguines of the Begijnhof Ter Hooie, and after her own death, she left them an astonishing total of 70 books. She demanded that the beguines should preserve the books well and lend them to her and Simon's friends. The beguines had to see to the books being well cared for and made available for the sake of her and/or their souls ('Dat sij (…) getrauwelic bewaert ende bescict tot salicheit der sielen').[40] Besides biblical material, i.e. Epistle and Gospel lessons and Paul's Letter to the Ephesians, the list contains saints' lives, examples, sermons, Passion literature, catechetical texts, and various other religious and devotional texts that are usually found in religious communities. However, these books all came from the personal property of a laywoman. Elisabeth's cousin Margareth of Varnewyc also left books to a convent in Ghent, more specifically two copies of the rhymed History Bible of Jacob of Maerlant and his *Spieghel historiael* to the Rich Clares or Urbanist Sisters. This we know from a chronicle of 1508, written by the confessor John Ysenbaert, which contains an

---

36   Brinkman, "Het Comburgse handschrift" 103–104. The number of 30 books is a calculation by Brinkman, based on the prices of books at that time.

37   Brinkman, "Het Comburgse handschrift" 104–105.

38   For example, a book list from the chapel of the hospital of Saint James in Ghent mentions several liturgical books, amongst others missals, an antiphonary and two Psalters, presumably in Latin. Derolez – Victor, *Corpus catalogorum vol. III* 104–105, no. 17.

39   Derolez – Victor, *Corpus catalogorum vol. III* 27–31, no 4. See also Stooker K. – Verbeij Th., *Collecties op orde: Middelnederlandse handschriften uit kloosters en semi-religieuze gemeenschappen in de Nederlanden vol. I*, Miscellanea Neerlandica 15 (Leuven: 1997) 291–292 and 344–345.

40   Both Derolez and Stooker – Verbeij read the word 'bescict' wrongly as 'bescut'. Cora Zwart brought this to my attention. Zwart C., *Lezen 'tot salicheit der sielen'. De betekenis en invloed van de nalatenschap van Elisabeth De Grutere († 03-08-1500) van zeventig religieuze volkstalige boeken aan het begijnhof Onze Lieve Vrouw Ter Hooie te Gent* (unpublished Master's thesis University of Groningen, 2013).

overview of the convent's books and their donors.[41] The same list mentions a Flemish Gospel book and another miscellaneous book containing Gospels donated by a religious woman named Catherine of Meersen, as well as a copy of the Epistle and Gospel lessons from an unknown donor.[42]

On the Use of Archival Sources

We could sum up many more examples of Bibles and biblical books in book inventories and wills, but then no room would be left for reflection on the methodological problems and possibilities of investigating inventories. For the study of lay readership of vernacular Bibles in the Low Countries, two things are important. First, the wills and inventories testify to the networks of religious and laypeople, who exchanged books by means of donation, sale and loan. Laypeople had a hand in the circulation and transmission of vernacular Bibles and biblical manuscripts. They were not passive receivers of books from religious institutions, but they participated actively in the appropriation and exchange of books. A couple of the aforementioned examples show that religious institutions received books from a private (lay) owner.[43] Not only archival sources, but also the surviving manuscripts bear witness to this phenomenon (see below, in the section on manuscripts). The data provided by archival sources complement the data given by the surviving manuscripts and show that lay readership and ownership of vernacular Bibles was even more common than the manuscripts suggest: of the 57 Middle Dutch Bibles we found in archival sources thus far, 19 items or 33% involve lay ownership, whereas only 13% of the surviving manuscripts with a known provenance were in the possession of laypeople (beguines are counted here as religious, although they, strictly speaking, were laywomen).[44] These different numbers can be explained by the nature of the sources: laypersons are probably better represented than religious persons in archival sources describing the estates of deceased persons, whereas manuscripts, presumably, have survived in greater

---

41   This book list was edited by Willems L., "De boekeninventaris van het klooster der Rijke-Claren te Gent in 1508", *Tijdschrift voor Boek- en Bibliotheekwezen* 9 (1911) 177–192, but I used the reprint of Derolez – Victor, *Corpus catalogorum vol. III* 32–44, no 5. See also Stooker – Verbeij, *Collecties op orde vol. I* 306–309 and 346–349, nos. 63 and 82.

42   Stooker – Verbeij, *Collecties op orde vol. I* 347–348 (nos. 62, 67, and 76).

43   Bakker also concludes that in the province and city of Groningen, laypeople and clerics left their books mainly to religious institutions. Bakker, "Handschriften" 2.

44   Folkerts, "Te 'duncker' voor leken?" 160.

numbers from religious institutions than from private collections, because they were kept under better circumstances.

Second, book lists reveal the function of books, just as the books themselves would. A fruitful way to explore book lists is to analyse their structure and division into sections. This is perhaps not so useful for the analysis of wills with only two or three books, but it is useful when studying the larger book lists. The organization and clustering of book titles and their classification by means of headings tell us something about the way they were used. Inventories of convent's books generally start with liturgical books, and subsequently mention Bibles, hagiography, and other genres. When separate book inventories existed for the convent library and the church, the convent library's book lists exclude liturgical books, because these belonged to the church or the sacristy. The book list of the convent of tertiaries of Saint Barbara in Delft says explicitly: 'These are the study books, which belong to the library' ('Dit sijn die studierboeken, die in die liberie horen').[45] This list does not contain Latin liturgical books, nor Books of Hours and Psalters, which functioned as personal prayer books. The latter were likely the personal belongings of the sisters. This is important to our theme of lay readership, because sisters could bequeath these books to family members and friends outside the convent.

Asides from churches and convent libraries, book lists sometimes refer to other places where books were kept, such as a school or a lay brothers' library. A well-known example from the Low Countries is the inventory of the Middle Dutch books of Rooklooster, a monastery of Canons Regular near Brussels.[46] This inventory was written around 1390 and includes, among other devotional and mystical literature, five Middle Dutch biblical items: a book of Gospels, a book of Epistles, another book of Gospels, the Psalms, and the books of Solomon.[47] They are not all grouped together, but the list starts with two biblical manuscripts, which seems to be a feature of inventories of convent libraries. It has often been stated that the list was the catalogue of the library of the lay brothers of Rooklooster, but Erik Kwakkel argues that this is not the case:

45   Moll W., "De boekerij van het St. Barbara-klooster te Delft, in de tweede helft der vijftiende eeuw", *Kerkhistorisch archief* 4 (1866) 209–285, here 224.

46   Kwakkel E., *Die dietsche boeke die ons toebehoeren: De kartuizers van Herne en de productie van Middelnederlandse handschriften in de regio Brussel*, Miscellanea Neerlandica 27 (Leuven: 2002).

47   Derolez A. – Victor B. – Bracke W., *Corpus catalogorum Belgii: The medieval booklists of the Southern Low Countries vol. VI: Provinces of Brabant and Hainault* (Brussels: 2001) 180–182, no 84. It is not clear whether 'book of Gospels' and 'book of Epistles' ('ewangeliboec' and 'epistelboec') refer to lectionaries with lessons of the liturgical year—the Epistle and Gospel lessons—or to the four Gospels and the Pauline and canonical letters.

the list is not a catalogue (i.e. it does not disclose a library) and it is written in a Latin manuscript—which, to our view, does not necessarily exclude lay readership.[48] The books or booklets were probably kept together in a closet or a chest, to be used by the clerics as well as the lay brothers.

If the titles in a book list appear to be randomly set down or completely lacking any order, this could indicate the physical presence of these titles at the table of the writer of the list and is not meaningless. These books were perhaps used together, just as texts in miscellanies functioned together.[49] This is argued by Renée Gabriël, who, inspired by the Material Philology, approaches book titles in book lists as she would texts in miscellanies. She used the book list of the magister Michael De Stoct, again, from Ghent, to demonstrate the possibilities of this approach. Michael composed a list of his books after he had left the abbey of Saint Bavo in Ghent, to live and work in Cologne. The list was sent to Ghent, in all probability because he was defending his possessions against a claim by the abbey. According to this list, Michael owned about 300 Latin and Middle Dutch books, including Middle Dutch Bibles and a *Life of Christ*.[50] The vernacular books were not arranged separately in the inventory as a set: some form a cluster with Latin works. Gabriël argues that Michael probably used both Latin and Middle Dutch works for his sermon writing projects, because they match thematically.[51] The book titles presumably were recorded in the order in which the books were found at the tables at which Michael was working.

Returning to lay owners of vernacular Bibles, a final book inventory is mentioned here as an example of the importance of the structure of book lists. It is a list of fourteen Middle Dutch devotional books, which is written in one of the manuscripts from the library of Mary of Loon and her husband John IV Count of Nassau (d. 1475). The list is attributed to Mary of Loon herself and was written between 1470 and 1502, the year of her death.[52] It gives only a selection

---

48   Kwakkel, *Die dietsche boeke* 29–30.

49   Gabriël R., "Boekenlijsten en *Material Philology*. Methodologische overwegingen bij de boekenlijst van Michael van der Stoct (ca. 1394)", *Queeste: Journal of Medieval Literature in the Low Countries* 16,2 (2009) 83–111, here 89–90.

50   This book list is edited in Derolez – Victor, *Corpus catalogorum vol. III* 53–71, no 10. The Middle Dutch Bibles are nos. [137] 'Item ewangelia in flamingo et in papiro' and [199] 'Item epistole per totum annum in theutonico'; the *Life of Christ* is no [189] 'Item van Christus levene ende passie in dietssche in papiro'. Note also no [43] 'Item de vita Christi in flamingo quam copulavi'.

51   Gabriël, "Boekenlijsten" 93–96.

52   Brinkman H., "The composition of a fifteenth-century aristocratic library in Breda: the books of John IV of Nassau and Mary van Loon", *Quærendo: a quarterly journal from the*

of their library and it is unknown why these works are mentioned on this list and with what purpose it was written. What the titles have in common is that they refer to vernacular devotional works, among which four Middle Dutch Bible manuscripts: the first part of the Bible, the second part of the Bible (these items probably refer to two volumes of the History Bible of Herne), the Gospel lessons for Sundays, and the Epistle and Gospel lessons.[53] The list also mentions a book with the Passion and the Ten Commandments, but it is not certain if these titles refer to biblical texts. Many books from John and Mary's library have survived, but none of the biblical manuscripts on this list. The two parts of the History Bible on the list cannot be identified with an existing copy of the History Bible that has their ex-libris note, because this copy has always been a single-volume manuscript.[54] Thus Mary and John must have had another copy of this History Bible in two volumes. Just like the book list from Rooklooster, Mary's list gives a selection of books out of a larger collection, which were either physically assembled, or perhaps only in the mind of the composer of the list. Herman Brinkman, who discovered the list, suggests that Mary and John's collection was scattered over different spaces and that the list describes the books in one room.[55] Following the attribution of the list to Mary herself, it is conceivable that this list was a personal reading list or a list of books she kept in her personal library, perhaps in her bedroom. However, even if we cannot reconstruct the reasoning behind the composition of Mary's list, it proves once more the extensive lay readership of Middle Dutch Bibles, and the great number of copies, which must have once existed but have now been lost.

A manuscript that turned out to be one of the books of the library of John of Nassau and Mary of Loon (but is not on the list) reveals another phenomenon that should be stressed here. This phenomenon is the tendency to attribute devotional books automatically to a monastic milieu. The manuscript contains works of the lay brother John of Leeuwen.[56] John of Leeuwen (d. 1378) was a cook who entered the convent of Canons Regular of Groenendaal, where he,

---

Low Countries devoted to manuscripts and printed books 23,3 (1993) 163–183, here 165, 168. Four of the fourteen titles are, however, written in another hand.

53   The list is edited in Brinkman, "The composition" 165–167. The titles mentioned are: 'Item eyn stuck van der bybelen dat eerste boech'; 'Item noch dat ander boech vander bybelen'; 'Item eyn sondaegs ewangely myt der gloesen'; 'Item eyn eyn [sic] ewangely vnd epystelen myt der gloessen'; 'Item de passy vnd x geboed eyn boech'.

54   Brinkman, "The composition" 167, n. 8, 178, no 4, 179, nos. 12–13. It concerns MS Copenhagen, KB, Thott 123 fol. (1442–1445).

55   Brinkman, "The composition" 169.

56   The manuscript is now MS Brussels, KBR, IV 401 and dates from around 1460. Brinkman, "The composition" 179, no 7.

according to his *vita*, learned to read and to write.[57] He even wrote more than twenty treatises, in which he combined the contemplative mystical teachings of John of Ruusbroec, his teacher and confessor, with the active daily life of a layperson. Although he wrote for both lay and religious readers, most of the copies of his work originate from monastic contexts.[58] The manuscript we are concerned with was discovered in a Dominican library and attributed to a nunnery on the basis of marginal notes like 'nota bene moeder' and 'nota virgo'.[59] However, these marginal notes could also refer to mother Mary and the Virgin. In the treatise 'Five ways of brotherly love' ('Van vijf manieren van broederliker minnen'), a note says: 'and shall not be read in general in any refectories and in particular those of women'.[60] However, later research with ultraviolet light, which revealed another note, proved that the manuscript originally belonged to the library of John of Nassau. Furthermore, another barely visible note says that the book was given by a lord of Nassau to the monastery of (probably) Vredenberch: 'This book my lord of Nass(…)w has (…) the Abbey of vredenb(…)ch (…). This (…)' and: '(…) lord of Nassau gives (…) to the Abbey of (…) which is (…)'.[61] Vredenberch was a nunnery near Breda, founded by Mary of Loon in 1476, one year after John of Nassau's death. In this case, a manuscript that, based on its contents and visible traces of use, fitted in a female monastic context, turned out to be of lay aristocratic origin. John of Nassau or, more likely, his pious wife and, later, widow Mary of Loon was interested in treatises on how to combine the contemplative life with the active life. Just like Elisabeth De Grutere used her 70 devotional books before she left them to the Begijnhof, Mary must have used the John of Leeuwen manuscript herself before it was donated, probably by her son, to Vredenberch. Devotional books like these, which bear no visible ex-libris notes, are too easily associated with religious convents. Some Middle Dutch Bible manuscripts are attributed to convents just because they contain biblical material, others because they contain a calendar with certain saints' names, and still others because they are owned by the Bibliothèque nationale de France in Paris, where many

57 Warnar G., "De weduwe, de kok en de ridder. Middelnederlandse kloosterteksten voor de lekenvroomheid", *Literatuur* 9 (1992) 279–285, here 281–282.

58 Desplenter Y., "Huis- tuin- en keukenmoraal? Jan van Leeuwen en de tien geboden", *Spiegel der Letteren* 52, 1 (2010) 1–29, here 24; Warnar, "De weduwe" 282.

59 Brinkman, "The composition" 181, n. 85.

60 'en salmen niet lesen int ghemeyn in ghenen reeftere ende sonderlinghe van vrouwen personen'. Brinkman, "The composition" 181, n. 85. English translation by Brinkman.

61 English translation by Brinkman, "The composition" 182.

monastic manuscripts ended up after the Revolution.[62] Another example is a Psalter, which, according to J.A.A.M. Biemans, possibly came from a convent of tertiaries in Weesp.[63] The manuscript was found in the Reformed Church in Weesp in 1837, where other manuscripts had been found as well, many of which had originated from the tertiaries. This kind of reasoning, as plausible as it may sound, excludes other scenarios. This manuscript, however, bears the sixteenth-century ex-libris note 'A. v. Paddensz', which gives cause to speculations about lay ownership as well. With these manuscripts, however, we have left the domain of archival sources and entered the domain of manuscript sources.

Lay Readership of Middle Dutch Bibles: Manuscript Sources

As book inventories and wills demonstrate, the exchange of religious books, including vernacular Bibles, took place in networks of lay and religious persons in which laypeople were often the providers of books. This is also visible in the surviving manuscripts themselves. Again starting in Ghent, we find a manuscript with a Dutch translation of the *Meditationes de passione Christi* of Jordan of Quedlinburg and the Passion from the Gospel of John in the Northern Middle Dutch translation.[64] It was donated to the Canonesses Regular of Our Lady in Galilea in Ghent by the founder of that convent, John Eggaert.[65] John Eggaert was lord of Purmerend and Spaarnland in Holland, and fulfilled

---

62   Biemans J.A.A.M., *Middelnederlandse bijbelhandschriften/Codices manuscripti sacrae scripturae Neerlandicae, Verzameling van Middelnederlandse bijbelteksten: Catalogus/Corpus sacrae scripturae Neerlandicae Medii Aevi: Catalogus* (Leiden: 1984) 29–30, no 17 (this manuscript has no ex-libris notes, but Biemans quotes C.C. de Bruin: 'De codex moet afkomstig zijn uit een klooster [...]'), 47–48, no 30 (an ex-libris note says 'Kathelijne Brie[...]', but on the basis of the stamps of the Bibliothèque nationale Biemans attributes the book to a religious convent).

63   Biemans, *Middelnederlandse bijbelhandschriften* 114–115, no 78.

64   Biemans, *Middelnederlandse bijbelhandschriften* 196–197, no 178; Deschamps J. – Mulder H., *Inventaris van de Middelnederlandse handschriften van de Koninklijke Bibliotheek van België (voorlopige uitgave)* 6 (Brussels: 2003) 24–26.

65   Scheepsma W., *Medieval Religious Women in the Low Countries: The Modern Devotion, the Canonesses of Windesheim, and their Writings*, transl. D.F. Johnson (Woodbridge: 2004) 199; Mingroot E. van, "Prieuré de Ten Walle à Elsegem", in *Monasticon belge vol. VII: Province de Flandre orientale vol. 4* (Liège: 1984) 677–730, here 692–693; Mingroot E. van, "Prieuré de Galilée à Gand", in *Monasticon belge vol. VII: Province de Flandre orientale vol. 4* (Liège: 1984) 761–794, here 768–769.

several functions at the court of Jacoba of Bavaria. In 1422 he fled to Ghent
when Jacoba came into conflict with opponents. In Ghent he devoted himself
to spiritual matters, and founded the convent of Galilea in 1431, which two of
his daughters joined. Around 1440 he also donated a collection of sermons of
the Dominican John Tauler to the convent.[66] Furthermore, a Latin obituary
of the Priory of Canons Regular of Galilea in Elzegem mentions John's death in
1452 and his donations of a 'bibliam, lectionarium et alios libros' for the choir
and the refectory.[67] It is uncertain if he bought books with the intention of
donating them immediately, or if the books were at his own disposal before
he donated them. According to Biemans, the manuscript with the Passion was
written around 1440, and this would mean that John bought it while he was
already living in Ghent.[68] According to Jan Deschamps and Herman Mulder,
the manuscript was written and decorated in Holland in the first half of the
fifteenth century, so it is more likely that John brought it from Holland and
owned the book a long time before he donated it to the sisters of Galilea.[69]

Middle Dutch manuscripts often circulated in a lay context not only before,
but also after they were in the possession of religious persons. A History
Bible of Herne that belonged first to the Canons Regular of Den Hem near
Schoonhoven in Holland was subsequently sold to John Gheritsoen, who in
turn gave it to the monastery of Emmaus.[70] The manuscript thus transferred
from religious into lay hands and again into religious. Vernacular books were
often donated to religious daughters, cousins and nieces, by family members
or by other pious laypersons. For example, Lambert 'the saddler' and his sister
Ghertrude donated two books, a Psalter and a New Testament, to their niece
Yde Henricks, who was a religious.[71] This book was produced in the Benedictine
monastery of Selwerd near Groningen. Another Psalter was given to the natural sisters Hynrick Schaffers and Cornelis, both tertiaries in the convent of

---

66   Scheepsma, *Medieval Religious Women* 206.

67   Derolez – Victor, *Corpus catalogorum vol. III* 25–26, no 3. John is called 'amicus vir venera-
       bilis Iohannes Egghert'.

68   Biemans, *Middelnederlandse bijbelhandschriften* 196.

69   Deschamps – Mulder, *Inventaris* 25.

70   MS Utrecht, UB, 1006 (c. 1470), f. 26or: 'Dit boec hoert totten reguliren buten schoenhouen
       inden hem'. Other, later hand: 'Ende jan gheritsoen heft et ghecoft'. Third, later hand:
       'ende jan gherrit soen heeftet die cellebroers in emaus te gou ghegheuen'. See Biemans,
       Middelnederlandse bijbelhandschriften 69–71, no 44.

71   Folkerts S., "The Cloister or the City? The Appropriation of the New Testament by Lay
       Readers in an Urban Setting", in Corbellini S. (ed.), *Cultures of Religious Reading in the Late
       Middle Ages. Instructing the Soul, Feeding the Spirit and Awakening the Passion*, Utrecht
       Studies in Medieval Literacy 25 (Turnhout: 2013) 175–199, here 182–183 (other examples of
       donations are also given here).

Saint Agnes or 'Oldeklooster' in Groningen, by their parents.[72] It was written in 1527 in Thesinge, just like Selwerd a Benedictine monastery in the present province of Groningen, by the nun Stine Dutmers.[73] Thérèse De Hemptinne writes about this phenomenon of book donations to religious women:

> In cities of the Low Countries, both lay and (semi-)religious women were the main consumers of books written in the vernacular. Moreover, I have the impression that books often procured links between the lay and religious worlds of those cities. [...] Like their sisters who remained 'in' the world, (semi-)religious women were supposed to honour their parents and relatives and to be useful for them, although they would do this quite differently: by living a devout life and by praying for them.[74]

Middle Dutch Bibles and other devotional books thus functioned as a connecting agent in networks of laypeople and religious. In exchange for books, (female) religious prayed for their family members. When we search for reciprocity, tertiaries (until 1468) and beguines, who were allowed to have private possessions, were especially important players on the 'market' of book exchange.[75] They left books to each other and to family members. The aforementioned manuscript Psalter of Hynrick Schaffers and her sister Cornelis was later in the possession of Lutgert of Dulck, presumably a beguine in Groningen—strictly speaking a laywoman [Fig. 1.1].[76] A Psalter, which was given by Sister Mouwersdochter,

---

72   'Item Dijt boek hoert suster hijnrick schaffers ende hoer suster cornelis toe welker datet crijghet nae horen dode Die bijdde voer hem ende hoer olders daert van ghecomen is'. MS Leiden, UB, Ltk 235 (1527), f. 211v. This colophon is struck through.

73   'God si gelouet Dit boeck ende solter is gheeyndiget in dat iaer ons heren dusent vijfhunder ende souenende twintich des vridaghes voer iubilate.s.d.'. MS Leiden, UB, Ltk 235, f. 211v. On the identification of Stine Dutmers, see Hermans J.M.M., "Glimpses from the North: Selwerd and Thesinge, Two Workshops in Groningen (ca. 1470–ca. 1530)", in Horst K. van der – Klamt J.Ch. (eds.), *Masters and Miniatures. Proceedings of the Congress on Medieval Manuscript Illumination in the Northern Netherlands (Utrecht, 10–13 December 1989)*, *Studies and facsimiles of the Netherlandish illuminated manuscripts* 3 (Doornspijk: 1991) 347–357, here 351–352.

74   Hemptinne Th. De, "Reading, Writing, and Devotional Practices: Lay and Religious Women and the Written Word in the Low Countries (1350–1550)", in Hemptinne Th. De – Góngora M.E. (eds.), *The Voice of Silence: Women's Literacy in a Men's Church*, Medieval Church Studies 9 (Turnhout: 2004) 111–126, here 122.

75   Simons, " 'Staining the Speech' " 99–100; Folkerts, "The Cloister" 182–183, 195.

76   'Item Dit boeck hoert suster [above with other hand: juffer] lutgert van Dulck vonende op de bredere kerckhof we dat vijnt de brenget my weder omme godes wille'. MS Leiden, UB, Ltk 235, f. 211v. The word 'juffer' is indicative of a beguine. Simons, " 'Staining the Speech' " 104.

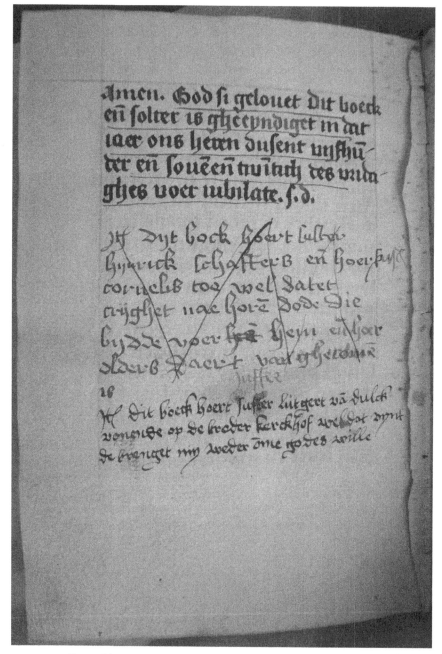

FIGURE 1.1   *Two ex-libris notes in a Psalter that was produced in the monastery of Thesinge near Groningen. Leiden, University Library, MS Ltk 235 (1527), f. 211v. Image © Author.*

a tertiary in Naarden, to Fye Anssendochter, a tertiary in Amsterdam, is yet another example.[77] A third is a manuscript with Epistle lessons, bequeathed by the beguine Magdalene Claesdochter to the convent of Saint Ghertrude at the Groot Begijnhof in Haarlem, for the benefit of all beguines.[78] These examples show the interaction between religious, 'semi'-religious and laypersons, and the role vernacular Bibles played in their networks. They support the evidence provided by archival sources, and vice versa.

Towards a Complementary Approach

Walter Simons, who has studied literacy and readership of beguines, and Thérèse De Hemptinne, who has done the same for women in the Low Countries in general, draw attention to archival sources such as convents' archives and convents' book inventories, inheritance records like wills and testaments, estates records, and accounts. We searched these kinds of sources for references to Middle Dutch Bibles in the possession of laypeople, both male and female. The preliminary results, on the basis of secondary literature, are promising. A substantial number of references to Middle Dutch Bibles in the possession of laypeople such as widows, glove-makers, physicians, brewers, aristocrats and beguines, shows the widespread circulation of Bibles. These references are complemented by the data provided by colophons of the surviving Bible manuscripts themselves. Although Middle Dutch Bibles have survived mainly in manuscripts from religious convents, archival sources suggest that a substantial quantity of manuscripts must also have circulated among urban networks of laypeople. Following De Hemptinne, we stress the function of these Bibles in the networks of laypeople and religious. Bibles cannot be seen as static objects, written in a convent or a workshop, and meant to stay

---

77 'Item dit boec hoert toe Fye anssen dochter woenende tot amsterledam totten elfdusent maechden Bidt. Bidt voer die ghene die hier een arm bezorghester of gheweest heeft om gods willen Suster mouwers dochter woenende te naerden tot sancta marien int cloester'. MS Amsterdam, UB, XV E 21 (before 1482), f. 9r. Biemans, *Middelnederlandse bijbelhandschriften* 142–144, no 116. See for a discussion of this Psalter, which has Latin incipits, Desplenter Y., "Songs of Praise for the 'Illiterate': Latin Hymns in Middle Dutch Prose Translation" in Hemptinne Th. De – Góngora M.E. (eds.), *The Voice of Silence: Women's Literacy in a Men's Church*, Medieval Church Studies 9 (Turnhout: 2004) 127–142, here 127–129.

78 MS Hamburg, SUB, Cod. 95 in scrinio (c. 1450). Biemans, *Middelnederlandse bijbelhandschriften* 215–216, no 201.

in a religious or secular context, respectively. They moved between those contexts, uniting people in their zeal for religious reading.

A third set of sources, which has not yet been mentioned but complements the evidence for lay readership of Bibles, is the evidence provided by the clergy. De Pauw and others who assumed that vernacular Bibles were forbidden or discouraged by the clergy ignored the treatises written by priests and clerics, which stimulated the reading of the Bible by laypeople. It is especially in the Low Countries, in the context of the reform movement of the *Devotio Moderna*, that we find such treatises.[79] Geert Grote, Gerard Zerbolt of Zutphen and Dirc of Herxen encouraged laypeople to read the Epistle and Gospel lessons before they went to church.[80] They did not think of these Bible texts as too complicated for laypeople, let alone as forbidden fruit. In addition, an anonymous Franciscan brother wrote in his 'Mirror or rule of the Christian faith' (*Spieghel ofte reghel der kersten ghelove*, around 1462) that everyone should teach their children well in the Christian belief, go to church on each holy day, and, if possible, read a lesson from the Bible every night before bedtime.[81] The archival sources reveal that laypeople actually had such Bibles at their disposal. The assumption, fed by the Protestant paradigm and still very much alive, that the vernacular Bible was forbidden or considered inappropriate for laypeople, should truly be laid to rest.

This contribution concludes with a manuscript that embodies a combination of both treated sources, namely a fifteenth-century Bible manuscript containing a book list. The manuscript contains the letters of Paul, which are preceded by a reading list with the lessons of the proper of the year and the proper of the saints.[82] In the back of the manuscript a book list was written [Fig. 1.2]. It contains, among other devotional book titles, the Pauline letters

---

79   For Dutch, Italian, French and German material on this topic, see Corbellini, "Instructing the Soul".

80   Folkerts, "The Cloister or the City?" 180–181; Beek L. van, *Leken trekken tot Gods Woord. Dirc van Herxen (1381–1457) en zijn Eerste Collatieboek, Middeleeuwse Studies en Bronnen* 120 (Hilversum: 2009) 125–126, 140–146.

81   'Voert so siet oec dat ghi uwe ondersaten ende uwe kinderen wel regyert ende die wet Gods wel leert also dat si alle jaer ten minsten die vier hoechtiden ten heilighen sacrament gaen ende alle heilighe daghe gheerne te kerken gaen ende dat woert Gods gheerne horen ende des savens te samen vercallen. Ende ist dat ghi tijt hebt soe leest alle avent een capittel van goeder leringhe der heiligher scriften eer ghi slapen gaet'. Bange P., *Een handvol wijsheden. Eenvoudig geloof in de vijftiende eeuw: de Spieghel ofte reghel der kersten ghelove* (Nijmegen: 2000) 87–88.

82   MS Leiden, UB, Ltk 243 III (first half 15th C.). Biemans, *Middelnederlandse bijbelhandschriften* 223, no 210.

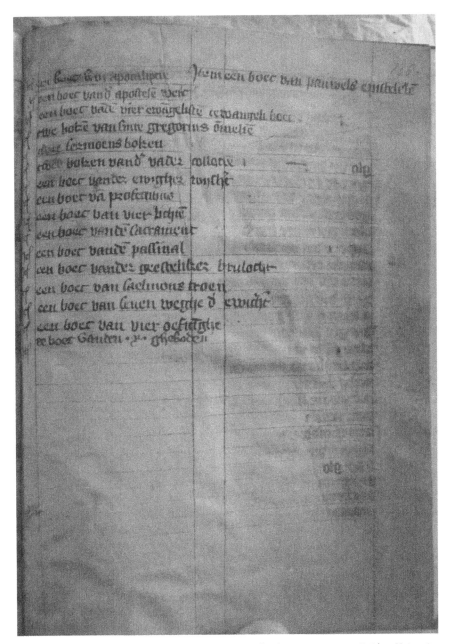

FIGURE 1.2 *Book list in a New Testament manuscript of unknown provenance. Leiden, University Library, MS Ltk 243 III (first half 15th c.), f. 138r. Image © Author.*

(which is the manuscript at hand), the Apocalypse, the apostles' works (i.e. the canonical letters and Acts), and the four Gospels.[83] Considering the devotional nature of the books on the list, does this list describe books of a religious convent? Or did the manuscript and the list, contrarily perhaps to what one might assume at first sight, come from the property of a layperson? The book lists of pious laypeople like Elisabeth De Grutere were not very different from the book collections of religious convents. Moreover, just like the list of Mary of Loon, this list was written in a manuscript, and not as a separate inventory, which may indicate a private book list.[84] Returning to the list of lessons in the front of the manuscript, we find an addition to the list, namely the lesson for the feast day of Saint Francis. Taken together, this suggests that this manuscript originated from a convent of tertiaries, which belonged to the Third Order of Saint Francis. In other manuscripts from tertiaries we find the addition of Saint Francis and Saint Clare's feast days as well. Or was the addition, as the suspicious reader might suggest, written by a layperson with a strong sympathy for Saint Francis? The confusion does not end there: from 1683 on, the manuscript was transmitted in a set with two other, complementary manuscripts from the Groot Begijnhof in Haarlem.[85] These two other manuscripts contain the Gospels and Acts, the apostolic or canonical letters, and Apocalypse, exactly the New Testament books complementary to the Pauline letters in the first manuscript. Possibly, they already belonged together before 1683, not long after their production in the first half of the fifteenth century. We know that one of

---

83   The other titles on the list are two books of Gregory's homilies, two sermons' books, two
      books of the *Collations* of the Fathers, Henry Suso's *Eternal Wisdom*, a book of 'profectibus',
      a book of 'four lights', a book of the sacraments, a Passion book ('vanden passinal'), John
      of Ruusbroec's *Spiritual Espousals*, Otto of Passau's *The Golden Throne*, a book of 'seven
      paths of eternity', a book of 'four meditations', and a book of the Ten Commandments.

84   Derolez writes that in the fifteenth and sixteenth centuries no book lists of institutions
      have been found in manuscripts from the Low Countries. This one in the Leiden manu-
      script may be the exception. Otherwise, we are dealing with a private book inventory.
      Derolez A., "Opmerkingen bij enkele Middeleeuwse catalogi uit de Nederlanden", in
      Hermans J.M.M. (ed.), *Middeleeuwse handschriftenkunde in de Nederlanden 1988. Verslag
      van de Groningse Codicologendagen 28–29 april 1988, Nijmeegse codicologische cahiers*
      10–12 (Grave: 1989) 271–283, here 278.

85   These manuscripts are MS Leiden, UB, Ltk 243 I (c. 1410) and MS Leiden, UB, Ltk 243 II
      (1431). Biemans, *Middelnederlandse bijbelhandschriften* 172–173, no 144 and 218, no 203.
      Lieftinck, however, clearly states that MS Leiden, UB, Ltk 243 III did not originate from
      the same convent as Ltk 243 I and Ltk 243 II. Lieftinck G.I., *Codicum in finibus Belgarum
      ante annum 1550 conscriptorum qui in Bibliotheca Universitatis asservantur vol. 1: Codices
      168–360 Societatis cui nomen Maatschappij der Nederlandsche Letterkunde, Bibliotheca
      Universitatis Leidensis, Codices manuscripti* V, 1 (Leiden: 1948) 60.

the other two manuscripts—and therefore the other one of the set presumably as well—was given by will by Catharine Willemsdochter and her natural sister Ave to their fellow sisters of the Begijnhof of Haarlem.[86] Transactions like these, between beguines themselves, between tertiaries and beguines, and also between religious and laypeople, were common. Although we do not know where exactly the book list in the manuscript with the Pauline letters was written, we do know that it was a witness of the lively exchange of books.

Evaluating the different sources for lay readership of Middle Dutch Bible manuscripts, we can conclude that they not only complement each other when it comes to providing numbers, for the items on book lists can almost never be identified with an existing exemplar, but they are also complementary in scope. As we have seen above, the surviving manuscripts reflect a lower number of lay owners than archival sources do. Archival sources, especially descriptions of estates, which are the written results of disputes and inheritance of goods, are more likely to come from lay circles, whereas manuscripts seem to have been better preserved in institutions. The sources that are used define to a certain extent the character of the readers that are found. The third set of sources, normative sources coming from the clergy, only gives indirect proof of lay readership of vernacular Bibles, but direct proof of the stimulating climate and clerical approval for laypersons reading the Bible by clergymen in the Low Countries.

Bibliography

Boone M., "De Gentse staten van goed als bron voor de kennis van de materiële cultuur: mogelijkheden en beperkingen (Late middeleeuwen-vroege moderne tijden)", in Daelemans F. (ed.), *Bronnen voor de geschiedenis van de materiële cultuur: Staten van goed en testamenten/ Sources pour l'histoire de la culture materielle: Inventaires après-décès et testaments. Handelingen van de studiedag te Bussel/ Actes de la journée d'étude de Bruxelles 24-10-1986, Archives et bibliothèques de Belgique/ Archief- en bibliotheekwezen in België: Numéro special/ Extranummer* 25,2 (Brussels: 1988) 51–73.

---

86   'Ghescreuen int iaer ons heren m. cccc ende xxxi opten viertienden dach in april'. MS Leiden, UB, Ltk 243 II, f. 202r. The rest of the colophon is erased, but Lieftinck was able to read it with ultraviolet light: 'Dit boec hebben besproken ende ghemaect kathrijn willems dochter ende aue haer suster den ghemenen susteren vanden seluen conuents huyse daer si in pleghen te wonen gheheten alijt florijs dochter couent aldaer totten huyse te bliuen ten ewighen daghen Bid voer haer beider sielen'. Lieftinck, *Codicum in finibus* 60.

Brinkman H., "Het Comburgse handschrift en de Gentse boekproductie omstreeks 1400", *Queeste: Journal of Medieval Literature in the Low Countries* 5,2 (1998) 98–113.

———, "Oude en nieuwe filologie bij Herman Pleij", in *Neerlandistiek.nl* 09.01c (May 2009) 1–10, http://www.neerlandistiek.nl (consulted on 1 September 2012).

Corbellini S., "Instructing the Soul, Feeding the Spirit and Awakening the Passion: Holy Writ and Lay Readers in Late Medieval Europe" in Gordon B. – McLean M. (eds.), *Shaping the Bible in the Reformation: Books, Scholars and Their Readers in the Sixteenth Century* (Leiden: 2012) 15–39.

Derolez A., "Opmerkingen bij enkele Middeleeuwse catalogi uit de Nederlanden" in Hermans J.M.M. (ed.), *Middeleeuwse handschriftenkunde in de Nederlanden 1988. Verslag van de Groningse Codicologendagen 28–29 april 1988, Nijmeegse codicologische cahiers* 10–12 (Grave: 1989) 271–283.

Folkerts S., "Te 'duncker' voor leken? Middelnederlandse bijbelvertalingen vanuit het perspectief van de gebruikers", *Jaarboek voor Nederlandse Boekgeschiedenis* 18 (2011) 155–170.

———, "The Cloister or the City? The Appropriation of the New Testament by Lay Readers in an Urban Setting", in Corbellini S. (ed.), *Cultures of Religious Reading in the Late Middle Ages. Instructing the Soul, Feeding the Spirit and Awakening the Passion*, Utrecht Studies in Medieval Literacy 25 (Turnhout: 2013) 175–199.

Folkerts S. – Gabriël R. (eds.), *A Bunch of Books. Book Collections in the Medieval Low Countries*, [thematic issue of] *Queeste. Journal of Medieval Literature in the Low Countries* 20,2 (2013).

Gabriël R., "Boekenlijsten en *Material Philology*. Methodologische overwegingen bij de boekenlijst van Michael van der Stoct (ca. 1394)", *Queeste: Journal of Medieval Literature in the Low Countries* 16,2 (2009) 83–111.

Gow A.C., "The Contested History of a Book: The German Bible of the Later Middle Ages and Reformation in Legend, Ideology, and Scholarship", *The Journal of Hebrew Scriptures* 9 (2009) 1–37.

———, "Challenging the Protestant Paradigm: Bible Reading in Lay and Urban Contexts of the Later Middle Ages", in Heffernan Th.J. – Burman Th.E. (eds.), *Scripture and Pluralism: Reading the Bible in the Religiously Plural Worlds of the Middle Ages and Renaissance*, Studies in the History of Christian Traditions 123 (Leiden – Boston: 2005) 161–192.

Guzzetti L., "Women's Inheritance and Testamentary Practices in Late Fourteenth- and Early Fifteenth-Century Venice and Ghent", in Kittell E.E. – Suydam M.A. (eds.), *The Texture of Society: Medieval Women in the Southern Low Countries* (New York: 2004) 79–108.

Hemptinne Th. De, "Reading, Writing, and Devotional Practices: Lay and Religious Women and the Written Word in the Low Countries (1350–1550)", in Hemptinne Th. De – Góngora M.E. (eds.), *The Voice of Silence: Women's Literacy in a Men's Church*, Medieval Church Studies 9 (Turnhout: 2004) 111–126.

Janssens J., "Begrijpen en begrijpen is twee . . . Een halve eeuw medioneerlandistiek", *Queeste: Journal of Medieval Literature in the Low Countries* 19,1 (2012) 1–19.

Kors M. – Claassens G.H.M. (eds.), *De Bijbel voor leken. Studies over Petrus Naghel en de Historiebijbel van 1361* (Turnhout – Leuven: 2007).

Kwakkel E., *Die dietsche boeke die ons toebehoeren: De kartuizers van Herne en de productie van Middelnederlandse handschriften in de regio Brussel*, Miscellanea Neerlandica 27 (Leuven: 2002).

Simons W., " 'Staining the Speech of Things Divine': The Uses of Literacy in Medieval Beguine Communities", in Hemptinne Th. De – Góngora M.E. (eds.), *The Voice of Silence: Women's Literacy in a Men's Church*, Medieval Church Studies 9 (Turnhout: 2004) 86–110.

CHAPTER 2

Manuscript Paratexts in the Making: British Library MS Harley 6333 as a Liturgical Compilation

Matti Peikola

British Library MS Harley 6333 is a Middle English Biblical manuscript from the fifteenth century. Its rich and uniquely designed set of liturgical paratexts makes for a case study of religious reading habits and techniques at the close of the medieval period. To interpret the function of the paratexts in their manuscript context, a materialist philolological approach is adopted in this paper, with a focus on the physical structure of the book as well as its thematic organisation. The paratextual design of MS Harley 6333 reflects the contents of the manuscript, which combine a gospel harmony (*Oon of Foure*) with Biblical books in the Later Version of the Wycliffite translation to form a complete New Testament. To understand the rationale of the compiler/scribe of the manuscript, I examine his creative responses to established paratextual conventions of the *Oon of Foure* and the Wycliffite Bible. Before scrutinising the manuscript evidence, I address theoretical concerns related to paratextuality and materialist philology.

Paratexts and Manuscript Culture

The original formulation of the concept of *paratext* by Gérard Genette was largely based on textual practices of the print culture, characterised by the speculative production of books in which individual copies are as a rule *not* custom-made to the order and specification of individual customers.[1] In that context, the various paratextual elements mediating a book to its reader

---

* The original version of this paper was presented at the International Medieval Congress in Leeds, 2011. I wish to thank the conveners and participants of the Leeds session and the editors of the present volume for their valuable comments. I am grateful to Dr. Mary Raschko for allowing me to read her at the time unpublished paper on *Oon of Foure*. Research for this article has been supported by the Academy of Finland, funding decision 136404.

1   Genette G., *Seuils* (Paris: 1987), transl. into English by J.E. Lewin as *Paratexts: Thresholds of Interpretation* (Cambridge: 1997); see especially 1–15 and the Foreword by R. Macksey. See also

emerge essentially as devices conveying ideas of the *author* and those of the *producer* (publisher, printer, translator, editor etc.) as to how the book and its texts are to be consumed. In manuscript production, however, which in fifteenth-century England continued to be largely based on individual acts of commissioning rather than on speculative trade, the paratextual packaging of a book may also, importantly, reflect the needs of a specific *consumer*—the individual (or collective) patron, owner, or reader.[2] For this reason, it can be argued, the paratexts of manuscript books can potentially provide more direct information concerning individual reading practices than can be inferred from their printed equivalents.[3]

Interpreting the role played by paratexts in manuscripts will benefit from the perspective provided by *materialist philology*, which emphasises the need to approach individual manuscript texts and variation between their different versions in the context of the artefacts (books) in which they were circulated.[4]

Genette G., *Palimpsestes* (Paris: 1982), transl. into English by C. Newman and C. Doubinsky as *Palimpsests: Literature in the Second Degree* (Lincoln, NE: 1997) 2–3.

2   Gillespie A. – Wakelin D. (eds.), *The Production of Books in England 1350–1500* (Cambridge: 2011) contains several important articles addressing the mode and organization of manuscript production. See especially Kwakkel E., "Commercial Organization and Economic Innovation" 173–191; Mooney L.R., "Vernacular Literary Manuscripts and Their Scribes" 192–211; Pouzet J.-P., "Book Production outside Commercial Context" 212–238. See also Pearsall D., "Introduction", in Griffiths J. – Pearsall D. (eds.), *Book Production and Publishing in Britain 1375–1475* (Cambridge: 1989) 1–10. For a detailed discussion of a bespoke book contract between a scribe and a priest in mid-14th-century York, see Hanna R., *Introducing Medieval English Book History: Manuscripts, their Producers and their Readers* (Liverpool: 2013) 166–192.

3   Poleg E., *Approaching the Bible in Medieval England* (Manchester: 2013) 108–151, discusses the role played by paratextual addenda in Late Medieval Latin Bibles; he points out that "[w]hile the layout was uniform, the addenda were varied and versatile, accommodating Bibles to personal tastes and rendering them invaluable for the medieval classroom, pulpit, or lectern" (112). Findings of the ERC-funded research project "Holy Writ and Lay Readers. A Social History of Vernacular Bible Translations in the Late Middle Ages" demonstrate how Biblical manuscripts often enjoyed a long afterlife during which they could move from one individual owner to another as well as from individual owners to institutions, and vice versa; see, for example, Corbellini S., "Vernacular Bible Manuscripts in Late Medieval Italy: Cultural Appropriation and Textual Transformation", in Poleg E. – Light L. (eds.), *Form and Function in the Late Medieval Bible* (Leiden: 2013) 261–281.

4   A seminal statement of the concerns of materialist philology is Nichols S.G. – Wenzel S., "Introduction", in Nichols S.G. – Wenzel S. (eds.), *The Whole Book: Cultural Perspectives on the Medieval Miscellany* (Ann Arbor: 1996) 1–6. Expanding Genette's original position, recent scholarship on paratextuality also emphasises the important semiotic role played by the materiality of the text in mediating the reader's reception; see, for example, Andersson B., "Female Writing in Manuscript and Print: Two German Examples from the Cultural and

In addition to the clues for contextual interpretation provided for example by the physical size, materials (writing support, binding), script, illumination and layout of the book, the materialist philological approach also seeks to examine the role played by individual texts in the design and thematic organisation of the whole book. According to Nichols and Wenzel, '[t]he manuscript agency (...) can thus offer social or anthropological insights into the way its texts were or could have been read by the patron or public to which it was diffused'.[5]

In particular, the materialist philological approach can help us gauge the degree to which the presence of specific paratexts in a manuscript book can be thought to reflect interaction between a specific producer and consumer. Absolute distinctions cannot be drawn, but it seems plausible to assume that paratexts that circulated with a text regularly and in fairly invariable form across different manuscript contexts are less likely to reflect such interaction than those occurring infrequently or even uniquely in the manuscript tradition, or those subject to considerable textual variation between individual copies. Paratexts of the first kind may have been included in a book routinely by producers, without much concern as to whether or not they would in fact serve the needs of their specific customers, let alone reflect customers' specific wishes about the contents. As an example of such paratexts one may think of the so-called *Interpretations of Hebrew Names*, a virtually standard element of the mass-produced thirteenth-century pandect Bibles that provided a key to the significance of thousands of proper names found in the Bible.[6]

In the weighting of the status of different manuscript paratexts, this criterion may be supplemented by codicological and paleographical evidence. The evidence may indicate, for example, that certain paratexts were often produced in self-contained structural units (quires or booklets) or written in a different hand from that of the main scribe of the manuscript. Especially when combined with the first criterion, such findings will strengthen the possibility that paratexts made available in this way were added to the manuscript at some

---

Political Context of Late Seventeenth-Century Sweden – Maria Aurora von Königsmarck (1662–1728) and Eva Margaretha Frölich (?–1692)", *Studia Neophilologica* 86, Supplement 1 (2014) 9–28.

5   Nichols – Wenzel, "Introduction" 2.

6   For the *Interpretations of Hebrew Names* and their paratextual functions, see Light L., "The Bible and the Individual: The Thirteenth-Century Paris Bible", in Boynton S. – Reilly D.J., *The Practice of the Bible in the Middle Ages: Production, Reception, and Performance in Western Christianity* (New York: 2011) 228–246, here 234; Poleg, *Approaching the Bible* 118–124; Poleg E., "The Interpretations of Hebrew Names in Theory and Practice", in Poleg E. – Light L. (eds.), *Form and Function in the Late Medieval Bible* (Leiden: 2013) 217–236.

point after its original production, for example to promote a specific mode of reading or use for the book preferred by its new owner. Liturgical calendars, for example, which specify the dates and grades of the saints' festivals month by month throughout the ecclesiastical year, often form a separate quire at the beginning of manuscripts, sometimes with their first and last pages left blank by the scribe. Especially when found appended to a type of book which does not usually contain a liturgical calendar, such as a complete medieval Bible or a New Testament, its presence suggests that the owner or reader wanted the text to be added to the manuscript for a specific reason.[7]

The *Oon of Foure* and its Paratexts

The Middle English translation of Clement of Llanthony's twelfth-century gospel harmony *Unum ex Quattuor*, usually known as the *Oon of Foure* (henceforth *OF*), is extant, in full or in part, in fifteen manuscripts paleographically dateable to a time extending from the end of the fourteenth century through the first half of the fifteenth. Paul Smith's detailed description of the manuscripts indicates the presence of several paratexts in them.[8] The most ubiquitous of these elements are Clement's own prologue, to which some additional comments were added by the anonymous translator of *OF*, and a summary of the contents of the twelve Parts that constitute the gospel harmony.[9] Both Clement's prologue and the summary were also standard elements of the

---

7   See, for example, Peikola M., "Instructional Aspects of the Calendar in Later Medieval England, with Special Reference to The John Rylands University Library MS English 80", in Peikola M. – Skaffari J. – Tanskanen S.-K. (eds.), *Instructional Writing in English: Studies in Honour of Risto Hiltunen* (Amsterdam: 2009) 83–104, here 90–91; Poleg, *Approaching the Bible* 112–113; Light L., "The Thirteenth-Century Pandect and the Liturgy: Bibles with Missals", in Poleg E. – Light L. (eds.), *Form and Function in the Late Medieval Bible* (Leiden: 2013) 185–215.

8   Smith P.M., "An Edition of Parts i–v of the Wycliffite Translation of Clement of Llanthony's Latin Gospel Harmony *Unum ex Quattuor* known as *Oon of Foure*", unpublished PhD thesis, University of Southampton (1985) xii–lxiii.

9   In his comments, the translator explains how he simplified Clement's method of systematically indicating in the text each instance where the Gospel source for the narrative changes. According to the translator, this was done to facilitate the 'simple' reader's understanding of the text ('lest þis ofte rehersing and medeling of þe names of þe Gospeleris among þe sentence shulde make þe sentence derk, and cumbre symple mennis wittes'. Quoted from Smith, "An Edition" 2).

manuscript transmission of the Latin text.[10] They occur together in ten of those eleven manuscripts that contain the complete *OF*, the summary always immediately following Clement's prologue; in one complete manuscript the prologue appears unusually without the summary (see Table 1).[11]

TABLE 1   *The major paratexts in the eleven complete manuscripts of OF. The headings of the columns correspond to the manuscript sigla used by Smith, "An Edition", as follows: A = London, British Library MS Arundel 254; B = Oxford, Bodleian Library MS Bodley 481; C = Oxford, Christ Church College MS Allestree L. 41; D = Oxford, Bodleian Library MS Bodley 771; E = Peterborough Cathedral MS 8; G = University of Glasgow Library MS General 223; H = London, British Library MS Harley 1862; L = London, British Library MS Harley 6333; O = London, British Library MS Royal 17 D. VIII; P = New York, Columbia University MS Plimpton 268; Y = Oxford, Bodleian Library MS Bodley 978. A black square indicates the presence of the paratext in the manuscript.*

	A	B	C	D	E	G	H	L	O	P	Y
Clement's prologue	■	■	■	■	■	■	■	■	■	■	■
Summary of the contents	■	■	■		■	■	■	■	■	■	■
1st additional prologue	■				■	■					
2nd additional prologue	■		■		■	■		■			
3rd additional prologue	■				■	■		■			
Table of lessons	■	■	■	■			■	■	■	■	■

---

10   For a description of a prototypical Latin manuscript with the usual paratexts accompanying the *Unum ex Quattuor*, see Smith, "An Edition", lxiv–lxv. Unlike Clement's prologue and the summary of the contents, a third regular paratextual companion of the Latin text—the so-called *Ratio Ordinis*—did not become part of the Middle English transmission. In the *Ratio*, the sequence in which the gospel harmony was compiled from the four gospels into a single narrative is carefully presented, chapter by chapter, in tabular form (see Smith, "An Edition" lxv, xc, xcii).

11   Of the four other surviving copies, Cambridge, St John's College MS G.25 (Smith's siglum J) and San Marino, Huntington Library MS HM 501 (N) only contain extracts from *OF*, while London, British Library MS Royal 17. C. XXXIII (R) and Dublin, Sir John Galvin MS 8 (M) are acephalous and all their front-matter is lost. See Smith, "An Edition" xii–lxiii.

In addition to the paratexts inherited from the Latin source text, a few manuscripts of *OF* contain additional prologues. These are not derived from the Latin tradition of the *Unum ex Quattuor*, but their contents and patterns of circulation associate them with Wycliffite Biblical scholarship in later fourteenth-century England.[12] The additional prologues occur together as a fixed set in three manuscripts of *OF*; a fourth manuscript contains two of them together; one is found on its own in a fifth manuscript (see Table 1). All three prologues are also extant in manuscripts that do not contain *OF*, used as prologues to individual Gospels in some manuscripts of the Wycliffite Bible and the Wycliffite *Glossed Gospels*. There is no evidence that they were originally designed to accompany *OF*. According to Hunt, 'they were clearly not a regular concomitant of the text'.[13] Codicologically, the additional prologues form a distinct production unit in at least two manuscripts of *OF*.[14] It is possible that they were interpolated in these codices to emphasise the status of the gospel harmony as Biblical translation.

As indicated in Table 1, altogether ten manuscripts of *OF* contain a table of lessons, helping the reader to find in the text of the gospel harmony the passages corresponding to the gospel pericopes read at Mass during the ecclesiastical year. Descriptions of extant manuscripts of the *Unum ex Quattuor* suggest that this liturgical paratext was not a usual element of the Latin version.[15] The high frequency of the table of lessons among the complete manuscripts

---

12   For a discussion of the additional prologues, see Hunt S., "An Edition of Tracts in Favour of Scriptural Translation and of Some Texts connected with Lollard Vernacular Biblical Scholarship," 2 vols., unpublished DPhil thesis, University of Oxford (1994) vol. 1 66–68, 92–97, 179–180, 190–196; see also Dove M., *The Earliest Advocates of the English Bible: The Texts of the Medieval Debate* (Exeter: 2010) xxxvii–xxxix, lxii–lxiii; Raschko M., "*Oon of Foure*: Harmonizing Wycliffite and Pseudo-Bonaventuran Approaches to the Life of Christ", in Johnson I. – Westphall A.F. (eds.), *The Pseudo-Bonaventuran Lives of Christ: Exploring the Middle English Tradition* (Turnhout: 2013) 341–373. Two of the prologues (the so-called second and third additional prologue) have been recently edited by Dove, *The Earliest Advocates* 103–105, 174–179; Hunt, "An Edition" vol. 2 363–364 contains an edition of the first additional prologue.

13   Hunt, "An Edition" vol. 1 67.

14   Hunt, "An Edition" vol. 1 67.

15   No critical edition of the *Unum ex Quattuor* exists. See Schmid U.B., *Unum ex quattuor. Eine Geschichte der lateinischen Tatianüberlieferung* (Freiburg: 2005) 48, 178–180. Smith, "An Edition" ccv, lists ten extant copies of the Latin text. Catalogue descriptions of five of the manuscripts available to me do not record the presence of a table of lessons in them (Cambridge University Library MS Dd.1.17; London, British Library MS Royal 3. A. 10; Oxford, Bodleian Library MS Hatton 61; Oxford, Merton College MS 40; Oxford, University College MS 19). Deanesly M., *The Lollard Bible and Other Medieval Biblical Versions*

of *OF* (see Table 1) could be taken to mean that it was a standard paratextual companion to the English gospel harmony, comparable to Clement's prologue and the summary of the contents. Codicological and paleographical evidence shows, however, that similarly to the additional Wycliffite prologues, the table of lessons too was sometimes a supplementary item appended to the book after its original production. On the basis of the collation formulae provided by Smith, in most of the manuscripts the table forms a self-contained structural unit, occasionally with blank leaves or a filler item at the end of the quire, and tends to occur as the very first item of the book, i.e. the position traditionally occupied by detachable liturgical calendars in Psalters and Books of Hours.[16] In at least two manuscripts (A, O), the table has been written in a different hand from that of the rest of the volume.[17]

In comparison to Clement's prologue and the summary of the contents, the *OF* tables of lessons show considerably more variation in their textual and visual features, including the referential systems used in them indicating how to locate each pericope in the text of *OF*. The tables circulated in more than one distinct redaction and were modified by individual scribes (and readers) according to their needs and expectations. To better appreciate the idiosyncratic features of the table of lessons in MS Harley 6333, it will be useful to briefly examine the typical elements of these tables in *OF* manuscripts, especially with an eye on their referential apparatus.

The most common type of referential apparatus represented by the *OF* tables of lessons (henceforth Type A) is illustrated in this figure from British Library MS Royal 17. D. VIII (O) [Fig. 2.1]. As shown in Fig. 2.1, the leftmost column identifies the liturgical occasion, i.e. the specific day on which the gospel pericope is read at Mass; the entry in the top line, for example, pertains to the Second Sunday after the Octave of Epiphany. For each occasion, the reference to the text of *OF* consists of four elements (exemplified here from the top line of Fig. 2.1 with abbreviations expanded silently): (1) the number of the Part of Clement's gospel harmony, from I to XII ('ii partie'); (2) the number of the Chapter within the designated part ('ix chapiter'); (3) the precise location of the lesson within the designated Chapter, identified with a subdividing letter of the alphabet that is repeated in the margin of the text at the appropriate

---

(Oxford: 1920) 303 reports, however, that the copy in Cambridge University Library is 'preceded by a table of lessons'.

16   Smith, "An Edition" xii–lxiii.
17   Smith, "An Edition" xxv–xxix.

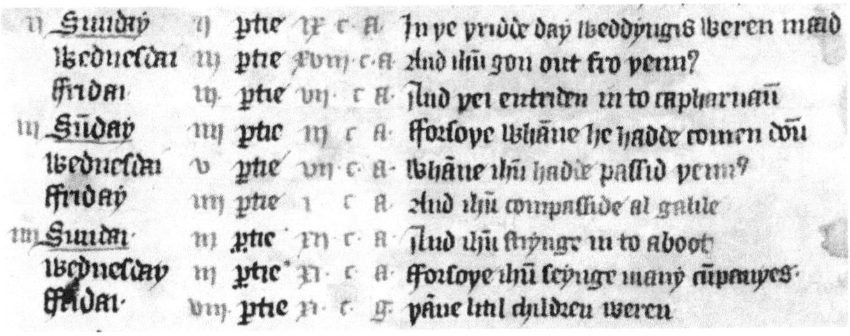
ii Sunday ii ptie ix c a In þe þridde day weddyngis weren maad
wednesdai iii ptie xiiii c a And ihũ gon out fro þenn?
Fridai iii ptie vii c a And þei entriden in to capharnaũ
iii Sũdai iii ptie iii c a Forsoþe whãne he hadde comen doũ
wednesdai v ptie vii c a Whãne ihũ hadde passid þenn?
Fridai iiii ptie i c a And ihũ compassede al galile
iiii Sundai ii ptie xii c a And ihũ stiynge in to a boot
wednesdai iii ptie xi c a Forsoþe ihũ seynge many cũpanyes
Fridai viii ptie xi c g Whãne litil children weren

FIGURE 2.1 Oon of Foure, *Table of liturgical lessons. London, British Library,* MS *Royal 17. D. VIII, f. 1v (s. xiv ex., Smith, "An Edition" xxv). Detail. Image © British Library Board.*

point ('a.');[18] (4) the opening words (*incipit*) of the lesson ('In þe þridde day weddyngis weren maad').

In addition to MS O, four other *OF* manuscripts contain a Type A table (A, B, C, G). Two tables (D and P) share another referential system (Type B), illustrated in the next figure from P [Fig. 2.2].[19] At first glance, the design of Type B seems to correspond to that of Type A in elements (1)–(3), but lack element (4), the incipit of the lesson (see Fig. 2.2). A closer comparison indicates, however, that the most substantive difference between the two types in fact has to do with element (3). Contrary to what its appearance suggests, the rightmost element in each line of Type B does not correspond to the alphabetical *distinctiones* used in Type A to signal chapter-internal subdivisions (see for example the letter 'I' in the top line of Fig. 2.2, compared to the same entry in Fig. 2.1). Instead, the letters in Type B stand for the first letter (sometimes the first two or three letters) of the opening word of the lesson, and should be viewed as highly truncated incipits rather than *distinctiones* proper. In the top line of

18 The alphabetical *distinctiones* subdivide the chapters of *OF* into virtual segments of roughly equal length beginning from the letter *a*. Only the distinctions corresponding to the beginning of gospel lessons are shown in the margins. For the origins and development of medieval systems of alphabetical *distinctiones*, especially with regard to Biblical texts, see Saenger P. "The British Isles and the Origin of the Modern Mode of Biblical Citation", *Syntagma* 1 (2005) 77–123; Saenger P., "The Anglo-Hebraic Origins of the Modern Chapter Division of the Latin Bible", in Burguillo F.J. – Mier L. (eds.), *La fractura historiográfica: Las investigaciones de Edad Media y Renacimiento desde el tercer milenio* (Salamanca: 2008) 177–202.

19 For an edition of the *OF* table from P, see Smith, "An Edition" 236–250.

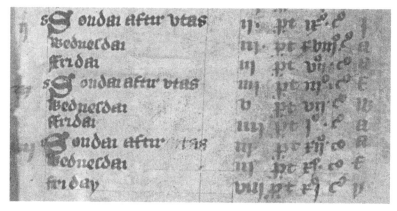

FIGURE 2.2 Oon of Foure, *Table of liturgical lessons. New York, Columbia University,*
MS *Plimpton 268, f. 2r* (s. xiv/xv, Smith, *"An Edition" xxxix*). Detail. Image
© *Columbia University Libraries.*

Fig. 2.2 for example, the 'I' corresponds to the first letter of the lesson 'In þe þridde day weddyngis weren maad' ('On the third day there was a wedding'). In the corresponding location in the text of *OF* in these manuscripts, the reader would find the truncated incipits repeated in the margin at the appropriate location as a visual cue, similar in function to the alphabetical *distinctiones* reproduced in the margins of copies furnished with a Type A table.

Neither in Type A nor in Type B does the referential apparatus of the table provide any information about the Biblical loci from which the gospel lessons for the various liturgical occasions have been derived; the reference simply pertains to the text of *OF*. This is wholly to be expected, since the primary para-textual function of the table is to enable the reader to locate the text of each lesson in the gospel harmony contained in the same manuscript. Information as to the Biblical loci would not seem to serve this purpose in any conceivable way. It is therefore worth particular attention that in three manuscripts of *OF* (H, L, Y) the table of lessons also identifies the precise Gospel source, in addition to referring to the Parts and Chapters of the gospel harmony as usual. The three tables are otherwise somewhat different in their features and not classifiable under a single type. Their design suggests scribal creativity to tailor the paratextual apparatus of the book in an individualised way. The table of lessons at the beginning of MS Harley 6333 (L) is a case in point.

MS Harley 6333 (L) and its Table of Lessons

L is a parchment manuscript of 365 leaves from the first half of the fifteenth century.[20] It originally formed a single codex, but was rebound in two volumes in 1966.[21] Several features testify to the professional quality of its design and execution: a spacious and regularly ruled double column layout; *littera duplex* initials with penwork border elements placed at the beginning of new books; the use of a formal *textualis quadrata* script of a style typically found in contemporary liturgical manuscripts written in Latin.[22] In addition to *OF*, accompanied by Clement's prologue and the summary of the contents as usual, the major textual contents of L comprise, in this order, the Pauline Epistles, Acts of the Apostles, Catholic Epistles, and the Apocalypse—all in the Later Version (LV) of the Wycliffite Bible. The Apocalypse is followed by the Epistle to the Laodiceans, which is not a standard constituent of Wycliffite Bible manuscripts, but is present in a relatively small proportion of them; it may have become part of the transmission of LV at a fairly late stage.[23] Another non-standard textual feature in the Wycliffite Bible materials in L is the presence of an additional

---

20   See the unpublished descriptions of the manuscript in Smith, "An Edition" xxx–xxxv and Hunt, "An Edition" vol. 1 172–175. While I am informed by these accounts, my textual, codicological and paleographical observations concerning the manuscript, unless otherwise indicated, are based on my own examination of the original and its digital reproduction. In comparison to the detailed information provided by Smith and Hunt in their doctoral theses, the published descriptions of the manuscript are superficial (see *A Catalogue of the Harleian Manuscripts, in the British Museum* (1808), vol. 3 358; Forshall J. – Madden F. (eds.), *The Holy Bible Containing the Old and the New Testaments with the Apocryphal Books, in the Earliest English Versions Made from the Latin Vulgate by John Wycliffe and his Followers* (Oxford: 1850) vol. 1 xliii).

21   Smith, "An Edition" xxx.

22   For the *littera duplex* initial, see Derolez A., *The Palaeography of Gothic Manuscript Books: From the Twelfth to the Early Sixteenth Century* (Cambridge: 2003) 41–42. *Textualis quadrata* is described, for example, by Roberts J., *Guide to Scripts Used in English Writings up to 1500* (London: 2005) 141.

23   Dove M., *The First English Bible: The Text and Context of the Wycliffite Versions* (Cambridge: 2007) 234 reports that the Epistle to the Laodiceans is found in twelve manuscripts (these are characterised on p. 207 as 'late LV MSS'). To the manuscripts listed by Dove should be added at least Dresden, Sächsische Landesbibliothek MS Od. 83; New York Public Library, MS MA 64; London, Dr Williams' Library MS Anc. 7; and Orlando, FL, Van Kampen Collection MS 640. Apart from L, no other manuscript containing the Epistle to the Laodiceans contains *OF*. Forshall – Madden, *The Holy Bible*, vol. 4 438–439 edited Laodiceans from L.

prologue to the Epistle to the Romans, placed on a separate quire of two leaves before the Epistle (f. 145r–146r); manuscript evidence suggests that the circulation of the Epistle to the Laodiceans may have been related to that of the additional prologue.[24] Although L does not contain the four Gospels as separate texts, the standard LV prologues for these Gospels have been placed in front of *OF* together with the second and third additional prologue, the former labeled in a rubric as 'a prolog vpon þe gospel of Mathew'.[25]

Looking at L as a complete book, it seems plausible to describe it as a New Testament in which the four Gospels have been replaced by the gospel harmony *OF*. L is not the only manuscript in which translations of Biblical books co-occur with *OF*. In addition to the extracts and selected passages from various Biblical books found in three manuscripts (D, N, R), two manuscripts contain the Catholic Epistles in the Wycliffite Early Version (A, G), and one has the Catholic Epistles, Acts and Apocalypse in LV (Y). Only in L, however, do these materials combine to emulate a complete New Testament. In fact, the paratextual packaging of L readily indicates that despite the presence in the manuscript of *OF* instead of the four Gospels, the model for the book was provided by Wycliffite New Testaments. A large number of the complete New Testaments contain a table for finding the gospel, epistle and Old Testament lessons according to the Use of Sarum, usually placed at the beginning of the book (cf. L, f. 1r–17r).[26] A number of manuscripts also include a full-text Old Testament lectionary, so that the book functions in effect as a complete English-language lectionary for the Mass pericopes of the year; in L, this text occupies almost sixty leaves at the end of the volume.[27]

Whether or not the use of *OF* in the book instead of the LV Gospels was a deliberate plan, it presented the scribe of L with an almost insurmountable

24   The additional prologue is no. 674 in Stegmüller F. – Reinhardt N., *Repertorium Biblicum Medii Aevi*, 11 vols. (Madrid: 1950–1980); it was edited from L by Forshall – Madden, *The Holy Bible*, vol. 4 301–303. Dove, *The First English Bible* 206 finds the prologue in nine manuscripts of the Wycliffite Bible. No fewer than six of them also contain the Epistle to the Laodiceans. I am currently working on scribal and other affiliations between these manuscripts.

25   Harley 6333, f. 18r.

26   For such tables, see Peikola M., "Tables of Lections in Manuscripts of the Wycliffite Bible", in Poleg E. – Light L. (eds.), *Form and Function in the Late Medieval Bible* (Leiden: 2013) 351–378; Poleg, *Approaching the Bible* 113–114.

27   Harley 6333, f. 307r–364v. For Old Testament lectionaries in manuscripts of the Wycliffite Bible, see Dove, *The First English Bible* 61–62.

paratextual problem.[28] The scribe—in the light of his active editorial engagement with the book, perhaps better termed *compiler*—devoted considerable effort to trying to ensure that the user of the manuscript would be able to locate in OF the whole text of each Gospel lesson similarly to the way they would be found in the four Gospels. A close examination of the table of lessons in L enables us to reconstruct his working methods.[29]

The textual details of the opening rubric (canon) of the table of lessons in L, as well as its order, layout and liturgical scope, indicate that the compiler had at his disposal (as an exemplar) a copy of a redaction of the LV table of lessons found in at least twelve other extant manuscripts.[30] In this table, references to the gospel lessons for each liturgical occasion comprised the following elements: the name of the Gospel; the number of the chapter within the Gospel; the letter corresponding to the alphabetical subdivision of each chapter by *distinctiones*; and the opening and closing words of the lesson. For a large majority of the gospel lessons copied in the table in L, the compiler seems to

---

28   Disagreeing with Smith's statement (in "An Edition" xxxiv) that L is written in a single hand, Hunt, "An Edition" vol. 1 175 argues that the quire containing the additional OF prologues and the LV prologues for the four Gospels (f. 18–22) is 'written in a different hand from *Oon of Foure* and its standard concomitants' (see also *ibid.* 68). He does not discuss the paleographical grounds for the argument. Although the quire in question shows inarguable signs of having been produced as a separate unit (as also observed by Hunt, "An Edition" 175)—similarly to several other sections of the volume—it is difficult to see any such compelling paleographical evidence between the handwriting of the quire and the rest of the manuscript that would substantiate Hunt's argument about a different hand (i.e. another scribe at work).

29   In addition to the table of lessons discussed here (f. 1r–17r), L also contains a liturgical calendar into which finding information for the lessons of the Sanctorale has been worked (f. 139r–144v). This text differs from the Sanctorale section of the table of lessons at the beginning of the manuscript as regards the saints it contains as well as in some of its readings. In this text too the gospel pericopes refer to OF.

30   Like L, one of these manuscripts contains the second and third additional prologue, the additional prologue to the Epistle to the Romans, and the Epistle to the Laodiceans (Dresden, Sächsische Landesbibliothek MS Od. 83, New Testament in LV). Other manuscripts with the same redaction of the table, all New Testaments in LV unless otherwise stated, include Cambridge, Emmanuel College MS 108; Cambridge Magdalene College MS Pepys 2073; Cambridge University Library, British and Foreign Bible Society MS 156; Cambridge University Library MS Dd.1.27 (complete Bible with Early and Later Version texts); London, British Library MS Harley 1212; London, British Library MS Royal 1. A. IV; London, Lambeth Palace MS 532; Manchester, John Rylands University Library MS English 80; New York, Pierpont Morgan Library MS M. 400; Oxford, Bodleian Library MS Laud Misc. 388; Oxford, Christ Church College MS 145 (complete Bible in the Early Version).

have lifted their opening and closing words (as well as the Biblical book and chapter reference) directly from the LV exemplar—regardless of the fact that owing to differences in the Middle English translation used in the LV table of lessons a number of its incipits and explicits do not in fact bear a very close linguistic resemblance to the corresponding passage in OF and the tables of lessons usually accompanying it. For example, the incipit in the table in L for the gospel lesson for the twenty-second Sunday after Trinity Sunday from *Matthew* 18:23–35 ('Þe kyngdom of') corresponds to 'Þer for þe rewme of heuenes is lijk to a man kyng' ('Therefore the realm of heaven is like a (man-)king') in the Type A table of MS Royal 17. D. VIII. In the text of OF in L, the same passage reads 'Þer fore þe rewme of heuenes is lickened to a man kinge' ('Therefore the realm of heaven is likened to a (man-)king').[31]

Although the incipits and explicits of the lessons copied from the LV exemplar often did not precisely match the text of OF, this was clearly not a matter of concern for the compiler. After all, the beginning of the lesson was also identifiable from the alphabetical distinction placed in the margin of the text at the appropriate location, and a double virgule (//) in the margin marked its ending.[32] What did give him great concern in designing the table, on the other hand, was to make sure that the reader would be able to find the complete text of each gospel pericope in the book. To achieve this, he undertook a most laborious checking procedure, comparing the full text of each pericope (as it was read according to the Use of Sarum) with the corresponding passage of OF (as it was referred to in his exemplar of the OF table by Part, Chapter and alphabetical distinction).[33] Upon ascertaining that the complete text of the pericope was indeed present in OF at the location specified by the reference in the table, he copied its incipit and explicit from the LV table at his disposal, adding the specific OF reference to the entry to complete it. This situation applied to a majority of the gospel pericopes. Fig. 2.3 illustrates how such regular entries in the table are structured on the manuscript page in L [Fig. 2.3]. In fifty or so instances the collation procedure undertaken by the compiler revealed that

---

31   Harley 6333, f. 91v.

32   Since the alphabetical distinctions for the gospel lessons in the LV tables correspond to the text of the four Gospels, it obviously made no sense to the compiler to copy them from that exemplar. It therefore seems likely that the compiler also had access to a table of lessons for OF, perhaps supplied together with an exemplar containing the text of OF, from which he copied the alphabetical distinctions proper to the gospel harmony (as well as the precise references to its Parts and Chapters).

33   Originally the rite of Salisbury cathedral, by the end of the fourteenth century the Use of Sarum had been adopted throughout most of southern England. See Pfaff R.W., *The Liturgy in Medieval England: A History* (Cambridge: 2009) 412–444.

FIGURE 2.3 Oon of Foure/*Wycliffite New Testament, Table of liturgical lessons. London, British Library, MS Harley 6333, f. 1v (s. xv¹, Smith, "An Edition" xxx). Detail. Image © British Library Board.*

the complete text of the pericope could not be located by means of the reference given in the standard *OF* table of lessons. To improve the referential integrity of the new table he was putting together, the compiler inserted into it a number of first-person comments and instructions to the reader as to how the continuous text of a lesson was to be assembled. These comments and instructions generally reflect the compiler's concern about the inadequacy of *OF* as a source for the Sarum pericopes.

The reader of the book is alerted to the presence of such textual complications already in the opening canon of the table of lessons (on f. 1r) to which the compiler added an extra paragraph after the standard rubric he copied from the LV table of lessons used as exemplar. The paragraph reminds the reader of the fact that—contrary to the standard opening rubric ('in þe rubrisch here afore write')—in the ensuing table ('kalender') the gospel lessons of the year have been referenced in a special way, following the organisation of *OF* ('write in ordre in þe stori called oon of foure which stori biginnneth after þis kalender').[34] The compiler's reference to the gospel harmony as a 'stori' highlights the perception of *OF* as a narrative.[35]

The compiler's metatextual observations and instructions transform some of the standard single-line entries of the table into 'mini-commentaries' spanning several lines of text in the manuscript, the longest one taking up no fewer than eight lines [Fig. 2.4]. The compiler's comments address various forms of textual discrepancy. In the gospel for the High Mass on Christmas Day, for

---

34   That is 'written following the order of the narrative called *Oon of Foure*, which begins after this table', Harley 6333, f. 1r. In quotations from the manuscript, abbreviations have been silently expanded.

35   See *Middle English Dictionary*, s.v. *stōrīe*, n.¹ 1 (http://quod.lib.umich.edu/m/med/).

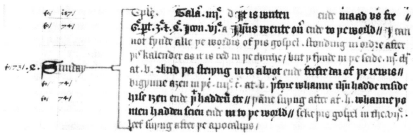

FIGURE 2.4   Oon of Foure/*Wycliffite New Testament, Table of liturgical lessons*. London,
British Library MS Harley 6333, f. 4v (s. xv¹, Smith, "An Edition" xxx). Detail. Image
© British Library Board.

example, the complete text of the lesson from the first chapter of *John* (1:1–14)
is available in OF in its entirety, but not as a continuous passage. Readers are
therefore instructed to assemble it from three separate passages. They should
start from the first Part and first Chapter of OF (a passage marked with the
alphabetical distinction *a*), proceed to the first Chapter in the second Part
(a passage marked with *b*), and then turn back to read the end of the pericope
in the first Chapter of the first Part from a location marked with a specific tie
mark (*signe-de-renvoi*) in the margin resembling the number 9 or the Latin
abbreviation for *con*.[36] If we check the appropriate passages in the text of the
OF in L, we find that the navigational pointers mentioned in the instruction
have been duly placed in the margin, including the compiler's tie mark on f.
30v, highlighted with a pointing hand (manicule) [Fig. 2.5].

It would seem that the manicule was not part of the compiler's original
design, but was inserted by a scrupulous Early Modern reader of the book.
The same reader foliated the whole manuscript and added folio references
to each entry in the table of lessons (as seen in Fig. 2.3 and Fig. 2.4), including the lessons to be assembled from more than one passage according to the
instructions of the fifteenth-century compiler. This facilitated considerably the

36   'I pt. I c. Joon I *a* In þe bigynnyng *ende* token not it// *þanne turne to þe firste chapiter in þe*
      secunde parti to .b. A man was sent of god *ende* born of god// *after turne aзen to þe forseide*
      firste chapiter of þe firste parti to þis figure .9. And goddis sone *ende* and of treuþe' ('I pt.
      I c. Joon I *a* In the beginning *end* took not it// *Then turn to the first chapter in the second*
      part to .b. A man was sent by God *end* born of God// *after this turn again to the previously*
      mentioned first chapter of the first part to this figure .9. And God's son *end* and of truth').
      Harley 6333, f. 2r. In the quotation, italics correspond to text written in red ink. For *signes-*
      de-renvoi, see Clemens R. – Graham T., *Introduction to Manuscript Studies* (Ithaca: 2007)
      37–39.

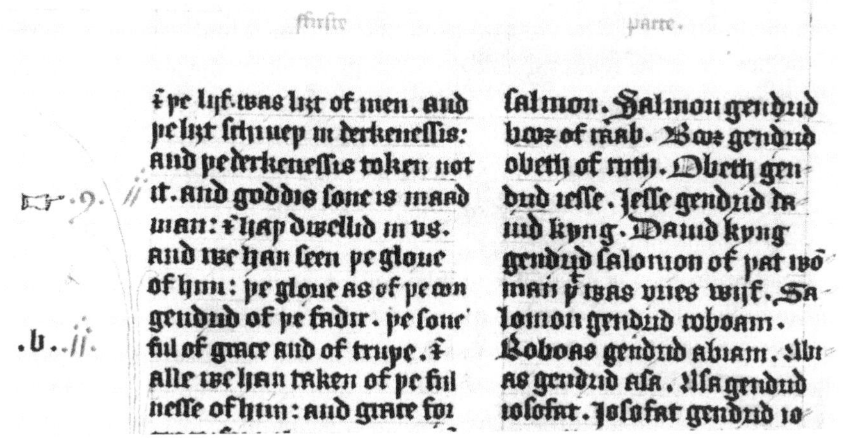

FIGURE 2.5   Oon of Foure, *part 1, chapter 1. London, British Library* MS *Harley 6333, f. 30v*
(s. xv¹, *Smith, "An Edition" xxx). Detail.* © *British Library Board (*MS *Harley 6333).*

reader's task of finding the pericopes in the bulky codex. Judging from a note placed at the end of the table, the foliator's work can be dated to 1581.[37] The precision of his undertaking strongly suggests that the book was at that date still used as a source of liturgical readings in some context.

The compiler's comments indicate that assembling the complete pericope from more than one passage proved to be impossible for a number of liturgical occasions, because parts of the pericope were missing altogether from the text of the gospel harmony. In his entry for the First Wednesday after the Octave of the Epiphany, for example, the compiler stated, with characteristic precision, that he was only able to find nine words from the beginning of the gospel lesson in the text of *OF* ('y can not fynde þis gospel in þe stori of oon of foure except .ix. wordis of þe bigynnyng').[38] He solved the problem of the missing text by designing a separate foliated section, to be placed after the Apocalypse, which contained the full text of thirty pericopes.[39] In his comments the

---

37   Harley 6333, f. 17r. '/ By henry <f>lyck/ anno/ 1581/ this folio was made/'. The word 'folio' here refers to leaf-numbering rather than the leaf itself (see *OED*, s.v. *folio*, n. 3).

38   Harley 6333, f. 2v.

39   Harley 6333, f. 297v–306r. The section is introduced by a rubric specifying its rationale: 'Because þat certeyn gospels stonden not in ordre word be word in þis stori of oon of foure/ but muste be souȝte in dyuers placis/ wherfore here after suen summe of þo gospels as þei ben red in þe chirche' ('Since in this narrative *Oon of Foure* the text of certain gospel lessons is not written consecutively but must be sought in different locations, some of those lessons follow here as they are read in the church') (f. 297v). The Apocalypse ends on f. 297r and is immediately followed by the Epistle to the Laodiceans and its prologue

compiler instructs the reader to consult that section to find the complete text of the pericope; the reader should, for example, look for the text of the lesson on the sixth leaf following the Apocalypse ('seke þat gospel in þe vjᵉ leef suyng after the apocalips').[40] An additional rubric placed at the end of *OF* also draws readers' attention to textual/liturgical deficiencies in *OF* and similarly exhorts them to consult the foliated section after the Apocalypse ('sertayn leeues after þe apocalips numbred in the heed').[41]

In addition to specifying the number of missing words in his comments, the compiler also measured the amount of absent text in lines. For example, on one occasion he pointed out that the text lacked six or seven lines ('vj. or vij. lynes') from the beginning of the lesson, and again referred the reader to the full-text section after the Apocalypse.[42] The compiler's observation about missing text here can be corroborated from the Sarum Missal, which shows that in modern terms *OF* lacks two verses from the beginning of the lesson derived from *Luke* 4:14–22.[43]

On a few occasions the compiler observed that there were additional words in the text of the gospel harmony which did not belong to the pericope. Unless there were also other problems in the text at that point, such as words of the pericope appearing in the wrong order in the text of *OF*,[44] he let such inaccuracies pass without providing the complete text of the pericope after the Apocalypse. The compiler's comments addressing the presence of additional words indicate that his primary intention was to provide the reader with the

---

(f. 297r–v) before the full-text lections begin. In addition to pericopes whose parts are missing altogether from *OF*, the section contains several pericopes which may be assembled following the instructions given by the compiler.

40   Harley 6333, f. 2v.

41   Harley 6333, f. 138v. The whole rubric reads 'ffor as miche as manye gospellis in þe ʒeer. whiche ben markid in þis forseid storie of oon of foure wiþ lettris of þe a. b. c. and also with wordis of þe biginnyng and þe eende of þo gospellis/ as þei ben red in þe chirche after þe vsse if salisburi; ʒitt in þo seid dyuers gospellis þe wordis stonden not in ordre. after þe writung of þe gospeller þat wrote hem firste/ wherfore seche þo gospellis ful out write after þe vsse of salisburi in sertayn leeues after þe apocalips numbred in the heed/' ('Considering that many gospel lessons of the year that have been marked in this preceding narrative *Oon of Foure* with letters of the ABC and also by their opening and closing words as they are read in the church according to the Use of Salisbury do not follow the text of the gospel as the evangelist first wrote it, seek those lessons fully written out according to the Use of Salisbury on the foliated leaves after the Apocalypse').

42   Harley 6333, f. 2v.

43   Friday (*feria sexta*) after the first Sunday after the octave of Epiphany. See Legg J.W. (ed.), *The Sarum Missal Edited from Three Early Manuscripts* (Oxford: 1916) 41n.

44   For such an instance, see f. 7v for the gospel for the Saturday after Whitsun.

complete *substance* of the text of the pericope; thus the presence of extra words might not matter as long as the meaning remained unchanged. In an entry for Ember Wednesday in the autumn, he noted that although the referenced passage contained 'manye mo wordis' (many more words) than are found in the pericope from the ninth chapter of *Mark* (9:16–28), it nonetheless seemed to him that the 'sentence' (meaning) of the pericope accorded with the Use of Sarum.[45] In this case the textual mismatch identified by the compiler resulted from the principles followed by Clement himself in compiling the *Unum ex Quattuor*. The narrative for the Chapter in question (Part VII, Chapter 8) was assembled from parallel accounts provided by the synoptic Gospels; thus the words of the pericope, as they would have been read in the Use of Sarum from the Gospel of Mark, had become conflated in *OF* with text from Luke and Matthew.

The textual structure of the foliated section placed after the Apocalypse sheds some further light on the working procedure followed by the compiler. Although one would expect the thirty pericopes of the section to follow the same liturgical order in which the entries are listed in the table of lessons (i.e. beginning from the Temporale pericopes of the Advent season), the section begins with the gospel for Easter Sunday. It then follows the usual liturgical order throughout the rest of the Temporale and the Sanctorale, returning to the beginning of the Temporale and completing the sequence with the gospel for Palm Sunday (the nineteenth full-text pericope of the section). Thereafter, a new sequence of nine pericopes begins from Lent, running through Eastertide and ending with the Wednesday following the fourth Sunday after Trinity. The last two pericopes of the section represent yet a third sequence with the gospels for the High Mass on Christmas Day and Annunciation. They differ from all previous pericopes of the section in that the corresponding entries in the table of lessons contain no metatextual direction for the reader to find them after the Apocalypse. In the case of Annunciation, the regular one-line table entry does not hint at the presence of textual problems in finding the complete text of the pericope as a single passage in *OF*—rightly so, because the whole pericope (*Luke* 1:26–38) corresponds to Part I, Chapter 4.[46]

---

45   'þouȝ in þis gospel after þis stori ben rehersid manye mo wordis þan ben red in þe chirche. ȝitt me seemeþ þe sentence is accordyng with þe vsse of salisburi' ('While in this narrative there are many more words to this gospel lesson than are read in the church, it seems to me yet that the meaning accords with the Use of Salisbury'). Harley 6333, f. 8v.

46   Harley 6333, f. 31v–32r.

In addition to indicating that the compiler seems to have begun his collation of the pericopes from Eastertide, the details of textual structure suggest
that the decision as to whether or not to provide a full-text substitute for a
defective pericope was by no means a clear-cut one. It appears that the compiler's original plan was to provide full-text substitutes for nineteen pericopes
only, but he extended his design twice during the preparatory stage, adding
first nine and then another two full-text pericopes to the section. He may also
have been prompted by a codicological incentive to copy more material into
unfinished quires of the full-text section. The regular quire of eight leaves
(f. 292–299) containing the end of the Apocalypse, followed by the Epistle to
the Laodiceans and its prologue, had space only for five full-text pericopes and
two thirds of the sixth, so the compiler first added a bifolium (f. 300–301) and
then a singleton (f. 302) to the section to accommodate the rest of the nineteen
pericopes of the first stage of the plan. When he finished the copying of the
nineteenth pericope in the right-hand text-column of f. 302v, nine empty lines
remained at the end of the column. This may have prompted the compiler to
expand the section with another nine pericopes. He filled the nine lines at the
end of f. 302v with the beginning of the first pericope of the extended set, continuing into a new added quire of four leaves (f. 303–306). The last of the nine
added pericopes ended on the verso of the third leaf of the quire (f. 305v).
As there was still a considerable amount of blank space remaining in the quire,
the 29th and 30th pericopes may have been further *ad hoc* additions to fill up
that space.[47]

It remains a mystery why the textually complete gospel for Annunciation
Day was copied here. Although the full-text pericopes of the section follow the
LV text *verbatim*, the differences between LV and *OF* are rather inconspicuous
in this locus (*Luke* 1:26–38), suggesting that the form of Biblical translation was
not the reason for copying the passage. That no cross-reference is made in the
table of lessons to the last two pericopes of the full-text section may indicate
that the compiler had completed the copying of the final version of the table
by the time they came to be added to the section. For the first twenty-eight
pericopes, however, the presence of accurate cross-references in the table to
their foliation (leaf numbers) in the full-text section must mean that the final
version of the table was made only after these pericopes had been copied into
the section and its foliation had been determined. On the whole, the working

---

47   Even with the 29th and 30th pericope added, most of the right-hand column of f. 306r and
      the entire f. 306v were left blank by the compiler.

procedure of the compiler established here indicates that he very likely first prepared a draft of the table before writing out its final version.[48]

Conclusion: Reading Practices

Following this detailed scrutiny of the work of the compiler, let us consider the design of Harley 6333 with regard to the kind of reading practice it seeks to promote. The signals offered by the book as to how it is to be consumed may seem contradictory. On the one hand, the gospel harmony *OF* is used as a substitute for the four Gospels; on the other hand, the book testifies to a very strong paratextual emphasis on liturgical readings—a purpose for which the inadequacy of *OF* is repeatedly stressed by the frustrated compiler. The sheer amount of labour and the degree of textual complexity involved in the compiler's revision of the table of lessons suggest that it would have been an easier solution to copy into the manuscript the LV Gospels instead of *OF* in the first place.

The full-text section of gospel lessons (following LV text) after the Apocalypse and the LV prologues of the four Gospels placed before *OF* indicate that the compiler very probably had access to the LV Gospels at the time he was copying these texts into the book and preparing the table of lessons at the beginning of the volume. We cannot be sure, however, whether he had access to these texts at an earlier stage of compiling the book. Combined evidence from the structure of the quires, the quire signatures, and the presence of blank leaves at the end of the quires suggests that the manuscript was assembled from several discrete codicological units, which initially may not necessarily have been planned to form a single coherent whole. In the light of this evidence it is perfectly possible that the paratextual sections containing the table of lessons and the added prologues, as well as the full-text lessons placed after the Apocalypse, were added to the book only when its final shape and contents came to be determined and the textual combination of *OF* with the LV material had already been confirmed.

By allowing for the possibility that the heavy liturgical emphasis may not have been part of the original design of the manuscript, the codicological

---

48   There is no compelling reason to assume that the compiler of L must have been identical with the scribe of the manuscript. It therefore remains a possibility that after the compiler had designed and drafted the material, he gave the draft to a professional scribe to be copied. The frequent references made in the comments to the structure and foliation of the book mean, however, that the compiler must have been intimately familiar with the manuscript.

evidence offers a reasonable way of making sense of the apparent contradictions in its design. It is, however, worth considering the possibility that even if the LV Gospels had been available to the compiler from the start, he nonetheless preferred to include *OF* in the manuscript—regardless of the liturgical problems this was to cause. In a nuanced discussion of the theology of *OF*, Mary Raschko surmises that Clement's gospel harmony presents a 'more comprehensive description of events than any individual Gospel and creates a more cohesive account of Christ's life, both by providing a chronology and by resolving apparent contradictions or ambiguities'.[49] These qualities, she argues, made *OF* more accessible than the Gospels, thereby facilitating lay devotion and religious edification.[50] Raschko refers to Bishop Reginald Pecock's mid-fifteenth century commendation of *OF* to lay readers for similar reasons.[51]

The inclusion of *OF* in the Harley manuscript instead of the four Gospels may well have been motivated by such considerations. As a gospel harmony *OF* differs from the most widely circulated representative of the genre in fifteenth-century England—Nicholas Love's *Mirror of the Blessed Life of Jesus Christ*—both in its comprehensiveness and in its lack of meditative metatext ('devout imaginations') merged with text obtained from the Gospels.[52] In a recent article, Elizabeth Schirmer juxtaposes *OF* and the *Mirror* as ideologically competing Middle English gospel narratives participating in 'a battle between two coordinated textual programs, Lollard (or Wycliffite) and anti-Lollard, designed to enact opposing models of the true church'.[53] She argues

---

49   Raschko, *"Oon of Foure"* 353.

50   Raschko, *"Oon of Foure"* passim. See also Schmid, *Unum ex Quattuor* 252–267.

51   Raschko, *"Oon of Foure"* 354. See also Hudson A., *The Premature Reformation: Wycliffite Texts and Lollard History* (Oxford: 1988) 268.

52   See Raschko, *"Oon of Foure"* 346–353. Cf. the prologue to the *Mirror*: 'it is to vndirstonde at þe bygynyng as for [a] pryncipal & general rewle of diuerse ymaginacions þat folowen after in þis boke þat þe discriuyng or speches or dedis of god in heuen & angels or oþere gostly substances bene only wryten in þis manere, & to þis entent þat is to saye as devoute ymaginacions & likenessis styryng symple soules to þe loue of god & desire of heuenly þinges' ('to start with, it needs to be understood as a principal and general rule for the various imaginations that follow in this book that the description, speech or actions of God in Heaven and angels or other spiritual entities are only written in this manner and purpose, that is to say as devout imaginings and likenesses, to direct simple souls towards the love of God and desire of heavenly things'). Quoted from Sargent M.G. (ed.), *Nicholas Love. The Mirror of The Blessed Life of Jesus Christ: A Reading Text* (Exeter: 2004) 10 (my translation into present-day English).

53   Schirmer E., "Canon Wars and Outlier Manuscripts: Gospel Harmony in the Lollard Controversy", *Huntington Library Quarterly* 73, 1 (2010) 1–36; quoted from p. 1.

that *OF* 'fitted squarely into the Lollard scriptural canon'.[54] Whether or not the Middle English translation of Clement's text originated among Wycliffite translators, the co-occurence of *OF* and books of the Wycliffite Bible in several manuscripts need not be seen as ideologically contradictory.[55] At the same time it is hardly a coincidence that despite the considerably larger number of surviving *Mirror* manuscripts in comparison to those of *OF*, none of them contains texts from the Wycliffite Bible.[56]

Returning, finally, to the uniquely designed paratextual apparatus in Harley 6333 and the mode of reading it seeks to promote, we may want to probe into the ultimate motive of the compiler for his revision of the table of lessons. What made him undertake such a formidable task in the first place? After all, judging by the number of surviving manuscripts, the earlier tables of gospel lessons tailored to *OF* (Types A and B) evidently served the needs of many readers who wished to have access to the Mass pericopes in the vernacular. The main difference in kind between the encounter with the text of the pericopes as promoted by the regular *OF* tables and the one in Harley 6333 is that the former only enable readers to locate the beginning of the pericope in *OF*, while the latter seeks to ensure that they will in fact be able to read each pericope through in its entirety and as accurately as possible with regard to the meaning of the text.

It is important to recognise, however, that the compiler's obsession with the accuracy of the Gospel text does not operate in terms of distinguishing between the words of Holy Writ and interpretive glosses—a concern voiced by many Wycliffite writers; what the compiler is concerned with, above all, is the faithfulness of the text of the pericopes to the liturgy of Sarum (although notably in English rather than Latin, the official liturgical language). Several comments made by the compiler indicate that the ultimate motive of his paratextual endeavours was to take the reader as close as reasonably possible to the text of the pericopes as they are 'red in þe chirche'.[57] Such a pervasive interest in liturgical detail might suggest that the compiler's voice belongs to a

---

54   Schirmer, "Canon Wars" 8.

55   See also Hudson, *The Premature Reformation* 267–268; Hunt, "An Edition" I 65–71; Smith P., "Could the Gospel Harmony *Oon of Foure* Represent an Intermediate Version of the Wycliffite Bible?", *Studia Neophilologica* 80,2 (2008) 160–176; Raschko, "*Oon of Foure*" 343–345.

56   The *Mirror* survives in sixty-four manuscripts (see Sargent, *Nicholas Love* ix). Descriptions of the manuscripts are available on the website *Geographies of Orthodoxy: Mapping English Pseudo-Bonaventuran Lives of Christ, 1350–1550* (http://www.qub.ac.uk/geographies-of-orthodoxy/).

57   See e.g. f. 2v, 4r, 4v, 6r, 8r.

cleric—perhaps one seeking to mediate the liturgical text accurately to select lay persons under his guidance; one instructing a clerical owner of the book in using it to obtain the text of the pericopes for his sermons; or even one giving instructions on how to read out the English translation of the pericope from the book to a congregation attending Mass. These settings involving direct mediation by a priest are obviously not the only possible contexts that may be envisaged for the meticulous work on liturgical paratexts witnessed in the Harley manuscript. Other conceivable Late Medieval contexts of use that might perhaps equally well explain the liturgical bent of the material include, for example, a convent (male or female), a hospital, a school, a confraternity, as well as the possibility of a Latinate lay reader (such as a lawyer) convinced of the importance of having access to the complete pericopes.[58] While there is no historical evidence to either corroborate or reject any one of such conjectures about the intended primary readership and specific liturgical (or quasi-liturgical) usage of MS Harley 6333, the materialist philological scrutiny of the book conducted in this article serves to remind us of the research potential of paratexts for the study of manuscript production and models for religious reading towards the end of the Middle Ages.

Bibliography

Boynton S. – Reilly D.J. (eds.), *The Practice of the Bible in the Middle Ages: Production, Reception, & Performance in Western Christianity* (New York: 2011).

Dove M., *The First English Bible: The Text and Context of the Wycliffite Versions* (Cambridge: 2007).

Genette G., *Seuils* (Paris: 1987), transl. into English by J.E. Lewin as *Paratexts: Thresholds of Interpretation* (Cambridge: 1997).

Hudson A., *The Premature Reformation: Wycliffite Texts and Lollard History* (Oxford: 1988).

Hunt S., "An Edition of Tracts in Favour of Scriptural Translation and of Some Texts connected with Lollard Vernacular Biblical Scholarship," 2 vols., unpublished DPhil thesis, University of Oxford (1994).

---

58 I am grateful to Margriet Hoogvliet for these excellent suggestions. For findings concerning the use of vernacular Biblical texts in France in some such settings, see Hoogvliet, M., "The Medieval Vernacular Bible in French as a Flexible Text: Selective and Discontinuous Reading Practices", in Poleg E. – Light L. (eds.), *Form and Function in the Late Medieval Bible* (Leiden: 2013) 283–306; for corresponding Italian contexts for using Biblical texts, see Corbellini, "Vernacular Bible Manuscripts".

Nichols S.G. – Wenzel S. (eds.), *The Whole Book: Cultural Perspectives on the Medieval Miscellany* (Ann Arbor: 1996).

Poleg E., *Approaching the Bible in Medieval England* (Manchester: 2013).

Poleg E. – Light L. (eds.), *Form and Function in the Late Medieval Bible* (Leiden: 2013).

Raschko M., "*Oon of Foure*: Harmonizing Wycliffite and Pseudo-Bonaventuran Approaches to the Life of Christ", in Johnson I. – Westphall A.F. (eds.), *The Pseudo-Bonaventuran Lives of Christ: Exploring the Middle English Tradition* (Turnhout: 2013) 341–373.

Schirmer E., "Canon Wars and Outlier Manuscripts: Gospel Harmony in the Lollard Controversy", *Huntington Library Quarterly* 73, 1 (2010) 1–36.

Schmid U.B., *Unum ex quattuor. Eine Geschichte der lateinischen Tatianüberlieferung* (Freiburg: 2005).

Smith P.M., "An Edition of Parts I–V of the Wycliffite Translation of Clement of Llanthony's Latin Gospel Harmony *Unum ex Quattuor* Known as *Oon of Foure*", unpublished PhD thesis, University of Southampton (1985).

Smith P., "Could the Gospel Harmony *Oon of Foure* Represent an Intermediate Version of the Wycliffite Bible?", *Studia Neophilologica* 80, 2 (2008) 160–176.

CHAPTER 3

Uncovering the Presence: Religious Literacies in Late Medieval Italy

Sabrina Corbellini

It is necessary to make an effort and to study diligently in order to learn the complete life of Jesus Christ and to have his life in every moment fixed in your memory. This will only be possible if you are ready to learn it thoroughly and carefully. It is thus essential to be acquainted with the life of Jesus Christ from the very beginning, the Nativity, until the moment of his Ascension, as it is narrated in the Gospels. And thus to know every deed, manner, stance and virtue in speaking and handling during the thirty-three years he spent in this world. You should have as a mirror before the eyes of your mind his life [...] And all these things should first be read and then printed in your mind in order to be able to meditate savouring the taste of devotion.[1]

---

1 'Per tanto si de' studiare con ogni sforzo e diligentia di sapere in tutto la vita di Giesu Christo: la qual vita tu habbi da ogni hora e tempo e fissa nella memoria ma tu non hauerai se essa vita bene e compitamente tu non saperai. Bisogna adunque sapere tutta la vita di Giesu Christo fino che lui stette in questa vita dal principio della sua natiuitade fino che llui ascese in cielo come narrano li Euangelii. Et così per quelli sapere tutti li atti e modi costume e vertude in parlare & operare le quali lui fece per trenta tre anni nelli quali per tuo amore stette in questo mondo. E così habbi come uno specchio dinanti dalli occhi della mente tua la vita sua [...] Le quali tutte cose è dibisogno sapere hauendole ben prima lette e perfettamente impresse nella mente tua acciocché le possi meditare con gusto di deuotione'. The text is translated from the original printed edition, *Giardino de oratione fructuoso* ([S.l.] 1496) f. 59v–6or (copy from Württembergische Landesbibliothek Stuttgart, available online, http://digital.wlb-stuttgart.de/purl/bsz346775906). As mentioned in this contribution, the author of the *Giardino* is still unidentified, although the text has been attributed to the Franciscan Niccolò da Osimo. In the prologue, the treatise is dated 1454. For an introduction to this treatise see Da Campagnola S., "'Il Giardino di Orazione' e altri scritti di un anonimo del Quattrocento. Un' errata attribuzione a Niccolò da Osimo", *Collectanea Fransciscana* 41 (1971) 55–59 and Ginzburg C., "Folklore, magia, religione", in *Storia d' Italia* 1 (Turin: 1972) 603–679, here 631–633. See also Corbellini S., "Instructing the Soul, Feeding the Spirit and Awakening the Passion: Holy Writ and Lay Readers in Late Medieval Europe", in Gordon B. – McLean M. (eds.), *Shaping the Bible in the Reformation: Books, Scholars and their Readers in the Sixteenth Century* (Leiden: 2012) 15–39, here 32–33.

With these words, the anonymous fifteenth-century author of the *Giardino de Oratione fructuoso* ('Fruitful Garden of Prayer') explains to his readers how to meditate on the life of Christ. If the reader is willing to follow a sequence of studious reading, memorizing and rethinking, he will be able to taste the 'fruits of his devotion'. While the description of this combination of reading and meditation could be considered to belong to a more generalized medieval practice, especially in monastic communities, the instructions for religious reading portrayed in this treatise offer an outstanding starting point for an investigation of religious literacies in late medieval Italy, in particular among lay readers literate in the vernacular.[2] In fact, the author proudly declares in the prologue that he has composed the treatise in the vernacular 'so that [the] simple, ignorant souls may understand prayer and practice it'. He then continues by stating that 'ignorance is more important than knowledge' because 'science makes the soul proud and [he wishes] to do something more useful than satisfying the vanity and curiosity of those who seek speech that is ornate, rhetorical and exquisite'.[3] This treatise should, moreover, be considered a real late medieval (and early modern) bestseller, as it was reprinted at least ten times in the late fifteenth and sixteenth centuries (between 1494 and 1563), thus crossing the traditional boundaries of late medieval and early modern religious education. In having done so it offers an exceptional perspective on religious literacy among 'unlearned' readers; that is, on their specific ability to

---

2 The strict interdependence between reading and meditating is expressed in Hugh of St Victor's *Didascalicon*, probably the first book dedicated to the art of reading. Hugh of St Victor (1096-1141) writes in his treatise that 'the things by which every man advances in knowledge are principally two—namely, reading and meditation', and he explains that 'meditation takes its start from reading but is bound by none of reading's rule and precepts. For it delights to range along open ground, where it fixes its free gaze upon the contemplation of truth, drawing together now these, now those causes of things, or now penetrating into profundities, leaving nothing doubtful, nothing obscure'. The text is cited from the English translation by Taylor J., *The Didascalicon of Hugh of St. Victor. A Medieval Guide to the Arts* (New York – London: 1961) 44, 92–93.

3 'Acciò che queste anime idiote e simplice possano avere intendimento di questa oratione ed in essa exercitarsi: hauendo più la vanità della scientia: la qual fa l'anima insuperbire e volendo più presto fare utilità che satisfare alla vanità e curiosità di quelli che cerchiano pur de haver parlamenti ornati Rhetorici e exquisiti'. *Giardino de oratione fructuoso*, f. A2v–A3r. For this passage, see also Caravale G., *Forbidden Prayer. Church Censorship and Devotional Literature in Renaissance Italy* (Farmham: 2011) 218.

approach and read religious texts and to transform the act of reading into a process of spiritual and moral growth.[4]

A brief examination of the *Giardino* and its meditational exercises will offer the opportunity to reflect on two seminal issues in the study of religious readership among laypeople: the combination of religious reading and the learning of and reflection on moral virtues, as well as the process of acquisition and assimilation of religious reading techniques by both lay individuals and communities of readers. In fact, as Wendy Scase recently stated, 'in the modern western world reading is considered to be a silent, solitary, individual, and private activity', while 'it is perhaps not going too far to say that medieval reading was, by contrast, always a community activity'.[5]

A Manual of Excellence

As Caravale summarizes, the *Giardino* was 'in fact a genuine manual on the excellence and singular and special virtues of prayer for unlearned readers', which taught the unlettered to respect 'the most ancient institutions', the 'most singular representation' and the 'most useful devotion' of the *oratione vocale* (vocal prayer) and *psalmodia* (psalmody). The prologue makes it clear to the readers that 'prayer [...] brings the soul closer to God' and introduces them

---

4   Caravale, *Forbidden Prayer* 216–217. According to Edit16, the online catalogue of sixteenth-century Italian books, the *Giardino* was printed for the last time in Venice (Al segno de la Speranza, 1563; http://edit16.iccu.sbn.it/web_iccu/eimain.htm). For devotional printing in early modern Italy, see Zarri G., "Note su diffusione e circolazione di testi devote (1520–1550)", in Zarri G., *Libri di Spirito. Editoria religiosa in volgare nei secoli XV–XVII* (Torino: 2009) 103–146. In Anglo-American scholarship, the term 'devotional literacy' is often used to define and describe the intersection of devotion and literacy. The term was introduced by Margaret Aston: Aston M., 'Devotional literacy', in Aston M., *Lollards and Reformers: Images and Literacy in Late Medieval Religion* (London: 1984) 101–133. In this contribution, which focuses on readers of religious texts, the more neutral term 'religious literacies' has been used. For a first attempt at exploring religious literacies among the late medieval laity, see the contributions in Corbellini S. (ed.), *Cultures of Religious Reading in the Late Middle Ages* (Turnhout: 2013). A pioneering study on this subject is Frioli D., "Tra oralità e scrittura. Appunti su libri e biblioteche dei laici devoti", *Quaderni di Storia Religiosa* (2001) 147–219.

5   Scase W., "Reading Communities", in Treharne E. – Walker G. (eds.), *The Oxford Handbook of Medieval Literature in English* (Oxford: 2010) 557–573, here 557. The reconstruction of reading communities is one of the main goals of the COST-Action "New Communities of Interpretation. Contexts, Strategies and Processes of Religious Transformation in Late Medieval and Early Modern Europe" (2013–2017). This research group is led and coordinated by the editors of this volume.

thus to the 'greatness and usefulness of divine contemplation'. Interestingly enough the author then contrasts the readers of his book who are sincerely willing to perform devotional practices with the 'professionals', who 'say the office in chorus because they have some temporary benefice of which they are slaves and they do not have enough freedom to hear the sweetness of the psalmody', and with those who 'say the psalms and the office because the Church obliges them, or because they have benefits, or because they hold holy office'.[6]

At the beginning of his work, the author of the *Giardino* thus summarizes the most fundamental features of a reading activity that has the potential to become an edifying experience and to morally improve its readers. As stated by Victor Nell, the prerequisites of such a reading experience are the voluntary nature of the reading act, the possibility of an affective identification between the reader and the events and characters described in the text (in this case the life of Christ), and the prospect of 'forgetting' reality and being completely involved in the narration.[7] Laypeople 'who have little knowledge and cannot understand books of literature and science and yet seek to come closer to God' are in some way the 'privileged' receivers of the divine message that is presented to them in their own vernacular language.[8]

---

6 Caravale, *Forbidden Prayer* 217.

7 Nell V., "The Psychology of Reading for Pleasure: Needs and Gratifications", *Reading Research Quarterly* 23, 1 (1988) 6–50; Nell V., *Lost in a Book: The Psychology of Reading for Pleasure* (New Haven: 1988). Nell's findings are summarized by Boyarin D., "Placing Reading: Ancient Israel and Medieval Europe", in Boyarin J. (ed.), *The Ethnography of Reading* (Berkeley – Los Angeles: 1992) 10–37, here 10.

8 Caravale, *Forbidden Prayer* 217. The emphasis on the vernacular and the criticism of the 'professional' users of the Scriptures could, according to Caravale, explain why the *Giardino* was put on the Index. See Caravale, *Forbidden Prayer* 217; Caravale G., "Illiterates and Church Censorship in Late Renaissance Italy", in Vega Ramos M.-J. – Nakládalová I. (eds.), *Lectura y culpa en el siglo XVI* (Barcelona: 2012) 93–106; and Caravale G., "Forbidding Prayer in Italy and Spain: Censorship and Devotional Literature in the Sixteenth Century. Current Issues and Future Research", in Vega M.J. – Weiss J. – Cesc E. (eds.), *Reading and Censorship in Early Modern Europe* (Barcelona: 2007) 57–78. The description of the 'simple souls' as the privileged recipients of the message of the Gospels is, however, a recurrent theme in late medieval religious literature, especially in the circles of Augustinian friars. See, for example Gagliardi I., "'Secondo che parla la Santa Scriptura'. Girolamo da Siena e i suoi testi di 'direzione spirituale' alla fine del Trecento", in Catto M. – Gagliardi I. – Parrinello R.M. (eds.), *Direzione spirituale tra ortodossia ed eresia. Dalle scuole filosofiche antiche al Novecento* (Brescia: 2002) 117–175; Corbellini S., "Vernacular Bible Manuscripts in Late Medieval Italy: Cultural Appropriation and Textual Transformation", in Poleg E. – Light L. (eds.), *Form and Function in the Late Medieval Bible* (Leiden: 2013) 261–281, at 272–273.

After the prologue, the author introduces the central themes in his treatise through a table of contents, which gives the readers the opportunity to select their reading material. The discontinuous and nonlinear reading of the text, offering the possibility of navigating through the text and selecting chapters and passages, lies at the very heart of the pragmatic function of the treatise entitled the 'Fruitful Garden of Prayer', as it gives its readers the opportunity to literally cherry-pick their way through the text, choosing from 'several fruits and tastes'.[9] After a general description of vocal and mental oration, the *Giardino* offers a selection of meditative exercises on several themes (ranging from sins to death, purgatory, hell, the Last Judgement and resurrection). The list of exercises does, however, have an overall focus on a central theme: Christ and various episodes from his life. The reader finds instructions on 'how to meditate on the life of Christ, following his virtues', and how to approach the meditation on specific episodes of his life, such as his birth, his Passion, his wounds, the shedding of his blood and his last words on the Cross.[10]

The first and 'most useful meditation' on the life of Christ functions as an instructive prelude to the whole corpus of Gospel meditations and instructs the reader in how to perform the exercises. At the outset, the life of Christ should be meditated on 'at a slow pace, pausing on each detail and ruminating in order to savour the fruit of the prayer' and an attempt should be made to focus on Christ's physical appearance, emphasizing his humanity and literally 'fall[ing] in love with him'.[11] Devotional activities need to be performed 'in a quiet place far away from noises and uproars', but not in the church as 'churches

---

9   *Giardino de oratione fructuoso* f. A3r. The terms 'nonlinear' and 'discontinuous' reading are used by Brown M.P., "The Thick Style: Steady Sellers, Textual Aesthetics, and Early Modern Devotional Reading", *Publications of Modern Language Association of America* 121, 1 (2006) 67–86. Although the terminology is developed to describe seventeenth-century Protestant reading habits, it can be readily applied to the description of reading activities in a late medieval context.

10   *Giardino de oratione fructuoso* f. A4r–v. Following the recent study by Michelle Karnes, these meditations can be described as 'gospel meditations', i.e. texts that 'are concerned less to recount Christ's life than to present individual episodes from it for meditation'. See Karnes M., *Imagination, Meditation, and Cognition in the Middle Ages* (Chicago: 2011) 4.

11   'Con riposo e dimoranza ogni cosa particolarmente ruminando altramente non senteresti frutto della tua orazione (…) nella mente tua ti formi uno huomo (…) ti possi innamorare più caldamente' *Giardino de oratione fructuoso* f. 6or. In order to help the reader reconstruct Christ's physical appearance, the author transcribes a fourteenth-century deuterocanonical text, the *Epistola Lentuli*. For a translation of the *Epistola Lentuli*, see Koerner J.L., *The Moment of Self-Portraiture in German Renaissance Art* (Chicago: 1993) 103.

are places dedicated to vocal oration'. He thus describes a form of domestic piety outside 'official' religious spaces, which can enhance a non-compulsory, 'de-institutionalized' form of reading and meditating that was not necessarily part of a daily routine and which was not automatically bound to the rules of a real or imagined collectivity, as in the case of religious institutions.

This affective relationship with the 'human Christ' could be further developed by recreating 'mental images' of the places where and the people with whom Christ lived, such as 'Mary Magdalene, Martha, Lazarus and the twelve Apostles'. In order to transform these characters into a real presence, the reader is asked to imagine them in the physical appearance of 'virtuous' acquaintances.[12] This emphasis on the humanity of Christ is reinforced by the request to focus on specific moments in his life, from his birth to his Passion, in chronological order.[13] It is quite evident that the reading techniques described in the *Giardino* require active participation in the reading process, through the selection of texts, the attention paid to reading at the right pace, the conscious pausing while reading the text and the 'rumination' on the most important details. They also stimulate the creativity of the reader, who is asked to create 'mental images' and 'local memories', to select the characters participating in the scene, and to project them into the spaces recreated in their imagination. Neither devotional objects nor devotional images are mentioned in the *Giardino*, with readers invited to use their own mnemonic and imaginative potential to savour the 'fruits of [their] meditation'.[14] As stated in studies by Ginzburg and Bolzoni, these instructions for religious reading and meditations are probably the first symptoms of a changing approach to religiosity—moving towards interiority and inwardness and with a stronger accent on

---

12 'Anchora ti sarà utile formarti nella mente li luoghi e terre e le stantie doue lui conversava. E le persone che singolarmente erano in sua compagnia. Come era la nostra Madonna, santa Maria Magdalena, Marta, Lazaro, e gli dodeci Apostoli'. *Giardino de oratione fructuoso* f. 6or.

13 The same technique is used by the author in the description of the meditation on the Passion (f. 69v). Also in this case, the events narrated in the Gospels are supposed to be linked to known persons and spaces in order to be able to completely transpose the biblical narrative into the daily living space of the reader. The use of short descriptions of episodes from the life of Christ in the form of a list in order to trigger the memory of his readers also characterizes the *Ordine della vita Cristiana* (The Organization of Christian Life) by the Augustinian friar Simone da Cascia. See Corbellini, "Vernacular Bible Manuscripts" 273–274.

14 Bolzoni L., *Il lettore creativo: percorsi cinquecenteschi fra memoria, gioco, scrittura* (Naples: 2012) 33.

personal engagement and responsibility—that will be fully developed in the sixteenth century.[15]

Moral Virtues: Self-scrutiny and Self-improvement

The final goal of the process of reading, meditation and visualization described in the instructions for the meditation is not, however, merely to reach a state of mystical union with Christ, but to equip the reader's mind with morals. According to the author of the *Giardino*, reading about and meditating on the life of Christ should assist the devout reader to reflect on seven virtues: Humility, Poverty, Simplicity, Self-denial, Charity, leading a model life and Fortitude.[16] By recognizing these virtues in the narration of Christ's life and using them as a mirror for their own spiritual and moral growth, readers can undergo a process of moral purification and thus transform themselves into a 'specchio & essemplo' (a mirror and an example) for other devotees.[17]

---

15   Ginzburg and Bolzoni see points of contact with the techniques propagated by the *Spiritual exercises* of Ignatius of Loyola (Ginzburg, "Folklore, Magia, Religione" 33; Bolzoni, *Il lettore creativo* 311).

16   'Humilita/Pouerta/Simplicita/Austerita/Charita/Essemplarita/Perpetuita'. *Giardino de oratione fructuoso* f. 61r. This emphasis on the goal of sacred reading as moral instruction is explained by Hugh of St Victor in the fifth book of his *Didascalicon*: 'Let whoever comes to sacred reading for instruction first know what kind of fruit it yields. For nothing ought to be sought without a cause, nor does a thing which promises no usefulness attract our desires. Twofold is the fruit of sacred reading, because it either instructs the mind with knowledge or equips it with morals'. See Taylor, *Didascalicon*, 126.

17   Although more research is needed to investigate this specific point, the emphasis on the importance of the acquisition of virtues and the conflation of meditation and moral training is somehow different from the instruction given to the readers of the Italian translation of the *Meditationes Vitae Christi*, probably the most widely read meditative text on the life of Christ. As a matter of fact, in the last chapter the reader is instructed on how to meditate on the text: 'Therefore you ought to know that it is enough to meditate only on what the Lord did or on what happened concerning him or what is told according to the Gospel stories, feeling yourself present in those places as if things were done in your presence, as it comes directly to your soul in thinking of them. The moralities and authorities that I placed in this work for your instruction need not to be used in the meditations, unless the virtue to be embraced or the vice to be avoided occurs of itself to your thoughts. Therefore, in this meditating, choose some quiet hour. Afterwards, later in the day, you can take the moralities and authorities and studiously commit them to memory. It is fitting to do so, for they are the most beautiful and can instruct you on the whole spiritual life'. The text is cited from Ragusa I. – Green R.B., *Meditations on the Life of Christ. An Illustrated Manuscript of the Fourteenth Century* (Princeton: 1961) 387.

The pivotal role assigned to moral training by the author of the *Giardino*, and the consequent blurring of meditation with moral education, fits perfectly into the process of the construction of new religious identities among the late medieval laity, in which the *vita contemplativa* and *vita activa* are combined and spiritual intimacy with God is mixed with social activity.[18] The combination of the *homo coelestis* and the *homo faber*, which implies an awareness of the fulfilment of the *vita beata*, can be found in the amalgamation of religious and civic virtues, which pleases each individual in a wider and collective social paradigm.[19] As Todeschini has recently explained, this contiguity is made possible by the strict connection between the 'theological language of election, salvation and spiritual profit' and the daily economic and professional practice of medieval urban dwellers. He writes:

> To understand this link it is sufficient to remember the relevance of many [Gospel] allegories, as the one depicted in the talents' parable, for the linguistic construction of medieval economic reflections on profit and loss or to keep in mind the influence exerted on theologians' and jurists' economic analysis by the widely diffused Christ's *agraphon* which established as a duty for the Christians to be 'similar to the skilled money-changer' that is able to make a distinction between good and wicked actions as one would be between legal or fake currencies.[20]

For a recent study of Italian *Meditationes Vitae Christi*, see Flora H., *The devout belief of the imagination. The Paris Meditationes Vitae Christ and Female Franciscan Spirituality in Trecento Italy* (Turnhout: 2009). For a discussion of the connection between biblical reading and ethics, see also Corbellini, S., "Looking in the Mirror of the Scriptures. Reading the Bible in Medieval Italy", in François, W. – Den Hollander A. (eds.), *"Wading Lambs and Swimming Elephants": The Bible for the Laity and Theologians in the Late Medieval and Early Modern Era* (Louvain 2012) 21–40.

18   On the discussion of the combination of *vita activa* and *vita contemplativa*, see Gilli P., "Vie active, vie contemplative chez les humanistes italiens du xvᵉ siècle. Du retrait volontaire à la retraite forcée", in Trottmann C. (ed.), *Vie active et vie contemplative au Moyen Age et au seuil de la Renaissance* (Rome: 2009) 425–442.

19   Artifoni E., "Tra etica e professionalità politica: la riflessione sulle forme di vita in alcuni intellettuali pragmatici del Duecento italiano", in Trottmann (ed.), *Vie active et vie contemplative* 403–423, in particular 408. See also Pirani F., "Moderazione del vivere cittadino: il Testamentum di Pietro da Fermo (1292)", *Archivio storico italiano* 169, 2 (2011) 343–371, here 351. The cultural vicinity between theological and urban and mercantile groups was recently described by Todeschini G., "Theological Roots of the Medieval/Modern Merchants' Self-Representation", in Jacob M. – Secrettan C. (eds.), *The Self-Perception of Early Modern "Capitalists"* (New York: 2008) 17–46.

20   Todeschini, "Theological Roots" 18–19.

The author of the *Giardino* invites his readers to transform the reading activities into action, not in the sense given by Anthony Grafton and Lisa Jardine in their famous article on Harvey's reading of Livy—that is, transformation into political action—but as an activity that is able to morally transform the reader.[21]

A case in point regarding this conflation of Gospel teachings and moral virtues is already visible in thirteenth-century Italy in the sermons given by the Italian *causidicus* (lawyer) Albertanus of Brescia (1190–after 1253), one of the most influential and widely read intellectuals in late medieval Italy.[22] Born in the 1190, Albertanus was 'the protagonist of important political events' of his time.[23] He is, moreover, the author of three tracts, the *Liber de Amore et dilectione Dei et proximi et aliarum rerum et de forma vitae* (1238; On the Love and Affection of God and Neighbours and Other Things and on the Form of Life), the *Doctrina Loquendi et Tacendi* (1245; On the Doctrine of Speaking and Remaining Silent) and the *Liber Consolationis et Consilii* (1246; Book of Consolation and Counsel), as well as at least five sermons, delivered in Genoa (1243; for the city lawyers) and in Brescia (before 1250; for the confraternity of fellow *causidici*). His first sermon, delivered in 1243 while attached as an 'assessor' to his fellow Brescian, Emmanuel de Madiis, who was *podestà* at Genoa, deserves attention due to its explicit linking of Gospel narrative and moral interpretation.[24] Albertanus starts his sermon to 'the advocates of Genoa and certain notaries on the confirmation of their life' by citing from the Epistles of

---

21   Jardine L. – Grafton A., "'Studied for Action': How Gabriel Harvey read his Livy", *Past and Present* 129, 1 (1990) 30–78.

22   The importance of Albertanus of Brescia in the reconstruction of lay religiosity, and a lay approach to religious literature in general and biblical literature in particular, cannot be overestimated. About manuscripts containing Italian vernacular Bible translations in combination with Albertanus' texts, see Corbellini S., "Vernacular Bible Manuscripts" 280–281.

23   Felice F., "Genovese Sermon", *Journal of Markets and Morality* 7, 2 (2004) 603–638, at 605. In this contribution, the works by Albertanus of Brescia are seen as stepping stones to the revision of the Protestant ethics theory as far as modern economic epistemology is concerned, 'which can thus make sense of market processes'. According to Felice, who bases his conclusions on the work of Oscar Nuccio, Albertanus 'adopts a thoroughly modern analysis of "human action", of a "double legitimization of work and profit" and of an "ethical consecration of utility"'.

24   The sermon has also been analysed by Andrews F., "Albertano of Brescia, Rolandino of Padua and the Rhetoric of Legitimation", in Alfonso I. – Kennedy H. – Escalona J. (eds.), *Building Legitimacy. Political Discourses and Forms of Legitimation in Medieval Societies* (Leiden: 2004) 319–340, in particular 328–329, and Powell J. M., *Albertanus of Brescia: The Pursuit of Happiness in the Early Thirteenth Century* (Philadelphia: 1992).

James (1:17) and from the Gospel of Matthew (10:29) and elaborates *in extenso* on a passage from the Sermon on the Mount (*Matthew* 5:13): 'You are the salt of the earth, but if the salt has lost its taste how shall its saltiness be restored? It is no longer good for anything except to be thrown out and trodden under foot by men'.[25] He then explains how the Gospel citation should be applied to the professional life of the listeners:

> Our Lord Jesus Christ addressed those words to his apostles. Nevertheless, by some sort of analogy the aforementioned words should be spoken to you wise men: You are the salt of the earth because, just as the apostles have brought back Christians to an appreciation of the faith and the love of eternal life, so you, as well, and by your wisdom should bring back all acts of men who come to you for advice and assistance to the appreciation of reason and a relish for justice and the love of the precepts of justice.[26]

As Andrews notes, this sermon not only 'highlights the crucial role of *causidici* as purveyors of reason, justice and wisdom [...] but also places Christian doctrine at the centre of [...] professional life'.[27] The careful and conscious fulfilment of daily activities could transform lawyers into apostles, able to disseminate the message of the Gospel through their own personal and professional life. Albertanus, who cites extensively from the Scriptures in his tracts and sermons (and thus was a fervent Bible reader who applied a process of selective reading of the text according to his own personal and professional needs), and values theological reflection particularly highly, shows very clearly how the reading of and the reflection on the sacred texts could be transformed into instructions for a moral life, and how the religious message could thus enter the world of the lay reader and be transformed into daily 'food for thought'.

As the author of the *Giardino* wishes and Albertanus exemplifies, the reading of and reflection on the sacred text could trigger a process in which the 'reader's energy is directed inward towards the self', leading to self-scrutiny and in particular to moral self-improvement.[28] It is indeed not by mere chance that

---

25   The text is cited from the translation in Felice, "Genovese Sermon" 3–4.

26   Felice, "Genovese Sermon" 4.

27   Andrews, "Albertano of Brescia" 329.

28   Stock B., "Minds, Bodies, Readers. I. Healing. Meditation, and the History of Reading", *New Literary History* 37, 3 (2006) 489–501, here 498. In Stock's reconstruction, the reading of religious literature and the experience of meditation may lead either to self-scrutiny and self-improvement or to literary expression, such as the writing of narrative

late medieval spiritual advisors constantly refer to the reading of religious literature as a shield against temptations and vices and as an instrument of spiritual welfare. Illustrations of this practice can be found in the letters sent by the
Augustinian friar Girolamo da Siena (around 1335–1420) to his spiritual daughters, who lived in religious communities and in the lay world.[29] Writing to an
anonymous nun, he advises her 'to read as much as possible' but only 'useful
books that can edify' her. He then specifies that she should leave aside 'vain
and worldly readings' and 'futile texts' that cannot enlighten her and instead
choose 'spiritual and devout readings [...] and in particular texts, which can
help her to fight vices and enflame her with love for God and virtues'.[30] The
widow Sigismonda is advised to 'take in the mirror of her mind the holy proph-
etess Anna', whose life is described in the Gospels and who was able to recognize Christ when he was presented at the Temple. Having lost her husband,
Sigismonda is advised to raise her mind to God and contemplate him, often
listening to God's Word and then, 'sitting in solitude, rethink it and memorize
the words she has listened to' and 'once [she] has placed these words in the
mouth of her memory, [she] should ruminate on them with the teeth of meditation', tasting 'the sweetness' of opening her heart to God. This practice will
comfort her and put an end to her troubles, but she must concentrate on God
and dedicate herself to prayer and other activities that can please her Saviour.[31]

Interestingly enough, references to the healing power of books are not
only the prerogative of religious men in their function as spiritual advisors.
Margherita Datini, wife of the merchant Marco Datini, uses the same language
in the letter she sends to her husband on 23 January 1395:

---

autobiographies. The only medieval figure able to combine these two aspects was, according to Stock, Petrarch.

29   The letters are edited by Girolamo da Siena, *Epistole*, ed. S. Serventi (Venice: 2004). For
      other examples of this practice, see Corbellini, "Instructing the Soul, Feeding the Spirit
      and Awakening the Passion".

30   'Leçi asai, ma più ora e leçi sempre [cose] utile che te possano hedificare. Lassa star ogni
      scriptura mondana e vana et ogni scriptura sença fructo e hedificatione di mente, e leçi
      scripture spirituale e devote. E speçialmente leçi volentiera scripture che te façano venire
      li vitii in odio e façate acendere in amore di Dio e de le vertù e de' boni costumi'. Girolamo,
      Epistole 157.

31   'Ana sanctissima prophetessa [...] e poi sedendo solitaria, specula e redute a memoria
      quelle cose che ài udito; e reduto che l' ài a la boca de la memoria, sì lo viene ruminando
      con denti de la meditacione e per dolceça di contemplacione spandi lo tuo cuore dinanci
      a Dio'. Girolamo, *Epistole* 201–204.

After the departure of Nanni di Santa Chiara's brother, we received a letter from you that has made me very anxious, because I see that you are worried, although I don't really know the reason. But, whatever it is, why dwell on it so much that you harm both body and soul? [...] If you were to place your faith in Him [in God] and accept what came, we wouldn't be subject to such passions. If we thought about death and how little time we have on this earth, we wouldn't worry as much as we do, and we would allow ourselves to be guided by Him and accept everything that happens. God doesn't like people who ignore Him. Remember the books that you read when you are here, and don't worry so much.[32]

Margherita's reference is cryptic, but it is known that Marco Datini had in that same year announced to his business partner Boninsegna di Matteo his decision to dedicate his spare time to the reading of religious literature (he mentions explicitly Gospels, Epistles, and the sayings and lives of the saints) in order 'to get nearer to God' and 'dedicate more time to God than [he has] done in the past'. To reach this goal, he decided to read the books he already had in his personal library and to have more copied.[33] There is, moreover, substantial evidence that Datini used his extended network, which included lay and religious individuals and communities alike, to acquire a substantial book collection with clear moral and religious contents.[34]

The decision to deepen his moral reflection and to dedicate more time to the reading of religious books, as announced in the letter to Boninsegna, has left clear traces in Datini's correspondence from the last years of his life (he died in 1410), showing how his religious reading could be transformed into moral lessons that he shared with his personal and professional network. He frequently cites from the Old and New Testaments, emphasizing the importance of the

---

32   Datini M., *Letters to Francesco Datini*. Trans. C. James – A. Pagliaro (Toronto: 2012) 160.

33   Cited by Brambilla S., "Libro di dio e dell'anima certamente. Francesco Datini tra spiritualità e commercio librario", in Manfredi A. – Monti C.M. (eds.), *L'Antiche e le moderne carte. Studi in memoria di Giuseppe Billanovich* (Rome: 2007) 189–246, here 192–193. The complete passage is translated in Corbellini S., "Reading, Writing and Collecting: Cultural Dynamics and Italian Vernacular Bible Translations", *Church History and Religious Culture* 93 (2013) 189–216, at 204–205.

34   About Datini's book ownership, see Brambilla, "Libro di dio e dell'anima certamente". The relationships with religious individuals and communities are thoroughly described in Brambilla S. (ed.), *'Padre mio dolce'. Lettere di religiosi a Francesco Datini. Antologia* (Roma: 2010).

citation by adding that the 'words [are] from God's mouth'.[35] Reflecting on his excessive focus on the importance of material goods and success, he refers to the parable of the House on the Rock (*Matthew* 7:24–27 and *Luke* 6:46–49):

> But I have built my wall on the sand, as the Gospel says, and then the rain came and the wind and it fell; but if I had built on the rock neither rain, nor wind or other accidents could have let it fall. I thank God for everything.[36]

Becoming conscious of making the wrong choices in his life ('òe erato quanto pùe poso nello mio vivere'), his inadequate moral conduct ('nmi sono male ghovernato') and his mistakes ('òe fatto male i fatti miei'), he decides to accept his fate and be patient in his suffering, just like Job, and to put his trust in God ('e mi sono chontento di portare la pena, ma vorei fare chome e' fece Giobo di chosa che lgli intervenise').[37] When he describes his relief in having resisted the temptation to be overambitious, he defines his impossible enterprises as 'a tower of Babel' and expresses his concern over putting so much effort into 'honouring people who did not deserve his admiration' ('di fare onore altrui'), rather than 'investing his hope, love and faith in the One who would never let [him] down' ('vorei avere mesa questa isperanza e questo amore e questa fede in Cholui che non si perde mai').[38]

In a letter to his wife Margherita, Francesco explained how he found consolation in rethinking the example of Christ and of the martyrs:

> All these efforts will make us better, as they will help us to admit our mistakes, especially mine. You know that God was killed out of envy and first falsely accused of having diabolic powers for all his miracles. All his apostles were killed and all the martyrs, and the female saints and the virgins; and then a great number of lords and worthy men in several countries have been killed and sent away out of envy and unjustly treated. All this has not just started, and this will last until the end of the world.[39]

---

35 'Dise Dio de la bocha sua'. Cited by Nanni P., *Ragionare tra mercanti. Per una rilettura della personalità di Francesco Datini (1335ca–1410)* (Pisa: 2012) 252.

36 Nanni, *Ragionare tra mercanti* 253. Datini uses the reference to this parable at least twice in his correspondence, see Nanni, *Ragionare di mercanti* 252.

37 Nanni, *Ragionare di mercanti* 252.

38 Nanni, *Ragionare di mercanti* 254–255.

39 'Tutte queste fatiche saranno per nostro melgl(i)o: farànoci richonosciere de' nostri errori, dicho de' mei. Tu sai che Idio fue per invid(i)a mor[to] e prima chalongnato, che d' ongni

The merchant is stimulated in his reflections by his religious correspondents. The Dominican Antonio Cancellieri, Master of Theology at the Florentine Santa Maria Novella, wrote him a letter announcing that he would 'send him ten peaches, to remind him of the Ten Commandments'. Some time later, Antonio announced the sending of a booklet 'with the seven penitential psalms' and a folium with the 'prayer that St Bridget read during the elevation of the Corpus Christi', and he added that the prayer should also be used to instruct Caterina, Margherita's niece.[40]

Communities of Readers

The epistolary exchange between Girolamo da Siena and his spiritual daughters and between Marco Datini and his correspondents sheds important light on one pivotal aspect of late medieval religious literacies: the emphasis in instruction books on reading and meditation, and on the need to choose a quiet time and place to stimulate the creation of 'mental places' and 'mental images', does not necessarily exclude communal reading experiences and the existence of real or imagined reading communities.[41] Girolamo da Siena explicitly asks that his letters will be copied and distributed among his disciples.[42] The books copied for and owned by Francesco Datini were probably used by members of his personal and professional network (and in the last instance they were bequeathed to the charitable institution he founded) and he felt the urge to communicate his reflections, which were evoked by the reading of religious texts, to the members of the same network.[43] As Scase emphasizes,

---

bene facea era detto facea per arte diabolicha. I suoi apostoli furono morti e tutti i marteri, apresso le sante e ll vergini; apresso molti singnori e valenti uomeni in pùe paesi sono stati morti e chaciati per invidia e fatti loro grande torto. Questo fatto no(n) chominc(i) a testé: in mentre che llo mondo durerà s'aran(n)o di queste chose'. Nanni, *Ragionare di mercanti* 255–256.

40 Brambilla, *'Padre mio dolce'* 17, 19.

41 The term 'imagined reading communities' is inspired by Anderson B., *Imagined Communities: Reflections on the Origin and Spread of Nationalism* (London: 1983). See also Scase, *Reading Communities*.

42 Girolamo, *Epistole* 20.

43 Brambilla, "Libro di Dio e dell'anima certamente" 42; Corbellini, "Reading, Writing and Collecting" 205. For an exploration of the idea of the household as a religious community, see Mertes R.G.K.A., "The Household as Religious Community", in Rosenthal J. – Richmond C. (eds.), *People, Politics and Community in the Later Middle Ages* (Gloucester – New York: 1987) 123–139. An example of an aristocratic household that can be described

'the study of medieval reading communities is relatively recent, and still very much in its early stage and much remains to be done before it will be possible to write a comprehensive history of medieval reading and its place in communities', but the importance of moving the research focus onto 'communities of readers' is paramount.[44] Indeed, this approach could help shed more light on the impact of religious reading activities on social and cultural transformation in late medieval and early modern Europe and would, moreover, contribute to a better understanding of the possibilities and limitations regarding laypeople's access to religious literature, an issue that lies at the very heart of discussions of European history and identities.

It is, for example, particularly important to acknowledge that access to texts and books was not restricted to a limited elite, but that books could be copied, circulated, bought second-hand, borrowed and also read by less affluent members of medieval society. An instance of this practice can be seen in the creation of networks for the loan and the exchange of manuscript books, such as the one established by Michele di Giovanni Guinigi in the first half of the fifteenth century in Lucca. According to his registers, he owned at least 100 manuscripts that were lent without charge to citizens of Lucca of different social backgrounds, including merchants, chancellors of the republic, religious men, schoolmasters, women and people with a less fortunate background.[45] As Michele systematically noted the name of the borrower and the title of the volume in his register, it is known that at least 141 borrowers benefited from the merchant's library, which consisted of vernacular and Latin manuscripts, ranging from primary school texts to Cicero, Ovid and Terentius. Vernacular religious books were mostly borrowed by female members of the network: 'monna Bartola' borrowed a book on the life of Christ; Michele's aunt Giannella read a Psalter (partially copied by Michele himself) and the Dialogues of St Gregory; and a nun, Battista, read works by Cassianus.[46]

---

as a node in the production and the exchange of manuscripts is investigated by Perry R., "The Clopton Manuscript and the Beauchamp Affinity: Patronage and Reception Issues in a West Midlands Reading Community", in Scase W. (ed.), *Essays in Manuscript Geography: Vernacular Manuscripts of the English West Midlands from the Conquest to the Sixteenth Century* (Turnhout: 2007) 131–159.

44   Scase, "Reading Communities" 557.

45   Polica S., "Le commerce et le prêt de livres à Lucques dans la première moitié du XVe siècle", *Médiévales* 14 (1988) 33–46. On the creation of book networks, see also Corbellini, "Beyond Orthodoxy and Heterodoxy"; and Corbellini S. – Hoogvliet M., "Artisans and Religious Reading in Late Medieval Italy and Northern France (ca. 1400–ca. 1520)", *The Journal of Medieval and Early Modern Studies* 43, 3 (2013) 521–544.

46   Polica, "Le commerce" 39.

It was, moreover, a common practice in medieval Italy to donate books to religious institutions and to confraternities. These 'testamentary schemes, in which books were left in wills, suggests a community constituted through personal links that extended beyond the lives of its individual members'.[47] A case in point is the will of the notary Pierfrancesco de Giovagne (Perugia, 31 July 1448), in which the books bequeathed to the Confraternity of St Jerome are described in great detail. Pierfrancesco owned:

- A book with the four Gospels and the four cardinal virtues
- The Epistles of St Paul, without 'the beginning and the end'
- The Epistles of St Jerome
- The Last Communion of St Jerome ('il transito di san Girolamo')
- All the sermons of the blessed Bernardino and other quires ('quaterne') on devout subjects concerning the Holy Writ and how to pray. This manuscript was lent to 'messer Petruccio da l'Aquila', one of Pierfrancesco's confraternity brothers.
- A book in which part of the Bible in the vernacular, the Gospels and the Acts of the Apostles and a list of popes and emperors from St Peter until that the year of composition of the manuscript had been copied by Pierfrancesco's father.[48]

Pierfrancesco decided that the books should be at the disposal of the members of the confraternities, as well as the brothers of the Observant convent of Monteripido who had become members of the confraternity. Moreover, he bestowed a lectionary on the same Observant community, stating explicitly that he 'had bought it [second-hand] in order to give it back to the original owners'. As he had failed to find the rightful owner, he asked the brothers to

---

47   Scase, "Reading Communities" 567. The importance of confraternities as nodes and nexuses where social and cultural networks intersected has already been emphasized in Corbellini S., "The Plea for Lay Bibles in Fourteenth and Fifteenth Century Tuscany: the Role of Confraternities", in Terpstra N. – Prosperi A. – Pastore S. (eds.), *Faith's Boundaries. Laity and Clergy in Early Modern Confraternities* (Turnhout: 2012) 87–112. New publications of sources related to inventories and catalogues of Italian medieval libraries have, however, made clear that the impact of confraternal organizations on the dissemination of biblical and religious literature is even more relevant and substantial. See, for example, the holdings of medieval confraternities described in the four recently published volumes of the *RICABIM*, the Repertory of Inventories and Catalogues of Medieval Libraries (Florence: 2011–2013).

48   Somigli E. (ed.), *Ricabim 3. Italia. Umbria, Marche, Abruzzo, Molise* (Florence: 2013) 83–84, nr. 287.

keep it until they were able to return it.[49] In the inventories of the confraternity, compiled in 1449, 1494 and 1532, the books left by Pierfrancesco indeed appear.[50] The other books owned by the notary (an unspecified number of law books and other juridical material) were also given to the confraternity to be sold. It is quite clear that Pierfrancesco's religious books were such an important aspect of his identity (probably much more than his function as a juridical professional) that he wanted to keep the collection intact and to continue his participation in the confraternal activities through his collection of religious books. It should also be noted that in his will he mentions that one of his manuscripts, a vernacular Bible, probably containing a part of the Old Testament, the Gospels and the Acts of the Apostles, had been copied by his father. This part of the family patrimony was also to be shared with the extended family of the confraternity brothers.

The registers of the confraternity of St Augustine in Perugia provide even clearer information about the creation of communities dedicated to the reading of religious texts, and testify to the sharing of books within and between confraternities. In a chronological record kept between 1426 and 1467, the borrowers of books that were exclusively religious in character and in the vernacular (*laudari*, devotional books, lectionaries, the seven penitential psalms, the *Vitas Patrum*, Gospels and Epistles) are all registered.[51] Among the borrowers we find a cloth maker, an Augustinian friar, an Augustinian prior, and unidentified members of the confraternity or possibly other confraternities in Perugia.[52] The description of one of the volumes loaned also reveals the possibility of the existence of a chained-book library located near the Church of St Augustine: in fact one of the manuscripts, the vernacular *Vitas Patrum*, is described as 'con assicielle e catenella' ('bound in wood and a small chain').[53]

As suggested by Somigli, the lending of these books could be related to the preparation and the staging of *sacre rappresentazioni*, 'holy performances'.[54]

---

49   Somigli, *Ricabim* 84.

50   Somigli, *Ricabim* 98–99, nr. 330–333.

51   Somigli, *Ricabim* 87–88, no. 300. The list of loans is edited by Nerbano M., "Cultura materiale nel teatro delle confraternite umbre", *Teatro e Storia* 12, 4 (1997) 293–346, at 329–346.

52   The inter-confraternity loan is suggested by Somigli, *Ricabim* 87.

53   On the confraternity libraries and the presence of chained books, see Corbellini, "The Plea for Vernacular Bibles". The idea that the confraternity could have created a small library is consistent with the role that confraternities played in the religious education of the laity and their sensitivity to the need of a growing number of literate members to read and copy religious literature.

54   The 'sacra rappresentazione' is a form of medieval Italian religious theatre. For a description of the characteristics of 'sacre rappresentazioni', see Marrone G. (ed.), *Encyclopedia of Italian Literary Studies* (New York: 2007) 1651–1653.

Although this specific use is not explicitly mentioned in the registers, and bor-rowers could have used the manuscripts to make a personal copy or to select reading material, it is particularly interesting to note that the same registers also recorded the loan of draperies, stage costumes and theatrical scenery for the performance of the *sacre rappresentazioni*. For example, Gniangne de Nicholò, who borrowed a book on the *Devotione* on 23 March 1429, received from the confraternity on 8 April, a 'Christ's crown of thorns', 'four beards' and 'five dresses', probably for a representation of the Passion of Christ. It is thus possible that the use of the manuscript and the staging of the Passion were strictly related, making the process of 'uncovering the presence' by reading the texts in the manuscripts particularly explicit: the salvific power of reading and meditating on religious texts could thus be shared even with those who had no access to books.[55]

Conclusion

This preliminary investigation of a broad range of textual sources, including a tract on the meditation of Christ, a sermon by a thirteenth-century law-yer, letters by religious men and lay merchants, registers of book loans and documentation on the donations of books, reveals the various possibilities for approaching and investigating religious literacies in medieval Italy (and in Europe more generally). All these sources register the dynamics of late medi-eval religiosity and emphasize the importance of reading, and reading activi-ties in lay circles, in the broadest sense of the word. The sources illustrate that reading activities were far from superficial and ephemeral and that lay read-ers were involved in a process of assimilation and transformation of religious content, which was integrated into their personal reflections and led to their spiritual growth. Moreover, once the 'presence was uncovered' and the reli-gious message had entered the readers' minds and lives, initiating the process of self-scrutiny and self-improvement, the experience then had to be shared, communicated and performed.

---

55   The combination of theatrical material and manuscripts is also present in the inven-tory of the confraternity of St Dominic in Perugia. The confraternity library contained the same type of texts described in the confraternity of St Augustine, i.e. manuscripts with *laude* and devotional literature, such as the *Specchio della croce* of the Dominican Cavalca, a book-long meditation on the Passion of Christ.

Bibliography

Andrews F., "Albertano of Brescia, Rolandino of Padua and the Rhetoric of Legitimation", in Alfonso I. – Kennedy H. – Escalona J. (eds.), *Building Legitimacy. Political Discourses and Forms of Legitimation in Medieval Societies* (Leiden: 2004) 319–340.

Bolzoni L., *Il lettore creativo: percorsi cinquecenteschi fra memoria, gioco, scrittura* (Naples: 2012).

Boyarin D., "Placing Reading: Ancient Israel and Medieval Europe", in Boyarin J. (ed.), *The Ethnography of Reading* (Berkeley – Los Angeles: 1992) 10–37.

Brambilla S., "Libro di dio e dell'anima certamente. Francesco Datini tra spiritualità e commercio librario", in Manfredi A. – Monti C.M. (eds.), *L'Antiche e le moderne carte. Studi in memoria di Giuseppe Billanovich* (Rome: 2007).

———— (ed.), *'Padre mio dolce'. Lettere di religiosi a Francesco Datini. Antologia* (Roma: 2010).

Brown M.P., "The Thick Style: Steady Sellers, Textual Aesthetics, and Early Modern Devotional Reading", *Publications of Modern Language Association of America* 121,1 (2006) 67–86.

Caravale G., *Forbidden Prayer. Church Censorship and Devotional Literature in Renaissance Italy* (Farnham: 2011).

Corbellini S., "Instructing the Soul, Feeding the Spirit and Awakening the Passion: Holy Writ and Lay Readers in Late Medieval Europe", in Gordon B. – McLean, M. (eds.), *Shaping the Bible in the Reformation: Books, Scholars and their Readers in the Sixteenth Century* (Leiden: 2012) 15–39.

————, "Looking in the Mirror of the Scriptures. Reading the Bible in Medieval Italy", in François, W. – Den Hollander A. (eds.), *"Wading Lambs and Swimming Elephants": The Bible for the Laity and Theologians in the Late Medieval and Early Modern Era* (Louvain 2012) 21–40.

————, "Reading, Writing and Collecting: Cultural Dynamics and Italian Vernacular Bible Translations", *Church History and Religious Culture* 93 (2013) 189–216.

Datini M., *Letters to Francesco Datini*. Trans. C. James – A. Pagliaro (Toronto: 2012).

Felice F., "Genovese Sermon", *Journal of Markets and Morality* 7,2 (2004) 603–638.

Frioli D., "Tra oralità e scrittura. Appunti su libri e biblioteche dei laici devoti", *Quaderni di Storia Religiosa* (2001) 147–219.

Gagliardi I., " 'Secondo che parla la Santa Scriptura'. Girolamo da Siena e i suoi testi di 'direzione spirituale' alla fine del Trecento", in Catto M. – Gagliardi I. – Parrinello R.M. (eds.), *Direzione spitituale tra ortodossia ed eresia. Dalle scuole filosofiche antiche al Novecento* (Brescia: 2002) 117–175.

Gilli P., "Vie active, vie contemplative chez les humanistes italiens du xve siècle. Du retrait volontaire à la retraite forcée", in Trottmann C. (ed.), *Vie active et vie contemplative au Moyen Age et au seuil de la Renaissance* (Rome: 2009) 425–442.

Ginzburg C., "Folklore, magia, religione", in *Storia d'Italia* 1 (Turin: 1972) 603–679.

Girolamo da Siena, *Epistole*, ed. S. Serventi (Venice: 2004).

Karnes M., *Imagination, Meditation, and Cognition in the Middle Ages* (Chicago: 2011).

Nanni P., *Ragionare tra mercanti. Per una rilettura della personalità di Francesco Datini (1335ca–1410)* (Pisa: 2012).

Nerbano M., "Cultura materiale nel teatro delle confraternite umbre", *Teatro e Storia* 12, 4 (1997) 293–346.

Pirani F., "Moderazione del vivere cittadino: il Testamentum di Pietro da Fermo (1292)", *Archivio storico italiano* 169, 2 (2011) 343–371.

Polica S., "Le commerce et le prêt de livres à Lucques dans la première moitié du xve siècle", *Médiévales* 14 (1988) 33–46.

Powell J.M., *Albertanus of Brescia: The Pursuit of Happiness in the Early Thirteenth Century* (Philadelphia: 1992).

Scase W., "Reading Communities", in Treharne E. – Walker G. (eds.), *The Oxford Handbook of Medieval Literature in English* (Oxford: 2010) 557–573.

Somigli E. (ed.), *Ricabim 3. Italia. Umbria, Marche, Abruzzo, Molise* (Florence: 2013).

Stock B., "Minds, Bodies, Readers. I. Healing. Meditation, and the History of Reading", *New Literary History* 37, 3 (2006) 489–501.

Taylor J., *The Didascalicon of Hugh of St. Victor. A Medieval Guide to the Arts* (New York – London: 1961).

Todeschini G., "Theological Roots of the Medieval/Modern Merchants' Self-Representation", in Jacob M. – Secrettan C. (eds.), *The Self-Perception of Early Modern "Capitalists"* (New York: 2008) 17–46.

Zarri G., "Note su diffusione e circolazione di testi devote (1520–1550)", in Zarri G., *Libri di Spirito. Editoria religiosa in volgare nei secoli XV–XVII* (Torino: 2009) 103–146.

CHAPTER 4

Evidence for Religious Reading Practice and Experience in Times of Change: Some Models Provided by Late Medieval Texts of the Ten Commandments

Elisabeth Salter

In studying the History of Reading in late Medieval and Early Modern England my particular focus is an exploration of evidence for popular reading practice and experience. I use a case study method in order to make detailed investigations of groups of manuscripts or books or particular texts in their differing contexts. A key aim is to extrapolate from this very particular evidence to some more general conclusions about reading practice and experience.

For this essay I begin by reviewing some issues pertinent to the study of reading practice and experience particularly in the context of Medieval and Early Modern England and with a focus on religious reading. In the second half of the essay, I proceed with the kind of case study that I propose as necessary for elucidating reading practice and experience, staying for these examples with a fifteenth century context whilst proposing how these examples might relate to a broader chronology of religious reading and change. Here, I take as my focus one text from the basic catechism, the Ten Commandments. I explore short, rhyming, versions of this text in one particular manuscript context (Lambeth Palace Library Ms 853) and I use this to postulate some possibilities for the ways that religious reading provides evidence for experiences of change or difference in two ways: in the first instance I use the manuscript example of two versions of a Ten Commandments poem in this one manuscript to explore the ways that acculturation may occur through familiarity. In the second instance, I use the same poems to propose a reader-centred model for engagement with heterodox (i.e. changed) ideas and practices.

The Study of Reading

The development of the field known as the History of Reading has brought renewed attention to studies of the manuscript and early printed book,

© KONINKLIJKE BRILL NV, LEIDEN, 2015 | DOI 10.1163/9789004290396_006

especially given the simultaneous revival of interest in material culture.[1] Indeed, one of the key scholars of the History of Reading, Roger Chartier, asserts the necessary connections between the material form of the text being read and the production of meaning by the reader.[2] Medieval devotional reading has received particular attention often in relation to the role of religious houses in the promotion of lay literate devotion, particularly in the period approaching the Reformation, which emerges as important for the transmission of books, and of ideas.[3]

Evidence for reading practice and experience can be elusive which perhaps encourages the tendency to discuss theories, rather than practices, of reading.[4] One of the key areas of concern is the problem of knowing what to do with the emancipated, creative, reader who necessarily breaks free from

---

1 See, for example, Price L., "Reading Matter", *PMLA* 121,1 (2006) 9–16; Cavallo G. – Chartier R. (eds.), *A History of Reading in the West*, trans. L.G. Cochrane (Oxford: 1999); see also, Chartier R., *The Order of Books: Readers, Authors and Libraries between the Fourteenth and Eighteenth Centuries*, trans. L.G. Cochrane (London: 1994). Thompson J. – Kelly S., "Imagined Histories", in Thompson J. – Kelly S. (eds.), *Imagining the Book: Medieval Texts and Cultures of Northern Europe* (Turnhout: 2006) 6. For other important references see Salter E., *Popular Reading in English c 1400–1600* (Manchester: 2012) Chapter 1.

2 Chartier R., *The Order of Books* ix; Chartier R., "Libraries Without Walls", *Representations, Special Issue: Future Libraries* 42 (1993) 38–52, here 48–49. The work to which he refers is McKenzie D.F., *Bibliography and the Sociology of Texts* (London: 1986); Chartier R., "Languages, Books and Reading from the Printed Word to the Digital Text", *Critical Inquiry* 31,1 (2004) 133–152, here 147. Chartier R., "Introduction: Aesthetic Mystery and the Materialities of the Written", in *Inscription and Erasure: Written Culture from the Eleventh to the Eighteenth Century*, trans. A. Goldhammer (Philadelphia: 2007) vii–xiii, vii–viii. On reading revolutions see, Darnton R., "What is the History of Books?", in *The Kiss of Lamourette: Reflections in Cultural History* (London: 1990) 107–135, here 133. For important recent work on materiality and reading see, for example, Sherman W., *Used Books: Marking Readers in Renaissance England* (Philadelphia: 2008); Richards J. – Schurink F. (eds.), *The Textuality and Materiality of Reading in Early Modern England*, Special Issue *Huntington Library Quarterly* 73,3 (2010).

3 See, for example, Sergeant M., "The Transmission by the English Carthusians of some late Medieval Spiritual Writings", *Journal of Ecclesiastical Studies* 27 (1976) 225–240; Gillespie V., "Vernacular Books of Religion", in Griffiths J. – Pearsall D. (eds.), *Book Production and Publishing in Britain, 1375–1475* (Cambridge: 1989); Gillespie V., "*Cura pastoralis in Deserto*", in Sargent M. (ed.), *De Cella in Seculum: Religious Secular Life and Devotion in Late Medieval England* (Cambridge: 1989) 161–181; and Hutchinson A., "Devotional Reading in the Monastery and in the Household", in Sargent M. (ed.), *De Cella in Seculum: Religious Secular Life and Devotion in Late Medieval England* (Cambridge: 1989) 215–227.

4 I have discussed this in Salter E., "'The Dayes Moralised': Reconstructing Devotional Reading, c. 1450–1560", in Lutton R.S.G. – Salter E. (eds.), *Pieties in Transition: Religious Practices and Experiences c 1400–1640* (Aldershot: 2007) 145–162, here 149–150.

the structural constraints of the written page.[5] Although there are limits to the freedoms of any reader at any moment in history, the heart of this problem is being able to understand the relationship between the products of discourse (e.g. the written text) and social practices (i.e. the uses or interpretations of that text).[6] William Sherman has recently proposed that there remains, a "more or less adversarial division between those who study 'imagined' 'implied' or 'ideal' readers and those who study the traces of 'real' 'actual' or 'historical' readers", which is a sign of the methodological distinctions between theorising and analysing practice.[7]

Roger Chartier has proposed that as part of a more general shift towards an appropriation-based model of cultural formation, there has been a general shift towards the analysis of practice. But this often seems to entail consideration of large data sets with relatively less consideration of, for example, the detail of an individual manuscript version.[8] In order to understand more about the reading practices and experiences of real readers in the Medieval and Early Modern period, I argue that more work which assesses the evidence of book and manuscript in some detail is needed.[9] There is a great inheritance of scholarship assessing reading habits, which is often based around specific manuscripts with associated evidence for ownership, provenance, circulation, transmission, and possible networks of readers.[10] There is a wide range

---

5   See for example, Chartier, *The Order of Books* 23; de Certeau M., *The Practice of Everyday Life*, trans. S.F. Rendall (Berkeley: 1984) 165–176.

6   Chartier R., *On the Edge of the Cliff: History, Language, and Practices*, trans. L.G. Cochrane (Baltimore and London: 1997) 1–10; Chartier, *The Order of Books* 1–23; Iser W., *The Act of Reading: A Theory of Aesthetic Response* (Baltimore – London: 1980) 132; Fish S., "Interpreting the *Variorum*", in Finkelstein D. – McCleery A. (eds.), *The Book History Reader* (London: 2001) 450–458, here 454.

7   Sherman W., *Used Books: Marking Readers in Renaissance England* (Philadelphia: 2008) 99–100; also, Brayman Hackel H., *Reading Material in Early Modern England: Print, Gender and Literacy* (Cambridge: 2005) 6–7.

8   Chartier, *On the Edge of the Cliff* 2; Chartier, "Texts, forms and interpretations" 83.

9   On the useful idea of the book as always being in process as both 'a material object and a cultural phenomenon', see Thompson – Kelly, "Imagined histories" 5.

10   See, for example, Riddy F., "'Women talking about the things of God' A Late Medieval Subculture", in Meale C. (ed.), *Women and Literatures in Britain, 1150–1500* (Cambridge: 1993) 106–111, and Boffey J., "Women Authors and Women's Literacy", in Meale C. (ed.), *Women and Literatures in Britain, 1150–1500* (Cambridge: 1993) 169–175, here 165–166; Thompson J., "Another Look at the Religious Texts in Lincoln Cathedral Library, MS 91", in Minnis A.J. (ed.), *Late Medieval Religious Texts and their Transmission, Essays in Honour of A.I. Doyle* (Cambridge: 1994) 169–187, here 172–173 for particular consideration of the

of useful recent work on laypersons' attitudes to devotional, moral, and fictive reading in Medieval and Early Modern society.[11] Much of this work tends to investigate evidence for ownership, which is not the same as evidence for reading.[12] Nevertheless, both ownership and provenance are often very significant in uncovering the likely readerships of a particular book and biographically orientated work on book ownership and readers has been a necessary precursor to approaches, such as mine, which prioritise the investigation of reading practice for readers whose identity is not necessarily known by name and social group.

For a consideration of religious reading in late Medieval and sixteenth century England there are some specific cultural conditions, which clearly had an impact on the availability, variety and circulation of text, especially literature in the English vernacular. During the years of suspicion about Wycliffism and Lollardy (particularly after Arundel's constitutions of the early fifteenth century and into the period of late Lollard persecution of the 1510s), the ownership of English religious texts, including catechetical and scriptural materials,

---

evidence for 'reading tastes'. On issues of book circulation see, for example, Minnis, *Late Medieval Religious Texts*, particularly Edwards, A.S.G., "The transmission and audience of Osbern Bokenham's legend of Hooly Wummen", in Minnis A.J. (ed.), *Late Medieval Religious Texts and their Transmission, Essays in Honour of A.I. Doyle* (Cambridge: 1994) 157–167, here 162 on the circulation of booklets; Powell S., "The transmission and circulation of *The Lay Folks' Catechism*", in Minnis A.J. (ed.), *Late Medieval Religious Texts and their Transmission, Essays in Honour of A.I. Doyle* (Cambridge: 1994) 67–84, here 73–74 on evidence for transmission and circulation, with mention of private reading of this text by Robert Thornton on p. 74; on evidence for book ownership see, Meale C., "'... alle the bokes that I have of latyn, englisch, and frensch': Laywomen and their books in late medieval England", in Meale C. (ed.), *Women and Literatures in Britain, 1150–1500* (Cambridge: 1993) 130–133. On the evidence which the last will and testament provides for book ownership, see also, Salter E., *Cultural Creativity in the Early English Renaissance: Popular Culture in Town and Country* (London: 2006) Chapter 7.

11 E.g. Gillespie V., "Mystic's Foot: Rolle and Affectivity", in Glascoe M. (ed.), *The Medieval Mystical Tradition in England* (Exeter: 1982) 212–220. On the significance of the private ownership of devotional books in the development of silent reading, as well as the broader political implications associated with lay independence from the clergy, see Saenger P., "Books of Hours and the Reading Habits of the Later Middle Ages", in Chartier R. (ed.), *The Culture of Print: Power and the Uses of Print in Early Modern Europe* (Cambridge: 1989) 143–145; Thompson J., *Robert Thornton and the London Thornton Manuscript: British Library MS. Additional 31042* (Cambridge: 1987) 1; see Salter, *Popular Reading* for references to other works.

12 Cavallo – Chartier, *History of Reading* 4.

comes with a set of debates concerning uncertainties and dangers.[13] Because of the threats posed by accusations of Lollardy against those owning and using English scriptural and catechetical writing, the years of Lollard persecution are generally considered a time of contention around the ownership and use of vernacular religious writings.[14] At the same time as some censorship or limitation the continued circulation of English Psalters and other devotional and catechetical texts is evidenced by numerous compilation manuscripts and other collections such as *Speculum Vitae*, Mirk's *Festial* and Mannyng's *Handlyng Synne*.[15] After the end of the main Lollard persecutions and at the start of the official reformation process, the years c. 1527–1530 have sometimes been identified as particularly crucial in the introduction of new vernacular (English) texts in print particularly through the medium of the Primer. This new phase of textual production is sometimes thought to have come to an abrupt end around 1529–1534 because of various prohibitions and statutes.[16] By 1534 there is thought to have been a revival in the production of English religious texts in print in England for an English market, some of which have a specifically reforming agenda.[17]

---

13   Clanchy M., "The ABC Primer: Was it in Latin or English?", in Salter E. – Wicker H. (eds.), *Vernacularity in England and Wales c. 1300–1550* (Turnhout: 2011) 17–39, here 11–12.

14   White H., *Tudor Books of Private Devotion* (Madison: 1951) 37–38. On the 'Lollard Inheritance', see, Loades D., "Books and the English Reformation Prior to 1558", in Gilmont, J.-F. (ed.), *The Reformation and the Book* (Aldershot: 1998), 264–291, here 264–265. See McSheffrey S., "Heresy, Orthodoxy and English Vernacular Religion 1480–1525", *Past and Present* 186 (2005) 47–80, 48 and n. 5. She uses these dates, 1500 being the restart of Lollard persecutions after a 'half-century hiatus' and 1525 being the 'approximate beginning of the reformation in England'.

15   White, *Tudor Books* 36–38. See, Thompson, "Another look" 177; on *Speculum Vitae* see Hanna R. (ed.), *Speculum Vitae* (Vol. 1) *A Reading Edition* (Oxford: 2008); on the contents of manuscripts CUL Ff 2/38 and Oxford Bodleian Ashmole 61 which is probably sixteenth century and may be copied from a printed text, Salter E., "Evidence for Devotional Reading in Fifteenth Century England: A Comparative Analysis of One English Poem in Six Manuscript Contexts", in Salter E. – Wicker H. (eds.), *Vernacularity in England and Wales c. 1300–1550* (Turnhout: 2011) 65–97; giving many examples of the circulation of literatures relating to the Bible, in the English vernacular, see Morey J., *Book and Verse: A Guide to Middle English Biblical Literature* (Urbana and Chicago: 2000).

16   Butterworth C.C., *The English Primers (1529–1545): Their Publication in Connection with the English Bible and the Reformation in England* (Pennsylvania: 1953) 14. On the 1534 statute, see Loades, "Books and the English Reformation" 278.

17   On 'The primer as an instrument of religious change', see White, *Tudor Books* 87–102. Erler M.C., "*The Maner to Lyve Well* and the Coming of English in Francois Regnault's Primers of the 1520s and 1530s", *The Library*, Series 6, 3 (1984) 229–243, here 237ff.

The issue of religious change and re-formation looms large in any consideration of reading practice and experience across the Medieval to early Modern period in England. And, indeed, the study of reading helps to contribute to a significant question: 'how was the average man [and woman] affected by the Reformation?'[18] The significant role of books and literature in the process and experience of reformation has been explored notably in relation to the role of the Prayer Book and the Bible on the absorption of Protestantism by the people in the Elizabethan era as well as in relation to the role of teaching for those who did not own books themselves.[19] Printing is still often implicated as a major tool in the spread of Protestantism through its production and circulation of English texts.[20] It is important to remember that print, in itself, did not cause or enable Protestantism and that, conversely, there was much religious literature, including vernacular works (English in this case), circulating in manuscript before printing became a practical alternative.

One of the other issues which often surfaces in a consideration of changing possibilities for reading practice and experience from the Medieval into the Early Modern period is a sense that reading styles changed (or developed) from group reading aloud to individual silent reading, particularly in the context of a popular consumption of literature. As with other models which find progress in any changes that occur in the transition from the Medieval to the Early Modern, this is problematic. And, interestingly, even in consideration of medieval practices of the 11th to 15th centuries, distinctions between private individual (and perhaps therefore silent) reading and public uses of text are awkward to sustain.[21] For many lay people, the book-centred reading of private devotion, for example, may well have taken place initially in the public space of the church; the subsequent 'use' or 'borrowing' of such books possibly being

---

18   Whiting R., "For the Health of my Soul: Prayers for the Dead in the Tudor South-West", in Marshall P. (ed.), *The impact of the English Reformation 1500–1640* (London: 1997) 121–142, here 121.

19   Maltby J., "'By this Book': Parishioners, the Prayer Book and the Established Church", in Marshall P. (ed.), *The impact of the English Reformation 1500–1640* (London: 1997) 257–278; Ryrie A., "Counting Sheep, Counting Shepherds: The Problems of Allegiance in the English Reformation", in Ryrie A. – Marshall P (eds.), *The Beginnings of English Protestantism* (Cambridge: 2002) 84–110.

20   See Hudson A., *The Premature Reformation: Wycliffite Texts and Lollard History* (Oxford: 1988) 510. I discuss these issues further in Salter E., "The Uses of English in Printed Religious Texts c. 1497–1547: Further Evidence for the Process and Experience of Reformation in England", *English: Journal of the English Association* 61/233 (2012) 1–22.

21   For some implications of silent reading in public, see Saenger P., *Space Between Words: The Origins of Silent Reading* (Stanford: 1997) 273–276.

through memory in the privacy of the home. But as Chartier identifies, it is also problematic to assume that collective reading is popular and elite reading is private.[22]

To consider the ordinary reader engaged in private reading in a public space requires questions to be asked about the imaginative world of the reader and how interactions between the daily life of public and private practice engage with the reading of such literature. In describing these types of engagement with reading matter it sometimes seems more appropriate to use verbs other than 'to read', such as 'to see', 'to use', 'to enjoy', 'to consume'. Indeed, some scholars of the History of Reading are currently choosing to move away from the term 'reading' in favour of the term 'use'.[23] Sherman's employment of 'use' is partly aimed at avoiding the word reading's 'associations with particular protocols and etiquettes—including privacy, linearity, and cleanliness'.[24] My suggestion is that all of these activities which seem to require other verbs should be understood as part of the broader sphere of popular reading and the business of being literate, where literacy is viewed as part of the process of cultural formation (or acculturation) and transformation.[25]

Based on research using a case study method, and drawing on this backdrop of research in the History of Reading, I argue for a model of surprising continuity in the forms and contents of popularly available religious reading matter across the great ideological changes of the English Reformation. There is evidence, for example, to indicate that certain forms of popular religious reading matter such as proverbial and doggerelised text remained popular in books with either a 'Catholic' or 'Protestant' emphasis. This tends to suggest a popular desire for continuity even if this was not directly or solely attached to religious ideology.[26] Alec Ryrie's proposition that 'most English people never experienced a dramatic individual conversion' is, therefore, probably appropriate in

---

22   Chartier, *The Order of Books* 18.

23   See, for example, Sherman, *Used Books* xiii–xiv.

24   Sherman, *Used Books* xiv. The date of his example is 1586. Commenting on Sherman's choice of 'use' and the history of the origins of this term with Robert Darnton's work see Richards J. – Schurink F., "Introduction: The Textuality and Materiality of Reading in Early Modern England", *Huntington Library Quarterly* 73,3 (2010) 345–361, here 345–346.

25   Fabian J., "Keep Listening: Ethnography and Reading", in Boyarin J. (ed.), *The Ethnography of Reading* (Berkeley – London: 1993) 80–97.

26   I have discussed this in Salter E., "What Kind of Horse is it? Popular Devotional Reading During the Sixteenth Century" in Hadfield A. – Dimmock M. (eds.), *Literature and Popular Culture in Early Modern England* (Aldershot: 2009) 105–120. For similar ideas concerning the continuities of taste and sensibility, Driver M., *The Image in Print: Book Production in Late Medieval England and its Sources* (London: 2004) 209–212.

relation to the changes and continuities in reading practice and experience.[27] There is strong evidence to suggest that, while there were many changes, there were also many continuities in the devotional texts being popularly consumed throughout the reforming years including their visual appearance and the languages in which they were produced.[28] There is also evidence that individual readers made changes to their devotional books according to the differing and changing requirements of Catholicism and Protestantism and the associated laws and statutes.[29] Of course, such action is not necessarily evidence that the same people actually believed something new or different (although I would not wish to argue that Protestantism had no impact on the people or that the people in general actively resisted Protestantism in favour of Catholicism).[30]

I would like to propose catechetical texts as a very useful example for a consideration of religious reading practice and experience across a broad chronological span of the Medieval to Early Modern, for example the period 1200–1700.[31] The encouragement by the Lateran councils of the late eleventh and early twelfth centuries to circulate these texts to a wide sector of the population, controversies over matters of vernacular spirituality during the era of Wycliffite and Lollard heresies, and the Protestant desire to circulate and disseminate a programme of religious knowledge all helped to sustain the production of catechetical texts across this long period of time.[32] There were of course some substantial changes during these centuries in the ways that

---

27   Ryrie, "Counting Sheep" 105.

28   I have discussed some continuities in Salter, "'The Dayes Moralised'" 145–162. The long print run of *The Shepherds Kalender* (c. 1506–1585) provides another example of such continuities. On this see Driver M., "When is a Miscellany not Miscellaneous: Making Sense of the 'Kalender of Shepherds'", *The Yearbook of English Studies* 33 (2003) 199–214.

29   See Duffy E., *Marking the Hours: English People and their Prayers, 1240–1570* (New York – London: 2006). Salter, "Which Horse is it?" 105–120. See also, Driver, *Image in Print* 194–204, here 212–214.

30   For the seminal text on traditional religion see Duffy E., *Stripping of the Altars: Traditional Religion in England, 1400–1580* (New York – London: 1994) 543. On the difference between participation and ideological commitment see Marshall P., "Introduction", in Marshall P. (ed.), *The Impact of the English Reformation 1500–1640* (London: 1997) 7, and on the possibility that 'gullible labourers' were the most easily swayed to conform with new directives, see Maltby, "'By this Book'" 271.

31   This essay is part of the first stages of developing a project on Reading the Catechism in England c. 1200–1700.

32   See, for example, Aston M., *England's Iconoclasts: Laws Against Images* (Oxford: 1988), 344–370; Green I., *The Christian's ABC: Catechisms and Catechizing in England 1530–1740* (Oxford: 1996).

catechetical texts were viewed. This includes the changing form of some (such as the order and numbering of the Ten Commandments which is discussed below) and an altered perception of what was valid or important (such as the increased interest, for Protestants, in scriptural elements like the Decalogue over elements such as the Seven Deadly Sins). Margaret Aston suggests that the expectations of how much of the (new) catechism should be learned also increased during Reformation.[33]

The Ten Commandments

Margaret Aston notes that great attention was given to the commandments in the thirteenth through to fifteenth centuries partly because of the central significance of this element of the catechism for confessional and penitential practice. Ecclesiastical constitutions, such as those of Walter Cantilupe (Bishop of Worcester, in 1240), and Archbishop Pecham's *Ignorancia Sacerdotum* (c. 1260), provided for regular instruction in key elements of the faith; and later medieval commentators such as Jean Gerson and Johann Nider wrote extensively on the Commandments as well as other catechetical elements.[34]

It has been noted that dissemination of the Ten Commandments became dangerous in the years after Arundel's constitutions and this includes ownership of books containing commandment texts (in English) or teaching this and other elements of the catechism. This is the case until at least 1519 when seven martyrs were created in Coventry.[35] Ten Commandments texts were in circulation in a wide variety of forms and variations and these included short and long rhymes, prose versions and commentaries, dialogues, mixed Latin and English texts, and versions with more clearly orthodox or heterodox content. Below are extracts from a small selection of the texts in circulation during the fifteenth and sixteenth centuries which is the period of time particularly relevant to the case study that follows.

---

33 Aston, *England's Iconoclasts* n. 13, 346–348.
34 Aston, *England's Iconoclasts* 344.
35 Aston, *England's Iconoclasts* 347; McSheffrey, "Heresy, Orthodoxy" 53–55.

Examples of Ten Commandments Texts

Example 1: A poem found in six manuscript contexts including Lambeth Palace 853.[36]

I warn eche liif þat liveþ in lond	(I warn each person living on earth
And do him dredlees out of were	To make him safe out of fear
Þat he must studie & undirstonde	That he must study and understand
Þe lawe of god to love & lere.	The law of god to love and learn
For þere is no man feer ne neer	For there is no man far nor near
Þat may him sillfe save unschent	That may himself save unharmed
But he þat castiþ him with conscience clere	But he that casts him with conscience
To kepe weel cristis comaundement	To keep well Christ's Commandments
Thou schalt have oon god & no mo	Thou shalt have one god and no more
And serve him boþe wiþ mayn & my3t	And serve him with both manner and might
And over al þing love him also	And over all things love him too
For he haþ lent þee liif and li3t	For he hath given thee life and light
If þou be noied bi day or ny3t	If thou be troubled by day or night
In peyne be meeke & pacient	In pain be meek and patient
And rewle þee ay bi resoun ri3t	And rule thyself with reason right
And kepe weel cristis comaundement.	And keep well Christ's Commandments
Lete þi nei3e boris, boþe freend & fo	Let thy neighbours both friend and foe
Freli of þi freendschip feele	Freely of thy friendship feel
In herte wilne þou hem also	In your heart desire them also
Ri3t as þou woldist þi self were wele	Right as thou would [for] thy own welfare
Helpe to save hem from unsele	Help to save them from mischance
So þat her soulis ben not schent	So that their souls be not harmed
And her care þou helpe to kele	And their care thou help to calm
And kepe weel cristis comaundement	And keep well Christ's Commandments
Goddis name in ydil take þou nou3t	God's name thoughtlessly take thou not

---

36   Furnivall F.J. (ed.), *Hymns to the Virgin and Christ and Other Religious Poems,* Original Series 24 (London: 1867) 107–113.

But ceesse & save þee from þat synne
Swere bi no þing þat god haþ wrou3t
Be waar his wraþe lest þou so wynne
But bisie þee evere her bale to blinne
Þat wiþ blaberinge ooþis ben blent
Uncouþe & knowen of þi kynne
And kepe weel cristis
    comaundement.

But cease and save thee from that sin
Swear by nothing that God hath made
Beware of his wrath lest you incur it
Be busy thee ever its evil to thwart
That with blabbering oaths are made
Uncouth and known of thy kind
And keep well Christ's
    Commandments).

Example 2: A poem found in two manuscript contexts including Lambeth Palace 853.[37]

Every man schulde teche þis lore
To his children with good entent
And do it himsilf evermore
To kepe weel goddis comaundement
Fals goddis schalt noon have
But worschipe god omnipotent
Make not þi god þat man haþ
    grave
Þis is þe firste comaundement
Goddis name in ydil take þou not
For if þou do þou schalt be scheent
Swere bi no þing that god haþ wrou3t
Þis is the secunde comaundement
Have mynde to helewe þin holi day
Thou & alle þine wiþ good entent
Leve servile werkis & nyce aray
Þis is þe þridde comaundement.

Every man should teach this law
To his children with good intent
And do it himself evermore
To keep well God's Commandments
False gods shall thou none have
But worship God omnipotent
Make not thy god that man has
    engraved
This is the first Commandment
God's name in vain take thou not
For if thou do thou shalt be damned
Swear by nothing that god hath made
This is the second Commandment
Have mind to hallow the holy day
Thou and all thine with good intent
Leave servile works and nice things
This is the third Commandment).

Example 3: A version found amongst 'moderate Lollard writings' in BL Ms Harley 2398.[38]

---

37   *Hymns to the Virgin* 104–105.

38   Jefferson J.A., "An edition of the Ten Commandments commentary in BL Harley 2398 and the related version in Trinity College Dublin 245, York Minster XVI.L.12 and Harvard English 738 together with discussion of related commentaries" (Unpublished PhD Thesis University of Bristol, 1995) 7. This is described as 'moderate lollard writings' in Gayk S., *Image, Text and Religious Reform in Fifteenth Century England* (Cambridge: 2006) 19–20.

Þou schalt have none alyene godes before me. Þou schalt nouȝt make þe an ymage grave by mannes honde, ne no lykenesse þat is in hevene above and þat is in eorþe byneþe, noþer of hem that beþ in waters under þe eorþe. Þou schalt nouȝt worschepe ne herye hem. Ich am þy Lord God a strange lover gelouse. Ich visyte the wykkednesse of fadres into here children into the þrydde and ferþe generacioun of hem that hateþ me, and I do mercy into a þousand kynredenys of hem þat loveþ me and kepeþ myn hestes.[39]

Example 4: A typical example from early printed matter, from *The arte or crafte to Lyve Well* (1505).[40]

One onely god y shalt wor shyppe / and love perfytly: God in vayne thou shalt not swere: ne by his sayntes verily The sondayes y shall kepe / in Servynge god devoutely.	(One only god thou shall wor/ship / and love perfectly God in vain thou shalt not swear: nor by his saints verily The Sundays thou shall keep/ in Serving God devoutly).

The Case Study: Lambeth Palace Library, London, Ms 853

The manuscript used here as the basis for the case study of Ten Commandments texts is Lambeth Palace Manuscript 853 which includes two rhyming versions of the Ten Commandments. The manuscript is a collection of 34 items of varying lengths predominantly in English. The book looks like a single product, using the same hand and style throughout. In character the texts are mainly religious, with quite a lot of didactic material, several giving a moralisation of the ages of man with other slightly more political texts commenting on the standard trope of the vanities of the world, and there are others with a slightly

---

39   'Thou shalt have no alien gods before me. Thou shalt not make thee an image graven by man's hands, nor any likeness that is in heaven above and that is in earth beneath, nor of them that are in waters under the earth. Thou shalt not worship nor heed them. I am the Lord God a strange jealous lover. I visit the wickedness of fathers onto their children unto the third and fourth generations of those that hate me, and I do mercy unto a thousand kin of those that loveth me and keepeth my behests'.

40   *The Crafte to Lyve Well* (1505), STC 792, f. 27r–v.

more contemplative tone.[41] The two poems of the Ten Commandments found in this manuscript are different and this demonstrates nicely that even doggerel adaptations of this text were various, even in one manuscript produced at one time. Extracts from the two commandment poems are given in the examples above. The first is given the title 'Kepe Weel Cristis Commandement' in the *Early English Text Society* [EETS] edition, after its repeated refrain. It is a poem with 13 stanzas of 8 lines with the first line being 'I warn each man that lives on land'. The second is given the title 'The Ten Commandments' in the same EETS volume. This is a poem of 11 four-line stanzas with the first line, 'Every man should teach this law'.[42] For clarity, I will use a shortened version of the first line of each poem in the following discussion. Alongside Lambeth MS 853, 'I warn' is also found in a range of other places with a few variations, including, Oxford, Bodleian Library, MS Eng.poet.a.1 (The Vernon Manuscript), London, British Library Add. 22283 (The Simeon Manuscript), British Library Harley 78 (incomplete), St George's College Windsor EII (now catalogued as SGC LIB MS 1), and Cambridge, Magdalene College, Pepys 1584). The only other identified manuscript context of 'Every man' is British Library, Harley 665.[43]

The opening stanza of each commandment poem gives a clear sense of their difference in tone: 'Every man' is less harsh than the warning tone of 'I warn' (see extract above). The focus on 'Every man' seems to be as a teaching text for children whereas 'I warn' is set up, as the first two words imply, as a warning of the perils of not keeping the Commandments. Seeming to confirm its role as a teaching text for children, 'Every man' clearly provides the number of each commandment as the last line of each of the 10 commandment stanzas (2 through to 11). In 'I warn', the numbering is less clearly articulated although each commandment has its own stanza and the first line of each of the commandment stanzas (2, 4 through to 12) clearly indicates to which it refers. (Stanza 3 has the addition on the neighbour from the New Testament). It is noticeable that the last line of the first stanza of 'Every man' seems to allude to the other poem with the line 'To keep well God's commandment', although in 'I warn' the poem has been Christianised (so, the keep well line becomes 'Keep well Christ's commandment').[44]

---

41   James M.R., *A Descriptive Catalogue of the Manuscripts in the Library of Lambeth Palace: The Mediaeval Manuscripts* (Cambridge: 1932).

42   Lambeth Palace Library Ms 853 47–50; Furnivall, *Hymns* 104–113.

43   See Mooney L. – Mosser D. – Solopova E., *The Digital Index of Middle English Verse* http://www.dimev.net.

44   Cawley A.C., "Middle English metrical versions of the Decalogue with Reference to the English Corpus Christi Cycles", *Leeds Studies in English*, n.s. 8 (1975) 129–145, here 133.

Instance 1: Manuscript Evidence for Religious Acculturation[45]

The existence of two versions of the same catechetical text in what seems to be a planned manuscript is not unique by any means, and it relates to the manuscript culture of copying. John Thompson noted this issue with reference to the Lincoln Thornton Manuscript miscellany and suggested the situation of 'two conflicting impulses that must have been encountered on numerous occasions by some late Medieval copyists and collectors of Middle English religious literature'; firstly an 'urge to be eclectic...to satisfy a voracious appetite for religious and moral reading'; and secondly an 'urge to be conservative, to limit and control the range of instructional and devotional material being made available to other listeners and readers'.[46] The existence of two versions of the Ten Commandments is not unique either for manuscripts produced at a very similar date to Lambeth Ms 853. The Simeon manuscript has the 'I warn' poem together with another version of the Ten Commandments although this other version is not a stand-alone poem but rather part of the *Somme le Roi* sequence. I have already described some of the differences in the two Commandments poems of Lambeth Ms 853 perhaps suggesting that each poem has its own function. It is also reasonable to suggest that the two poems are in the same book by choice, therefore, because they offer a different perspective or a different tone. But given that my interest is in understanding more about reading practice and experience using material evidence such as this, I want to propose a possible model for what we might describe as 'religious acculturation' stimulated by this piece of evidence.

The Ten Commandments (like much popular religious text) is very familiar territory for the reader from a wide range of literate occasions that involve reading a book as well as some of those other activities I mentioned in the first half of the essay (listening, seeing, using, thinking). It is possible to say, therefore, that people were already 'accultured to' The Ten Commandments. So with regard to the practice and experience of using Lambeth MS 853, some questions to ask are: how might these two poems be used (together or separately)? What, if anything, does this suggest about the nature of religious thinking or reading? Can this help with making a model for acculturation through religious reading more generally?

---

45   I am grateful for discussion of this issue at the 'Religious Acculturation' meeting held at Queen's University Belfast in June 2012, and at Leeds IMC in sessions organised by Pavlina Rychterova (Vienna) and Sabrina Corbellini (Gronigen).

46   Thompson, "Another look" 177.

Drawing on some anthropological work on the making of popular history, I propose the following scenario: in using this book, and others like it, the individual reader or member of a reading group turning the pages has the experience of, 'Oh this is the poem where we teach our children about the precepts', whereas 'This one beginning "I warn" is where we acknowledge our responsibilities in fear of peril'. Why not also then: 'Do you remember the time that we read the warning poem and there was a great clap of thunder—this could have been a sign about the actions of N.N. who didn't return after he was discovered . . .'.

I am borrowing here from the ethnographic work of Johannes Fabian who constructed an excellent model for understanding the cultural processes surrounding the making of popular history, or 'historiology'.[47] I suggest that we might be able to understand aspects of religious acculturation as analogous to the making of popular history. One of the key elements to take from Fabian's work is the (very simple) concept of the ways that knowledge is produced rather than re-produced through the retelling of events in, for example, the stories, myths, or images that are so important in historiology.[48] In his agenda-setting work on the construction of popular history through the combination of pictorial and oral narrative he gives examples of the ways that the performance of popular history might use 'variations in stress, pitch, volume, speed, intonation patterns, register and even linguistic code' as well as various 'audible gestures'; alongside this are instances where the historiologer 'performs little sketches', recalling particular actions, one example is concerned with a telephone not working and having to crank it over and again, which is told with the cranking action.[49] Fabian describes these instances as moments where 'performative takes over from informative talking'.[50] A key point, for my purposes, is that it is in the familiarity of the telling and the re-enactment that the popular history comes alive.

Acculturation through Familiarity

On the broader issue of how religious acculturation occurs across the reforming era, perhaps it is possible to take a similar model to the one proposed above.

---

47   Fabian J., *Remembering the Present: Painting and Popular History in Zaire* (Berkeley – London: 1996).
48   Fabian, *Remembering* 251.
49   Fabian, *Remembering* 253.
50   Fabian, *Remembering* 253.

This is a model that has broader implications for understanding the processes of change associated with religious reading practice and experience across the reforming era. I suggest that the process of incorporating and accepting changing ideologies in a popular context is similar (analogous) to the business of making popular historiology (where a key element is the very familiarity of the cultural product involved, in this instance the text of the Ten Commandments). The scenario looks rather like this: 'Do you remember the time that . . ., do you remember our parents reading this poem and crossing themselves each time Christ was mentioned. . . . This time/now when we read/tell it we didn't/don't cross ourselves. Do you remember the time when we stopped crossing ourselves? Do you remember the time when we were worried to say the "hath grave" line in the children's poem? Now we emphasise "hath grave" in the second stanza because there's no fear that this phrase sounds Lollard'.

In the first half of the essay, I noted my finding of the very continuity in reading practice and experience across the reforming era and that means the surprising continuity of actual texts in circulation and also in styles of 'popular' text being produced and circulated. This includes macaronic forms (Latin and English in this case), rhyming versions of biblical and catechetical material such as the Ten Commandments, doggerel rhyme more generally. Continuity is, I suggest, key to the processes of religious acculturation that I propose here for popular religious reading. I suggest, therefore, that this connection between familiarity and acculturation has broader implications for understanding the experience or nature of change in popular culture.

Instance 2: Ten Commandments and Wycliffism/ Lollardy[51]

My second model explores the possibility that a text such as the Ten Commandments as found in rhyme in Lambeth Ms 853 might be open to, or stimulate, a range of interpretations that include potentially heretical understandings. So, for this example, I take the notion of change to mean the mutability of the meanings of one particular text in the imagination of the reader who may, in this fifteenth century context, be seeking out heterodox or sectarian views. The Ten Commandments lends itself to such a consideration because it was a controversial text in the fifteenth century. Anne Hudson identified that Decalogue texts receive frequent mention in heresy trials and one reason for this was that the prohibition on the making of graven images

---

51   I am grateful for discussion of these issues at Leeds IMC 2012 in my paper at the session sponsored by The Lollard Society.

'offered such an obvious place, and obvious hunting place, for Lollard views'.[52] The graven images phrase was not officially sanctioned in English (printed) text until 1539 / (1545).[53] It is significant, then, that the Decalogue texts identified as Wycliffite or Lollard (or Lollard-leaning) tend to make specific reference to graven images. One such version is given as Example 3 above. This version is described as a controversial heterodox view of Commandments found in a manuscript with more traditional texts.[54]

In England in the fifteenth and early sixteenth centuries, the Ten Commandments in English is potentially quite a dangerous text to own, then, at certain times of visitation and depending on which region of England the text is owned in. *Dives and Pauper* is also mentioned as a dubious book on a number of occasions (as discussed by Hudson, for example). Perhaps its explicit use of the 'graven images' phrase does not help to reassure authorities of its orthodoxy at this time.[55] At the same time there is also evidence to suggest that not all ownership of such a text needed to be kept under wraps. One such example of open reference to a book containing the Ten Commandments which, being given an English title one might assume is actually an English text, is found in the last will and testament of a carpenter called William Basse of Southwark near London in 1488, as follows:

> Item I bequeathe unto William Hylle of the Citte of Caunterbury a maser with a foote carvyd and with a knoppe of silver and gilt a book with x comaundementes and other diverse things therynne a gowne of Grene and a cloth of Grene for a bedde of tapstry werk and with portatrwys of men and women in the same.[56]

This situation of one text having potentially orthodox and heterodox connotations points to an issue of current interest in studies of Wycliffism and

52   Hudson, *Premature Reformation* 484; Gayk, *Image, Text* 11.

53   See Aston, *England's Iconoclasts* 344ff, and discussion in Salter, "Uses of English" 128–129.

54   The text identified by Thomas Arnold as quintessentially Wycliffite (using Oxford, Bodleian 789) has very similar phraseology for this commandment; Arnold T., *Select English Works of John Wyclif edited from original Manuscripts*, 3 vols. (Oxford: 1871), Vol. 3 "Miscellaneous works" 82–92.

55   Hudson, *Premature Reformation* 485.

56   'Item I beaqueath to William Hill of the City of Canterbury a maser [cup] with a foot carved and with a knob of silver and gilt a book with 10 commandments and other diverse things therein a gown of Green and a cloth of Green for a bed of tapestry work and with portraits of men and women on the same)'. The National Archive, London PROB 11/8/38/306.

Lollardy which is that there are many similarities between the texts and ideas used and valued by those in the 'mainstream' and those who hold 'sectarian' beliefs.[57] Another way of looking at this is to identify the 'plasticity of the categories of orthodoxy and heresy'.[58] And as Rob Lutton's work shows, if we are viewing sectarian behaviour as polysemic, we should remember that orthodox behaviour was multifarious too.[59] McSheffrey has described the ways that the ownership of certain English texts, especially catechetical and scriptural material, was sometimes part of an accusation of heretical practice. At other times the very orthodoxy of the common reader owning, using, and learning English catechetical material was emphasised.[60] This issue of the heterodox, or Lollard leaning, or orthodox, nature of the mixture of texts in some manuscripts has been taken up more recently, for example, in the work of Amanda Moss on Westminster Manuscript 3 where there are various Ten Commandments texts, as well as in other studies of what have been termed 'cosmopolitan' or 'lollard friendly' texts and their readerships.[61] Anna Lewis's discussion of a 'catechetical hinterland' with reference to the heterodox range of *Pater Noster* texts in circulation during the fifteenth century demonstrates more evidence for the interconnectedness between the mainstream and the Lollard or Wycliffite.[62]

---

57   Somerset F., "Afterword", in Bose M. – Hornbeck II P.J, *Wycliffite Controversies*, Medieval Church Studies 23 (Turnhout: 2012) 319–333, here 327.

58   McSheffrey, "Heresy, orthodoxy" 49.

59   See, for example, Lutton R.G.A., "Lollardy, Orthodoxy, and Cognitive Psychology", in Bose M. – Hornbeck II P.J, *Wycliffite Controversies*, Medieval Church Studies 23 (Turnhout: 2012) 97–119.

60   See, for example, McSheffrey, "Heresy, orthodoxy" 59.

61   Hudson, *Premature Reformation* 271; Moss A. "Context and Construction: The Nature of Vernacular Piety in a Fifteenth-Century Devotional Anthology", in Salter E. – Wicker H. (eds.), *Vernacularity in England and Wales c. 1300–1550* (Turnhout: 2011) 41–64; Johnson I., "Vernacular Theology/ Theological Vernacular: A Game of two Halves?", in Gillespie V. – Ghosh K. (eds.), *After Arundel: Religious Writing in Fifteenth Century England,* Medieval Church Studies 21 (Turnhout: 2012) 73–88, and Perry R. – Kelly S., "Devotional Cosmopolitanism in Fifteenth century England", in Gillespie V. – Ghosh K. (eds.), *After Arundel: Religious Writing in Fifteenth Century England,* Medieval Church Studies 21 (Turnhout: 2012) 363–380.

62   Lewis A., "Textual Borrowings, Theological Mobility, and the Lollard Pater Noster Commentary", *Philological Quarterly* 88,1 (2009) 1–23. On Lollard appropriations of mainstream discourses see also Gayk, *Image, Text* 18. Another similar example is discussed in Patwell N, "Canons and Catechisms: The Austin Canons of South-East England and Sacerdos Parochialis", in Gillespie V. – Ghosh K. (eds.), *After Arundel: Religious Writing in Fifteenth Century England,* Medieval Church Studies 21 (Turnhout: 2012), 381–393, here 388–389.

And as Mary Dove recently demonstrated, the whole catechism was really part of the Wycliffite pastoral agenda.[63] All of which recent work constitutes a problematisation (sometimes a deconstruction) of what constitutes Wycliffite or Lollard texts and behaviours and a demonstration of the mutual interests in catechetical writings of mainstream and sectarian readers.

Reflecting on this issue of the problems of differentiating between mainstream and sectarian practices and ideas, Fiona Somerset has recently identified a further issue in defining what constitutes heresy. She suggests book use or sharing as an area of practice that prevails for Lollards and that this might be relatively less concerned with doctrine than with group identity. As she says: 'One might imagine defendants bemused by "inquisitors" insistent focus on the precise doctrine of the Eucharist, for example, and far more concerned among themselves with a sense of group identity and of mission drawn from group reading of the Ten Commandments'.[64] Choosing to focus more on distinctions than similarities in the 'catechetical hinterland' (and demonstrating the minute differentiations in textual form that this might entail), Matti Peikola has discussed evidence for what he describes as the 'late medieval contest between two catechetical programmes—a contest in which the lexical minutiae of even the most elementary items of faith, such as the *Pater Noster*, the *Ave Maria*, and *Creed*, were regarded as significant, and were consequently carefully scrutinised and if necessary modified by scribes'.[65]

My tentative proposition takes up this current trend to deconstruct what constitutes a 'mainstream' or a 'sectarian' text, and is based on the evidence from Lambeth Ms 853, to suggest a reader-focussed consideration of the possible heterodoxy of a text. And I draw, here, on Peikola's proposition about the significance of short phrases as 'hot links' which point towards an issue more fully explicated elsewhere in Lollard texts.[66] The piece of evidence in Lambeth Ms 853 is one phrase found in the children's text of the Commandments ('Every man') for which the seventh line is: 'Make not þi god þat man haþ grave'. In the fifteenth century, as I have indicated above, the 'hath grave' phrase signalled an issue of major contestation with regard to sectarian and mainstream versions of the Ten Commandments. This hot phrase is admittedly rather 'innocuously'

63   Dove, M., "The Lollards' three-fold Biblical agenda", in Bose M. – Hornbeck II P.J, *Wycliffite Controversies*, Medieval Church Studies 23 (Turnhout: 2012) 211–226, here 220.

64   Somerset, "Afterword" 327.

65   Peikola M., "'And after All, Myn Ave Marie Almost to the Ende': Pierce the Ploughman's Crede and Lollard Expositions of the Ave Maria", *English Studies* 81,4 (2000) 273–292, here 290.

66   Peikola, "And after All" 277. For an analogous discussion of distinctions in Lollard discourse on images see Gayk, *Image,Text* 20, 23.

used in a ditty which might seem aesthetically very far from Lollard-sounding.[67] But my reader-focused proposition is that this phrase could function as a stimulus towards Lollard thinking or as a connection to other texts exploring this issue at greater length. For a reader dissatisfied by orthodox thinking about images at this time or for a 'wannabe Lollard', or for a confirmed Lollard experiencing fear of persecution, this little phrase in this poem might either acculturate him or her into sectarian thinking or enable him/her to pursue heterodox practice and ideas in secret. Such an approach has broader implications for understanding the transmission of non-orthodox (or changed) views of religious literature.[68]

Conclusion

This essay presents two models for understanding the ways that medieval manuscripts can provide evidence for the experience and practice of religious reading during a time of change. Each instance is concerned with very specific pieces of evidence using one manuscript as the source for this case study. Each model also has wider applicability, particularly with reference to understanding more about cultural processes and the ways that processes such as ideological change and transition might have been understood and experienced in medieval society through religious reading. While I review the general background to my approach to religious reading in English Medieval and Early Modern Society in the first half of the essay, the case study focuses on catechetical texts (specifically the Ten Commandments in this instance) which were widely circulated and intended for the widest spectrum of readers and users. By examining the evidence offered by the occurrence of two versions of a doggerel Ten Commandments poem in one manuscript of the fifteenth century, I hope to have demonstrated the ways that evidence from popular forms, innocuous words, and basic rhymes might enable much greater understanding of the nature and experience of religious reading.

---

67   The role and uses of rhyme is the subject of a forthcoming article. But for a re-examination of Lollard aesthetics and rhyming text see, Gayk S., "Lollard Writings, Literary Criticism, and the Meaningfulness of Form", in Bose M. – Hornbeck II P.J., *Wycliffite Controversies*, Medieval Church Studies 23 (Turnhout: 2012) 145–152, here 137, 152; Peikola, "And after All" 277, where 'Innocuous' is to discuss the phrase 'almost to the ende' in *Pierce Ploughman's Creed*.

68   I am currently developing this model for consideration at greater length.

Bibliography

Arnold T., *Select English Works of John Wyclif edited from original Manuscripts*, 3 vols. (Oxford: 1871).

Aston M., *England's Iconoclasts: Laws Against Images* (Oxford: 1988).

Bose M. – Horbeck II P.J., *Wycliffite Controversies*, Medieval Church Studies 23 (Turnhout: 2012).

Butterworth C.C., *The English Primers (1529–1545): Their Publication in Connection with the English Bible and the Reformation in England* (Pennsylvania: 1953).

Cavallo G. – Chartier R. (eds.), *A History of Reading in the West*, trans. L.G. Cochrane (Oxford: 1999).

Cawley A.C., "Middle English metrical versions of the Decalogue with Reference to the English Corpus Christi Cycles", *Leeds Studies in English*, n.s. 8 (1975) 129–145.

Chartier R., *On the Edge of the Cliff: History, Language, and Practices*, trans. L.G. Cochrane (Baltimore – London: 1997).

——— (ed.), *The Culture of Print: Power and the Uses of Print in Early Modern Europe* (Cambridge: 1989).

———, *The Order of Books: Readers, Authors and Libraries between the Fourteenth and Eighteenth Centuries*, trans. L.G. Cochrane (London: 1994).

Darnton R., "What is the History of Books?", in *The Kiss of Lamourette: Reflections in Cultural History* (London: 1990) 107–135.

Driver M., *The Image in Print: Book Production in Late Medieval England and its Sources* (London: 2004).

Duffy E., *Stripping of the Altars: Traditional Religion in England, 1400–1580* (New York – London: 1994).

———, *Marking the Hours: English People and their Prayers, 1240–1570* (New York – London: 2006).

Fabian J., "Keep Listening: Ethnography and Reading", in Boyarin J. (ed.), *The Ethnography of Reading* (Berkeley – London: 1993).

———, *Remembering the Present: Painting and Popular History in Zaire* (Berkeley LA, London: 1996).

Furnivall F.J. (ed.), *Hymns to the Virgin and Christ and Other Religious Poems, Original Series, 24* (London: 1867).

Gayk S., *Image, Text and Religious Reform in Fifteenth Century England* (Cambridge: 2006).

Gillespie V. – Ghosh K. (eds.), *After Arundel: Religious Writing in Fifteenth Century England*, Medieval Church Studies 21 (Turnhout: 2012)

Green I., *The Christian's ABC: Catechisms and Catechizing in England 1530–1740* (Oxford: 1996).

Griffiths J. – Pearsall D. (eds.), *Book Production and Publishing in Britain, 1375–1475* (Cambridge: 1989).

Hudson A., *The Premature Reformation: Wycliffite Texts and Lollard History* (Oxford: 1988).

Iser W., *The Act of Reading: A Theory of Aesthetic Response* (Baltimore – London: 1980).

James M.R., *A Descriptive Catalogue of the Manuscripts in the Library of Lambeth Palace: The Mediaeval Manuscripts* (Cambridge: 1932).

Jefferson J.A., "An edition of the Ten Commandments commentary in BL Harley 2398 and the related version in Trinity College Dublin 245, York Minster XVI.L.12 and Harvard English 738 together with discussion of related commentaries" (Unpublished PhD Thesis University of Bristol, 1995).

Lewis A., "Textual Borrowings, Theological Mobility, and the Lollard Pater Noster Commentary", *Philological Quarterly* 88, 1 (2009) 1–23.

Lutton R.S.G. – Salter E. (eds), *Pieties in Transition*: *Religious Practices and Experiences c 1400–1640* (Aldershot: 2007).

Marshall P. (ed.), *The impact of the English Reformation 1500–1640* (London: 1997).

McSheffrey S., "Heresy, Orthodoxy and English Vernacular Religion 1480–1525", *Past and Present* 186 (2005) 47–80.

Meale C. (ed.), *Women & Literatures in Britain, 1150–1500* (Cambridge: 1993).

Minnis A.J. (ed.), *Late Medieval Religious Texts and their Transmission, Essays in Honour of A.I. Doyle* (Cambridge, 1994).

Mooney L. – Mosser D. – Solopova E., *The Digital Index of Middle English Verse* http://www.dimev.net.

Morey J., *Book and Verse: A Guide to Middle English Biblical Literature* (Urbana – Chicago: 2000).

Peikola M., "'And after All, Myn Ave Marie Almost to the Ende': Pierce the Ploughman's Crede and Lollard Expositions of the Ave Maria", *English Studies* 81,4 (2000) 273–292.

Ryrie A. – Marshall P. (eds.), *The Beginnings of English Protestantism* (Cambridge: 2002).

Saenger P., *Space Between Words: The Origins of Silent Reading* (Stanford: 1997).

Salter E., *Popular Reading in English c. 1400–1600* (Manchester, 2012).

Salter E. – Wicker H. (eds.), *Vernacularity in England and Wales c. 1300–1550*, Utrecht Studies in Medieval Literacy (Turnhout: 2011).

Sargeant M., "The transmission by the English Carthusians of some late medieval spiritual writings", *Journal of Ecclesiastical Studies* 27 (1976) 225–240.

———— (ed.), *De Cella in Seculum: Religious Secular Life and Devotion in Late Medieval England* (Cambridge: 1989).

Sherman W., *Used Books: Marking Readers in Renaissance England* (Philadelphia: 2008).

Thompson J., *Robert Thornton and the London Thornton Manuscript: British Library MS. Additional 31042* (Cambridge: 1987).

Thompson J. – Kelly S. (eds.), *Imagining the Book: Medieval Texts and Cultures of Northern Europe* (Turnhout: 2006).

White H., *Tudor Books of Private Devotion* (Madison: 1951).

CHAPTER 5

'Car Dieu veult estre serui de tous estaz': Encouraging and Instructing Laypeople in French from the Late Middle Ages to the Early Sixteenth Century

Margriet Hoogvliet

In February 1522 an inventory was made of the possessions of the recently deceased printer Jehan Janot, including the stock of unfolded and unbound printed leaves in his home in Paris.[1] Apparently Janot's business was successful in editing religious books in French, because besides literary and pragmatic texts, the inventory not only lists hundreds of copies of saints' lives, biblical texts and religious song books (*Noëlz*) in French, but also countless devotional and catechetical works in the vernacular:

> 1,200 copies of the *Livre de Meditacion sur la Passion*,[2]
> 400 of the *Lucidaire*,[3]
> 240 of the *Jardin Spirituel*,[4]

---

1 The post-mortem inventory is preserved in the Archives Nationales in Paris, Minutier Central, CXXII,4. The inventory of books has been edited in abridged form by Runnalls G., "La vie, la mort et les livres de l'imprimeur-libraire parisien Jean Janot d'après son inventaire après décès (17 février 1522 n.s.)", *Revue belge de philologie et d'histoire* 78,3–4 (2000) 797–851. An earlier edition can be found in Doucet R., *Les bibliothèques parisiennes du XVIe siècle* (Paris: 1956) 91–104. For this article I have also consulted an unpublished transcription of the entire inventory made by the Institut de Recherche et d'Histoire des Textes (IRHT) in Paris.

2 Identified by Runnalls as: Jehannot Estienne, *Meditation tresdevotte pour chascune heure du jour sur la Passion* (Paris, Veuve Jean Trepperel et Jean Janot: s.d.). Many French works of this kind are translations and adaptations of Pseudo Bonaventura's *Meditationes vite Christi* (c. 1336–1364).

3 Several translations of Honorius Augustodunensis's *Lucidarius* into French survive; the earliest dates from the thirteenth century and it was frequently reprinted from 1479 onwards. This edition might be: *Le lucidaire en francoys* (Paris: [veuve Jean Trepperel: 1520]).

4 Identified by Runnalls as Bougain Michel, *Le Jardin spirituel de lame devote* (Paris, Alain Lotrian: s.d.). This is an elaborated version of Pierre d'Ailly's *Jardin amoureux de l'âme dévote*, dating from the early fifteenth century, of which 22 manuscripts are known. D'Ailly's text

125 of the *Mirouer de contemplacion*,[5]
500 of the *Theologie spirituelle*,[6]
200 of the *Eschelle d'amour divine*,[7]
120 of a *Manuel Sainct Augustin*,[8]
400 of the *Cueur crucefie*,[9]
70 of the *Orloge de devocion*,[10]
250 of the *Livre de bonnes meurs*,[11]
300 of the *Commandemens de Saincte Eglise*,[12]
450 of the *Myrouer de lame pecheresse*,[13]

---

has been edited by Glorieux P., ed., *Jean Gerson, Oeuvres compètes, vol. 7/1 L'oeuvre fran-çaise* (Paris: 1966) 144–154.

5   The text is probably that of: *Le Mirouer de contemplation fait sur la très-sainte mort et pas-sion de nostre seigneur Jésus Crist* (Paris, for Guillaume Eustache: 1517). No other editions are presently known.

6   The text is probably similar to that of: *La Théologie spirituelle, extraicte du livre sainct Denis, translatée de latin en françoys par ung vénérable religieux de l'ordre des Frères mineurs de l'observance, très utille et prouffictable à tout homme et femme tendant à perfec-tion, soit séculier ou régulier, pour facillement unir son cueur en amour de Dieu son créateur* (Paris, G. Soquand: [ca. 1527]).

7   Identified by Runnalls as: Sauvage Jehan, *L'Eschelle d'amour divine* (Paris, Veuve Jean Trepperel et Jean Janot: s.d.).

8   This is probably the *Manuale* attributed to Pseudo-Augustine, edited by Migne J.P., *Patrologiae latinae* vol. 40, col. 951–968. No French translation of this text is presently known. I owe the identification to Sabrina Corbellini.

9   Identified by Runnalls as: Regnart Pierre, *L'Exercice du Cueur Crucifié* (Paris, Lescu de France: s.d.).

10 French translation of *Zeitglöcklein des Lebens und Leidens Christi nach dem 24 Stunden aus-geteilt/ Horologium devotionis circa vitam Christi*, attributed to Bertholdus Friburgensis. One manuscript: Paris, Bibliothèque nationale de France (hereafter: BnF), MS fr. 1849 (fifteenth century). The only surviving printed edition is the translation by Quentin Jean, *L'orologe de devotion profitable pour exciter lame endormie par paresse* (Paris, Jean Trepperel: [c. 1505]).

11 Identified by Runnalls as: Legrand Jacques, *Le Livre de bonnes moeurs* (Paris, Veuve Jean Trepperel: s.d.). This text was written by the Augustine friar Jacques Legrand between 1404 and 1410; it survives in c. 75 manuscripts and 20 printed editions before 1578. For a modern edition, see: Beltran E. (ed.), *Jacques Legrand, L'Archilogie Sophie, Le livre de bonnes meurs* (Geneva: 1986).

12 Identified by Runnalls as: *Les commandemens de saincte eglise et la confession generale du jour de Pasques par les paroisses. Le petit traicte de maistre Jehan Gerson qui aprent a bien mourir* (Paris, Veuve Jean Trepperel et Jean Janot: s.d.).

13 The text is most likely that of *Le miroir de l'âme pêcheresse* translated by Jean Miélot. Frequently reprinted from c. 1481 onwards.

300 of the *Imitacione Christi*,[14]
66 of the *Myrouer de la Redemption*,[15]
250 of the *Doctrinal de sapience*,[16]
780 *Ordinaires*.[17]

Several of these titles also appear in the catalogue of a *marchand libraire* in Tours, made in the late fifteenth century,[18] together with a considerable amount of other devotional and catechetical works, both manuscript and printed, such as, for instance, *La somme le roy*,[19] *L'orloge de sapience*,[20] *L'esguillon d'amour divine*,[21] *La fleur des vertus mondaines*,[22] and many works by the chancellor

---

14 French translation of Thomas of Kempen's, *Imitatio Christi*. Frequently reprinted, also with the title *Internelle consolation* or *Eternelle consolation*. See: Delaveau M. – Sordet Y., *Edition et diffusion de L'Imitation de Jésus-Christ 1470–1800* (Paris: 2011).

15 A French translation of the *Speculum humanae salvationis*. Frequently reprinted until c. 1505; no surviving edition by Jehan Janot.

16 Identified by Runalls as: *Le doctrinal de sapience* (Paris, Veuve de Jean Trepperel et Jean Janot: s.d.). This catechetical text with numerous references to the Bible, also with the title *Le doctrinal aux simples gens*, dates from the mid-fourteenth century. The long version was written in 1388 and in the early fifteenth century Guy de Roye, Archbishop of Reims, added a prologue.

17 Runnalls reads *Ordonnances*, but the transcription by the IRHT suggests *Ordinaires*. This could be the *Ordinaire des Crestiens* (Rouen, Guillaume le Talleur: [ca. 1485]). Several reprints until 1530; an updated version was published in 1580 by René Benoist. See: Dhotel J.-Cl., *Les origines du catéchisme moderne, d'après les premiers manuels imprimés en France* (Paris: 1967) 35–36.

18 Edited by Chéreau A., *Catalogue d'un marchand libraire du XVᵉ siècle à Tours* (Paris: 1848).

19 This treatise on the virtues and vices was written in 1279 by frère Laurent, the Dominican confessor of the French King Philippe III. The text survives in 94 manuscripts, and was printed until c. 1510 (also with the title: *Le chapelet des vertus et des vices*). The later printed editions might also borrow from the Italian *Fiore di virtù*.

20 French translation of Henry of Suso's *Horologium sapientiae* (c. 1339) made by an anonymous Dominican translator in 1389. The French version survives in 55 manuscripts; two printed editions are known before 1500, and it was reprinted until 1533.

21 Several French translations of the thirteenth-century Franciscan text *Stimulus amoris* have been made (by an anonymous translator, Jean de Brixel, Jean Gerson and Simon de Courcy). It was printed until 1606 (with a new translation by Blaise de Vigenère). On the Latin and German versions, see: Eisermann F., *Stimulus amoris. Inhalt, lateinische Überlieferung, deutsche Übersetzungen, Rezeption* (Tübingen: 2001).

22 Possibly a translation of the anonymous Italian *Fiore di virtù*. Corbellini S., *Italiaanse deugden en ondeugden: Dirc Potters "Blome der doechden" en de Italiaanse "Fiore di virtù"* (Amsterdam: 2000).

Jean Gerson (such as *Le livre de la mendicité spirituelle, La montaigne de contemplation*, and several shorter texts).[23]

Fifteenth- and early sixteenth-century wills and post-mortem inventories from the towns of northern France indicate that these religious works in the vernacular were read by all levels of society, from members of the nobility, the urban patriciate, laypeople with university training (such as lawyers, notaries, surgeons, unordained clerics), priests, canons, monks, nuns, merchants, to sometimes even craftsmen, servants and impoverished widows. There are a great many examples that could be quoted here, but a few will have to suffice: in his will dated 23 August 1390, Jean de le Warde, *parmentier* (tailor) in Tournai, bequeathed a book with *La somme le roy*,[24] and in the inventory from 1468 of the estate of *sire* Philippe Tanart, also living in Tournai, includes a copy of *Le livre de bonnes meurs*.[25] Slightly later, the inventory of the goods owned by Jehenne le Scellier, wife of a merchant, made on 28 April 1509 in Amiens, mentions a copy of *L'ordinaire des crestiens*,[26] and the inventory of Antoine de Coquerel, *procureur* (lawyer) made on 13 August 1518 in Amiens includes 50 books,[27] among which *La fleur des commandements de Dieu*,[28] *Le miroir de la vie humaine*,[29] *L'ordinaire des crestiens, Le doctrinal aux simples gens*,[30] *L'imitation de Nostre Seigneur, La mendicité spirituelle*, and *L'aiguillon d'amour divine*.

This small sample of the available historical sources gives a good first impression of the enormous number of books with religious texts in the French vernaculars that must have been in circulation during the fifteenth and early sixteenth centuries, as well as their accessibility, even for less wealthy audiences. Some of these texts were 'best-sellers' on a European scale, many

---

23   Edited by Glorieux, *Jean Gerson*.

24   Vanwijnsberghe D., *"De fin or et d'azur". Les commanditaires de livres et le métier de l'enluminure à Tournai à la fin du Moyen Âge (XIVe–XVe siècles)* (Leuven: 2001) T 62; Derolez A. (ed.), *Corpus catalogorum Belgii: the medieval booklists of the southern Low Countries. Vol. IV: Provinces of Brabant and Hainault* (Brussels: 2001) nr. 155.

25   Vanwijnsberghe, *"De fin or"* T 191; Derolez, *Corpus* nr. 189.

26   Amiens, Archives communales, FF 154/2, 8 books in total. I owe the transcription of this inventory to the generosity of Mary Jane Chase. For book ownership and lay religiosity in Amiens, see: Labarre A., *Le livre dans la vie amiénoise du seizième siècle. L'enseignement des inventaires après décès du XVIe siècle* (Paris: 1971); Chase M.J., *Popular piety in sixteenth-century Picardy: Amiens and the rise of private devotions, 1500–1540* (diss. Columbia University: 1992).

27   Amiens, Archives communales, FF 161/15.

28   No manuscripts are presently known of this text. It was printed between 1496 and 1548.

29   A translation of the *Speculum humanae salvationis*; see note 15.

30   *Doctrinal de sapience* in the inventory.

of them originating from Germany, the Low Countries and Italy, such as the *Speculum humanae salvationis*, the *Meditationes vite Christi*, the *Stimulus amoris* and the *Imitatio christi*.[31] Conversely, some French texts found in translation large audiences elsewhere in Western Europe, such as *La somme le roi* and Jean Gerson's *Montaigne de contemplation*. Compared to other European regions, devotional and catechetical works in the French vernaculars intended for the instruction of laypeople appeared in relatively high numbers from the early thirteenth century onwards, including works as *La carité* et *Le miserere* by the hermit of Molliens (verse, c. 1224 and c. 1230),[32] *Le miroir du monde* (prose, shortly after 1279),[33] *Le miroir de l'âme* (thirteenth century),[34] *Le dialogue du père et du fils* (before 1267).[35] Most striking when browsing through historical book lists and modern catalogues of manuscripts and early prints is the impressive variety of original French religious texts, many of them surviving in only a few copies. All these sources testify to a lively textual culture in late medieval and early modern France, with religious and lay readers demanding texts especially adapted for a wide variety of religious and devotional practices.

Many of these texts are didactic and catechetical works written for laypeople (although frequently addressing religious men and women too), giving them information about the Bible, the Church and religion, or devotional instructions, and often a combination of both. Some texts exhort laypeople to turn away from a sinful and worldly life and to do penance; others are manuals for confession at Easter or on the deathbed. There are texts that instruct laypeople how to behave and what to think during Mass, or give the basic knowledge that each Christian should have, such as the Ten Commandments, the Lord's Prayer, the Apostle's Creed, the Hail Mary and the seven mortal sins, all translated into the French vernacular. Yet another group of texts gives instructions for religious meditations, often scheduled according to the Hours, or the seven days of the week, and in some cases laypeople could find suggestions there on how to combine a religious life with work, marriage and household. Finally,

---

31   Late medieval pious 'best-sellers' in the vernacular are presently being investigated from a European perspective by the ERC Starting Grant project OPVS directed by Géraldine Veysseyre (Paris, IRHT). See: www.opvs.fr.

32   Hamel A.-G. van, *Li romans de carité et Miserere du Renclus de Moiliens: poèmes de la fin du XIIe siècle* (Paris: 1885).

33   Incipit: 'On siot dire que envis muert qui apris ne l'a. Aprent a morir si saras vivre'. Unedited, survives in 38 manuscripts.

34   Incipit: 'Audi Domina et vide. Oyez, Dame, veez et entendez et enclinez vostre oraille'. Unedited, survives in 4 manuscripts.

35   Incipit: 'C'est du pere qui son filz enseigne. Et du filz qui au pere demande ce qu'il ne scet'. Unedited, survives in 24 manuscripts.

a striking characteristic is the textual instability and the use of sampling techniques: existing texts were often rewritten and adapted, while useful fragments were frequently borrowed from other works.

In the past, historians have believed that the Roman Catholic Church prohibited laypeople from reading religious texts in the vernacular, out of fear of heresy and in order to keep them ignorant. It has also been suggested that the medieval Church only valued the complete dedication of monastic life, and that a religious life suitable for laypeople was never developed: they had to make do with a much diluted version of the monastic ideal, in the form of simple prayers, to be recited mechanically without really understanding them, and Books of Hours. However, the widespread presence of an enormous variety in religious texts in the French vernaculars during the late Middle Ages and the sixteenth century evoked above, confirms recent publications about the high degree of lay participation in religious life, most notably during the fifteenth century. During the past decades a completely different image of lay religiosity and religious texts in the vernacular has started to emerge: Lawrence C. Duggan has argued that laypeople did actively participate in religious life during the late Middle Ages,[36] John Van Engen, Eamon Duffy and Klaus Schreiner have pointed towards the richness of lay devotion and the active participation of laypeople in matters of religion during the fifteenth century,[37] and religious texts in the vernacular have been positively valued as 'vernacular theologies'.[38]

---

36   For examples and a critical discussion of these hypotheses, see: Duggan L.G., "The Unresponsiveness of the Late Medieval Church: A Reconsideration", *Sixteenth Century Journal* 9,1 (1978) 3–26. For the vitality of the pre-Reformation Church, see: Swanson R.N., "The Pre-Reformation Church", in Pettegree A. (ed.), *The Reformation World* (London: 2000) 9–30.

37   Van Engen J., "Multiple Options: The World of the Fifteenth-Century Church", *Church History* 77,2 (2008) 257–284; Duffy E., *The Stripping of the Altars. Traditional Religion in England, c. 1400–c. 1580* (New Haven: 1992); Schreiner K., "Laienfrömmigkeit – Frömmigkeit von Eliten oder Frömmigkeit des Volkes? Zur Sozialen Verfasstheit laikaler Frömmigkeitspraxis im späten Mittelalter", in Schreiner K. – Müller-Luckner E. (eds.), *Laienfrömmigkeit in sozialen und politischen Zusammenhängen des Späten Mittelalters* (Munich: 1992) 1–78.

38   For a discussion of this terminology and references to earlier literature, see: Georgianna L., "Vernacular Theologies", *English Language Notes* 44 (2006) 87–94; Gillespie V., "Vernacular Theology", in Strohm P. (ed.), *Middle English* (Oxford: 2007) 401–420. In Germany the same phenomenon is referred to as "Frömmigkeitstheologie", see most recently: Hamm B., *Religiosität im späten Mittelalter: Spannungspole, Neuaufbrüche, Normierungen* (Tübingen: 2011). For late medieval and early modern catechisms in German, see also: Bast R.J., "Strategies of Communication: Late-Medieval Catechisms and the Passion Tradition", in MacDonald A.A. – Ridderbos H.N.B. – Schlusemann R.M. (eds.), *The Broken*

As will be demonstrated below, many of these vernacular theologies in French were strongly didactic in character and very accommodating for laypeople, allowing them to perform shorter religious exercises when they could not free themselves from work, while at the same time stressing that it was their duty to do more if time and intellectual abilities allowed for it.

A number of these texts were written and distributed at the request of reforming bishops that were active in France and who sought to improve the level of religious knowledge of the laity by providing them with biblical texts in the vernacular, catechetical works and directions for a contemplative life; to name only a few: Guy de Roye (c. 1340–1409), Archbishop of Reims, Jean Gerson (1363–1429), chancellor of the Sorbonne, Étienne Poncher (1446–1524), Bishop of Paris and Archbishop of Sens, François d'Estaing (1460–1529), Bishop of Rodez, and Guillaume Briçonnet (1470–1534), Bishop of Meaux (the latter is often considered as a proto-Protestant, but, in reality he never left the Catholic Church).[39] In fact, during the late Middle Ages and the early sixteenth century, the Gallican Church of France was a multifaceted institution that included multiple opinions. Pierre Imbart de La Tour has distinguished three main currents in France during this period: conservative, with some disdain for the religiosity of laypeople (non-reforming); humanistic, evangelical and reformist (reforming, but non-schismatic); and reformed (reforming and schismatic).[40] During the French Wars of Religion the 'reforming, but non schismatic' current did not disappear, but has been largely overlooked by modern historians. Thierry Wanegffelen has recently demonstrated the existence of religious 'middle groups' during the French Wars of Religion of the sixteenth century, whose members were sympathetic to some of the ideas of the Reformation, but who did not want to leave the Catholic Church.[41] Luc Racaut has pointed to 'moderate voices' and orthodox Catholics who sought to defeat Calvinism with its own weapons: vernacular Bible reading and the religious education of

---

Body. Passion Devotion in Late-Medieval Culture (Groningen: 1998) 133–144; Ehrenpreis, S., "Teaching Religion in Early Modern Europe: Catechisms, Emblems and Local Traditions", in Schilling H. – Tóth I.G. (eds.), *Cultural Exchange in Early Modern Europe, vol. 1: Religion and Cultural Exchange in Europe, 1400–1700* (Cambridge: 2006) 256–273. For texts in English, see: Salter E., "The Dayes Moralised: Reconstructing Devotional Reading c. 1450–1560", in Lutton R. – Salter E. (eds.), *Pieties in Transition: Religious Practices and Experiences, c. 1400–1640* (Aldershot: 2005) 145–162.

39   Reid J.A., *King's Sister – Queen of Dissent: Marguerite of Navarre (1492–1549) and her Evangelical Network* (Leiden: 2009) 153–180.

40   Imbart de la Tour P., *Les origines de la Réforme*, 4 vols (Paris: 1905–1935).

41   Wanegffelen Th., *Ni Rome ni Genève. Des fidèles entre deux chaires en France au XVIe siècle* (Paris: 1997).

the laity.[42] I will argue here that already during the fifteenth century 'orthodox reform' was supported by the kind of religious texts in the French vernaculars that I will present below. This is very similar to the orthodox reform in the British Isles after the Arundel Constitutions, during the fifteenth century, that used the vernacular as a means of expression, as has been shown recently by Vincent Gillespie.[43]

Because of the enormous variety in texts and the complexity of the textual tradition, a complete overview of all religious texts in the French vernaculars from the period under consideration here is still lacking. Geneviève Hasenohr has done important pioneering work for texts surviving in manuscripts from the period stretching from the thirteenth to the end of the fifteenth century. She has identified many forgotten works, and thanks to her publications scholars can get a first grasp of the exceptional richness of this late medieval religious literature in French.[44] Studies concentrating on printed religious

---

42 Racaut L., *Hatred in Print: Catholic Propaganda and Protestant Identity during the French Wars of Religion* (Aldershot: 2002); Racaut L., "Nicolas Chesneau, Catholic Printer in Paris during the French Wars of Religion, 1558–1584", *Historical Journal* 52 (2009) 23–41; Racaut L., "Education of the Laity and Advocacy of Violence in Print during the French Wars of Religion", *History* 95 (2010) 159–177; Racaut L. – Ryrie A. (eds.), *Moderate voices in the European Reformation* (Aldershot: 2005). For Catholic reform, see also: Taylor L., *Heresy and Orthodoxy in Sixteenth-Century Paris: François Le Picart and the Beginnings of the Catholic Reformation* (Leiden: 1999) 151–186.

43 Gillespie V., "Chichele's Church: Vernacular Theology in England after Thomas Arundel", in Gillespie V. – Ghosh K. (eds.), *After Arundel: Religious Writing in Fifteenth-Century England* (Turnhout: 2012) 3–42. It would be wrong, however, to qualify the orthodox reform initiatives during the fifteenth century generically as 'pre-Reformation'; see: Vénard M., "Réforme, Réformation, Préréforme, Contreréforme. Étude de vocabulaire chez les historiens récents de langue française", in Joutard P. (ed.), *Historiographie de la Réforme* (Paris: 1977) 352–365.

44 Hasenohr G., "La vie quotidienne de la femme vue par l'Église: l'enseignement des "journées chrétiennes" de la fin du Moyen Age", in Brauneder W. (ed.), *Frau und spätmittelalterlicher Alltag* (Vienna: 1986) 19–101; Hasenohr G., "Aperçu sur la diffusion et la réception de la littérature de spiritualité en langue française au dernier siècle du Moyen Âge", in Wolf N.R. (ed.), *Wissensorganisierende und wissensvermittelnde Literatur im Mittalalter* (Wiesbaden: 1987) 57–90; Hasenohr G., "La littérature religieuse", in Poirion D. (ed.), *Grundriss der Romanischen Literaturen des Mittelalters*, vol. VIII/1: *La littérature française aux XIVᵉ et XVᵉ siècles* (Heidelberg: 1988) 266–305; Hasenohr G., "Aspects de la littérature de spiritualité en langue française (1480–1520)", *Revue d'histoire de l'Église de France* 77 (1991) 29–45; Hasenohr G., "Religious Reading Amongst the Laity in France in the Fifteenth Century", in Biller P. – Hudson A. (eds.), *Heresy and Literacy, 1000–1530* (Cambridge: 1994) 205–221; Hasenohr G., "Les prologues des textes de dévotion en langue

texts from the sixteenth century usually do not start before about 1520 and tend to privilege Protestant examples, often based on the traditional coupling of Protestantism and the dissemination of religious books in the vernacular among laypeople.[45] Consequently, orthodox texts published before about 1540 in France have received less scholarly attention,[46] with some paragraphs by Jean-Claude Dhotel,[47] and articles by Henri Hauser,[48] Francis Higman,[49] Karen Maag,[50] Virginia Reinburg[51] and Agnès Passot-Mannooretonil[52] among the rare exceptions.

Concentrating on the period between the 1400s and the 1530s allows for a closer examination of the continuities between late medieval religion and the period of the Reformation, something that has been suggested earlier, but

française (xiiie–xve siècles): formes et fonctions", in Hamesse J. (ed.), *Les prologues médiévaux* (Turnhout: 2000) 593–638.

45 See, for instance: Higman F., *Piety and the people: Religious Printing in French, 1511–1551* (Aldershot: 1995); Gilmont J.-F. (ed.), *La Réforme et le livre: l'Europe de l'imprimé (1517–v. 1570)* (Paris: 1990); Gilmont J.-F. – Kemp W. (eds.), *Le livre évangélique en français avant Calvin: études originales, publications d'inédits, catalogues d'éditions anciennes* (Turnhout: 2005). For critical remarks, see: Pettegree A. – Hall M., "The Reformation and the Book. A Reconsideration", in Pettegree A., *The French Book and the European Book World* (Leiden: 2007) 221–249.

46 The production of new catechetical texts in French before 1550 is even denied by Lemaître N., "Renouvellement et réformes au sein de l'église établie", in Benedict Ph. et al. (eds.), *La Réforme en France et en Italie. Contacts, comparaisons et contrastes* (Rome: 2007) 183–2001, here 197–198.

47 Dhotel, *Les origines* 27–47.

48 Hauser H., "Petits livres du xvie siècle", in Hauser H., *Études sur la Réforme française* (Paris: 1909) 253–298.

49 Higman F., "Premières réponses catholiques aux écrits de la Réforme en France, 1525–c. 1540", in Higman F., *Lire et découvrir. La circulation des idées au temps de la Réforme* (Geneva: 1998; first published in 1988) 497–514; Higman F., "Theology for the Layman in the French Reformation", *The Library: A Magazine of Bibliography and Literature, Sixth Series* 9 (1987) 105–127.

50 Maag K., "Education and works of religious instruction in French", in Pettegree A. – Nelles P. – Conner Ph. (eds.), *The Sixteenth-Century French Religious Book* (Aldershot: 2001) 96–109.

51 Reinburg V., "Books of Hours", in Pettegree A. – Nelles P. – Conner Ph. (eds.), *The Sixteenth-Century French Religious Book* (Aldershot: 2001) 68–82; Reinburg V., *French Books of Hours. Making an Archive of Prayer, c. 1400–1600* (Cambridge: 2012).

52 Passot-Mannooretonil A., "La spiritualité catholique à destination des mondains: mobilité des choix entre education morale et dévotion dans le genre des miroirs", in Burnett Ch. – Meirinhos J. – Hamesse J. (eds.), *Continuities and Disruptions between the Middle Ages and the Renaissance* (Louvain-la-Neuve: 2008) 37–62.

rarely substantiated with historical sources. In this article, I would like to concentrate on three aspects in particular: Firstly, instructions for a religious and sometimes contemplative life intended for laypeople, living in the world and adapted to a life of work and in the household. Secondly, I will discuss several paragraphs from these texts that encourage laypeople to read religious texts and that give them instructions what to read, how to read it and when. Thirdly, I will briefly examine orthodox religious reading during the period after the rise of Lutheranism (from the 1520s onwards). I will argue that French laypeople did not stop reading religious texts in the vernacular, not even after the first censoring measures by the Sorbonne and the *Parlement de Paris*: religious texts of a non-dissenting nature continued to be produced and read. In some cases both confessions at times even shared the same texts.

Religious Texts for Laypeople (and Clerics)

'I have been asked several times by many men and women to give them a certain manner by which they can live according to God and the Christian law and to write it down'.[53] This is one of the first phrases of a religious text in French, entitled the *Epistre du mirouer de crestiente*, written towards the end of the fourteenth century by Jean de Varennes, hermit in the chapel of Mont Saint-Lié near Reims. It makes clear that transferring religious knowledge to laypeople and their participation in religious life was not a one-way process initiated by members of the Church, but that laypeople were actively demanding access to religious knowledge and that they required directions for a religious life that could be combined with the obligations of work, trade and family life. The inventories of Jehan Janot and the bookseller from Tours, quoted in the introduction, are another indication that the production of religious texts in the vernacular was determined by a great demand by laypeople and that the production and distribution of the books was in their hands as well.

The author of the *Epistre du miroir de crestientie* continues that he intended to write directions for 'a religious life that is common to all true Catholics in general, regardless of their religious status',[54] and he explains that it is 'car dieu

---

53   'par diuerses foiz de plusieurs seigneurs et dames ay este requis que je leur deisse et escripsisse vne certaine maniere par la quelle ilz puissent viuvre selon dieu et la loy crestienne'. Brussels, KBR, MS 10394–10414, f. 38v. For this prologue, see also Hasenohr, "Les prologues" 622.

54   'Et ainsi je me sui ymagine pour cause de briefte de compiller vne petite fourme de viure commun a tous vrais catholiques en general de quelque estat que ilz soient'. Brussels, KBR, MS 10394–10414, f. 38v.

veult estre serui de tous estaz' ('because God wants to be served by all orders of society'). Several other religious texts in French also simultaneously addressed an audience of laypeople and clerics, such as the widely read *Doctrinal aux simples gens*, which was intended 'for simple priests who have no knowledge of Sacred Scripture and for simple laypeople'.[55] Remarks such as these indicate that the authors, usually clerics, had an inclusive vision of religion and believed that the Church did not only consist of those who were officially ordained, but that laypeople were an important part of it and that their participation was required. They also indicate that the boundaries between laypeople and religious were not as sharply defined during the late Middle Ages and the early sixteenth century as in the post-Tridentine Church.

A genuine effort seems to have been made to reach laypeople of all kinds: in a text printed in the early sixteenth century, the anonymous author states in the introduction that merchants can best be reached by discussing trade with them. Hence his book is entitled *La marchandise spirituelle*, 'to which our Lord in the Gospel not only invites male and female merchants, but also all male and female Christians regardless of their religious status or their social class, speaking to them in this manner: *Negociamini dum venio*. Do your spiritual trade in this world until I will come to search for you at your death'.[56]

The growing demand for religious texts in the French vernaculars also went hand in hand with a changing theological conceptualization of the life of laypeople and the *vita activa* during the fifteenth and early sixteenth centuries, to such a point that it and the monastic life were presented as equally valuable: both ways of life could lead to salvation.[57] A testimony of this new theology of

---

55 'pour les simples prestres qui nentendent pas les escriptures, comme pour les simples gens'. Le doctrinal de sapience (= Le doctrinal aux simples gens) (Lyon, Guillaume Le Roy: 1485) sig. aiii verso.

56 'La marchandise spirituelle a laquelle nostre seigneur en leuangille inuite non point seullement les marchans et marchandes / mais aussi tous chrestiens et chrestiennes de quelque estat et condition quilz soient en leur disant en cest maniere: *Negociamini dum venio*. Marchandez spirituellement en ce monde iusque a ce que ie vous vienne querir a vostre mort'. Quoted from *La marchandise spirituelle* (Paris: [1529]), sig. ai verso; but it is very likely that the text was written earlier, in the late fifteenth century.

57 For artisans as readers, authors and disseminators of religious texts in the vernacular, together with the changing theological conceptualization of work, see: Corbellini S. – Hoogvliet M., "Artisans and Religious Reading in Late Medieval Italy and Northern France (c. 1400–c. 1520)", *Journal of Medieval and Early Modern Studies* 43,3 (2013) 521–544. For the *vita activa* and the mixed life in English texts, as well as the patristic sources, see Steele F.J., *Towards a Spirituality for Lay-Folk: The Active Life in Middle English Religious Literature from the Thirteenth Century to the Fifteenth* (Lewiston: 1995).

the *vita activa* can be found in a sermon from 1525, printed as a reading text
with the title *Le fagot de myerre*:

> This is why, by means of God's Scripture, I do not know any road as sure
> and necessary to arrive from the sea of this world in the haven of Paradise
> for those from the class of the contemplative live, which I understand
> as prelates, religious people and churchmen, as well as the class of the
> active life, either members of the nobility, lawyers, merchants, married
> or bachelors, living in the world.[58]

In an earlier text, the *Ordinaire des chrestiens*, probably written in 1467, the
author stated first that the *vita contemplativa* is superior to the *vita activa*, but
he continued by underlining that both ways lead to salvation because they
require equally hard work. Moreover, only the *vita activa* allows for charitable
actions, such as donations to the poor.[59]

Because of the theological revaluation of the *vita activa*, the life of laypeople
could even become a model for ordained religious to follow. For instance, in
his allegorical work written for religious women, *Le livre du jardin de contemplacion*, the author Jehan Henry urged his female readers to come out of the
garden of the contemplative life in order to enter the active life, because only
the latter allows for charitable actions.[60] The *vita activa* was also increasingly
identified as a necessary condition in order to be able to enter the contemplative life. For instance, in the thirteenth-century work *La somme le roi*, the
author frère Laurent states unambiguously that 'no one can come to the contemplative life if he has not first been thoroughly tested in the active life', while
referring to the authority of St Gregory.[61] A very similar point can be found in
Jean Gerson's *Montaigne de contemplation*: 'the active live that is composed
of hardship and bodily work, must be taken before the contemplative live, as

---

58   'Parquoy par les escriptures de dieu ne congnois chemin si seur et necessaire pour arriuer
de la mer de ce monde au port de paradis a lestat de la vie contemplatiue soubz laquelle
ientens les prelatz gens de religion et gens deglise et a lestat de la vie actiue soit des
nobles, de gens de iustice, marchans et mariez ou non mariez au monde viuans'. *Le liure
intitule le fagot de myerre* (Paris, Yolande Bonhomme: 1525), *sig.* A iii recto.

59   *Lordinaire des crestiens* (Paris, André Vérard: 1490) f. 65v–68r.

60   'Pareillement fault maintenant que la verite des choses diuines que as en ce jardin par
la doctrine de ma seur soy conceu et entendu conuertisses et emplies es operations et
action humaines auxquelles es appelle par vie actiue'. Paris, BnF, MS fr. 997, f. 102v.

61   'car nus ne puet venir a la vie contemplative se il n'est premierement bien esprovez en la
vie active'. Brayer E. – Leurquin-Labie A.-F. (eds.), *La somme le roi par frère Laurent* (Paris:
2008) 330.

a road leading to it and as a preparation'.[62] Moreover, Gerson continues, both forms of life cannot do without one another

> because nobody is so absorbed by the active life that he or she does not have to think every now and then about God, his or her conscience, confession and repentance; and on the other hand there is nobody so contemplative that he or she can do without any form of labour.[63]

During the fifteenth century, clerics started to value the simple and direct religiosity they attributed to simple and devout laypeople over the arid theological subtleties of university-trained men. One of the most explicit statements of this point of view comes from Jean Gerson in his treatise *La montaigne de contemplation*: the pride of learned theologians sometimes prevents them from humbling themselves, something that is indispensable for entering the contemplative life. On the other hand, Gerson indicated that it was possible for laypeople to be very well predisposed for a life of solitude and continuous contemplation of their salvation without any worldly occupations: 'And we have seen it and still see it by many experiences with holy hermits and certain women that have had more profit from the love of God by this contemplative life than several great clerics do or have done'.[64]

A similar example from the early sixteenth century can be found in the anonymous work entitled *Une petite instruction et maniere de vivre pour une femme seculiere*. In a short introductory story we read about the encounter of a highly learned cleric and a married young woman. At first the cleric treats the laywoman very condescendingly, but when she tells him about her daily

---

62   'De ces dist saint Gregoire et les autres sains, que la vie active qui gist en affliction et labeurs corporelz, doibt estre prise avant la contemplative, comme voie et disposition a icelle'. Glorieux, *Jean Gerson*, 27.

63   'Car n'est personne si donnée a vie active qui ne doie aucunes fois penser a Dieu et a sa conscience et a soi confesser et repentir; et d'aultre part n'est personne si contemplative a qui ne face besoing aucun labeur'. Glorieux, *Jean Gerson*, 28.

64   'Et nous l'avons veu et veons par tant d'experiences es sains hermites et en aulcunes femmes qui plus ont pourfité en l'amour de Dieu par ceste vie contemplative que ne font ou ont fait plusieurs grans clers'. Glorieux, *Jean Gerson*, 18. There has been much debate about the complexity of Gerson's attitude towards the spirituality of laypeople: he was basically encouraging, but warned against superficiality and excesses; see: Hobbins D.B., "Gerson on Lay Devotion", in McGuire B.P. (ed.), *A Companion to Jean Gerson* (Leiden: 2006) 41–78. On Gerson's inclusive vision of the Church and religiosity, see: Burger C., *Aedificiatio, Fructus, Utilitas. Johannes Gerson als Professor der Theologie und Kanzler der Universität Paris* (Tübingen: 1986) 183–193.

devotional exercises and the role she plays in the religious education of her children and her husband, he changes his attitude and acknowledges her superiority: 'O dear lady, you are on the right track and know that I have worn this theologian's hat for fifty years and I am called master in holy theology and I have not yet come to this perfection'.[65]

In some of the religious texts in French laypeople could find directions on how they could integrate prayer and contemplation into the obligations of their daily life. One strategy was to create a quiet moment for withdrawal during daytime or the night. For instance, a text with instructions for an unmarried young woman in a manuscript from the fourteenth century suggested to

> take for the hour of prime the moment when you see the day and do not go immediately out of your bedroom in order to start your duties, but rather start to pray and think how your lover was brought before Pilatus at the same moment.[66]

In a fifteenth-century treatise married women were told that 'marriage and household' cannot be used as an excuse for not being able to fulfil religious exercises,[67] and the author advised them to

> always have dinner early, for instance between five and six in the afternoon, if circumstances do not prevent it – but I leave that to your own good judgement. And after your meal, relax until seven o'clock in your house, or in the courtyard while looking at your servants working. And later, when your family will be in good order, enclose yourself in your bedroom and start your meditation while thinking about your sins of that day in particular and of those of the past in general.[68]

---

65   'O bonne dame tu es en la droicte voye et saichez que iay porte ceste chappe cinquante
        ans. Et suis appelle maistre en saincte theologie et touteffois encores ne suis ie point venu
        en ceste parfection'. *Une petite instruction et maniere de vivre pour une femme seculiere*
        (Paris, [veuve Jean Trepperel: 1512–1517]) *sig.* [a5v].

66   'Apres en matin que praing pour leure de prime quant tu le verras ne va pas tantost hors
        de ta chambre por besoignier ancois te met a oroison et a penser comment ton ami a cele
        eure [...] fu menez deuant pilate'. Paris, BnF, MS fr. 1802, f. 82v.

67   'Contre celles qui pour mariage se veulent excuser de tenir la regle dessusdict' and
        'Commant mariage ne mesnage ne empeschent point a venir a ceste parfection'. Paris,
        Bibl. de l'Arsenal, MS 2176, f. 94r and f. 95r.

68   'Mais pource que vous auez mary mesnage enfans et famille je vous conseille que vous
        souppez tousiours a haulte heure comme entre cinq et six heures en tout temps se occa-
        sion de necessite ne vous empesche laquelle necessite ie laisse a jugier a votre bonne

Another possibility was to pray during work and other daily activities. The *Doctrinal aux simples gens*, for instance, exhorts the reader as follows: 'You should know that in all places and during all sorts of occupations, one can pray to God and serve Him and everyone is obliged to do this'.[69] The inclusion of laypeople in the obligation of prayer for all Christians, together with the suggestion to pray continuously, also occurs in the *Ordinaire des crestiens*:

> Likewise it is necessary to pray continuously, as Jesus Christ says in the Gospel, after vocal or mental prayer, performed at a suitable place and moment, we will always be in the love and fear of God and we will be occupied in a saintly manner; in doing so we pray to God continuously, because the good desire of the heart is for God a loud clamour.[70]

In *La maniere de bien vivre devotement et salutairement par chascun jour pour hommes et femmes de moyen estat*, a short and cheap treatise of only eight pages, written by Jean Quentin and first printed in 1491, the reader was invited to 'dedicate yourself to their work or household until dinner and while doing that with zeal, think every now and then that the pain that you are suffering in this world is nothing compared to the pains of purgatory'.[71] The reader should 'employ his or her daytime for work in praise of the Lord'.[72] Besides that, he or

---

discrecion. Et puis apres votre refection du soupper esbatez iusques a vij heurs par vostre maison ou par la court en regardant voz gens besoigner. Et puis quant votre famille sera bien ordonnee enfermez vous en votre chambre et commances votre meditacion en pensant voz pechez de la iournee par especial et en general de tout le temps passe'. Paris, Bibl. de l'Arsenal, MS 2176, f. 110r.

69 'Tu dois scauoir que en tous lieux et en toutes places et en toutes oeuures peut et doit on dieu prier et seruir'. *Le doctrinal*, sig. e iii verso.

70 'Toute creature raysonnable qui a aage discrecion competens est obligee par le droit de nature a faire oraison a dieu son createur. [...] Si nous est necessite tousiours de prier ainsi que dit ieuscrist en leuangile. cest assuoir que apres oryason vocale ou mentale faicte en lieu et en temps selon bonne congruite nous nous tenons tousiours en lamour et crainte de dieu et sainctement occupez et en ce faisant nous prirons dieu sans cesser car le bon desir du cueur est deuant dieu vne haulte clameur'. *L'ordinaire*, f. 154v.

71 'Apres que vous seres retourne de leglise en vostre maison entendes a vostre mesnage iusques au disner et en y entendant penses aulcune fois que la paine que vous souffres en ce monde nest rien au regard de la paine de purgatoire'. Quentin Jean, *La manière de bien vivre dévotement par chascun jour* (Paris, Antoine Caillaut: 1491) sig. [a4r].

72 'Le demourant du iour emploies le a vostre mesnage a la louenge de dieu'. Quentin, *La manière*, sig. [a4v].

she should 'think often of Christ and consider what he did at that time during the day of his Passion'.[73]

The earlier-mentioned printed text from the early sixteenth century, *Une petite instruction et maniere de vivre pour une femme seculiere*, advised women to turn the situation to their profit when their children prevented them from doing devotional exercises and to think about how the 'very worthy mother of God the Creator held the blessed and little infant Jesus in her arms and that she was so taken away thinking that he was who she held and that she covered his whole body with her tears'.[74] This same text suggests a very original weekly devotional exercise, especially adapted to laypeople, with every day of the week having its own special theme connected to laypeople mentioned in the Gospels:

> On Mondays think about the poor and sinful woman to whom Our Lord forgave her sins, on Tuesday humble yourself with the centurion, on Wednesday with Mary Magdalene, on Thursday with the woman of Canaan, on Friday with the Roman tax collector and Saturday with the prodigal son.[75]

Another striking aspect of these religious texts in French is that they are, in fact, very accommodating for laypeople, thus testifying an understanding of the circumstances of their daily life and a willingness to make space for their special needs. For instance, Jean de Varennes was aware that poor people were not in a position to attend church every day, but on Sundays 'even poor people'

---

73   'Consideres souuent de iour ou de nuit quant vous vous esueillies quelle chose faisoit nostre sauueur au iour de la passion et ou il estoit a telle heure'. Quentin, *La manière*, sig. [a5r].

74   'Et apres ma seur pourtant quil vous semble que vous estes fort empeschee de deuotion pour vos petis enfans ie vous asseure que vous les aiez bien tournee a deuotion et en faire vostre proffit spirituel. Souuiengne vous et penses comment la tresdigne mere de dieu le createur tenoit le benoist et petit enfant iehus entre ses bras elle estoit si rauye en pensant quil estoyt celuy que elle tenoit que elle luy arrosoit tout le corps de ses larmes'. *Une petite instruction*, sig. aiiiv–[a4 r].

75   'Et le lundy vous humilieres auecques la pouure femme prinse en peche a qui nostre seigneur pardonna. Et pensez que vous auez tant de foys rompu la foy que vous auez promise a nostre seingeur iheuschrist au sacremen de baptesme qui est espoux de vostre ame. Et le mardy vous humileres auec le centurion. Le mercredy auecques la benoise magdaline. Le ieudy encores auecques la chananee. Le vendredy auecques le publicain. Le samedy auec et comme lefilz prodigue'. *Une petite instruction*, sig. [b4 r].

were expected to go to Mass.[76] Jean Quentin, too, acknowledged that laypeople did not always have the time in order to perform all exercises he prescribed and he proposed shorter exercises for them instead: 'and if you cannot stay in church for such a long time because of other reasonable occupations, only say grace to God and his good works'[77] and 'say when you can the vigils of the death during festive days if you do not have enough time to say them during the other days'.[78]

Texts such as the ones alluded to here – and they are by no means exceptional – helped laypeople fulfil their religious duties in such a way that they could be combined with their worldly obligations. They also testify that there was a current in the late medieval Church whose representatives understood the pressures of laypeople's life and collaborated with them in order to find solutions. The religious texts in the French vernaculars are witnesses testifying to the inclusiveness of late medieval religion and the emergence of new forms of religious life where work, family life and charity could become a form of worship. This process of the sanctification of the work and daily life of laypeople was supported by members of the Church, and even sometimes imitated by them. It is noteworthy that reading in the vernacular played a key role in this important cultural change taking place during the fifteenth and early sixteenth centuries.

Reading and the Transfer of Religious Knowledge

An implicitly expressed intention underlying all religious texts in the French vernaculars is that they want to be read, their lessons to be known and their knowledge transferred to a wide audience. Moreover, several texts contain explicit remarks encouraging their audience to read, because reading was considered an important religious activity besides prayer and meditation, not only for clerics, priests, monks and nuns, but also for laypeople. Frequent religious reading was also considered important as a means to internalize the

---

76 'mais le dymenche riches ne poures nen sont excusez se pour necessite ou chose tres ou plus prouffitable aux ames ne le laissent'. Brussels, KBR, MS 10394–10414, f. 39r.

77 'Vela les pensees que ie veul que vous ayes en leglise et se par aultre occupation raisonnable vous ne poues estre si longuement a leglise que dit est cy dessus rendes seulement graces a dieu de ses biens'. Quentin, *La manière*, sig. [a4r].

78 'Quant a vostre seruice dites iusques a tierce deuant disner acheues le tout deuant souper et dites quant vous pourres vigiles de mors au mains es iours de feste se vous naues bonne espace de les dire les autres iours a trois lecons'. Quentin, *La manière*, sig. [a4v].

religious knowledge transferred by the texts, for it to be recalled during meditative exercises. Moreover, accumulating religious knowledge through reading, and transferring that knowledge to others by reading aloud for them was often encouraged during the fifteenth and early sixteenth centuries.

French-speaking laypeople were invited to participate in religious reading quite early. For instance, in a treatise attributed to Pierre de Beauvais entitled *Les trois séjours de l'homme et la vertu de la récitation des Psaumes*, written in the second half of the thirteenth century for both clerics and laypeople, reading the Psalms is called an obligation for everyone who could read: 'Men and women who know how to read, must read the Psalms that remove the sins. Psalms have great virtues; it is a bad thing when one withholds them from his or her eyes when one knows how to read and does not read them'.[79]

Religious reading was considered an important element of a devotional life, including that of laypersons. In the late fourteenth-century *Livret* attributed to Pierre de Luxembourg (1369–1387), the lay reader is advised to withdraw to his or her bedroom after dinner, in order to 'study there some good scripture that is beneficial to your soul' as a part of the daily routine.[80] In his *Montaigne de Contemplation* Jean Gerson prescribed to his sisters (and to other readers who desired to follow their example) reading religious works as an indispensable part of the contemplative life: 'But also Sacred Scripture and the examples of good books, listening to them and thinking about their lessons, often chase this love of worldly things'. He later adds: 'Every day you should read together a part of some good book'.[81]

A fifteenth-century text with instructions for meditations on Christ's Passion, suggests to the female lay reader a meditative form of reading: 'read it often and meditate, think and concentrate at every point or every page'.[82] Moreover,

---

79   'Cil et celes qui lire seuent / Lour siaumes qui les pechiez lieuent / Sachent questre doivent en grant / De lire car vertu ont grant / Trop de mal a son oes elit / Quil les set lire sil nes lit'. Paris, BnF, MS n.a. fr. 13521, f. 66r.

80   'Quant tu auras dit graces tu ten yras en ta chambre et estudieras en aucune bonne escripture salutaire pour lame'. Paris, Bibl. de l'Arsenal, MS 2036, f. 396v.

81   'Mais aussi la sainte escripture et les exemples des bons liure, ouir et penser, chassent souvent ceste amour mondaine' and 'Item soit chascun jour lut une partie d'aucun bon liure entre vous'. Glorieux, *Jean Gerson*, 24 and 56. For a recent discussion, see: Hobbins, "Gerson on Lay Devotion", 72–75. As with all religious matters, Gerson was cautious about excesses stemming from laypeople misinterpreting biblical and religious texts. However, modern research has had an almost exclusive attention for Gerson's concerns, while examples where he explicitly encourages lay reading have remained understudied.

82   'Ce beau petit liuret que je vous envoie regardes le bien souuent et medittes penses et vous arestes sur chascun point ou feuillet'. Valenciennes, Bibl. municipale, MS 126, f. 306r.

the text should be read often so that it will be 'inscribed in your heart and that you can remember it in private and in a secret place'.[83] Repetitive reading is very often encouraged, in combination with the exhortation to memorize the content of the text and to create moments of withdrawal during one's daily activities in order to recall it during meditative exercises. A fifteenth-century text with religious instructions contained in a miscellany manuscript with sermons and a life of Christ suggests to its readers: 'Consequently and in order that you obey all these things and that you will not become negligent, read this writing two times every week. That is on Saturday and on Wednesday'.[84] Other texts give practical advice on making space for reading in a working life, such as these reading instructions inserted after a life of Christ in a fifteenth-century manuscript:

> And take one hour every day the time to think about this without being occupied by mundane things. And later during other hours you can read the lessons from this book, or listen to them. And memorize them carefully, because they are necessary for those who want to come to a spiritual life.[85]

For meditative reading by laypeople, see: Huot S., "A book made for a queen: The shaping of a late medieval anthology manuscript (B.N. fr. 24429)", in Nichols S.G. – Wenzel S. (eds.), *The Whole Book: Cultural Perspectives on the Medieval Miscellany* (Ann Arbor: 1996) 123–143; Huot S., "Polytextual Reading: The Meditative Reading of Real and Metaphorical Books", in Chinca M. – Young C., (eds.), *Orality and Literacy in the Middle Ages: Essays on a Conjunction and its Consequences in Honour of D.H. Green* (Turnhout: 2005) 203–222; Bryan J., *Looking Inward: Devotional Reading and the Private Self in Late Medieval England* (Philadelphia: 2008).

83 'Chiere sueur je ne vous ay point escript touttes ces choses pour nyent. Ne affin que vous le lysies vne fois, mais affin que vous le lisies si souuent que y soyent escriptes en vre ceur et que les ramenteues et recordes a part en quelque lieu secret comme se vous veissies faire ceste doleur a vostre amy et doulx espeulx ihesus'.Valenciennes, Bibl. municipale, MS 126, f. 310r.

84 'Doncques et afin que tu gardes bien toutes ces choses et que tu nen faces negligence liz cest escript deux fois en la sepmaine. Cest assauoir le samedj et le mercredi'. Paris, Bibl. de l'Arsenal, MS 2109, f. 193r.

85 'Et une heure du jour prens aucune espace que tu ayes loysir dy penser sans toy occuper en aucunes choses mondaines. Et apres es autres heures pourras lire et entendre les auctoritez et enseignemens de ce liure. Et le retien diligentement en ta memoire. Car elles sont tres necessaires a celuy qui veult venir a vie espirituelle'. Paris, Bibl. de l'Arsenal, MS 2036, f. 388v.

The earlier-mentioned printed text *Une petite instruction et maniere de vivre pour une femme seculiere* gives several very interesting reading instructions. The female reader should read the text often in order to be incited to devotion and to put it into practice; the author suggests, for instance, that she should copy a part of it on a small piece of paper and paste it into her Book of Hours, and read it every day as a preparation for Mass. Moreover the author insists that the devout woman should read his text carefully by savouring it in her heart and in her mind.[86]

Other texts were adapted to the time-consuming daily life of laypeople by means of abridgement, because it would have been easier for them to make time for reading shorter texts. The 'modern' predilection for shorter texts is a recurring theme, as for instance in an explanatory poem at the end of the printed *Miroir dor de lame pecheresse* (c. 1482–1484): 'You all should learn how to live well in this world / Don't forget to mirror yourself in this book / It only contains seven chapters / Alas, sinners, recall them often / So read one of them every day'.[87]

Besides its meditative and reclusive aspects, reading was also a collective activity in order to share and disseminate religious knowledge. One of the early reforming bishops, Guy de Roye, ordered that all priests in his diocese should possess a copy of the *Doctrinal aux simples gens* and that they should read a few chapters from it every Sunday at the rood screen. Besides this, he also promised twenty days of indulgences to everyone who read the text aloud to someone else.[88]

---

86 'Et si vous seroit bien prouffitable de le lire souuent pour vuous inciter a deuotion et a le mettre en oeuure. Et aussi il vous seroit bon de en reciter en vng petit papier ce qui est a dire tous les iours comme la preparation que vous debuez faire tous les matins et la maniere de oyr la messe. [...] Et mettez cela dedans vos heures que vous portez a leglise. [...] Et quant vous lirez pensez bien a ce que vous dictes en le sauourant en vostre cueur et entendement. Car plusieurs lisent en courant qui ny pensent ne ny prouffitent gueres'; and: 'Et tout le moins vne fois le iour lisez vng fueilet ou deux de quelque deuot liure pour la refection de vostre ame'. *Une petite instruction*, sig. Aiii recto and [B6 verso].

87 'Cy apres sensuit en brief la declaration des chapitres de ce liure: Aprenes tous en ce monde bien viure / Nomblies pas vours mirer en ce liure / Tant seulement sept chapitres comprent. / Helas pechers recordes les souuent / Or en lises vn par chascun iour'. *Miroir dor de lame pecheresse*, [Paris, Antoine Caillaut: c. 1482–84].

88 'Et a ordonne et commende le dit reuerent pere par grant deuocion que on chascune paroche de la cite et diocese de Reins il ait vn tel liuret. Et que les cures et chappellains dez dictes paroches en lisent chascun dimenche au prosme deux ou trois chapitres se aucuns en vueillent oir. [...] Le dit resreuerent pere en dieu [...] a donne et attroie a touz ceulx qui seront en estat de grace qui de ce liuret liront a autrui .xx. jours de pardon'.

Institutions with intensive lay participation, such as the parish, the school, the hospital and also the household, were identified as places where religious knowledge was communicated to wider lay audiences, even including those that could not read at all. For instance, Jean de Varennes stipulated that little children should learn his *Epistre du mirouer de crestiente* in school. Moreover, men and women who knew how to read should possess a copy, and priests should read from it at the rood screen.[89] Jean Gerson, too, wrote that his vernacular work with the basics of religious knowledge, entitled *Le miroir de l'âme* (1400–1401), was intended to be 'published in a public place, entirely or partially, and to be attached to parish churches, schools, religious houses and hospitals in books or on tablets'.[90] Very similar recommendations were repeated in a printed version of several of Gerson's vernacular works from 1507: all schools, hospitals and religious houses in the diocese of Paris were obliged to possess a copy of this work. Moreover 'parents and other Christians who do not have a great knowledge of their salvation should have this work of doctrine at least in French and if they know how to read. And when they study it often they will benefit from it'.[91] The readers of the treatise *La marchandise spirituelle* were also encouraged to share their religious knowledge with others: 'Sacred Scripture teaches us how we should teach others'.[92]

In the examples evoked above, the family and the household were mentioned several times as a place for religious instruction through collective reading. Jean Gerson discusses this topic even more clearly in the chapter of his

---

Reims, Bibl. municipale, MS 614, f. 173r. This is generally thought to have been Guy de Roye's personal copy. The prologue occurs in most manuscripts with the long version and in the printed editions.

89 'Et ceste petite espistre les petis enfans en faueur de nostre foy doiuent aprendre a lescole. Les hommes et les femmes qui sceuent lire la doient auoir en escript et les curez la doiuent plusieurs fois prononcier a leurs prosne au peuple'. Brussels, KBR, MS 10394–10414, f. 47v.

90 'En tout ou en partie escripte publiee et atachiee es paroices, es escoles, es religions et es hospitauz par liure et par tableaus en lieu publique'. Glorieux, *Jean Gerson*, 57, 193–206.

91 'Voulons aussi et ordonnons que en toutes escolles et hospitaulx et maisons dieu et maladeries on ait ceste doctrine par escript. [...] En exhortant peres et meres et tous bons chrestiens qui nont plus grant congonissance de leur salut auoir sils peuuent la doctrine dussusdict au moins en francois et silz scauent lire. Et quant souuent ilz y estudiereont bien leur en prendra'. *L'instruction des curez pour instruire le simple peuple, suivi du Livre de Jésus. S'ensuivent les trois vérités composées par maître Jean Gerson* (Paris, S. Vostre: 1507) f. iiii r.

92 'Secondement la sainte escripture enseigne comment on doibt enseigner les autres'. *La marchandise spirituelle*, sig. E.iii verso.

Miroir de l'âme about the third commandment concerning Sundays: besides the obligations of attending Mass and the abstinence from work, good Christians should 'listen to God's word and other teachings' during the rest of the day. On the same occasion 'parents should teach their sons and daughters and others who are under their guidance'.[93] Jean Gerson was not the only one to identify lay circles as places of transfer of religious knowledge. For instance, in the *Livre de bonnes meurs* Jacques Legrand encouraged laypeople to discuss religious subjects by referring to a wise layman ('un preudomme'), who according to Cassiodorus's *Historia tripartitus* converted several heathens. Immediately after this the author addresses the lay reader directly:

> But you will say that you are not a learned cleric at all and that you cannot give sermons. To this I give you a reply and I say to you that if you are good in your affection the Holy Spirit will give you good and profitable words.[94]

The examples quoted here all indicate that religious reading, as a means of acquiring knowledge and as a meditative practice, was an important part of the religious life of laypeople during the fifteenth and early sixteenth centuries. It also shows that the domestic space was increasingly identified as the main place for religious reading, either in a secluded place for private meditation, or in a collective setting for the transfer of religious knowledge. It is also striking that laypeople were explicitly invited to actively function as mediators of religious knowledge by reading religious texts to other laypeople and to speak among them about religious matters, well before Luther and the Reformation. This suggests that the strong polarization of the later sixteenth century might have masked certain continuities between practices of the late medieval Roman Catholic Church and those of the Reformed churches.

Orthodox Reading in France after Luther

When Luther's writings started to appear in France during the early 1520s, the theologians of the Sorbonne reacted almost immediately with censoring

---

93   'On doibt lors oyr la parole de Dieu et bons enseigenemens selon ce que on peut. [...] Et doibt on enseignier ses filz et filles et serviteurs et aultres que on ha en gouuernement'. Glorieux, *Jean Gerson*, 197–198.

94   'Mais tu diras que tu n'es mye clerc pour preschier. A ce je te respons et di que se tu es bon en ton affection le Saint Esperit t'amenistrera parole bonne et prouffitable'. Beltran, *Jacques Legrand*, 346.

measures.[95] Modern research has had much attention for the texts that were under suspicion, condemned, confiscated or even burnt, to such a degree that the phenomenon of orthodox reading has been almost completely neglected, and it seems as if after this moment hardly any religious texts in French were printed and sold. However, the prohibitions of texts judged as heretical by the Sorbonne and the *Parlement de Paris* only became truly effective when they gained support from the French crown after the *affaire des placards* of 1534, and a complete ban on all religious texts in the vernacular was never issued. Quite to the contrary, several prelates and members of religious orders started to promote religious reading by laypeople as an effective tool against heretical ideas.

An example of this strategy is the didactic work *Le viat de salut necessaire et utile a tous chrestiens pour parvenir a gloyre eternelle*, written by Guillaume Petit, Bishop of Paris, and printed from 1527 onwards. In the colophon Petit stipulated that priests, schoolmasters and heads of hospitals should possess a copy and that they should read the text to children and illiterate laypeople. Petit also stated that he gave this text to all his subjects and he promised forty days of indulgences for every time it was read or listened to:[96] this strategy was already started a century earlier by Guy de Roye, as described above. Petit's main goal was that simple laypeople 'who do not have perfect knowledge of the Holy Gospels (as clerics do have) can no longer pretend to be ignorant about their salvation'.[97] Besides this, Petit's work was also destined for clerics, and for them he had added 'healthy and solid doctrines', while 'the milk, the simple doctrines, were intended for the common people; the latter group should only take what they could chew and understand'.[98] Although Petit's

---

95   Higman F.M., *Censorship and the Sorbonne: A Bibliographical Study of Books in French Censured by the Faculty of Theology of the University of Paris, 1520–1551* (Geneva: 1979).

96   'A tous curez chapellains vicaires et maistres descolle auoir ce present liure. Pour le lire ou le faire lire au prosne les dimenches et festes. Et aux escolles aux enfans capables de lentendre. Et a cest fin a donne ledict reuerend a tous ses subgectz qui deuotement liront ce present liure ou escouteront lire. Auec bon propos de foy amender et viure selon la doctrine de nostre seigneur: quarante iours de vray pardon toutes les foys quantes qui le liront ou escouteront lire'. Petit Guillaume, *Le viat de salut necessaire et utile a tous chrestiens pour parvenir a gloyre eternelle* (Troyes, Jehan Lecoq: [1527]) sig. [a1 recto]. On this work by Petit, see also: Higman, "Premières réponses catholiques", 500–503. However, Higman emphasizes mainly the restrictive aspects of Petit's introduction.

97   'Le simple peuple [....] lesquelz nont pas parfaicte intelligence des sainctes euangiles (comme les clercz) ne pretendent ignorance de leur salut'. Petit, *Le viat de salut*, sig. [a1 verso].

98   'De adiouster et mettre bonnes saines et solides doctrines pour les clercz et du laict cest adire doctrines simples pour le commun populaire. Les simpes donc prendront ce quil pourront macher et entendre'. Petit, *Le viat de salut*, sig. aij recto.

words testify to a concern about possible abuses stemming from uneducated laypeople misinterpreting theological subjects, there is no question of censorship at all. Quite to the contrary, this bishop provided laypeople with 'solid doctrines' in the vernacular, destined for clerics, and left it to the judgement of his lay readers if they were capable of understanding it properly.

Petit was certainly not the only person from the orthodox side who was convinced that educating the laity was the most effective weapon against the Lutheran heresy. Some ten years later the Dominican friar and doctor in theology Pierre Doré (c. 1500–1569) wrote in the post scriptum to his vernacular work *Les voies de Paradis*, first printed in 1538, that

> It seemed good to me to give in French some good books as a medicine against the pestilent teachings that one can take out of the dangerous books that are being printed in several places in the vulgar language, which is something pernicious that greatly damages the Christian republic, against which I only can give an antidote: a useful book for the simple people that is not against our faith.[99]

A similar strategy was proposed by Nicole Grenier from the monastery of Saint-Victor in his *Bouclier de la foy*, first printed in 1548. Grenier wrote that since ignorance was the greatest cause of heresy, he proposed a work in the French vernacular based on Sacred Scripture ('extraict de la saincte Escripture') together with explanations by theologians 'in defence of our faith, and in order to inform and fortify people with little education so that they will reject errors opposed to the truth'. This work was explicitly intended to inform laypeople with commercial or domestic obligations who did not have the time to read all

---

99 'ma semble bon et convenable donner en francoys quelques bons liures comme anthidote contre les pestiferes enseignemens quon peult prendre es meschans liures qui en diuers lieux se impriment en langue vulgaire qui est chose trespernicieuse et qui fort endommaige la Republique chrestienne: a quoy ne puis remedier (comme le desireroye) sinon que en baillant le contrepoison. Cest a dire liure utile au simple peuple lequel ne discorde a nostre foy'. Pierre Doré, *Les voies de paradis* (Paris: 1538) '*Au lecteur catholique*'. A similar argument in the preface to Doré's *Dyalogue instructoire des chrestiens en la foy* (Paris: 1538). For Doré, see: Higman F., "La réfutation par Pierre Doré du catéchisme de Megander", in Colin P. et al. (eds.), *Aux origines du catéchisme en France* (Paris: 1989) 55–66; Higman, "Premières réponses catholiques", 509–513; Higman, *Piety and the people*, 177–190; Crouzet D., *Les guerriers de Dieu. La violence au temps des troubles de religion, vers 1525–vers 1610* (Seyssel: 1990) 374–376.

books on the subject.[100] As Luc Racaut has shown earlier for the period after c. 1560, the guardians of the Catholic orthodoxy in France did not simply prohibit all religious texts in the vernacular; instead the reading of orthodox religious texts in the vernacular by laypeople was proposed by several clergymen as an effective counter strategy aimed against Lutheran and Calvinist teachings.[101]

While it is true that certain texts were censored during the sixteenth century, other religious texts in French were printed without encountering restrictive measures from the side of the Sorbonne, the *Parlement de Paris* or the French monarchy. Religious texts in the vernacular that continued to be printed in France included those by Pierre Doré and Nicole Grenier, but also many of the texts that were read earlier by laypeople. For instance, the French *Lucidaire* was reprinted until 1648; Jacques Legrand's *Livre de bonnes meurs* until 1578; the *Myrouer dor de lame pecheresse* until 1578; the *Doctrinal aux simples gens* until 1680; the *Ordinaire des Crestiens* until 1580; *L'esguillon d'amour divine* until 1606; *Une petite instruction et maniere de vivre pour une femme seculiere* until 1560 or 1574; several of Gerson's works well into the 1560s and beyond; the French translation of the *Imitatio Christi* was reprinted frequently during the sixteenth and early seventeenth centuries; and Gospel-based stories of Christ's life and Passion, often together with sermons or instructions for meditative and devotional exercises, continued to be disseminated in high numbers throughout the sixteenth century and beyond. The books possessed by laypeople in Amiens during the sixteenth century reveal similar patterns: in spite of the restrictive measures proposed by the Sorbonne, laypeople possessed surprisingly high numbers of religious and biblical texts in the vernacular, including polemical texts emanating from both the Protestant and Catholic sides.[102]

100　'L'ignorance, ou non vraye intelligence [de la saincte escripture], a seduict plusieurs et faict tomber en heresie' and 'Ce petit traicté, couché en langue vulgaire, compilé des sainctes escriptures, exposées et declariées selon la vraye et saine intelligence des sainctz et anciens docteurs de l'eglise, en faueur et defence de nostre foy, pour mieulx informer et fortifier gents de simple literature, à repoulser les erreurs contraires à verité [...] Et aussi pour soulager ceulx qui par occupation des negoces temporelles et domesticques, n'ont loysir et espace de lire et reuoluer plusieurs volumes ou traictez sur ce faictz et mis en public'. Nicole Grenier, *Le bouclier de la foy en forme de dialogue extraict de la saincte Escripture et des saincts Pères*, (Paris: 1548). *sig.* aa iij recto and [aa 8 r].

101　Racaut, *Hatred in Print*, 7–22; Racaut, "Nicolas Chesneau"; Racaut, "Education of the Laity". See also Crouzet, *Les guerriers de Dieu*, 366–373 for vernacular mysticism as a counter strategy.

102　Febvre L., *Au coeur religieux du XVIᵉ siècle* (Paris: 1957) 327–333.

The historical polarization, together with the current conceptualization by modern historians of two strictly separated confessional blocks,[103] has resulted in the similarities of the textual cultures and the sharing of texts being over-looked for a long time. For instance, along the complete confessional spectrum from conservative Catholics, through humanistic and evangelical middle groups to fanatic Protestants, there was a great concern to teach to the young or illiterate laypeople the basics of Christian knowledge: the Ten Commandments (although there was disagreement about the Second Commandment), the Lord's Creed, the Credo and the Ave Maria. Texts with the basic knowledge for each Christian proliferated during the late Middle Ages, especially as books intended for beginning readers; Jean Gerson's *ABC des simples gens* was one of the most widely read examples. During the sixteenth century an even greater variety of this type of text was distributed and in higher numbers, both from Catholic and Protestant perspectives,[104] the latter also in the form of ABC books.[105]

More religious texts in French were read by surprisingly wide audiences, such as the *Livre de vraye et parfaicte oraison*, first printed in Paris in 1528. This work most likely originated from the surroundings of Lefèvre d'Étaples and it incorporated, among other texts, an exposition on the Ave Maria, but also texts by Guillaume Farel and a French translation of parts of Luther's *Betbüchlein*. In spite of the Protestant connotations of most of its texts, the work was often reprinted in France until 1545, it was widely disseminated and the historical readers included non-dissenting Catholics who used it in a way similar to that of a Book of Hours.[106] Another example is the *Sommaire des livres du vieil et nouveau testament*—a collection of the elementary principles of Christian faith, based on quotations from the Old and New Testament, followed by the Ten Commandments—originally written in Latin by the Parisian printer Robert Estienne and first printed in 1532 with the title *Haec docent sacra bibliorum scripta*. Despite the Protestant associations with Robert Estienne and

---

103   Nicholls D., "Heresy and Protestantism, 1520–1542: questions of perception and communication", *French History* 10,2 (1996) 182–205.

104   For the Catholic perspective, see Nicholls, "Heresy and Protestantism".

105   Maag, "Education and works of religious instruction"; Milway M., "Forgotten Best-Sellers from the Dawn of the Reformation", in Bast R.J. – Gow A.C. (eds.), *Continuity and Change: The Harvest of Late Medieval and Reformation History* (Leiden: 2000) 113–142, discussion of ABC-books on 132–135.

106   Higman F., "Luther et la piété de l'église gallicane: Le livre de vraye et parfaicte oraison", *Revue d'histoire et de philosophie religieuses* 63 (1983) 91–111; Reinburg, "Books of Hours", 80–81.

this text, it is not explicitly polarizing with Roman Catholic doctrine. A French translation was often added as a prologue to Protestant Bibles, but, surprisingly, it also served as a prologue to Catholic Bibles in the vernacular; such as a preface to the French Bible printed in 1534 in Antwerp by Martin Lempereur (this is the translation attributed to Lefèvre d'Étaples) with the title *Instructions pour les chrestiens*, and in the French Bible for Catholics by René Benoist, first printed in Paris in 1566, entitled *La somme de tout ce que nous enseigne la Saincte Escriture*. In addition, it was printed as an independent work from 1542 onwards by Étienne Dolet in Lyon with the title *Le sommaire des livres du Vieil et Nouveau Testament. Les dix parolles, ou Commandements de Dieu*.[107]

The evidence discussed here shows that the lively religious reading culture in the French vernacular of the fifteenth century continued well into the sixteenth century, mainly because the Catholic and Protestant sides both used religious texts in the vernacular and the instruction of laypeople as an effective propaganda tool. Moreover, from the perspective of textual culture, the distinction between Catholic and Protestant is not always very clear. This is also a confirmation of the hypotheses concerning the existence of religious middle groups and orthodox reform during the sixteenth century, already mentioned in the introduction.

Conclusion

'Car dieu veult estre serui de tous estaz'—this phrase, written by Jean de Varennes in the last years of the fourteenth century, epitomizes the increasing importance that was attached to the participation of laypeople in church and in religious life. The circulation of a great variety of religious and catechetical texts in the French vernaculars, in high numbers of copies and often explicitly opening possibilities for laypeople to combine the *vita activa* with a contemplative life, shows that the century preceding the Reformation was not characterized by the religious exclusion of laypeople, or by their resistance towards the religion of the Church. Religious reading in the vernacular played an important role in the participation of the laity and in the transfer of religious knowledge, either by private reading as a meditative activity, or by giving voice to the religious texts by reading them aloud to others, thus turning laypeople into mediators of religious knowledge. Besides the parish church, the home

---

107   Gilmont J.F., "Le Sommaire des livres du Vieil et Nouveau Testament de Robert Estienne", in Gilmont J.F., *Le livre et ses secrets* (Geneva: 2003) 245–263.

and the workplace were also increasingly becoming places for prayer, worship, religious reading and the exchange of knowledge.

The richness and liveliness of the French religious reading culture of the late fifteenth century did not come to an end during the sixteenth century, but was continued by the Protestants, by non-schismatic evangelical reform movements and even by the Catholic Church. This latter phenomenon of orthodox religious reading in the vernacular has for a long time been overlooked, but texts such as those by Pierre Doré and Nicole Grenier, together with the continuing reprinting and dissemination of late medieval vernacular theologies, reveal that religious reading in the vernacular was by no means a monopoly of the adherents to Lutheranism and Calvinism. Finally, the sharing of texts by readers from the entire confessional spectrum indicates that the dividing line between the categories Catholic and Protestant was not always clearly demarcated. This shows that approaching the religious culture of the late Middle Ages and the early sixteenth century from the perspective of religious reading in the vernaculars results in new information that modifies the traditional perception of early modern religiosity, written from the perspective of institutional history.

Bibliography

Dhotel J.-Cl., *Les origines du catéchisme moderne, d'après les premiers manuels imprimés en France* (Paris: 1967).

Duffy E., The *Stripping of the Altars. Traditional Religion in England, c. 1400–c. 1580* (New Haven: 1992).

Duggan L.G., "The Unresponsiveness of the Late Medieval Church: A Reconsideration", *Sixteenth Century Journal* 9,1 (1978) 3–26.

Georgianna L., "Vernacular Theologies", *English Language Notes* 44 (2006) 87–94.

Gillespie V., "Vernacular Theology", in Strohm P. (ed.), *Middle English* (Oxford: 2007) 401–420.

———, "Chichele's Church: Vernacular Theology in England after Thomas Arundel", in Gillespie V. – Ghosh K. (eds.), *After Arundel: Religious Writing in Fifteenth-Century England* (Turnhout: 2012) 3–42.

Hamm B., *Religiosität im späten Mittelalter: Spannungspole, Neuaufbrüche, Normierungen* (Tübingen: 2011).

Hasenohr G., "La vie quotidienne de la femme vue par l'Église: l'enseignement des "journées chrétiennes" de la fin du Moyen Age", in Brauneder W. (ed.), *Frau und spätmittelalterlicher Alltag* (Vienna: 1986) 19–101.

————, "Aperçu sur la diffusion et la réception de la littérature de spiritualité en langue française au dernier siècle du Moyen Âge", in Wolf N.R. (ed.), *Wissensorganisierende und wissensvermittelnde Literatur im Mittalalter* (Wiesbaden: 1987) 57–90.

————, "La littérature religieuse", in Poirion D. (ed.), *Grundriss der Romanischen Litteraturen des Mittelalters*, vol. VIII/1: *La littérature française aux XIVᵉ et XVᵉ siècles* (Heidelberg: 1988) 266–305.

————, "Religious Reading Amongst the Laity in France in the Fifteenth Century", in Biller P. – Hudson A. (eds.), *Heresy and Literacy, 1000–1530* (Cambridge: 1994) 205–221.

————, "Les prologues des textes de dévotion en langue française (XIIIᵉ–XVᵉ siècles): formes et fonctions", in Hamesse J. (ed.), *Les prologues médiévaux* (Turnhout: 2000) 593–638.

Hauser H., "Petits livres du XVIᵉ siècle", in Hauser H., *Études sur la Réforme française* (Paris: 1909) 253–298.

Higman, F., "Premières réponses catholiques aux écrits de la Réforme en France, 1525–c. 1540", in Higman F., *Lire et découvrir. La circulation des idées au temps de la Réforme* (Geneva: 1998; first published in 1988) 497–514.

Higman F., "Theology for the Layman in the French Reformation", *The Library: A Magazine of Bibliography and Literature, Sixth Series* 9 (1987) 105–127.

Imbart de la Tour P., *Les origines de la Réforme*, 4 vols. (Paris: 1905–1935).

Maag K., "Education and works of religious instruction in French", in Pettegree A. – Nelles P. – Conner Ph. (eds.), *The Sixteenth-Century French Religious Book* (Aldershot: 2001) 96–109.

Pettegree, A. – Hall M., "The Reformation and the Book. A Reconsideration", in Pettegree A., *The French Book and the European Book World* (Leiden: 2007) 221–249.

Racaut L., *Hatred in Print: Catholic Propaganda and Protestant Identity during the French Wars of Religion* (Aldershot: 2002).

————, "Nicolas Chesneau, Catholic Printer in Paris during the French Wars of Religion, 1558–1584", *Historical Journal* 52 (2009) 23–41.

————, "Education of the Laity and Advocacy of Violence in Print during the French Wars of Religion", *History* 95 (2010) 159–177.

Racaut L. – Ryrie A. (eds.), *Moderate voices in the European Reformation* (Aldershot: 2005).

Reinburg V., "Books of Hours", in Pettegree A. – Nelles P. – Conner Ph. (eds.), *The Sixteenth-Century French Religious Book* (Aldershot: 2001) 68–82.

————, *French Books of Hours. Making an Archive of Prayer, c. 1400–1600* (Cambridge: 2012).

Salter E., "The dayes moralized: Reconstructing devotional Reading (1450–1560)", in Lutton R. – Salter E. (eds.), *Pieties in Transition: Religious Practices and Experiences, c. 1400–1640* (Aldershot: 2005) 145–162.

Schreiner K., "Laienfrömmigkeit – Frömmigkeit von Eliten oder Frömmigkeit des Volkes? Zur Sozialen Verfasstheit laikaler Frömmigkeitspraxis im späten Mittelalter", in Schreiner K. – Müller-Luckner E. (eds.), *Laienfrömmigkeit in sozialen und politischen Zusammenhängen des Späten Mittelalters* (Munich: 1992) 1–78.

Swanson R.N., "The Pre-Reformation Church", in Pettegree A., ed., *The Reformation World* (London: 2000) 9–30.

Van Engen J., "Multiple Options: The World of the Fifteenth-Century Church", *Church History* 77,2 (2008) 257–284.

Vénard M., "Réforme, Réformation, Préréforme, Contreréforme . . . Étude de vocabulaire chez les historiens récents de langue française", in Joutard P. (ed.), *Historiographie de la Réforme* (Paris: 1977) 352–365.

Wanegffelen Th., *Ni Rome ni Genève. Des fidèles entre deux chaires en France au XVIe siècle* (Paris: 1997).

CHAPTER 6

Books, Beads and Bitterness: Making Sense of Gifts in Two Table Plays by Cornelis Everaert

Bart Ramakers

Like all other authors in their time, historical playwrights were readers. They did not compose their plays *ex nihilo*, but were inspired by, and made use of, what they had read or what had been read to them, and by what they had seen or otherwise perceived. Then, like now, being literate entailed more than just being able to read and write. Literacy also meant the ability to understand other forms of communication, including visual and body language—and, for that matter, drama. It was especially the practice of this genre that required authors not only to read and write, but also to speak, to listen and to see, with which is meant not just the ability to use the senses *per se*, but to use them coherently, for whatever purpose, intellectual or otherwise. Of course, the same applies to viewers or spectators. They, too, had to be literate in all the aforementioned ways.

The definition of literacy as a composite activity has led scholars in modern literacy studies to speak of 'performative literacy', by which they mean a set of reading practices through which readers can grow in knowledge and literacy.[1] These practices or actions include, among others, a capacity for sustained attention while reading, the willingness to read and reread repeatedly, and the ability to argue for a particular reading of a text, but at the same time be open to an alternative one.[2] Being literate in this sense means one treats reading, like writing, as a process of textual construction, whereby the meaning process may eventually be visualized through writing.[3]

This concept of performative literacy is much akin to that of 'performative reading', a term used to describe historical, especially medieval, reading practices.[4] It can be defined as a way of reading that invites an active process of

---

1 Blau S., "Performative Literacy: The Habits of Mind of Highly Literate Readers", *Voices from the Middle* 10 (2003) 18–21.

2 Blau, "Performative Literacy" 19–21.

3 Blau, "Performative Literacy" 21.

4 Brantley J., *Reading in the Wilderness. Private Devotion and Public Performance in Late Medieval England* (Chicago & London: 2007) 1–6, 14–16; Gertzman E., "Introduction: the spectrum of

reenactment,[5] the result of which is not only the constitution of meaning, but also the affirmation of individual and cultural values.[6] Studying performative reading is not as much about the meaning of the text as it is about the reader's response to a combination of text and images, and in addition to rubrics and layout (mise-en-page).[7] This response, often intended and explicitly required by the text, can be very active and practical, especially where devotional texts are concerned.

A third term, recently developed in medieval theatre studies and informed by cognitive theory, is that of 'performance literacy'.[8] The word 'literacy' here does not refer so much to reading, but to seeing, the term denoting a strategy of seeing whereby laypeople derive devotional meaning from their encounter with an image's material presence. They are able, or they learn or are taught to be able (hence the word 'literacy') to engage, on a regular basis, with their bodies (hence the word 'performance') in rituals or devotional practices vis-à-vis images (statues as well as paintings and prints) that reflect, assume and activate that same corporeality, because they are (representations of) bodies themselves—of Christ, of Mary or of some saint. It is supposed that historical drama stimulated this particular kind of literacy by providing models for these encounters.[9]

Aim and Set-up

This paper aims to illustrate all three types of reading or literacy with plays by Cornelis Everaert (d. 1556), a member and possibly the principal poet—*factor*—of the chambers of rhetoric The Holy Ghost and The Three Saints from Bruges. Everaert earned a living as a fuller and dyer, but also acted as a clerk of the Bruges drapers' guild and of the city's archers' guild of St Sebastian. He is the author of a substantial body of work for the stage (35 plays in all), written and performed in the first three decades of the sixteenth century, handed

---

performances", in Gertsman E. (ed.), *Visualizing Medieval Performance. Perspectives, Histories, Contexts* (Aldershot – Burlington, VT: 2008) 1–13; Sheingorn P., "Performing the illustrated manuscript: great reckonings in little books", in Gertsman, *Visualizing*, 57–82, here 57–58.

5 Gertsman, "Introduction" 1.

6 Gertsman, "Introduction" 2.

7 Gertsman, "Introduction" 4.

8 Stevenson J., *Performance, Cognitive Theory, and Devotional Culture. Sensual Piety in Late Medieval York* (New York: 2010) 9, 41–43, passim. Also see Brantley, *Reading* 7–8.

9 Stevenson, *Performance* 2, 12, 15–16, 24, passim. On this subject also see Newman B., "What Did It Mean to Say 'I Saw'?", *Speculum* 80 (2005), 1–43, here 16.

down in a carefully written manuscript, now in the Royal Library of Belgium in Brussels.[10] Although a minority of his plays are on comical, political, dynastical and socio-critical subject matters, his dramatic oeuvre mainly consists of religious plays.[11] This concerns plays that are attached to, and are predominantly written for, the observation of central devotions, or address religious life more or less directly: a Biblical play, a miracle play, a morality play, five so-called *comparaties* ('comparations' or 'comparisons')[12] and seven so-called *tafelspelen* ('table plays').[13] The latter are short allegorical plays performed indoors, during a banquet. Table plays were often called 'present plays', because they were geared towards and culminated in the presentation of a gift to the person or persons in whose honour the banquet was given. That might be a newlywed couple, but also, as is the case with Everaert's plays, a newly ordained priest, a Franciscan tertiary celebrating his fiftieth jubilee of religious life, or the newly installed king of a trade or militia guild. Everaert wrote five table plays on the occasion of such installations, which took place during these guilds' annual feasts, usually the feast days of their patron saints. The guilds involved were the already mentioned guild of St George, the Bruges milliners' guild and the chamber of rhetoric The Holy Ghost itself.[14]

---

10   For an edition of Everaert's plays according to the Brussels manuscript as well as the most recent biographical and bibliographical information on the author, see Hüsken W.M.H. (ed.), *De Spelen van Cornelis Everaert*, 2 vols. (Hilversum: 2005). Further information on the plays in Hüsken W., "Cornelis Everaert and the community of late medieval Bruges", in Hindley A. (ed.), *Drama and Community. People and Plays in Medieval Europe*, Medieval Texts and Cultures of Northern Europe 1 (Turnhout: 1999) 110–125.

11   For a discussion of those plays written on political and dynastical events, see Mareel S., *Voor vorst en stad. Rederijkersliteratuur en vorstenfeest in Vlaanderen en Brabant (1432–1561)* (Amsterdam: 2010).

12   Ramakers B., "Discerning Vision. Cognitive Strategies in Cornelis Everaert's *Mary Compared to the Light* (c. 1511)", in Melion W.S. – Wandel L.P. (eds.), *Image Theory and Incarnation Doctrine*, Intersections: Interdisciplinary Studies in Early Modern Culture (Leiden – Boston: 2015) (forthcoming).

13   On the genre generally, see Pikhaus P., *Het tafelspel bij de rederijkers*, 2 vols. (Ghent: 1988). The eight table plays are numbered 1B15, 1B24, 1B26, 1B27, 1B29, 1B31, 1B32, and 1B34 in Hummelen W.M.H., *Repertorium van het rederijkerdrama 1500–ca. 1620* (Assen: 1968). Also see Pikhaus, *Tafelspel* 39–40. For editions of these plays, see Hüsken, *Spelen* I, no. XIV; II, nos. XXIII, XXV, XXVI, XXVIII, XXX, XXXI, XXXIII. As a matter of fact, according to Hüsken, one play is not a real table play. Hüsken W., "De gelegenheidsdichter Cornelis Everaert en zijn tafelspelen in enge en ruimere zin", *Verslagen en Mededelingen van de Koninklijke Academie voor Nederlandse Taal- en Letterkunde* (1992) 62–78, here 73.

14   Two of the guilds for which he wrote table plays are not identified in the text of the plays.

It is especially in his *comparaties* that Everaert's erudition is revealed in full glory, because in them he demonstrates a wealth of knowledge of the physical (both natural and man-made) and metaphysical realms—knowledge he must have at least partly acquired through reading.[15] Here, however, we will deal with two of his table plays. These lead us to the heart of late medieval lay piety, that is to the devotion to Christ and Mary, two devotions which, of course, were strongly intertwined, and moreover were embedded in local Bruges observances. Like in so many other cities, public veneration of both Mother and Son manifested itself almost on a daily basis. Bruges knew a special veneration of the Passion of Christ through the relic of the Holy Blood.[16]

The plays in question demonstrate Everaert's performative literacy, in the sense that they were clearly informed by his reading experience of devotional treatises and by his ability to visualize this experience through writing, in this case through the composition of these two plays. The treatises involved called for a performative reading, which, as previously stated, is to say that they invited an active process of reenactment. Finally, the plays stimulated the audience's performance literacy, in the sense that they demonstrated how to encounter and deal with an object's (or image's) material actuality, *in casu* dealing with the gift that was presented.

Making sense of these gifts in an intellectual manner of course implied the active use on behalf of the audience of the senses of sight and hearing, so elementary to the understanding of drama in general. But in the case of these particular plays the senses of smell, taste and touch were referred to as well. Not that the banqueters were asked to actually smell, taste and touch the objects revealed and presented in the course of the action, but explicit reference is made to their sensual characteristics, which the spectators knew about through either reading or experience, or both. What we are dealing with in Everaert's table plays is what Elizabeth Williamson succinctly circumscribes as 'properties in action' or 'the materials of performance'.[17] In daily life the use of these material objects, some devotional in nature, was closely intertwined with the—sometimes systematic—reading of devotional texts, including

---

15   Ramakers, "Discerning Vision".

16   Brown A., *Civic Ceremony and Religion in Medieval Bruges c. 1300–1520* (Cambridge: 2011) passim. On manifestations of the city's Marian devotion, see Strohm R., *Music in Late Medieval Bruges* (Oxford: 1990) passim.

17   Williamson E., "Mere Properties. The Materiality of Religious Objects", in Williamson E. (ed.), *The Materiality of Religion in Early Modern English Drama* (Farnham – Burlington, VT: 2009) 1–32, here 23, 27.

prayer and contemplation.[18] Not only was this reading performative in character, it also was informed by performative and performance literacy in the aforementioned meanings. In their descriptive and explanatory technique, the plays clearly build on the audience's devotional reading experiences. It is even possible that in the case of one play an actual book or booklet was presented, and thus functioned as property in action or as material in performance.

A Rosary

In the first play, called *Een Tafelspeilken up een Hoedeken van Marye* (A Table Play on the Chaplet of Mary),[19] the gift is a rosary, which in the course of the play is handed to the newly installed king of the Bruges milliners' guild. Probably the play was performed during the guild's 1531 Epiphany banquet.[20] According to a stage direction, the rosary was contained in 'a small case or casket' ('een cleen cofferkin ofte forchierkin'; after v. 195). According to that same stage direction the rosary itself consisted of either coral or amber beads.[21] In dealing with this play and the way it was perceived, it is necessary to stress that the meaning of the rosary was not in the object as such, but in the context; that is, in the performance of the act of praying and meditation that the use

---

18   On these objects as material expressions of religion, see Keenan W.J.F. – Arweck E., "Introduction: Material Varieties of Religious Expression", in Arweck E. – Keenan W.J.F. (eds.), *Materializing Religion. Expression, Performance and Ritual* (Farnham – Burlington, VT: 2006) 1–20.

19   Hüsken, *Spelen* II, 785–802, no. XXV. Everaert wrote another play on the rosary, *Tspel van Maria Hoedeken*; Hüsken, *Spelen* I, 74–126, no. I. Also see on this play Hüsken W., " 'Van Incommen en begheert men Scat noch Goet': Cornelis Everaert and the Rosary", in Gosman M. – Walthaus R. (eds.), *European Theatre 1470–1600. Traditions and Transformations*, Mediaevalia Groningana 18 (Groningen: 1996) 119–129, here 122–123 (on devotion to the rosary in Bruges).

20   Hüsken, *Spelen* II, 787; Dumolyn J. – Haemers J., " 'Let each man carry on with his trade and remain silent'. Middle-class ideology in the urban literature of the late medieval Low Countries", *Cultural and Social History* 10 (2013) 169–189, here 175.

21   About the materials of the beads and their characteristics, see Ritz G., "Der Rosenkranz", in *500 Jahre Rosenkranz* (Cologne: 1975) 51–101, here 74, 88, 100; Kramer B., "Verbondenheid verbeeld. Over de uitbeelding van een rozenkranssnoer op een schilderij van de Meester van Sint-Goedele", *Ons Geestelijk Erf* 82 (2011) 136–159, here 153–156; King R., " 'The Beads with Which We Pray Are Made from It': Devotional Ambers in Early Modern Italy", in De Boer W. – Göttler C. (eds.), *Religion and the Senses in Early Modern Europe*, Intersections: Interdisciplinary Studies in Early Modern Culture 26 (2012) (Leiden – Boston: 2013) 153–175, here 168–174 (on the tactile and olfactory characteristics of amber).

of the rosary implied. During the late Middle Ages, and still in the sixteenth century, praying the rosary meant more than just reading—aloud, murmuring or silent—Hail Marys and Our Fathers, or the Latin versions of these prayers. It also involved the meditation through visualization of scenes from the life of Mary and Christ. The cult of the rosary was instituted to supplement the public celebration of Mass and the observance of the Hours. Rosary confraternities stimulated lay association and private devotion in its honour.

The rosary itself became the instrument or practical attribute that helped the individual believer to perform a series of mental, particularly imaginative operations that were learned and became more or less embodied through the reading of a variety of treatises, many of them illustrated. They started to appear in the late decades of the fifteenth century and continued to be printed in the sixteenth.[22] This period could be considered the heyday of the rosary.[23] Sales went up after several popes granted indulgences for saying the prayer.[24] They became popular gifts, too, with many people owning more than one.[25] The partly overlapping scenes from the life of Mary and Christ were divided over the five decades or series of ten beads a normal rosary consisted of. So every decade was devoted to another scene to be meditated upon during the prayer of ten Hail Marys. Sometimes additional prayers referring to that particular scene were said after each decade.

The praying of a full rosary involved fifteen decades; that is, three times the length of a normal prayer bead. Consequently fifteen scenes were contemplated during the praying of a full cycle.[26] This number links the rosary to another devotion, namely the joys and sorrows of Mary, usually divided into a series of seven or fifteen uplifting or agonizing moments of her life.[27] This devotion, too, was stimulated by booklets describing and depicting the scenes involved, providing texts for prayer and meditation. The sorrows of Mary involved many scenes from the Passion,[28] among them the seven blood-sheddings, the moments in Christ's life when blood had dripped from his body—the topic of another of Everaert's table plays, to be discussed in a moment.

---

22   Winston-Allen A., *Stories of the Rose. The Making of the Rosary in the Middle Ages* (University Park, PA: 1997) 25–26.

23   Ritz, "Der Rosenkranz" 94.

24   Winston-Allen, *Stories of the Rose* 28, 140.

25   Ritz, "Der Rosenkranz" 94–95.

26   Ritz, "Der Rosenkranz" 65.

27   Schuler C.M., "The Seven Sorrows of the Virgin: Popular Culture and the Cultic Imagery in Pre-Reformation Europe, *Simiolus* 21 (1992) 5–29, here 18, 23–24.

28   Schulten W., "Das Rosenkranzgebet", in *500 Jahre Rosenkranz* (Cologne: 1975) 122–127, here 122; Kramer "Verbondenheid verbeeld" 146–153.

More than just the instrument or practical attribute of the prayer to and meditation on the lives and sufferings of Mary and Christ,[29] depictions of the rosary in paintings and prints became the graphic symbol or sign for the actual performance of these prayers and meditations. So, when we see a lay donor in an altarpiece or a layman or laywoman in a single portrait holding a rosary, we may assume the portrayed person to be praying—again aloud, murmuring or silently—and to have scenes from the Passion before their real eye, as in the case of an altarpiece,[30] or before their mind's eye, as in the case of a single portrait. Especially these individual portraits—showing well-to-do city-dwellers in three-quarter view, who are looking or staring into the distance while inconspicuously handling a rosary, hardly noticeable between their fingers,[31] and half disappearing behind the lower picture frame—suggest they have Mary and Christ on their mind. It is particularly in male portraits that we discern not only a unostentatious use of rosaries, but rosaries that are themselves unostentatious. One sixteenth-century portrait from the Low Countries, a copy after Jan Cornelisz. Vermeyen (c. 1504–1559), dated 1545, may serve as an example [Fig. 6.1]. Vermeyen and his contemporaries portrayed many well-to-do city dwellers, who, although presented as men of the world, through rosaries demonstrated their religiosity. The specimens involved always concern simple, short loops with relatively large beads, or linear strings, counting a limited number of beads, maybe even one-decade specimens, so-called tenners. These were favoured by men.[32] They might not even have a cross at the end, only a tassel, such as the one carried by the sitter in the aforementioned portrait or hanging on the wall at the back of *The Arnolfini Portrait* by Jan van Eyck [Fig. 6.2]. This unostentatiousness, as regards both the object and its handling, suggests that these men were praying and meditating while going about their daily affairs.

It is important to mention that in Everaert's play the gift is not shown and presented until two-thirds into the dialogue—that is after two hundred of a total of three hundred lines. Before that, the kind and value of the gift is only hinted at, whereby the case or casket is shown, certainly, but its lid is kept closed.

---

29   Schulten, "Das Rosenkranzgebet" 124; Winston-Allen, *Stories of the Rose* 16, 26.

30   See for a discussion of such altarpieces and other devotional images, Kramer, "Verbondenheid verbeeld" 137–144. On image and sensory experience in general, see Harbison C., "Visions and Meditations in Early Flemish Painting", *Simiolus* 15 (1985) 87–118; Williamson B., "Sensory Experience in Medieval Devotion", *Speculum* 88 (2013) 1–43.

31   Ritz, "Der Rosenkranz" 91.

32   Ritz, "Der Rosenkranz" 65, 69, 72; Winston-Allen, *Stories of the Rose* 112; Kramer, "Verbondenheid verbeeld" 153; King, "The Beads" 160.

FIGURE 6.1   *Copy after Jan Cornelisz. Vermeyen,* Portrait of a Man with a Rosary *(1545). Oil on*
wood, 50.8 × 41.3 cm. New York, The Metropolitan Museum of Art, The Jack and
Belle Linsky Collection, 1982. Image © The Metropolitan Museum of Art.

The character that holds it is called Reason (Redene). According to a stage
direction she is dressed like 'an eminent lady' ('een houde matroone'; after v.
56). Two characters appear at her side: Sensuality (Zinnelicheyt), meaning the
senses, and Willpower (Wille). The sex of the first is not indicated, but it is

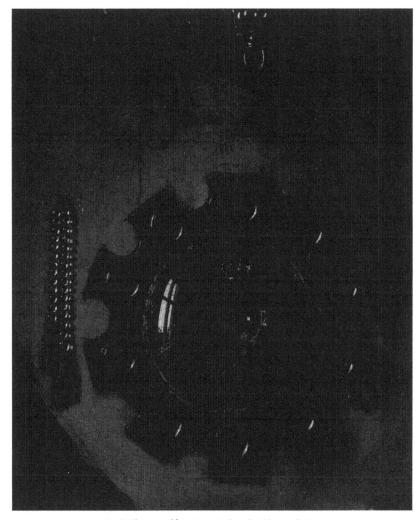

FIGURE 6.2 *Jan van Eyck,* The Arnolfini Portrait *(1434). Oil on oak, 82.2 × 60 cm.*
London, The National Gallery. Detail of mirror and rosary. Image
© The National Gallery.

probably a man. The second is referred to as female.[33] Table plays are not only
short, they count no more than two or three characters on average. The latter
two enter the playing area first, one shortly after the other, the playing area
being the hall where the company meets, before or between the dinner tables.

_____

33   Below v. 8.

They, too, carry gifts for the king. These are—appropriately—two hats, again with allegorical names. One hat is called Temporary Novelty (Tydelicke Nyeuwicheyt), the other Anticipative Discretion (Voorsieneghe Disscrecie). Temporary Novelty is Sensuality's gift, while Anticipative Discretion comes from Willpower. The choice of a rosary as a gift is appropriate as well, for the Middle Dutch word for chaplet, *hoedeken*, literally means 'little hat'. The modern Dutch word *hoedje* may still refer to the coronet, crown or garland of roses by which the rosary is allegorically described and represented.[34] Additionally the rosary that Reason eventually presents to the king has a symbolic name: Fiery Devotion (Vierighe Devocie).

Through the application of allegorical characters and objects, body and matter are charged with symbolic meaning, or, conversely: through the acts these characters perform with these objects they enable the unseen or unperceivable to become accessible to the audience, to be experienced, understood and remembered by them. However sober its dramaturgy, however light-footed and comic at times the language of its characters, and however straightforward the message it wants to convey, still the play is quite sophisticated in the way it represents the mental operations involved in living a virtuous life. The three characters represent three parts of the soul: reason, willpower and sensuous appetite. These parts sometimes clash, as they more or less do in this play, be it in the light and playful manner appropriate to the festive occasion. A person may crave or have an appetite for something—Sensuality speaks of herself and is described by Willpower as being prone to the sins of the eyes—yet resist that craving with willpower.[35] A justly acting soul requires the highest part, reason, to control the lowest part, appetite, with the help of willpower. All three are presented in this play as indispensable for the good acts of man, in this case the good functioning of the king of the milliners' guild, who, as we are about to see, is a man of the world—such as the man in the portrait after Vermeyen [Fig. 6.1]. Reason is the last to enter the playing area and more or less settles the dispute between Sensuality and Willpower about the need for the senses to be curbed. Her opening line actually entails a popular saying: 'Reason serves all play' ('Redene tot allen spele dient'; v. 57). In other words, man should act with discretion in all circumstances.[36]

---

34   Ritz, "Der Rosenkranz" 57. Also see Winston-Allen, *Stories of the Rose* 15.

35   Vv. 47–54.

36   Vv. 93–110.

Hats

The gifts—the hats—through their name and content reflect the relation-ship between the characters that present them. Temporary Novelty forms the basis for trade and prosperity, according to the text. The millinery industry, like any other trade, is reigned by fashion. For what else does fashion mean than 'temporary novelty', desired by man through the senses? He who cre-ates such temporary novelty (and for that purpose one has to use the senses, and thus be sensual) will be assured mercantile success. With that message Sensuality hands his hat to the king. Next, Willpower's gift has a mitigating effect on that of Sensuality. After all, it is the task of willpower to direct and control the senses. The two of them express their mutual relationship explic-itly: Willpower describes Sensuality as someone whose conduct is determined by outward appearances, who is driven by curiosity, has a craving for enjoy-ment and is prone to envy.[37] Sensuality retorts that it is the will—the free will, of course—that stimulates man to either an unbridled or a cautious use of his senses.[38] Willpower's gift exemplifies this controlling function: Anticipative Discretion is the ability to avoid adversity, mitigate suffering and increase patience—truly a fine quality in a real king.[39] A tradesman, too, may benefit from it: it reduces losses and increases profits. In physical terms the hat may protect him from wind, rain and sun—an indispensable piece of clothing for a travelling businessman, one would think. Before presenting him with the hat, Willpower allows Sensuality to put it on. That, according to the text, the latter either does wrong, or the hat does not fit or suit him. In either case it is clear that sensuality and discretion are difficult to reconcile. At the end of the verbal exchange this second gift is presented to the guild's king as well. It should liter-ally cover his will, Reason concludes.

In order to impress the allegorical meaning of both hats on the audience, their names, particularly the central nouns *nyeuwicheyt* ('novelty') and *diss-crecie* ('discretion'), are repeated over and over again. The same happens in the part of the play—much longer than the previous ones—devoted to the gift by Reason; that is, the rosary called Fiery Devotion. As soon as she has revealed its name, she starts repeating it, both the whole name, the word *devocie* ('devo-tion'), and the word *hoedeken*, thus clearly establishing the link among the object and its use, which must have immediately or gradually triggered the

---

37   Vv. 19–42.
38   Vv. 43–56.
39   Vv. 111–165.

correct identification of the 'little hat' among the audience, an identification Sensuality and Willpower fail to make—a clear example of dramatic irony.

This 'little hat', thus Reason starts her enigmatic explanation, is sweet, virtuous and valuable, hinting, of course, at the spiritual meaning of the expressions used.[40] Its virtuousness can hardly be described. It leads Willpower to suppose that it is produced abroad, and Sensuality to guess that it contains precious stones. Both are wrong, according to Reason. In that case, Willpower retorts, it cannot be a hat that one can wear on his head or carry in his hand or on his belt. But indeed one can, says Reason. If he is talking about a real hat that is neither foreign nor beset with jewels, how, then, can it be more valuable than the one presented by Willpower, Sensuality wants to know. Because, says Reason, its value lies in its virtue. When carried inside—in the heart—it has the power to cast away all foes. When Reason then refers to his present as a *hoedekin van minnen* ('little hat of love'; v. 190), Willpower suspects he means a garland of flowers, of roses or daisies, such as a lover would present to his beloved; a token, that is, of worldly instead of spiritual love, thus unknowingly getting closer to the truth.

When Reason brings out the casket but still does not open it, Sensuality in particular reveals his surprise: such a small box cannot contain a real hat! Reason continues to describe the gift: it is worthier of praise than anything in the world. Then it must be embedded with gems and pearls, Sensuality proposes. Willpower says to Reason: you speak in *parabelen* ('parables'; v. 208) and tries to get closer to the truth by asking who manufactured the chaplet. Its religious meaning now gradually emerges. It was made, says Reason, by a powerful king (he means God or Christ) who sent it to a particular maiden (Mary, of course) out of love. Sensuality now threatens to become angry if Reason does not immediately disclose the name of his gift. Reason gives in: it is called Fiery Devotion,[41] the kind of devotion that every king, like every human being, should show to God. Through its name the rosary is explicitly linked to its spiritual use, that is, fiery devotion. Willpower asks what kind of hat that is. Reason's answers become even more cryptic now: in honour of the maiden who received this hat, he says, we should present to her that same hat (he means the prayer), which was created by her fiery devotion. Sensuality can no longer wait and demands to see it, to let it be shown. Then Reason opens the casket and shows its content: this precious jewel, she says, worth more than any hat, brought from heaven.

Willpower finally mentions its real name, its source and destination, its maker, bringer and receiver: Mary's hat, brought from heaven to Nazareth as

---

40   Vv. 166–169.

41   V. 216.

a salutation from the Trinity. The three of them extemporize on the rosary's spiritual meaning, most poignantly described by Reason as a hat to be worn internally, in one's memory, with fiery devotion. Then he presents the casket with the rosary to the king, calling it a diadem stemming from fiery devotion, which makes the soul glorious before God's eyes. He should praise Mary with it every day. There is no sweeter devotion than to 'read' this hat. Reason sets up the conclusion by calling upon the king to keep and preserve all three presents internally, after which all three characters repeat their own names, those of their gifts and their meaning for him who receives them.[42]

Platter, Spices and Comfit

The second table play to be discussed is the *Play on the Seven Blood-Sheddings* (*Esbatement van de Zeven Bloetsturtinghen*),[43] also dated 1530, written for the installation of the king of an unknown Bruges guild.[44] It is about as long as the previous one: a little over 300 lines. In this play, however, the gift is already revealed—actually, it is being carried into the assembly room—after only 73 lines. The remaining text is used to interpret its meaning. That is done by two characters: a man, Joyous Will (Blyden Wille), and a woman, Happy Deed (Jonsteghe Daet).[45] The complexity of this table play lies not in the relation between the concepts indicated by their names. They are alluded to by the characters in a straightforward manner: the will precedes the deed, and one cannot work without the other.[46] Only towards the end of the play are their names loosely associated with the presented gifts, in the sense that these names add to the gifts' potential and actual effects.

What these gifts are seems evident at first but becomes more complicated once the two characters start to describe them. They play a role in a multi-layered exposition of the meaning of Christ's blood-sheddings. The following moments from his life and suffering are mentioned: the circumcision, the sweating of blood in the Garden of Gethsemane, the flagellation, the coronation with thorns, the ripping off of his clothes, thus tearing open his wounds, the stretching of his body on the cross and the following crucifixion and, finally, the piercing of his side by Longinus. This devotional topic, too, must

---

42   Vv. 270–296.

43   Hüsken, *Spelen* II, 852–871, no. XXVIII.

44   V. 66.

45   Cf. the exchange in vv. 44–48.

46   Vv. 1–42.

have been informed by Everaert's religious reading and must have appealed to his audience.

One of the gifts is identified by Joyous Will as a platter or dish, probably in majolica, the edge of which is decorated with what he describes as *vaenkens ofte bannyeren* ('flags or banners'; v. 76). He is likely referring to a pattern of triangle-shaped banners, as can be seen on a dish in the Robert Lehman Collection in The Metropolitan Museum of Art [Fig. 6.3]. Initially, though, it seems that the decorated platter is not the gift, but rather a collection of seven exotic spices, contained in pots or jars: namely zedoary, ginger, pepper, spikenard, cinnamon, clove and cardamom. As in the previous play, their meaning or value is explained predominantly in medicinal terms, and is connected directly to the receiver, the king of the guild. He is someone who, as Happy Deed explains, regularly travels to faraway places.[47] The spices, says Joyous Will, will strengthen his body, comfort his soul and protect him from pain.[48] In the Middle Ages, 'spices were luxurious, exotic, foreign, and expensive'.[49] They could only be imported at considerable cost and became items of conspicuous consumption, which the well-to-do liked to use in various dishes.[50] Their high price and distant origin—close to Paradise; some even, such as spikenard, were mentioned in the Bible—enhanced their reputation in both medicine and religion, and this depended for a great deal on their flavour and aromatic characteristics.[51]

Instead of starting to name and explain the meaning of each of the spices, Happy Deed begins by mentioning the Sweet Name of Jesus,[52] a popular late medieval devotion,[53] more or less presenting the name as the first spice because of its sweetness. Although nothing in the text indicates this, it seems likely that he simultaneously points at what may have been an IHS monogram

---

47   V. 85

48   Vv. 89–90, 92–94.

49   Freedman P., *Out of the East. Spices and the Medieval Imagination* (New Haven – London: 2008) 39. Also see Winter J.M. van, *Spices and Comfits. Collected Papers on Medieval Food* (Blackawton, Totnes: 2007) 94, 131, 141.

50   Freedman, *Out of the East* 6, 19–24, 42. On the concept of conspicuous consumption generally, see Veblen T., *The theory of the leisure class. An economic study of institutions* (New York: 1961 [1934]).

51   Freedman, *Out of the East* 13–18, 52–55, 76–78, 81–82. On the spiritual meanings of fragrances and flavours, also see Falkenburg R.L., *The Fruit of Devotion. Mysticism and the imagery of love in Flemish paintings of the Virgin and Child, 1450–1550* (Amsterdam – Philadelphia: 1994) passim.

52   V. 95. It is again referred to towards the end of the play (v. 305).

53   For its establishment in England, see Pfaff R.W., *New Liturgical Feasts in Later Medieval England* (Oxford: 1970) 62–83.

FIGURE 6.3   *Disk (c. 1510). Majolica, diameter 43.5 cm. New York, Metropolitan Museum of Art,*
            Robert Lehman Collection, 1975. Image © The Metropolitan Museum of Art.

or other abbreviation of Christ's name and symbol of the devotion to his
Sweet Name, painted on the platter. Many examples of such platters have sur-
vived, such as another dish in the Robert Lehman Collection [Fig. 6.4].[54] Next
Happy Deed mentions seven liquid sweets that dripped from his body, seven

---

54   On depictions of majolica pottery in early Netherlandish painting, including examples
       carrying the IHS monogram, see Jékely Z., "Majolica Jugs in late Medieval Painting", in

FIGURE 6.4 *Dish for a ewer (c. 1530–1540). Majolica, diameter 32.7 cm, New York, The*
Metropolitan Museum of Art, Robert Lehman Collection, 1975. Image © The
Metropolitan Museum of Art.

sweets displeasing to Satan. Then they hint that these are related to the seven
blood-sheddings. They are described as pardon, forgiveness, grace, peace,
concord, remission of sin and the opening of heaven.[55] The sweets refer to
(or are referred to by) what Joyous Will describes as *de zevenderhande tregye*
('the seven layer comfit'; v. 103) consisting of several fruits, nuts and spices:
oranges, pineapple seeds, hazelnuts, ginger, coriander and cinnamon.[56] Being
a dessert,[57] it was probably presented towards the end of the banquet. Like

---

Balla G. – Jékely Z. (eds.), *The Dowry of Beatrice—Italian Majolica Art and the Court of King*
Matthias (Budapest: 2008) 55–66.

55   Vv. 100–102.

56   Fruit was rarely eaten raw, but usually dried or sugared or made into comfits, adding nuts
      and spices. Freedman, *Out of the East* 41. On comfits and their place in medieval cuisine,
      see Van Winter, *Spices and Comfits* 242, 346, 350–352.

57   Van Winter, *Spices and Comfits* 299.

the fluid sweets dripping from Christ's body, they drive out 'de smaecke der bitterheyt ende corruptien' ('the taste of bitterness and corruption'; v. 108).[58] Is it possible that not only the seven spices but also this comfit was presented on the platter with the IHS monogram or a comparable acronym? The analogy between comfit and Christ not only illustrates the application of the metaphor of food consumption to the process of mystical unification,[59] but also says something about the high social value attributed to the particular kind of food involved in the comparison. Being able to afford and eat such fine comfits— fine enough to be compared to the body of Christ—contributed to the guild's prestige and unity,[60] as did gift-giving and, for that matter, banqueting in general.[61] The comfit with its differently-coloured ingredients possibly presented a visual attraction, too, thus adding to the comparison's appeal.[62]

Its sweetness refers to Jesus, says Happy Deed, who is brought to the king 'in figuere' (v. 110), which can mean two things: figuratively, that is by means of figurative speech, or by means of material illustration, using real images, either two-dimensional, in paint or print, or three-dimensional, in the form of living images (tableaux vivants) or plays.[63] It turns out that Joyous Will and Happy Deed do both: they use figurative speech in addition to material illustration, to which they add the pots with exotic spices. It is their intention to compare Christ's seven blood-sheddings with these seven spices. Whereas the latter preserve the body, the former preserve the soul.[64]

---

58 On the spiritual associations of sweet and bitter smells and tastes in relation to consumption, see Falkenburg, *The Fruit of Devotion* 12, 60, 66.

59 Falkenburg, *The Fruit of Devotion* 56–76 (chapter 3).

60 Scholliers P., "Meals, food narratives, and sentiments of belonging in past and present", in Scholliers P. (ed.), *Food, drink and identity. Cooking, eating and drinking in Europe since the Middle Ages* (Oxford & New York: 2001) 3–22, here 10–11; Tomasik T.J. – Vitullo J.M., "At the table. Metaphorical and material cultures of food in medieval and early modern Europe", in Tomasik T.J. – Vitullo J.M. (eds.), *At the table. Metaphorical and material cultures of food in medieval and early modern Europe* (Turnhout: 2007) XI–XX, here XV–XVI.

61 Dumolyn – Haemers, "'Let each man'" 175–176. On gift-exchange in general, see Thoen I., *Strategic Affection? Gift Exchange in Seventeenth-century Holland* (Amsterdam 2007) 18–20.

62 On the sensual aspects of food and their link with Eucharistic devotion, see Bynum C.W., *Holy Feast and Holy Fast. The Religious Significance of Food to Medieval Women* (Berkeley – Los Angeles: 1987) 60.

63 Ehrstine G., "Framing the Passion: mansion staging as visual mnemonic", in Gertsman, *Visualizing Medieval Performance* 263–277, here 63–65. Also see Ehrstine G., "Passion Spectatorship between Private and Public Devotion", in Gertsman E. – Stevenson J. (eds.), *Thresholds of Medieval Visual Culture: Liminal Spaces* (Woodbridge: 2012) 302–320.

64 Vv. 114, 117.

How exactly the sufferings of Christ were presented remains unclear. Joyous Will explicitly says that the comparison 'will appear before the eye' ('voor ooghen mach blycken'; v. 115). Were the scenes painted on the edge of the platter, like on the frame of the convex mirror in *The Arnolfini Portrait* [Fig. 6.2]? Or did the characters show a series of woodcuts to the audience depicting the seven blood-sheddings? Or were these scenes mimed by actors? The last option certainly would have made the staging of this table play a much more ambitious and costlier affair. On closer inspection the blood-shedding must have been visualized in some way. It would be illogical not to materially represent the thing to be compared (the *comparans*) and to only show one of the elements it was being compared with (the *comparandum*). If the spices had been the only visual objects in the comparison, it would have made more sense mnemotechnically to describe them first. Moreover, at the fifth stage of each cluster, when the presenters directly address the king, they sometimes use words that suggest that the sufferings of Christ were indeed not only aurally but also visually perceived. Thus, he is instructed to 'see' ('siet'; vv. 155) or 'notice' ('merct'; v. 181) the actions performed by or directed towards Christ. After the seventh and last cluster he is asked to 'impress them' (prentse'; v. 288) on his heart, and to 'lock' (sluut'; v. 301) Jesus's Passion there, as if it were a treasure vault. Even if the life of Christ was only referred to in words, the performance—due to the broad familiarity of contemporary lay audiences with illustrated descriptions of the joys, sorrows and sufferings of Mary or Christ, varying in number—would have stimulated these scenes to appear before the inner eye of the audience, a process prompted by the systematic set-up of the sevenfold comparison and the fact that at the end of each of them Joyous Will and Happy Deed imperatively call upon the king to take its content at heart, to follow Christ's example and not to fall into the deadly sin associated with the taste or effect of the given spice.

A Print or a Charm

Thus, the play is very much like a devotional treatise acted out on stage. In fact, the figurative demonstration follows a fourfold scheme in which, first, a blood-shedding is presented; which then is connected to a particular spice, its taste (in three cases) and medicinal effect (in six cases); after which this sensual experience is associated with one of the seven cardinal sins; and, finally, with one or more Old Testament characters who committed that sin.[65] Properly

---

65   Vv. 119–288. In the following each blood-shedding is followed by a spice, its taste (if mentioned; otherwise a dash is used) and medicinal effect (if mentioned; otherwise a

speaking, there even is a fifth level of explanation, namely that of the moral admonitions to the king. Whereas the spices are recommended as natural cures against bodily injury, the blood-sheddings are praised as a spiritual remedy or medicine against the temptation of sin.[66] Ultimately the gifts are presented to the king while Joyous Will and Happy Deed pronounce an eight-line rondel.[67] (They also may themselves be the presenters.) Because of the fact that in this rondel the king is explicitly called upon in three repeated lines to receive the blood-sheddings—'Accept [it]' ('Neimpt'; vv. 297, 300, 303)[68]—it is hard to imagine that they were not presented in any material way, as an object of some sort. The first line after the rondel refers to the Name of Jesus again, calling upon the king to receive it in his heart. This way the platter that possibly contained the IHS monogram was included in the gift offering as well.

Two lines down Happy Deed admonishes the king to keep 'this small image' ('dit beildekin'; v. 307) as a memory of those who gave it to him.[69] The word *beildekin* may refer to a devotional print, a broadsheet representing Christ in one or more scenes from the Passion or maybe the IHS monogram, again hinting at the devotion to his Holy Name. During the late fifteenth and early sixteenth centuries these kinds of woodcuts combining devotional images and prayers were in high demand, especially those related to popular devotions such as the rosary and the Holy Name of Jesus.[70] Perhaps the print depicted all seven blood-sheddings. After all, the first of them was seen as the moment of

---

dash is used), a cardinal sin, and the Old Testament characters who committed that sin: 1) *circumcision*: zedoary / bitter / for children with threadworms / lust / Reuben, Amnon, Lot, David, Solomon; 2) *sweating of blood*: ginger / hot and salty / – / gluttony / Haman, Esau, Isaac, Job's children, the Amalekites; 3) *flagellation*: pepper / – / for the healing of wounds / envy / Rachel, Abimelech, Jacob; 4) *crowning with thorns*: spikenard / – / for embalming bodies / pride / Adam, Rehoboam, Sennacherib; 5) *ripping off of clothes*: cinnamon / sweet and dry / medicinal, used in recipes / greed / Achan, Gehazi, Samuel's sons; 6) *crucifixion*: clove / – / invigorating, strengthens the body / sloth / Elijah, Sisera; 7) *piercing of side*: cardamom / – / consumes pain, both inside and outside / wrath / Cain, Miriam, Jezebel, Saul.

66   Vv. 290–292, 294–296.

67   Vv. 297–304.

68   The opening and closing lines of the rondel read: 'Neimpt danckelic, heer conync, te desen termyne / den blyden wille met de jonsteghe daet' ('Accept [it], Lord King, at this very moment / both joyous will and happy deed'; vv. 297–298, 303–304), thus linking the blood-sheddings and probably also the spices to the names of the play's two characters in the sense that both in the blood-sheddings and the spices one may discern the aspect of potential or intention (will) and effect or working (deed).

69   Vv. 307–308.

70   Scribner B., "Popular Piety and Modes of Visual Perception in Late-Medieval and Reformation Germany", *The Journal of Religious History* 15 (1989) 448–469, here 449–456.

his name-giving, Jewish circumcision being the equivalent of Christian baptism. Both Passion and Holy Name were referred to in the preceding lines.[71] Or does 'beildekin' refer to a small three-dimensional representation, a statue or a charm in the form of a cross, a crucifix or a medallion with one of the aforementioned subjects on it? In any case it must have been a portable gift, since the final lines suggest the king should take it with him on his journeys: 'Wherever you travel, in villages, in towns, / keep it with you forever' ('Waer ghy reyst, in doorpen, in steden, / houdet eeuwich by hu'; vv. 310–311).[72] This would mean that he not only received the decorated platter and the set of pots or jars with exotic herbs, but also a small token to carry with or on him, somehow depicting or representing one or more scenes from Christ's life or Passion.

A Book?

Various devotional books printed in the last quarter of the fifteenth and in the first half of the sixteenth centuries linked contemplation of and prayer to the Virgin to the rosary, or at least the saying of Our Fathers and Hail Marys, either in Latin or the vernacular. Prayers to the Passion, especially to the blood-sheddings, as well as short meditations on their content, usually ended with a rubric indicating that one or more Our Fathers and Hail Marys should be said. In many of these booklets—which all had a practically sized octavo format— these prayers or meditations were divided among the days of the week, which in the case of the blood-sheddings stimulated the choice for a cycle of seven, as well as the combination with prayers or meditations on a sequence of events that were closely linked to the blood-sheddings: the seven sorrows of the Virgin. Going by the number of editions and extant copies of some of these titles, they must have been widespread and very popular. A rough survey yields at least nine of them. It seems worthwhile to dwell on their structure and content, in order to illustrate how believers, with their help, could in an almost matter-of-fact manner incorporate devotion to (the sufferings of) both Mary and Christ, a kind of devotion heavily imbued with corporeal and performative elements, into their daily lives. Although many of these titles were originally written for (semi-)religious persons, especially women, since in some we find explicit ref-

---

On the use of such woodcuts generally see Areford D.S., *The Viewer and the Printed Image in Late Medieval Europe* (Farnham – Burlington, VT: 2010).

71 Vv. 301, 305.

72 Also see v. 286: 'dach ende nacht, waer ghy ghaet, vaert of ryt' ('day and night, wherever you walk, sail or ride').

erences to female readership they must have reached laypeople as well. They fit into a tradition of 'shaping and training of the self though some kind of reading', and helped to create 'forms of identity [that] were anchored by an appeal to inner experience'.[73]

One such booklet is *Onser lieuer vrouwen croon* (Our Blessed Lady's Crown). It consists of a series of 23 benedictions of parts of Mary's body, starting with her head and ending with her feet. Each blessing ends with a rubric indicating an Ave Maria.[74] The preface advises the blessings to be read on Saturdays especially and on all Marian feasts, and to pray as many Hail Mary's as one likes, kneeling in private before a statue of the Virgin or before an altar devoted to her.[75] The title of the consulted edition suggests that the work contained two more treatises: *Onser liever vrouwen souter* (Our Blessed Lady's Psalter) and *Onser liever vrouwen mantel* (Our Blessed Lady's Mantle). Apparently, the book's printer, Jan Seversz. from Leiden, used to issue all three in one edition, but this time only included the first.[76] Separate editions of *Onser liever vrouwen souter* appeared as well. This work, falsely attributed to St Bernard of Clairvaux (a great way, for sure, to increase its popularity), consists of 150 meditations on the Virgin, divided over the week, each separated, again, by an Ave Maria.[77] The number of meditations made the book comparable to the real Psalter (hence its name), facilitating its use as a lay alternative to the Liturgy of the Hours, and additionally offering the opportunity to pray three rosaries of fifty Ave Maria's, adding a Pater Noster to each decade.

Moreover, praying the rosary in this manner was called 'our Blessed Lady's psalter' in *Die costelike scat der geesteliker rijckdoem* (The Precious Treasure of Spiritual Richness).[78] It defines a proper rosary as consisting of five decades, a number corresponding to the length of many sets of medieval prayer beads. It contains, among other things, a list of 55 'articles or points' ('articulen oft punten'), topographical locations related to Christi's life and Passion to be precise, where the reader may imaginatively halt and pray (parts of) the

---

73   Bryan J., *Looking Inward. Devotional Reading and the Private Self in Late Medieval England* (Philadelphia: 2008) 5.

74   Leiden, Jan Seversz., after 1513; ex. The Hague, Royal Library, KW 228 G 1 (NK 437).

75   F. A2r.

76   One example of an edition containing all three treatises is: Delft, Christiaen Snellaert, 1490; ex. The Hague, Royal Library, 150 E 18.

77   Leiden, Hugo Jansz. Van Woerden, after 1495; ex. The Hague, Royal Library, KW 227 G 32 [1] (NK 288).

78   Zutphen, Thieman Petersz. Os van Breda, 1518; ex. The Hague, Royal Library, KW 228 G 30 (NK 1806) f. K7v.

rosary.[79] Cross signs in the right margin apparently have the function of reminding the reader to move on to the next bead [Fig. 6.5]. When the sequence arrives at the Road of the Cross, a rubric says that the points (or stations) are described so lively 'as if those [who halt there imaginatively] were present in Jerusalem themselves' ('oft sy toe Jerusalem selven tseghenwoerdich weren').[80] The book is presented as being profitable to 'all Christian people' ('allen Kersten menschen') and includes a description of the origins of the cult of the rosary, referring, among others, to Alanus de Rupe (1428–1475), the cult's fervent advocate and founder of the first confraternity devoted to its propagation.[81] In fact, the book contains the list of regulations of that confraternity as a ready-to-apply model for any new chapter to be established, including a list of indulgences stimulating the praying of the rosary.[82] At the end two other confraternities are mentioned that pray the rosary as part of their devotion: that of the seven sorrows and that of the Sweet Name of Jesus. In the latter's case an indulgenced prayer cycle is defined in which each Pater Noster and Ave Maria should be preceded by a prayer to the Sweet Name of Jesus. Its beginning is marked by a woodcut representing the Virgin and Child with St Anne surrounded by a rosary, with five roses separating the decades [Fig. 6.6].

It was also possible to interweave the praying of the rosary with the contemplation of Christ's sufferings, Mary's seven sorrows partly overlapping with these. Another version of *Onser liever vrouwen souter*, for example, includes a prayer on the rosary consisting of a Pater Noster with ten Ave Marias, each alternating with a short description of a Passion scene.[83] This brings us to late medieval treatises that stimulated devotion to Christ's blood-sheddings. In his introduction to Everaert's play, its editor Wim Hüsken mentions several booklets whose content may have inspired him, or better yet, perhaps: whose content paralleled in print what Everaert tried to achieve on stage.[84] One option is the *Oefeninghen in die seven bloetstortinghen* (Exercises on the Seven Blood-Sheddings) by Godschalc Rosemondt (c. 1480–1526).[85] It links each of Christ's sufferings to a particular day of the week, a cardinal sin, its opposite and a

---

79   F. K1v.

80   F. K4r.

81   F. K8v.

82   *Onser liever vrouwen souter* also includes an indulgence (f. A2r-v).

83   Amsterdam, Doen Pietersz., c. 1520; ex. The Hague, Royal Library, KW 227 G 9 (NK 294) f. H8v–Y4r.

84   Hüsken, *Spelen* II, 852–853.

85   Antwerp, Henrick Eckert van Homberch, 1516; ex. The Hague, Royal Library, KW 229 G 7 (NK 1828).

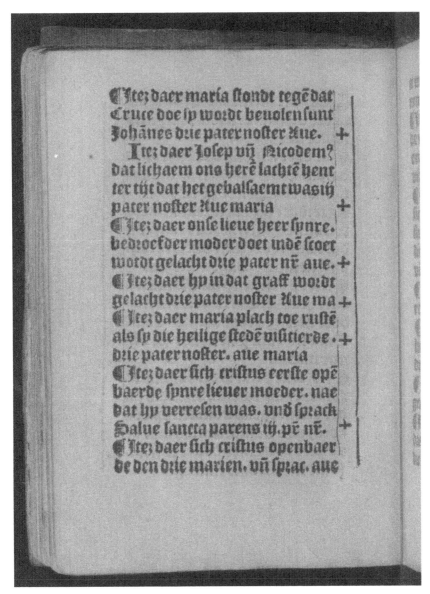

FIGURE 6.5 *Fragment of "The fifty-five articles or points of the Passion".* Die costelike scat
der geesteliker rijckdoem (*Zutphen, Thieman Petersz. Os van Breda: 1518*),
The Hague, Royal Library: KW 228 G 30, f. K5v. Image © ProQuest LLC.

FIGURE 6.6 *"Virgin and Child with St Anne surrounded by a rosary", woodcut illustration*
to Die costelike scat der geesteliker rijckdoem (*Zutphen, Thieman Petersz.*
Os van Breda: 1518). *The Hague, Royal Library: KW 228 G 30, f. M5r. Image*
© *ProQuest LLC.*

summoning to contemplate a particular anagogic element. Thus the fifth sequence connects Thursday to the carrying of the cross, gluttony, temperance and the contemplation of eternal punishment. However, compared to Everaert's play, the circumcision is missing. Instead, the treatise lists the aforementioned carrying of the cross. Moreover, it connects Wednesday to three instances or aspects of the ripping off of Christ's clothes, linking each to a particular form of greed. Finally, references to the days of the week and the virtues are altogether missing in Everaert's play. Another option would be a treatise that also deals with the seven blood-sheddings and does include the circumcision: *Een devote oeffeninge tot eenen Yegelycke choor der engelen* (A Devout Exercise on Each of the Choirs of Angels).[86] However, this booklet does not link Christ's sufferings to any of the cardinal sins. As far as the blood-sheddings are concerned, Everaert might also have drawn inspiration from a treatise on the fifteen blood-sheddings: *Die xv. bloetstortinghen Ons Lieven Heren Jhesu Christi* (The Fifteen Blood-Sheddings of Our Dear Lord Jesus Christ),[87] which consists of a series of prayers to these sufferings interspersed by one Pater Noster and one Ave Maria. All seven blood-sheddings that Evaert mentions are found among the fifteen listed here. All prayers, though, refer to sinning in a general way, and none makes a specific connection between a blood-shedding and a cardinal sin.[88]

Yet what comes closest in approach to Everaert's play is a small treatise whose title does not betray any connection to the seven blood-sheddings at all: *Die figuren vanden seven kercken van Romen* (The Figures of the Seven Churches of Rome).[89] On its first page it says that it concerns a number of prayers said within the confraternity of the Dominican friars of Haarlem, which are each connected with a particular indulgence. It was meant to help its readers gain indulgences by mentally visiting the seven pilgrim churches of Rome. They were stimulated to do so by looking at seven woodcuts, printed on each left page of the open booklet, representing these churches [Fig. 6.7]. Their walls are carved open like stages in order to allow the reader to look inside and meditate on two scenes depicted in each of them. One is related to the church's patron saint, the other is a representation of one of Christ's blood-sheddings.

---

86   Delft, Henric Pietersz. Lettersnijder, 1508–1511; ex. Amsterdam, University Library, OTM: Ned. Inc. 86 (NK 1610).

87   Antwerp, Jan van Ghelen, 1524; The Hague, Royal Library, KW 229 G 23 (NK 425).

88   A comparable list appears in the *Hortulus anime in duytsche* (Garden of the Soul in Dutch), Antwerp, Willem Vorsterman, 1526; The Hague, Royal Library, KW 151 D 26 (NK 4241).

89   Utrecht, J. Berntsz., c. 1526 or earlier; The Hague, Royal Library, KW 228 G 28 (NK 1283).

FIGURE 6.7   *"The Church of St Sebastian", woodcut illustration to* Die figuren
vanden seven kercken van Romen (*Utrecht, J. Berntsz., c. 1526 or earlier*).
The Hague, Royal Library, KW 228 G 28, f. A6v. Image © ProQuest LLC.

On each right page two prayers are printed, one to Christ and one to the patron
saint. Not only does each prayer contain a graphic description—however
short—of each of Christ's sufferings, thus stimulating the devotees' immersion
in his Passion, but they also start with a reference to one of the seven cardinal
sins.[90] The blood-sheddings are mentioned in the same order as in Everaert's

---

90   The woodcuts are similar to those in a treatise with a virtually identical title: *Van die
seven kercken van Romen* (About the Seven Churches of Rome), attributed to Robertus
Coelen, that is, the Benedictine monk Rupert of Deutz (c. 1075–1130); Antwerp, Willem

play, and are connected to almost the same vices. Whereas Everaert connects the flagellation to envy and the piercing of the side to wrath, the treatise does it the other way around.[91] Apart from the printed prayers, readers had to say one of the seven penitential psalms and meditate on one of the Stations of the Cross.[92] They were stimulated to do so by the woodcuts, each of which, apart from a pilgrim church, depicted a Station. As Stations the author chose the seven blood-sheddings. Not being a Station of the Cross, the circumcision was left out.

Conclusion

It seems likely that Everaert's table plays were informed by his reading experience of devotional treatises and by his ability to visualize this experience through writing, in this case through the composition of plays. This seems particularly true in the case of the play on the seven blood-sheddings. The booklets mentioned clearly called for a performative reading. They invited an active process of reenactment through visualization. They certainly incited their readers to action, by saying prayers. Both table plays intended to stimulate their audience's performance literacy, in the sense that they demonstrated how to encounter and deal with a devotional object's (or devotional image's) material actuality, *in casu* with a rosary or a representation—in one form or another—of the Passion of Christ.

Vorsterman, 1521; ex. The Hague, Royal Library, KW 2901 E 25 (NK 3313). This work can be called devotional in the sense that it provides the potential pilgrim to Rome with a description of these churches, a travel guide almost, adding details of indulgences to be gained by visiting them. The description is preceded by a calendar listing all indulgences connected to various stations and locations in Jerusalem, as well as the feasts of various saints. Although this treatise represents the blood-sheddings in an almost identical manner as its near namesake, it does not mention them, nor does it contain prayers and references to the vices.

91   It should be noted that two blood-sheddings are represented in the wrong order. The fourth woodcut (lettered E instead of D) shows the ripping off of clothes (and not the crowning with thorns), whereas the fifth (lettered D instead of E) shows the crowning with thorns (and not the ripping off of clothes). The woodcuts in *Van die seven kercken van Romen* show the blood-sheddings in the correct order: the crowning with thorns first, and then the ripping off of clothes. However, in this series the sweating of blood is shown before the circumcision.

92   On the performative praying of the penitential psalms, see Sutherland A., "Performing the Penitential Psalms in the Middle Ages", in Gargnolati M. – Suerbaum A. (eds.), *Aspects of the Performative in Medieval Culture* (Berlin – New York: 2010) 15–37. On their role in penitential practice, see King'oo C.C., *Miserere Mei. The Penitential Psalms in Late Medieval and Early Modern England* (Notre Dame, IN: 2012) 8–19.

Table plays fit into the sixteenth-century *convivium* tradition, meaning that the content of these plays supposedly became the subject of conversation and deliberation among the audience after the performance had ended. Already during its staging the dinner guests were challenged to get intellectually involved by trying to unravel the identity of the presents and to understand their allegorical meanings and connections. One could say that the dramatic performance constituted a play within a play, the latter being the banquet itself, with the banqueters as actors.[93] The guild's king was the main character in both, as the principal dinner guest probably sitting in the middle of the table and as addressee of the play. Especially in the *Play on the Seven Blood-Sheddings*, he is being involved in it almost from the outset. The plays, again especially that on the blood-sheddings, belong to the kind of vivid demonstrations—in line with the rhetorical principle of *enargeia*—that enlivened the early modern dinner party.[94]

Bibliography

Areford D.S., *The Viewer and the Printed Image in Late Medieval Europe* (Farnham – Burlington, VT: 2010).

Blau S., "Performative Literacy: The Habits of Mind of Highly Literate Readers", *Voices from the Middle* 10 (2003) 18–22.

Brantley J., *Reading in the Wilderness. Private Devotion and Public Performance in Late Medieval England* (Chicago – London: 2007).

Brown A., *Civic Ceremony and Religion in Medieval Bruges c. 1300–1520* (Cambridge: 2011).

Bryan J., *Looking Inward. Devotional Reading and the Private Self in Late Medieval England* (Philadelphia: 2008).

Bynum C.W., *Holy Feast and Holy Fast. The Religious Significance of Food to Medieval Women* (Berkeley – Los Angeles: 1987).

Dumolyn J. – Haemers J., " 'Let each man carry on with his trade and remain silent'. Middle-class ideology in the urban literature of the late medieval Low Countries", *Cultural and Social History* 10 (2013) 169–189.

Ehrstine G., "Framing the Passion: mansion staging as visual mnemonic", in Gertsman, *Visualizing Medieval Performance* 263–277.

———, "Passion Spectatorship between Private and Public Devotion", in Gertsman E. – Stevenson J. (eds.), *Thresholds of Medieval Visual Culture: Liminal Spaces* (Woodbridge: 2012) 302–320.

---

93   Goldstein C., *Pieter Bruegel and the culture of the early modern dinner party* (Farnham – Burlington, VT: 2013) 5, 78.

94   Goldstein, *Pieter Bruegel* 26.

Falkenburg R.L., *The Fruit of Devotion. Mysticism and the imagery of love in Flemish paintings of the Virgin and Child, 1450–1550* (Amsterdam – Philadelphia: 1994).

Freedman P., *Out of the East. Spices and the Medieval Imagination* (New Haven & London: 2008).

Gertsman E. (ed.), *Visualizing Medieval Performance: Perspectives, Histories, Contexts* (Aldershot – Burlington, VT: 2008).

———, "Introduction: the spectrum of performances", in Gertsman, *Visualizing Medieval Performance* 1–13.

Goldstein C., *Pieter Bruegel and the culture of the early modern dinner party* (Farnham – Burlington, VT: 2013).

Harbison C., "Visions and Meditations in Early Flemish Painting", *Simiolus* 15 (1985) 87–118.

Hummelen W.M.H., *Repertorium van het rederijkerdrama 1500–ca. 1620* (Assen: 1968).

Hüsken W., " 'Van Incommen en begheert men Scat noch Goet': Cornelis Everaert and the Rosary", in Gosman M. – Walthaus R. (eds.), *European Theatre 1470–1600. Traditions and Transformations*, Mediaevalia Groningana 18 (Groningen: 1996) 119–129.

———, "De gelegenheidsdichter Cornelis Everaert en zijn tafelspelen in enge en ruimere zin", *Verslagen en Mededelingen van de Koninklijke Academie voor Nederlandse Taal- en Letterkunde* (1992) 62–78.

———, "Cornelis Everaert and the community of late medieval Bruges", in Hindley A. (ed.), *Drama and Community: People and Plays in Medieval Europe*, Medieval Texts and Cultures of Northern Europe 1 (Turnhout: 1999) 110–125.

——— (ed.), *De Spelen van Cornelis Everaert*, 2 vols. (Hilversum: 2005).

Jékely Z., "Maiolica Jugs in late Medieval Painting", in Balla G. – Jékely Z. (eds.), *The Dowry of Beatrice – Italian Maiolica Art and the Court of King Matthias* (Budapest: 2008) 55–66.

Keenan W.J.F. – Arweck E., "Introduction: Material Varieties of Religious Expression", in Arweck E – Keenan W.J.F. (eds.), *Materializing Religion. Expression, Performance and Ritual* (Farnham – Burlington, VT: 2006) 1–20.

King R., " 'The Beads with Which We Pray Are Made from It': Devotional Ambers in Early Modern Italy", in De Boer W. – Göttler C. (eds.), *Religion and the Senses in Early Modern Europe*, Intersections: Interdisciplinary Studies in Early Modern Culture 26 (2012) (Leiden – Boston: 2013) 153–175.

King'oo C.C., *Miserere Mei. The Penitential Psalms in Late Medieval and Early Modern England* (Notre Dame, IN: 2012).

Kramer B., "Verbondenheid verbeeld. Over de uitbeelding van een rozenkranssnoer op een schilderij van de Meester van Sint-Goedele", *Ons Geestelijk Erf* 82 (2011) 136–159.

Mareel S., *Voor vorst en stad. Rederijkersliteratuur en vorstenfeest in Vlaanderen en Brabant (1432–1561)* (Amsterdam: 2010).

Newman B., "What Did It Mean to Say 'I Saw'?", *Speculum* 80 (2005) 1–43.

Pfaff R.W., *New Liturgical Feasts in Later Medieval England* (Oxford: 1970).

Pikhaus P., *Het tafelspel bij de rederijkers*, 2 vols. (Ghent: 1988).

Ramakers B., "Discerning Vision. Cognitive Strategies in Cornelis Everaert's *Mary Compared to the Light* (c. 1511)", in Melion W.S. – Wandel L.P. (eds.), *Image Theory and Incarnation Doctrine*, Intersections: Interdisciplinary Studies in Early Modern Culture (Leiden – Boston: 2015) (forthcoming).

Ritz G., "Der Rosenkranz", in *500 Jahre Rosenkranz* (Cologne: 1975) 51–101.

Scholliers P., "Meals, food narratives, and sentiments of belonging in past and present", in Scholliers P. (ed.), *Food, drink and identity. Cooking, eating and drinking in Europe since the Middle Ages* (Oxford – New York: 2001) 3–22.

Schuler C.M., "The Seven Sorrows of the Virgin: Popular Culture and the Cultic Imagery in Pre-Reformation Europe, *Simiolus* 21 (1992) 5–29.

Schulten W., "Das Rosenkranzgebet", in *500 Jahre Rosenkranz* (Cologne: 1975) 122–127.

Scribner B., "Popular Piety and Modes of Visual Perception in Late-Medieval and Reformation Germany", *The Journal of Religious History* 15 (1989) 448–469.

Sheingorn P., "Performing the illustrated manuscript: great reckonings in little books", in Gertsman, *Visualizing Medieval Performance* 57–82.

Stevenson J., *Performance, Cognitive Theory, and Devotional Culture. Sensual Piety in Late Medieval York* (New York: 2010).

Strohm R., *Music in Late Medieval Bruges* (Oxford: 1990).

Sutherland A., "Performing the Penitential Psalms in the Middle Ages", in Gargnolati M. – Suerbaum A. (eds.), *Aspects of the Performative in Medieval Culture* (Berlin – New York: 2010) 15–37.

Thoen I., *Strategic Affection? Gift Exchange in Seventeenth-century Holland* (Amsterdam: 2007).

Tomasik T.J. – Vitullo J.M., "At the table. Metaphorical and material cultures of food in medieval and early modern Europe", in Tomasik T.J. – Vitullo J.M. (eds.), *At the table. Metaphorical and material cultures of food in medieval and early modern Europe* (Turnhout: 2007) XI–XX.

Veblen T., *The theory of the leisure class. An economic study of institutions* (New York: 1961 [1934]).

Williamson B., "Sensory Experience in Medieval Devotion", *Speculum* 88 (2013) 1–43.

Williamson E., "Mere Properties. The Materiality of Religious Objects", in Williamson E. (ed.), *The Materiality of Religion in Early Modern English Drama* (Farnham – Burlington, VT: 2009) 1–32.

Winston-Allen A., *Stories of the Rose. The Making of the Rosary in the Middle Ages* (University Park, PA: 1997).

Winter J.M. van, *Spices and Comfits. Collected Papers on Medieval Food* (Blackawton, Totnes: 2007).

CHAPTER 7

Some Aspects of Male and Female Readers of the Printed *Bible Historiale* in the Sixteenth and Seventeenth Centuries

Éléonore Fournié

A publication on the relations between lay religiosity and the practices of vernacular reading during the Middle Ages and the beginning of the modern era would not be complete without a discussion of the French *Bible historiale*. A typical medieval work, it was printed at the end of the fifteenth century in Paris by Antoine Vérard, most likely at the request of the French King Charles VIII.[1] During the first half of the sixteenth century, another 27 editions would follow. At this moment 163 printed copies have been preserved across the world, all dated between 1498 and 1545. This richness in sources entails a problem, because the bibliography on this subject is scarce and most studies are limited to the necessary basic surveys of copies and their dating.[2] As a result, the challenges of this study are twofold: firstly to throw more light on a major part of the literature diffused during the fourteenth to seventeenth centuries and, secondly, to determine what reading practices of laypeople were associated with it. We should ask what transformations could have been caused by the media change of the printing press. It should also be established who possessed, read and annotated this work, and we should try to understand his or her attitude towards this 'old' (or at least medieval) version of the Bible during a period where new and Protestant translations imposed themselves. Who were those readers who still appreciated a version of the Bible that in the end might have been a bit archaic? This essay will firstly present the *Bible historiale*, followed by an overview of the identified owners, in order to arrive at some first conclusions concerning reading practices during the early modern period.

---

1 For the *Bible historiale*, see: Berger S., *La Bible au XVIᵉ siècle: étude sur les origines de la critique biblique* (Paris: 1879); Fournié E., "La Bible historiale", *L'Atelier du Centre de recherches historiques* 3,2 (2009), http://acrh.revues.org/1845, consulted 6 June 2012. See also Winn M.B., *Anthoine Vérard, Parisian publisher 1485–1512, prologues, poems and presentations* (Geneva: 1997) 104–123.

2 I would like to express my warmest thanks to all library staff, who have been so kind in helping me with the research necessary for this article.

© KONINKLIJKE BRILL NV, LEIDEN, 2015 | DOI 10.1163/9789004290396_009

The *Bible Historiale*, a Medieval Manuscript Printed in the Sixteenth Century

The printed versions of the *Bible historiale* are based on a long and rich textual production during the Middle Ages. At the end of the thirteenth century, when Guyart des Moulins, a cleric from Picardie, for reasons still largely unknown to us, undertook translating the Bible into French, he leaned on two of the greatest canonical texts of the period: the *Historia Scholastica* of Peter Comestor and St Jerome's *Vulgata*. Between 1292 and 1295 Guyart seems to have made a first version of his text (the original is unfortunately now lost), which he appears to have taken up again in order to deliver an improved version towards 1297. This latter version of the *Bible historiale* would have borne more resemblance to a chronicle of the events of the Bible than to a Bible in the post-Tridentine theological sense of the word. Guyart loved historical explications and the juicy details with which Peter Comestor larded his *Historia scholastica*. On the other hand, he often simplified the text and omitted those digressions by Comestor that were too learned, in favor of those of St Jerome. When this work appeared on the Parisian book market during the 1310s, it was quickly associated with the *Bible du XIIIe siècle*, another great success of the period, to form what is nowadays known as the *Bible historiale complétée*. In this manner, during the fourteenth and fifteenth centuries numerous and often very sumptuous manuscripts were produced. We still do not always know for whom they were made, but some of them have belonged to the greatest political figures of the period, including kings (Jean II le Bon, Charles V and Charles VI of France, Edward IV of England)[3] and princes (Jean de Berry, Philippe de Croÿ).[4] The *Bible historiale* was also part of more 'modest' libraries, such as those of important persons from the nobility: Hervé VIII de Léon (1341–1363), Lord of French Brittany; Guillaume de la Baume (d. 1495), Lord of Illeins in Switzerland; and Jean III le Meingre (d. 1490), Lord of Bridoré in Touraine.[5] Some families had their coat of arms painted in their manuscripts: the rich Bohier family from Burgundy, the Rochechouart family and the de Pompadour family—who between 1490

---

3   For instance: London, British Library, MS Royal 19 D II; Cambridge, Mass., Harvard University, MS Typ. 555; The Hague, Museum Meermanno, MS 10 B 23; Brussels, KBR, MS 9001–9002, London, BL, MS Royal 15 D I and Royal 18 D IX–X.

4   Paris, Bibliothèque nationale de France, MS fr. 159; Jena, Friedrich-Schiller Universität, Thüringer Universitäts und Landesbibliothek, MS El., f. 95–96.

5   Respectively: Paris, Bibliothèque Sainte-Geneviève, MS 22 and MSS 20–21; New York, Public Library, MS Spencer 4.

and 1582 also inscribed the dates of birth and baptism of their children.[6] This work has also belonged to women, such as the princesses Jeanne de Bourgogne (1293–1349), Marguerite de Bavière (1363–1413) and Marie de Berry (1375–1434).[7] Finally, in a number of copies, the names remain illegible and the owners unidentified.[8] Long absent from clerical libraries, Guyart des Moulin's translation only entered into monasteries and convents at a very late date.[9]

Judging by its form, its spirit and its contents, the *Bible historiale* is a manifestly medieval work. It success is based on the fact that it was written in prose and in French and because it recounts a somewhat fictionalized and didactic history of the Bible, which was also richly illustrated. If 143 manuscripts have survived until today, it can be reasonably expected that many more were produced. Faced with this (relative) abundance, why was there a need and a willingness to edit this text in print? The initiative probably goes back to the French King Charles VIII, who, unlike to his father, loved books and wished to collect a royal library for himself. As is indicated by the short dedicatory epistle, which

---

6 Montpellier, Bibliothèque municipale, MS 49; New York, Pierpont Morgan Library, MS 322–323; Berlin, Staatsbibliothek, MS Phillips 1906.

7 On top of the fact that increasingly significant numbers of women knew how to read, the presence of women corroborates a devotional practice where married women teach and diffuse religious knowledge in their households. The importance of the female reading public is confirmed by a scribal note that warns the potential female readers of their intellectual limits: 'Note that the Book of Wisdom is very obscure to read and even more so when hearing, because of the vice of the copyist who did not understand it; it is not profitable for women to amuse themselves with it, because it is no more than a violation of the text' ('Nota que le livre de la Sapience est tres obscur a lire et pis encore d'entendre parle, par le vice de l'escrivan qui pas ne l'entendoit, non profitable aux femes d'elles y amuser, car ce n'est que rompement de teste'. Reims, Bibliothèque municipale, MS 60 f. 18r).

8 Who are the mysterious 'Donay' (Cambridge, Fitzwilliam Museum, MS 9, first and last folios); 'Thomas Zowchen, Henry Zowche, Helen Zowche and P (?) Barlowe' inscribed in pale ink from the 16th century (Edinburg, University Library, MS 19); or the signatures from the 15th c. of 'Henry de Fresnoy' and 'N. Beauvarlet' (Reims, BM, MS 60, f. 283v). Sibylline phrases such as: 'My lady Powys, I you pray / reaymabayr me wayn yow may' (London, Britsh Library, MS Royal 15 D III) allow us to conclude that the work was already in the British Isles during the 15th century, but little more.

9 Cambrai, Abbaye du Saint-Sépulcre (Cambrai, Bibliothèque municipale, MS 398–399–400); Paris, Abbaye de Saint-Germain-des-Prés (Paris, Bibliothèque nationale de France, MSS fr. 15391, 15392, 15393, 15394, 15395, 15396); Paris, Abbaye Sainte-Geneviève (Paris, Bibliothèque Sainte-Geneviève, MSS 20–21, 22); Troyes, Abbaye de Clairvaux (Troyes, Bibliothèque municipale, MS 59); Paris, Couvent des Mimines (Paris, Bibliothèque Mazarine, MS 311).

is unique for this work,[10] he chose the same Bible as his famous forebears and commissioned the first printed edition towards 1498 from Antoine Vérard.[11] And yet, while several collaborative projects were undertaken between this Parisian printer and the princes of his time,[12] strangely no other edition of the *Bible historiale* was initiated by kings or princes. Even worse, we do not know of any sixteenth-century copies that once belonged to members of the royal family or to the high aristocracy—while one contemporary manuscript belonged to the close circle surrounding the French King François Ier.[13] Nevertheless, the *Bible historiale* was a commercial success: it is the only complete translation of the Bible printed in France before 1524,[14] reprinted 27 times between 1498 and 1545 in Paris, but also in Lyon, and in a large number of copies—if one relies on the number of surviving examples.[15]

---

10   'En perseverant tousiours de bonne affection vouloir acomplyr et fyare vos bons plaisirs et
      commandemens. Mon tres Souverain seigneur Charles huytiesme de ce nom tres chres-
      tien Roy de france A la louenge de la benoiste trinite de paradis et de vous chier sire.
      Apres que par vous me a este commande, vous ay fait la bible hystoryee contenant deux
      volumes ou sont les hystoires scolastiques. Lesquelz livres historiaux furent iadiz trans-
      lates par ung excellent docteur de latin en françoys comme vous pourrez veoir cy apres en
      ensuivant'. Undated and unsigned, quoting without reference to Guyart des Moulins, this
      dedication would have been written by Jean de Rély. Quoted after Brussels, KBR, Inc C 141.

11   This first edition is not dated. Several possibilities have been suggested, between 1487 and
      1499. See Fournié, "La Bible historiale".

12   Antoine Vérard worked for kings and regents such as Anne de Beaujeu, François
      d'Angoulême, Henri VII, and Louis XII.

13   Oxford, Corpus Christi College, MS 385–386.

14   In Paris the first edition of the Latin Bible was published between July 1476 and July 1477
      by Ulrich Gering, Michel Friburger and Martin Crantz Fering. Taking into account that the
      University did not attach importance to biblical studies, there were only a few editions of
      the Latin Bible at the end of the 15th century. In Lyon the situation is markedly different:
      from 1479 to 1500 eight Latin editions follow one another. The versions of the vernacular
      Bible are never complete editions.

15   List of all 27 editions: Paris, Antoine Vérard: c. 1498; Paris, Antoine Vérard: 1505; Lyon,
      Claude Davost, 1506; Paris, Antoine Vérard: 1510; Paris, Barthélemy Vérard: c. 1514; Paris,
      Barthélemy Vérard and François Regnault: 1517; Lyon, Jacques Sacon: 1518; Paris, François
      Regnault and Jean Petit: 1520; Lyon, Jacques Sacon and Pierre Bailly: 1521; Paris, François
      Regnault and Jean Petit: 1529; Lyon, Pierre Bailli, 1531; Paris, Jacques Bonnemère: 1537–
      1538; Paris, Madeleine Boursette, Ambroise Girault and Oudin Petit: 1541; Paris, Madeleine
      Boursette and Pierre Regnault: 1543; Paris, Madeleine Boursette, Pierre Regnault and Jean
      Bignon: 1543–1544; Paris, Oudin Petit, Thielman Kerver, Guillaume le Bret, Rémy Boyset
      and Pierre Sergent: 1545; Paris, Pierre Regnault: 1544–1546.

The printed versions look like the manuscripts: they are heavy volumes,[16] often in two parts and incorporating very many of illustrations; the text is that of the *Grande Bible historiale complétée* of the early fifteenth century, its most popular and most complete form.[17] But there are also numerous differences— and the comparison is even more easily performed because two manuscripts were produced at the beginning of the sixteenth century.[18] The printed versions have neither the aesthetic grandeur nor the iconographic harmony of the earlier manuscripts. Aside from introducing black and white, the technology also allowed for a great—even excessive—number of woodcuts, which are repeated tirelessly.[19] A transformation had taken place, though incomplete, as general aspects persist: broadly speaking, the printed versions were more in tune with the present than the manuscripts, which were rather the heirs of a past ideal. This phenomenon is even more striking because the two technologies existed simultaneously.

Male and Female Readers of the Sixteenth and Seventeenth Centuries

Besides the fact that the documentation on this subject is very poor, the actual sources are not without their own problems. On the one hand, taking into account the geographical dispersal of the 163 surviving printed copies over the entire world, it has not yet been possible to examine them all in detail; on the other hand, some copies are incomplete or fragmented and crucial information has surely disappeared. Finally, in some cases, certain inscriptions remain illegible, crossed out or erased. Taking into account the limits of this analysis

---

16   As the manuscripts, the printed copies are in folio; except for the later edition, from 1543 and 1543–33, which are small octavos. The copies consist of 512 to 1088 leaves.

17   The textual content of the first edition reflects, until the Books of Kings, the work of Guyart des Moulins. See Dupuigrenet Desroussilles F., *Dieu en son royaume: la Bible dans la France d'autrefois, XIIIe–XVIIIe siècle* (Paris: 1991) 22–23. The texts printed between 1498 and 1545 have not yet been the subject of scholarly publications; a first essay has been effectuated with the text of Ecclesiasticus, see Collet A., "L'*Ecclésiaste* à la fin du Moyen Âge: édition du texte extrait de la *Bible historiale complétée* (impression de Paris, Antoine Vérard, *circa* 1495)", in Gross G. (ed.) *La Bible et ses raisons: diffusion et distorsions du discours religieux, XIVe–XVIIe siècle* (Saint-Étienne: 1996) 47–76.

18   Oxford, Corpus Christi College, MS 385–386 and Paris, Bibliothèque nationale de France, MS Fr. 15370–15371.

19   The presence of woodcuts varies from one edition to the other. The first edition is the richest with 391 woodcuts; the others have an average number of 180 woodcuts. Only the copy owned by Charles VIII was decorated with paintings.

and the relative weakness of the proof submitted here, the conclusions will be put forward with the utmost prudence.

As it now stands, of the 163 surviving copies—stemming from the 27 editions now known to us—44 include annotations; this represents 27 percent of the total known copies, thus a good quarter. It is likely that an exhaustive study would yield more results, but this essay will be based on these 44 copies. Most of them contain inscriptions from different periods: 22 notes date from the sixteenth century, 20 from the seventeenth, 9 from the eighteenth and 4 from the nineteenth century. Finally, 48 are not dated. The following table presents those of the sixteenth century.

Shelfmark	Edition	Name	Date	Place	Inscription
Aix-en-Provence, Bibl. Méjanes, In Fol. 328	Lyon: 1521	Guilhen Lenansoy	16th c.	1st f. vol. I	'aquest libre es de guilhen Lenansoy'
Angers, BM, Rés. T 311	Paris: 1498	FrèresAugustins d'Angers	Late 16th c	Title page.	'Pour les freres Augustins d'Angers'
		Beauvau-Précigny family	Early 16th c.?	Last page vol. of II	2 coats of arms[20]

---

20   According to Marc-Édouard Gautier, vice-director of the Library of Angers: 'It is a painting, occupying a quart of the page, of an unknown coat of arms in the form of a losenge divided per pale that I would read as follows: per pale, in dexter, argent with two lyons, armed, langued and coronated guled, marked with a star of eight rays in azur; in senester, azur with two boar's heads, erased, in or, with teeth in argent. The dexter part represents without any doubt the arms of the Beauveau-Précigny family, descending from Bertrand de Beauveau, captain of the Castle of Angers and steward of Anjou, who died in 1474. He was an acknowledged bibliophile of whom we know several illuminated manuscripts, among which probably a breviary offered to the Augustinians of Angers, where he was buried next to his first two spouses. I cannot identify the senester part. However, the eldest of the Beauveau-Précigny family who was alive during the publication of this

Shelfmark	Edition	Name	Date	Place	Inscription
Antwerp, Plantin Moretus Museum, O.B.11.3	Lyon: 1506	J. De … ville	Late 16th c.?	Vol. I	'J. De … ville'
		Françoys de la Conet	1562	Vol. II	
Avignon, Bibliothèque Ceccano, Fol. 213	Lyon: 1518	Spirit Achard	c. 1576	f. 213r	'Apres tous lez possesseurs qui pourront estre escriptz dens la presente bible de dernier et legitime suis moy Spirit Achard qui l'ay acheptee en ceste ville de Tretz l'an 1576 et le premier de mars en foy de.. Signé Spirit Achard pretre'
		Spiritus Achard	1580	*not indicated*	'Ex libris Spiritus Achardi et amicorum 1580'
		Pidou Domand	19 February, 1537	*not indicated*	'1537 et XIX de fevrier fori batize moy Pidou Domand'
		Pidor Domand	1570	*not indicated*	'Se presant libro et a moi monsen Pidor Domand de Rians 1570'
		Not identified	1571	*not indicated*	'1571 em demourant a Marignane'
		Noël Bau(rel) ?	1593	*not indicated*	'Noel Bau[rel] 1593?'
Avignon, Bibliothèque Ceccano, Fol. 269	Lyon: 1531	Monsieur de Beauchamp	1564	*not indicated*	'De Beauchamps d'Avignon'

Bible towards 1498, Louis (d. c. 1527) was married to Regnaude de Hure of whom whe could have here the canting coat (*une hure* means a boar's head). The Bible Rés T 311 of Angers has probably belonged to Regnaude de Hure before she, or one of her descendants (the branch did not survive beyond 1597), donated it to the convent of the Augustines of Angers to which this family was particularly related since the founder himself'.

TABLE (*cont.*)

Shelfmark	Edition	Name	Date	Place	Inscription
Bordeaux, BM, T 129	Paris: 1544– 1546	*Not identified*	1547	Title page	'Ce pressante bible et amoy pre[…] [an erased name and a word that has been cut off]; fol[…?] le moy de mars 1547 [a signature]'
Lyon, BM, Rés. 20074	Lyon: 1531	Antoine de Villard Adrien Galoys	1560	At the beginning of the volume.	'Ceste presente Bible appartient a venerable et discret religieux frere Adrien Galoys, reiligieux et secretain au couvent nostre dame des Carmes de Chalon sur Saulne, 1560. Donne aud. Frere Adrien par Messire Anthoine de Villard le jour de feste Sainct Pierre et sainct Pol, lui estant vicaire à Lux (?), diocèse de Chalon'. Several handwritten ex-libris notes by Anthoine de Villard on the verso side of the fly leaf. 'A sire Nicole Verdeau pbre'
Paris, BnF, Rés. A 270	Paris: *c.* 1498– 1499	Guillaume de Saint Martin Guillaume de Guéret	16th c.	*not indicated*	'Guillaume de Saint-Martin demeurant à Rouen, au vieil marché en la paroisse Saint Sauveur et Guillaume de Guéret, marchand et bourgeois demeurant à Rouen en la paroisse Saint Jean, XVIe siècle'.

Shelfmark	Edition	Name	Date	Place	Inscription
Paris, Arsenal Fol. T. 141	Paris: 1510	François Dobray Perette Dobray Marie le Tonnelier	March, 1518 7 June 1552	*not indicated*	'François Dobray' à sa sœur 'Perrette Dobray', mars 1518; 'Perrette Dobray' à sa nièce 'Marie Le Tonnelier', 7 juin 1552.
Paris, BnF, Rés. A. 2277	Lyon: 1531	Jan Sondreval Nicolas Renart Jehan Passavant Frère Christophe Passavant	1546 1565 1579	*not indicated* *not indicated*	'Jan Sondreval' 'Nicolas Renart, demeurant à Armance (Meurthe-et-Moselle) vend cette Bible en 1565 à Jehan Passavant, clerc juré en la justice d'Amance ; en 1579 elle est la propriété de frère Christophe Passavant, demeurant au Pont au Mousson'.

Several conclusions can be drawn from this table: those who have inserted their ex-libris notes in the printed versions of the sixteenth century are male, and chiefly lay.[21] It is difficult to establish with certainty if these readers were the first owners of the copies, but in some cases the very small time span between the date of printing and the date of an inscription allows this supposition.[22] The others remain silent. There is a member of an aristocratic family (the family of Beauveau-Précigny)[23] and some merchants;[24] the others remain silent. The four clerical 'elements' identified as such are somewhat more informative: Spirit Achard is a priest,[25] friar Adrien Galoys is 'a venerable and a discreet

---

21   There would have been no more than four clerical owners.
22   In Paris, Arsenal, Fol. T 141 the oldest inscription dates from 1518; thus eight years after the edition.
23   Angers, BM, Rés. T 311.
24   Paris, BnF, Rés. A. 270.
25   Avignon, Bibl. Ceccano, Fol. 213.

religious (…) humble secretary';[26] and as far as Jehan Passavant is concerned, he is 'a sworn-in cleric'.[27] The readers are not easily identifiable. In the signatures, the most important information is the name, followed by the date and finally, in some cases, the manner of transmission (purchase or gift)[28] or the profession. In the majority of cases it is clerics who give details about their status; the others do not specify anything about this subject.

If we compare these rare bits of information with those mentioned above for the manuscripts, two major trends become clear: it is a work that is always present in 'modest' libraries, and a large presence of individuals is not, or not easily, identifiable. The habit of inscribing one's name continues, but without much attention given to the ex-libris. The *Bible historiale* is a work situated 'in-between' not precious enough for being the subject of sumptuous dedications, but sufficiently important for being personalized. As stated above, apart from the copy realized for Charles VIII, not one single copy concerns royal or princely circles. Indeed, the modern and printed *Bible historiale* seems to lose in presence among the nobility what it wins in general popularity— and this is apparently as true for its physical appearance as it is for its audience. It should be noted that copies printed in Lyons are over-represented in this sample. Did these volumes—less voluminous, more polished in their presentation and in the choice of woodcuts—have more success in the sixteenth century?

A table of the readers of the seventeenth century allows us a glimpse of the first developments:

---

26   Lyon, BM, Rés. 20074.

27   Paris, BnF, Rés. A. 2277.

28   Purchase (Avignon, Bibl. Ceccano, Fol. 213 and Paris, BnF, Rés. A.2277) or gift (Lyon, BM, Rés. 20074).

Shelfmark	Edition	Name	Date	Place	Inscription
Aix-en-Provence, Bibl. Méjanes, In Fol. 328	Lyon: 1521	Berenguier	17th or 18th c.	vol. II, f. 1r.	'Berenguier'.
Antwerp, Plantin Museum, O.B.11.3	Lyon: 1506	Society of Jesus in Louvain	'MDCI' (1601)	vol. I and II	'Lovanij Societatis Jesu'.
Avignon, Bibl. Ceccano, Fol. 213	Lyon: 1518	Degeorges	1666	f. 213r	'et le dernier possesseur.. Degeorges prestre achetée le 1er mars 1666'.
		Eryc de Bremond Françoyse de Mouton Rychard de Sisteron	1 December, 1613	*not indicated*	'Ceste presante byble est a moy quy m'apelle Eryc de Bremond segneur de Rosset et m'a esté lézé. Par damoiselle Françoyze de Mouton ma belle mere laqeulle luy avoit esté donnée par Mons. Rychard de Sisteron . . . sygné le premyer desambre 1613'.
Avignon, Bibl. Ceccano, Fol. 267	Lyon: 1521	Famille Gente: Charles Gente, Gaspard Gente, Gaspard Estienne	17th c.	*not indicated*	'Gente' ; 'ceste presante bible m'a esté donnee par feu monsieur Gaspard Gente bourgeois d'Avignon mon beau père, fils de Jean, petit fils de Gaspard Gente lequel (Gaspard) Estienne fict rellier la presante bible passant par Lyon – Charles'.
Dijon, B.M., Est. 48	Paris: 1544–1545	Jean Maignien[29]	Early 17th c.	1st flyleaf Title page	'Apartient a Jean maignien marchant a Dijon devant le palais'. 'Maignien apartient ceste bible'.

---

29   Jean Maignien was a printer was active in Dijon between 1601 and 1607.

TABLE (*cont.*)

Shelfmark	Edition	Name	Date	Place	Inscription
Geneva, Bibl. de Genève, Bb 91	Lyon: 1521	Francoys Cyviez	17 December, 1601	f. 173v	'Je Francoys Cyviez habitant de Lyon asseure en visite avoyr monstre la presante bible a pere Esprit Gaudin du Convent des Cappuchins de ceste ville lequel la tenue bonne cellon l'Eglyse Catholicque apostolicque Romayne et en foy de ce jay escript ce signe le [ ] memoyre de ma main et sein accoustume. Fait le dixseptiesme decembre mil six cens ung.' Signé 'F. Cyviez'. On the verso side of the following folio (signed yy [vi]) has been written upside down (the book has to be turned in order to be able to read it: 'Memoyre soit a moy et aulx miens que la presante bible a esté visitee et tenue bonne cellon la Relligion Catholicque appostholicque Romayne par pere Esprit Gaudin du Convent des peres Cappuchins a quy je lay monstre dans sa chambre entre les deux portes de l'Eglise de saincte Croix de Lyon daultant quil preschoit pendant la Caresme en lad. Eglise et ce jourdh[uy] samedy dixseptiesme jour du moys de mars mil six cens et ung en [ ] et foy de ce je francoys Cyviez habitant dud. Lion ay escript ce signe le [ ] pour memoyre de ma main et sain accoustume'. Signed 'F. Cyviez'.
Le Mans, BM, Th. 177	Paris: 1529	Frère André Leheu[30]	c. 1602	Title pages of vol I and II	'F. Andre Leheu'; 'Frere Andre Leheu religieux du Perray neuf'.

30   Frère André Le Heu was cantor in the abbey of Perray Neuf (Précigné).

Shelfmark	Edition	Name	Date	Place	Inscription
Lyon, BM, Rés. 100025	Lyon: 1521	Jean Baptiste Bordey	15 March, 1683	Leaf after the tables of content of vol. II	'Ceste Bible 1685. Qui l'auras apres luy priera Dieu pour luy. Cette Bible apartien a Jean baptiste Bordey qui l auras apres luy priera Dieu pour luy ce 15me mars 1683'.
				ff. 26r, 92r and 133r of vol. II	'Jean Baptiste Bordey'.
		La sœur Lucresse Cluny	13 September, 1684	*not indicated*	'Dans le mois de Xbre 1682, la sœur lucresse cluny a donne cette presente bible a jean baptis Bordey cordonier de la maison de la charite pour lamistiee quelle luy temogners Laditte sœur et morte le 15 mars entre 7 et 8 heure 1683. Tellement que cette bible et a luy qui l'aura apres luy priera Dieu pour luy Jean Baptise Bordey. Le tous pour la grande gloire de Dieu. ce 13 7bre 1684 (signed) Bordey Jesus.Maria.Joseph'.
		Jehan Chouquard	1625	Leaf after the tables of content	'en l'annee 1586 la (illegible) vallait sept sols et quatre deniers. A Jehan Chouquard apartient ceste bible achetee en l'annee 1625. priez pour luy apres sa mort ceux qui l'auront apres luy. J. Chouquard. (deux phrases illisibles)'.
			1631	Verso dernier f. of the 2nd vol.	'Apres la mort de feu mons. (illisible), j'ai achepte ceste bible en l'annee 1631 dont je me suis signé. Dieu fasse ceulx passes ainsy soit il Chouquard (further down) Choccard / Vinber femme de Pierre'.

TABLE (*cont.*)

Shelfmark	Edition	Name	Date	Place	Inscription
Orléans, BM, 2°Rés. A 123	Paris: 1498	Dominus Amabilis Choqs	1676	*not indicated*	'Ex-dono Domini Amabilis Choqs, pastoris Stae Catharinae et Ecclesiae Cathedralis poeniten-tiarii, anno 1676'.
Paris, BnF, Rés.g.A. 22	Paris: 1505	The son of Antoine Reydelles (François ?)	1616	*not indicated*	'Cette presente bible demeura en l'hoirie de Me Antoine Reydelles mon pere et m'advint en partage estant presque en folios et toutte (sic) escartee. Je le feitz relier à Me Jean Le Teinturier … Lannée mil six cent et seize. Je luy payey de la relieur deux livres quinze sols. Reydelles'.
		Pierre Daviollet	8 April (?) 1648	*not indicated*	'Appartient a present à Mre Pierre Daviollet, curé de Lalleyriat auquel en a esté faict don par Sr Françoys Reydelles Sr du Verloz son cousin le 8 apl 1648. Daviollet'.
Paris, BnF, Rés. A 274	Paris: 1514	Louis II de Bourbon-Condé	17th c.	Binding	Reliure aux armes de Louis II de Bourbon-Condé
Paris, BnF, Rés. A.277	Paris: 1529	Louis II de Bourbon-Condé	17th c.	Binding	Binding with the arms of Louis II de Bourbon-Condé
Paris, Bibl. Saint-Germain, Fol.A.174 inv.181 Rés.	Paris: 1544–1546	Guillaume de Flécelles[31]	1673	*not indicated*	Ex-dono inscriptions
Valognes, BM, R 230	Lyon: 1518	Saint Martin du Tourp Séminaire de Valognes	1625, 1628, 1658, 1660 17th c.	*not indicated* *not indicated*	'pour saint Martin du Tourp'.

---

31   Abbot at the Abbey of Sainte Geneviève.

Firstly, during the seventeenth century the inscriptions are longer and more developed; they give more information about the owners—this time clerics and laypeople alike. Next to the date, the most interesting information concerns the way in which the work has been acquired: inheritance, gift, and sometimes purchase.[32] This means that the *Bible historiale* was still being transmitted, and that most often the handwritten annotations were added at the moment of transmission. It is also interesting to observe that in a few (too few) cases the price of the acquisition or the restoration of the binding has been specified—but without any evidence whether this is an accurate or outrageous price.[33] This is followed by indications concerning the profession or the social-economic status of the owners, resulting in a nice sample of the social hierarchy of laypeople, from the shoemaker ('cordonnier') to collectors of royal blood, and from townspeople ('bourgeois') to the lord ('seigneur') or the merchant.[34] Thus, this work of the late thirteenth century appears to interest all and it can be owned by (almost) everyone. Women also seem to be emerging: one of them is quoted as a link between two men;[35] another, a religious woman, Lucresse Cluny, bequeaths at her death her copy to a shoemaker friend;[36] in the same book, a certain 'Vinber wife of Pierre' ('Vinber femme de Pierre') indicates her presence in a note just after one by her husband's hand. Did she wish to make clear that this book also belonged to her and that she could make use of it? While this is our only example of a female marking her own presence, indications of female usage seem to become more frequent during the seventeenth century.[37] A better and more systematic examination of the sources and a refinement of the datings could adjust this observation.[38]

It is however clear that these examples emphasize that the *Bible historiale* was read by both sexes, revealing a similar diversity as we have seen with social categories above.

---

32   Avignon, Bibl. Ceccano, f. 213, Paris, BnF, Rés.g.A.22, Lyon, BM, Rés. 20074 and Rés. 100025.

33   Lyon, BM, Rés. 100025 and Paris, BnF, Rés.g.A.22.

34   The shoemaker: Jean-Baptiste Bordey (Lyon, BM, Rés. 100025); the prince of the blood: Louis II de Bourbon-Condé (Paris, Arsenal, Fol. T 142 and Paris, B.n.F., Rés. g.A.11); the 'bourgeois': Gaspard Gente (Avignon, Bibl. Ceccano, Fol. 267); the 'segneur': Eryc de Bremond, seigneur de Rosset (Avignon, Bibl. Ceccano, Fol. 213); the merchant: Jean Maignien (Dijon, BM, Est.48) who was most likely a printer.

35   Françoyze de Mouton (Avignon, Bibl. Ceccano, Fol. 213).

36   Lyon, BM, Rés. 100025.

37   'Perette Dobray' and her niece 'Marie Le Tonnelier' in 1518 and 1552 (Paris, Arsenal, Fol. T 141).

38   To my knowledge there are two other notations by women that are not dated: 'Jeanne Coutier' (Dijon, BM, Est. 48) and 'C'est a moy V. Mauricette' (Paris, BnF, Rés. A. 273).

But if laypeople remained in the majority, little by little clerical circles were catching up, consisting of both religious institutions (associations, seminary, convent) and individuals (friars, parish priests).[39] But the two worlds are by no means completely separate or impermeable. Quite to the contrary—exchanges between the two seem to occur frequently. In this manner, the sister Lucresse Cluny mentioned above gives her Bible to her friend Jean-Baptiste Bordey, 'shoemaker of the house of charity for the friendship of which she wants to testify to him' ('cordonier de la maison de la charite pour lamitié quelle luy temoigners');[40] another instance of a gift—this time within the same family— can be found in the transmission of possession from a lord to his cousin, a parish priest.[41] These two examples clearly show that the gift could be conveyed from cleric to layperson, as well as from layperson to cleric. Finally, a long (double) quotation emphasizes that a cleric and a layperson have both read the same item at the same moment: Francoys Cuvier, living in Lyon, makes assurances that he has shown his Bible to a father of the convent of the Capuchin monks of Lyon, who confirmed that the content was conform 'the Apostolic Roman-Catholic religion' ('cellon la Relligion Catholicque appostholicque Romayne').

This latter example is striking: it clearly reveals the emergence of several changes in the practices of religious reading. In addition, it shows that by the early seventeenth century the *Bible historiale* lost its medieval status that had made it one of the better translations of Sacred Scripture. Challenged by the reforming currents of the sixteenth century, it now appeared problematic due to its content, most likely because from the Middle Ages and, consequently, was suspected at best of archaism, at worst of heresy. This suspicion with regard to the biblical text must, however, not be taken entirely at face value, because the *Bible historiale* never seems to have been strongly condemned.[42]

The quoted examples instead suggest that clerics and laypeople read Guyart's translation together and discussed it; moreover, it seems that this reading was encouraged by the ecclesiastic authorities. This evidence also reveals a practice of an intimate religion, such as among family or friends, and between clerics and laypeople in the early modern period. In addition it shows

---

39   A priest: Marc Antoine Degeorges (Avignon, Bibl. Ceccano, f. 213); a friar André Le Heu (Le Mans, BM, Th. 177); a parish priest: Pierre Daviollet (Paris, BnF, Rés.g.A.22), etc.

40   Lyon, BM, Rés. 100025.

41   Paris, BnF, Rés.g.A.22.

42   To my knowledge there are two other inscriptions, both of them undated, by members of the Inquisition who approve of the *Bible historiale*: 'f.ardi inquisitor' (Avignon, Bibl. Ceccano, f. 217) and 'Permettons à monsieur de Beauchamp et non a autre la lecture de ceste presente bible—F.E. Lemaire inquisiteur général de la Ste foy' (Avignon, Bibl. Ceccano, f. 269).

an exchange of actions and words surrounding a shared object: a didactic Bible, richly illustrated.

It is not possible to establish with certainty if the *Bible historiale* was more popular than other devotional books or why a reader would have wanted to acquire it—there is no note giving an indication of this. It is difficult to know how the religious text was experienced and if people read it alone in silence, or collectively by reading out loud. Apart from two small editions in-octavo that suggest an individual use, the others, in-folio, could only have been placed on a pulpit and, consequently, should have instead had a more collective use. But while the devotional practices concerning Books of Hours have been studied in detail, the daily use of this biblical literature has not been documented. Likewise, we do not know much about the value accorded to this publication in the Reformed religion and the attention that has been given to it in the ideological debate between Catholics and Protestants. Nevertheless, this text has all the characteristics that would render it unacceptable for the Calvinist theologians.[43]

Finally, it should again be emphasized that the copies of the Lyon editions are over-represented; having been reprinted less often, more of them have manuscript inscriptions. The post-medieval editions become less frequent in the eighteenth century. They can be divided into two groups: on the one hand those that belonged to the collectors, who appended their ex-libris,[44] and on the other hand those of religious brotherhoods, who were now marking the manuscripts as frequently as laypeople.[45] Had the *Bible historiale*, until this

---

43 It is amusing to note that Edouard Reuss (1804–1891), professor of Protestant Theology at the University of Strasbourg and author of a fundamental article ("Fragments littéraires et critiques relatifs à l'histoire de la Bible française. Seconde série. Les Bibles des XIVᵉ et XVᵉ siècles et les premières éditions imprimées", *Revue de théologie et de philosophie chrétienne* 14 (1857) 129–160), owned a printed copy of the *Bible historiale* imprimée (Strasbourg, University Library, E 122).

44 The Marquis de Méjanes, 1729–1786 (Aix-en-Provence, Bibliothèque Méjanes, In Fol. 328); Pierre-Daniel Huet, 1630–1721 (Paris, BnF, Rés.A.5835 (1–2)); the Marquis de Paulmy, 1694–1757 (Paris, Arsenal, Fol. T 509 (1)); the Reverend Lionel Gatford, 1642–1715 (Paris, B.n.F., Rés.g.A.11), or Anne-Thérèse Philippine, countess of Yve, 1738–1814 (Paris, BnF, Rés. A. 273). The collectors of the 19th century are also present, as 'J.F. Vandevelde' (Antwerp, Plantin Moretus Museum, O.B.11.3), Charles de L'Escalopier, 1811–1861 (Amiens, Bibl. Louis Aragon, LESC 33/Rés. 312 D), or Edouard Reuss, 1804–1891 (Strasbourg, University Library, E 122).

45 The Abbey of Sainte-Geneviève (Paris, BSG, Fol A 172 inv. 178 Rés.); the convent of the Récollets (Orléans, BM, 2°Rés. A 123) or the convent Sainte Marie du Salut (Bordeaux, BM, T 128); the seminary Sainte Irénée (Lyon, BM, Rés. 100024), or David Ferry for the Society of Jesus (Paris, BnF, Rés.A.273).

point could predominantly be found in the profane world, gradually pene-
trated religious libraries? An acknowledgment of this possible shift should be
tentative because of the great number of undated inscriptions that remain to
be studied.[46]

Conclusion

Even if we have been able to spot sporadic information about the male and
female readers of the *Bible historiale* based on elements gleaned from its suc-
cessive pages, important areas still remain unsure. It will take a long time in
order to write this history from the original monastic reading in the Collegial
Church of Guyart des Moulins to the equally religious consultation in a library
during our modern era, not to mention numerous other forms of consultation:
the reading practices vary greatly and remain in several aspects mysterious.
More time, study and research are required in order to throw more light on
this subject. Nevertheless, as a conclusion it is possible to suggest several lines
of reflection.

Firstly, in this abundant production of printed editions (and manuscripts),
each single copy has its own history and is a unique object in itself; there is
no standard historical itinerary—and consequently, no standard reader.
Furthermore, the technological change from manuscript to print results in a
qualitative and quantitative transformation and in a wider diffusion, which
has incontestably contributed to a new relation to the book. However, this
idea of a 'democratization' of Sacred Scripture, even if it is completely correct, should be tempered. As has been stated above, the *Bible historiale* seems
to have had an 'in-between' status: at times it was just as likely to have been
found in the possession of a simple shoemaker as in the hands of kings. From
its conception onwards, the *Bible historiale* has been perceived as a 'demo-
cratic' work—or this was in any case the intention of Guyart des Moulins,
who 'recounts/translates' the history of the Bible in the vernacular language.
Moreover, the study of the fourteenth and fifteenth centuries confirms its presence in libraries outside those of the nobility, which persists in the following
centuries. It was appreciated by all and diffused across society (regardless of
gender or social-professional categories). Furthermore, it seems that the *Bible
historiale* was appreciated during the sixteenth and seventeenth centuries

---

46   By way of example, in the copy of Bourg-en-Bresse, BM, 28–135: ex-libris of the Trolliet
        family, ex-libris of the Convent of the Capucines in Bourg-en-Bresse, intertwined initials
        that cannot be identified.

because it was ancient, and derived its legitimacy and its popularity from this prestigious antiquity.[47] We ignore everything concerning its possible archaism or the prospect of it being rejected by the reforming currents. Thus, in its own way, the *Bible historiale* contributes to the formation of a religious identity during the sixteenth and seventeenth centuries, perpetuating in this manner an already ancient function. It is a heritage Bible, a family Bible, a Bible of laypeople and clerics—even a source of discussion between these two; costly without being prohibitively expensive; impressive and yet still an everyday object; and it is it is transmitted, bearing the marks of ownership. Approaching the huge sacred history pedagogically, it was probably read over the course of an entire lifetime. A medieval book that withstood time, it could have been a bedside Bible used by all, so widely present that it was not even noticed anymore, and eventually forgotten.

Bibliography

Bedouelle G. – Roussel B., *Le Temps des Réformes et la Bible* (Paris: 1989).

Berger S., *La Bible au XVIe siècle: étude sur les origines de la critique biblique* (Paris: 1879).

Collet A., "L'*Ecclésiaste* à la fin du Moyen Âge: édition du texte extrait de la *Bible historiale complétée* (impression de Paris, Antoine Vérard, *circa* 1495)", in Gross G. (ed.) *La Bible et ses raisons: diffusion et distorsions du discours religieux, XIVe–XVIIe siècle* (Saint-Étienne: 1996) 47–76.

Dupuigrenet Desroussilles F., *Dieu en son royaume: la Bible dans la France d'autrefois, XIIIe–XVIIIe siècle* (Paris: 1991).

Gros G. (ed.), *La Bible et ses raisons: diffusion et distorsions du discours religieux, XIVe–XVIIe siècle* (Saint-Étienne: 1996).

Komada A., *Les illustrations de la Bible historiale. Les manuscrits réalisés dans le Nord* (Université Paris-IV: 2000).

Winn M.B., *Anthoine Vérard, Parisian publisher 1485–1512, prologues, poems and presentations* (Geneva: 1997) 104–123.

Spencer E.P., "Antoine Vérard's illuminated vellum incunables", in Trapp J.B. (ed.), *Manuscripts in the fifty years after the inventions of printing. Some papers read at a colloquium in Warburg Institute on 12–13 March 1982* (London, 1983) 62–65.

---

47   A handwritten and undated inscription would seem to suggest this: 'Cette bible doit être conservée à cause de son antiquité' (Paris, Bibl. Sainte-Geneviève, Fol. A 172 (2) inv. 179 Rés (edition: Paris, 1520).

CHAPTER 8

From Nicholas Love's *Mirror* to John Heigham's *Life*: Paratextual Displacements and Displaced Readers

Ian Johnson

Paratexts are an agent as well as a symptom of the cultural changes that affect the production and reading of religious texts. This essay is about paratextuality *en mouvance*. It involves three textual representatives of the vernacular English tradition of the *Meditationes vitae Christi*: Nicholas Love's *Mirror of the Blessed Life of Jesus Christ* (c. 1410); the 1606 Douai edition (and partial adaptation/modernisation) of Love's work printed by C. Boscard; and the 1622 revision of the *Mirror* by the lay recusant, polemicist and book smuggler John Heigham, published by him in St Omer, and also printed by Boscard.[1]

The *Meditationes vitae Christi* was one of the most important works of Latin devotional literature in medieval Europe, and it enjoyed a huge number of translations in many vernaculars, including English.[2] Love's rendering

---

1 Love N., *Nicholas Love's Mirror of the Blessed Life of Jesus Christ. A Critical Edition Based on Cambridge University Library Additional* MSS *6578 and 6686*, ed. M.G. Sargent (Exeter: 2005); *The Miroure of the Blessed Life of our Lorde and Savioure Iesus Christe* (Douai, C. Boscard: 1606) STC 3269, accessed as EEBO TCP02A.00014580; Heigham J., *The life of our blessed Lord and Sauiour Iesus Gathered, out of the venerable and famous doctor, Saint Bonauenture, and out of diuers other rare, renowned and Catholique doctors* (St Omer, C. Boscard: 1622) STC 13034, accessed as EEBO TCP02A.00015594. For information on Heigham's life, piety, career with books and the historical context, see Allison A.F., "John Heigham of S. Omer (c. 1568–c. 1632)", *Recusant History* 4,6 (1957–1958) 226–240; and Scheck T., "The Polemics of John Heigham and Richard Montagu and the Rise of English Arminianism", *Recusant History* 29,2 (2008) 22–29. See also, for further information and an interpretation of the evidence of relationships amongst the post-medieval English texts in the Pseudo-Bonaventuran tradition, Doyle A.I., "Recusant Versions of the *Meditationes Vitae Christi*", *Bodleian Library Record* 15 (1994–1996) 411–413. For bibliographical details of Heigham's publishing career, see Allison A.F. – Rogers D.M., *The Contemporary Printed Literature of the English Counter-Reformation between 1558 and 1640. An Annotated Catalogue*, 2 vols. (Aldershot: 1989–1994) vol. 2, 82–85, no. 420. The work discussed in this essay is the second edition of the work. Allison and Rogers note, however, that 'no copy of the first edition has been identified' (83).

2 For the *Meditationes vitae Christi*, see *Opera omnia sancti Bonaventurae*, ed. A.C. Peltier, 15 vols. (Paris: 1864–1871), XII (1868) 509–630, here 510. This edition, which from now on will be cited by page number in the main body of the text, is used by Sargent for his edition of the

was born into an early fifteenth-century world dominated by the Church's drive against Lollardy, and it accordingly adds anti-Wycliffite polemic and an appended Treatise on the Sacrament, in the form of an orthodox defence of the Eucharist. Many copies of the work also contain a memorandum that around the year 1410 Love presented his work to Archbishop Arundel, Chancellor of England and persecutor of Lollards. Arundel publically commended the work as a set text for the whole nation to the confutation of false Lollards and heretics. Love's work exists in more manuscripts than any prose Middle English religious work other than the Wycliffite Bible, and it enjoyed many early prints. It was a culturally central and highly mainstream text for which there was clearly much demand and a longstanding public well into the sixteenth century.[3]

Paradoxically, however, in the early seventeenth century, the *Mirror* was both central and marginal: central inasmuch as it still reflected a perfectly routine mainstream Catholic tradition of meditating on the life of Christ under the supervision of a priestly guide narrating, moralising, drawing affective lessons and inviting the imagining reader into the *mise-en-scène* of the spiritual work; marginal, in being now suspiciously papist-looking to a Protestant England, and now appealing to a restricted and enfeebled readership of disempowered Catholics. Both the 1606 and the 1622 Pseudo-Bonaventuran works were texts consigned to the margins: anglophone groups of assorted laity and religious exiled to the French-speaking Spanish Netherlands—in other words people like Heigham and the community of Poor Clares to whom he addressed his

---

Mirror because it is nearer to what Love used than any other modern edition. St Bonaventure has not for a long time been thought of as the author of the *Meditationes*, but his association with the work has left it with a 'pseudo-Bonaventuran' identity, despite John de Caulibus, a Franciscan of San Gimignano, generally being cited as the author of the work, originally made in Latin. More recently, however, Sarah McNamer has argued that the earliest version was not in Latin but in Italian, and probably by a woman; see McNamer A., "The Origins of the *Meditationes vitae Christi*", *Speculum* 84 (2009) 905–955. Peter Tóth and David Falvay have, however, taken a different view and brought to light another authorial possibility, a certain James of Cortona; see Tóth P. – Falvay D., "From the Apostle Peter to Bonaventure the Cardinal: Rethinking the Date and Authorship of the *Meditationes Vitae Christi*", in Kelly S. – Perry R. (eds.) *Devotional Culture in Late Medieval England and Europe. Diverse Imaginations of Christ's Life* (Turnhout: forthcoming, 2015). For a wide-ranging and up-to-date collection of studies of the medieval English pseudo-Bonaventuran tradition, see Johnson I. – Westphall A. (eds.), *The Pseudo-Bonaventuran Lives of Christ. Exploring the Middle English Tradition* (Turnhout: 2013).

3   For this, and further information, see in general the introduction of Sargent's edition of Love's *Mirror*. See also the Queen's University Belfast-St Andrews *Geographies of Orthodoxy* Arts and Humanities Research Council project web site at: http://www.qub.ac.uk/geographies-of-orthodoxy/.

St Omer version of 1622. (It was strangely fitting that Heigham should dedicate his work to Poor Clares, for in thirteenth-century San Gimignano a *dilecta filia* of this order was the first recipient of the original.)

This essay explores, through comparative analysis, changes in the paratext of the English *Meditationes vitae Christi* in Love's version of c. 1410; the 1606 Douai reprint, and John Heigham's revision.[4] While the text of Love's work has been accorded much scholarly and critical attention in recent years, the texts of the two later adaptations have not to date enjoyed the same degree of attention (if any), even though useful work has been done on the historical context of English recusancy in this part of the continent.[5]

We start, then, by looking at the Douai *Mirror*, and the significance of its differences from Love's work.

Douai and Love: The Natures of Christ and the Natures of Texts

Love's *Mirror* starts by quoting the celebrated and much-used *carte blanche* for reading or writing what one wishes to read or write, St Paul's assertion in *Romans* 15. 4 that all that is written is written for our doctrine, so that by patience and consolation of the Scriptures we have hope.[6] Love, it must be said, restores the importance of the theological virtue and human experience/emotion of hope to the understanding of this biblical verse:

> Quecumque scripta sunt ad nostram doctrinam scripta sunt vt per pacienciam & consolacionem scripturarum spem habeamus, ad Romanos xv° capitulo.
>
> Þese ben þe wordes of the gret doctour and holy apostle *Powle* consideryng þat the gostly leuyng of all trewe crysten creatures in þis world

---

4   I will, for ease of reference from this point, use abbreviated references after quotations from Love's *Mirror*, from the 1606 Douai print, and from Heigham's version, referring to them respectively as 'Love', 'Douai' and 'Heigham'.

5   The major study of the *Mirror* is still Salter E., *Nicholas Love's 'Myrrour of the Blessed Lyf of Jesu Christ'*, Analecta Cartusiana 10 (Salzburg: 1974). Excellent bibliographical information on a full range of topics is to be found in Sargent's edition. See also Ghosh K., "Nicholas Love", in Edwards A.S.G. (ed.), *A Companion to Middle English Prose* (Cambridge: 2004) 53–66.

6   For discussion of this liberal use of *Romans* 15:4, see Gillespie V., "From the Twelfth Century to c. 1450", in Minnis A. – Johnson I. (eds.), *The Cambridge History of Literary Criticism*, vol. II, *The Middle Ages* (Cambridge: 2005) 145–235, here 200.

stant specialy in hope of þe blysse & the lyfe þat is to come in another worlde.[7] (Love 9)

The Douai reprint at first seems to be following the fifteenth-century text in its initial paraphrase of the Vulgate, but substantive change enters quickly enough in the later work's treatment of Love's extrapolation of this biblical *auctoritas*:

¶ Ande for also mich as tweyne þinges pryncipaly noryschen & strenkþen þis hope in man þat is pacience in herte & ensaumple of vertues and gude liuyng of holy men writen in bokes⁓ Ande souereynly þe wordes and þe dedis writen of oure lord Jesu criste verrei god and man for þe tyme of his bodily liuyng here in erthe⁓ [...].[8] (Love 9)

And for asmuche as two thinges principally noryscheth & strengthneth this hope in man, that is pacience in him selfe & good exsamples of vertu to others, therefore of this haue many holy men wryten many bokes and to this purpose chiefly were spoken and wrought the wordes & dedes of oure lord Iesu Christ al the time of his liuinge here on earthe [...].[9] (Douai 3)

The divergences are worthy of comment. Douai has taken two clauses that in Love's original are subsequently completed by a resolving statement that the Apostle Paul said what he said with good purpose in order to strengthen humanity in hope of happiness in the life heareafter.[10] This statement is

---

7 'Whatever is written is written for our doctrine/instruction, so that by patience and con-solation of the Scriptures we may have hope. Romans, chapter 15. These are the words of the great Doctor and holy apostle *Paul*, considering that the spiritual living of all true Christian creatures in this world stands especially in the hope of the bliss and the life that is to come in another world'.

8 'And inasmuch as two things principally nourish and strengthen this hope in man, that is patience of heart and the example of the virtues and the good living of holy men written in books, and sovereignly the words and the deed written of Our Lord Jesus Christ very God and man for the duration of his bodily living here on earth [...]'.

9 'And inasmuch as two things principally nourish and strengthen this hope in man, that is his own patience and good examples of virtue for the benefit of others, therefore many holy men have written many books about this, and to this purpose chiefly were spoken and wrought the words & deeds of Our Lord Jesus Christ during the whole time of his liv-ing here on earth [...]'.

10 '[...] þerfore to strenkeþ vs & comfort vs in þis hope spekeþ the Apostle þe wordes aforseid to this entent seying þat all thynges þat ben written generaly in holi chirche ande specialy

in Douai too but, as can be seen above, before this, instead of two hanging clauses, Douai offers a complete sentence in which the 'holy men' are no longer those with exemplary lives but those who have written many books that support hope. Evidently, the only holy liver needed in the 1606 version is the supreme example of Christ. Also, whereas in Love's *Mirror* Christ is designated as 'our lord Jesu criste verrei god and man', in the later text the incarnational designation is dropped and the formula is shortened to 'oure lord Iesu Christ'. Love declared Christ 'verrei god and man' at this point in order to remind his readership of the role of the Incarnation in the process of salvation—on which hope focuses and depends: not so in the later work. The incarnational nature of Christ is, of course, referred to elsewhere in the Douai version, but its omission of the incarnational designation at this point restricts the local field of reference to the idea and identity of Christ as, first and foremost, a moral example.

Very soon after this in Love's *proheme* is a passage in which he renders and combines sentences from various locations in St Augustine's *De agone christiano*. In this passage Love tells his readers, through Augustine, that Christ took on human form and became the medicine of humanity, and that individual deadly sins are all curable by the opposing virtues contained in, and represented by, His life. Love then proceeds, in the saint's englished words, to inform us that Christ's life, in which God's Son gave Himself as an example of good living, protects against all sin for those who behold, love and follow that life:

> ¶ Ande more ouer þer is no synne or wickednesse, bot that he schal want it and be kept fro it þe whiche byholdeth inwardly & loueþ & foloweþ þe wordes & þe dedis of that man in whome goddes sone ȝaf himself to vs in to ensaumple of gode leuyng.[11] (Love 910)

The Douai version works some noteworthy changes to this. The idea of beholding ('byholdeth') disappears—which is perhaps odd in a discourse on the value of meditating:

---

of oure lorde Jesu cryste þei bene wryten to oure lore that by pacience and conforte of holi scriptures we haue hope that is to say of the Life & Blysse that is to come in anothere worlde'. (Love 9). ('[. . .] therefore to strengthen us and comfort us in this hope the Apostle speaks the aforesaid words to this intent, saying that all things that are written generally in Holy Church—and especially of Our Lord Jesus Christ—are written for our instruction, so that through patience and by the consolation of the Holy Scriptures we may have hope, that is to say, of the life and bliss that is to come in another world'.)

11   'And, moreover, there is no sin or wickedness, but that he shall be without it and be kept from it who beholds inwardly and loves and follows the words and the deeds of that man in whom God's Son gave himself to us as example of good living'.

and more ouer there is no sinne or wickednesse but that he may be
defended and kepte from it, the whiche inwardly loueth and foloweth
the blessed wordes and deedes of Christ, who gaue himself chieflie for a
pattern vnto vs in exsample of good liuinge.[12] (Douai 4–5)

The medium and practice of meditation are, to say the least, made less explicit
here. In this passage, as was the case earlier, the Incarnation ('that man in
whome goddes sone ȝaff [*gave*] himself') is again dropped. Now it is 'Christ',
not God's incarnate Son, 'who gaue himself': this gift is still described as a
self-giving, but it is no longer specified at this point as a combination of the
sacred and the human. As with the previous occasion, the moral exemplarity
of Christ remains to be given a showing. This is not the first time that this kind
of change has occurred. That it has happened twice suggests either a subtle
shift of priorities—or a difference of personal valuation and emphasis—on
the part of whoever made the changes. Indeed, the description of Christ being
exemplary is rephrased tellingly; for Love's 'ȝaff himself to vs in to ensaumple
of gode leuyng' becomes, emphatically, 'gaue himself chieflie for a pattern vnto
vs in exsample of good liuinge'. In Love's text, Christ is hailed as exemplary.
Exemplariness is by definition something on which to model oneself, but the
later text makes this even more explicit, with the word 'pattern' formalising
and reifying the instrumental functionality of this gift of exemplarity—which,
as a 'pattern', is thus a gift of method. It is not just that Christ's behaviour is
exemplary—He Himself is a template of exemplarity.

Further shades of change show themselves in the modifications of Love's
statement about the capabilities of his target audience and the suitability of
the *Meditationes vitae Christi* for them. Love highlights his work as partaking in
a potent tradition of texts combining Scripture and other writing. His work, he
indicates, is rich with clear teaching and sovereignly edifying to the relatively
uneducated:

> þe whiche scripture ande wrytyng for þe fructuouse matere þerof steryng
> specialy to þe loue of Jesu ande also for þe pleyn sentence to comun
> vndirstondyng semeþ amonges oþere souereynly edifiyng to symple
> creatures, þe whiche as childryn hauen nede to be fedde with mylke

---

12   'And, moreover, there is no sin or wickedness, but that he may be protected and kept from
     it who inwardly loves and follows the blessed words and deeds of Christ, who gave himself
     chiefly as a pattern for us as example of good living'.

of lyȝte doctryne & not with sadde mete of grete clargye and of hye contemplacion.[13] (Love 10)

The later edition re-identifies the nature of the text and the terms of its operation: the important distinction, 'scripture (i.e. biblical text) ande wrytyng' (i.e. parabiblical commentary, hagiography, devotional matter), is mutated into a rather different term: 'worke':

> the whiche worke for þe fructuous matter therof mouinge specialy to þe loue of oure lorde Iesu Christ, and also for the playne sense thereof to comon vnderstandynge semeth amonge other soueraignely edifyenge to symple people. The whiche as children haue neede to be fedde with mylke of lyght doctryne and not with sadde mete of greate & of hyghe contemplacyon.[14]

Love's self-consciousness about the biblical-parabiblical hybridity of his text, and his re-advertising of the conventions by which Holy Church combines Holy Writ with works that augment it and adjudicate its meanings and applications, is swept away in favour of a single word that connotes not just 'a work' in the sense of a 'text', but also 'work' as spiritual labour. When Love refers to the 'pleyn sentence' of the *Meditationes* he is referring to its teaching, spiritual import and wider application. Douai reduces this to an issue of exemplary clarity of meaning in the source: 'the playne sence thereof'. Evidently, by the early seventeenth century, the word 'playne' had lost touch with its French-derived Middle English meaning of 'full' or 'rich'. ('Prose pleyne', in earlier times, was that species of extrapolated glossatory prose that unpacked the meaning and the *sententia* from authoritative sources and their commentaries: such fecund plenitude is not to be found in Douai's 'playne'.)

---

13   'Which scripture and writing for its fructuous matter stirring especially to the love of Jesus and also for its clear and full meaning and teaching for the purpose of common understanding seems amongst other things to be sovereignly edifying to simple creatures, who as children need to be fed with the milk of light instruction and not with the solid meat of great learning and high contemplation'.

14   'Which work, for its fructuous matter moving especially to the love of Our Lord Jesus Christ, and also for its plain sense to common understanding, seems amongst other works to be sovereignly edifying for simple people, who as children need to be fed with the milk of light instruction and not with the solid meat of great and of high contemplation'. (Douai 5–6)

Other issues emerge in the shifts undergone by this passage. Love's 'symple creatures' are now 'symple people'. 'Creatures' (a conventional-enough humble (self-)label in late medieval devotional texts) are called thus because they are created by God, and owe all to Him. The collective noun, 'people', on the other hand, encompasses not only individuals but also a notion of a collectivity of individual Christians—in this case the marginalised and exiled recusant community of souls for whom this new print of the *Mirror* is intended. The term 'people' has a greater possibility of reflecting a communal solidarity and sounds more dignified than its predecessor, to be sure.

Why, one wonders, does the later text seemingly dispense with the notion of clerkly skill and learning in 'sadde mete of grete clargye and of hyghe contemplacion' by replacing it with 'sadde mete of greate & of hye contemplacyon'? The wording of the later version is grammatically and syntactically sound, but the awkwardness of the preposition 'of' being repeated in '*of* greate & *of* hyghe' might be evidence for simple accidental omission of 'clargye' at some point in the process of transmission. On the other hand, deliberately omitting it might have been seen as a means of creating a simplified but usefully clean distinction between two kinds of disciplined activity: basic instruction on the one hand and advanced contemplation on the other. The term 'clargye', true enough, can refer to skill, but it also conjures up the idea of a body of scholarship—a corpus and a tradition rather than disciplined mental action. The main meaning of 'clargye', of course, perhaps even riper for suppressing, was, at this time as it is now, the body of people ordained by, and working for, the Church. Perhaps Love's use of the term might have looked a bit odd to early seventeenth-century readers, or even been potentially misleading—in which case whoever adapted this text might simply have decided to exclude the word in order to avoid confusion or unnecessarily archaic arcaneness.

Scholastic Valorising?

Love's *proheme* is written in the late medieval tradition of the academic prologue, and accordingly deploys the idioms and attitudes of the *accessus* in the ways in which it packages and offers the work to the world and to its readers. The *Mirror* also, throughout its length, employs the scholastic discourses of *compilatio* and *ordinatio* in its representation and treatment of its *materiae*. It is noteworthy, therefore, that there is something scholastic in the manner of the Douai version's adaptation of Love's *proheme*. When it comes to the passage in the Middle English work where Love tells us his readers that he has added to and expanded some of his sources but also cut out materials,

the early modern work chooses to change significantly Love's description
of his mode of textual procedure, and it does so in a rather scholastically
analytical way:

> Wherfore at þe instance & þe prayer of some deuoute soules to edifica-
> tion of suche men or women is þis drawynge oute of þe forseide boke of
> cristes lyfe wryten in englysche with more putte to in certeyn partes &
> also wiþdrawyng of diuerse auctoritis and maters as it semeth to þe wry-
> ter hereof moste spedefull & edifyng to hem þat bene of symple vndir-
> stondyng.[15] (Love 10)

> therfore at the instaunce and prayer of some deuoute soules and to the
> edifycacyon of such men or women is this drawen out of þe forsaid boke,
> specyfyenge & declarynge the blyssed lyfe of our sauyour and redeemer
> Iesu Chryst writen in our English and vulgare tonge, and put into such
> order and method as semeth to the wryter therof most meete & edyfienge
> to them that be but of symple vnderstandynge and frayle entendement.[16]
> (Douai 6)

The earlier work's 'with more putte to in certeyn partes & also wiþdrawyng
of diuerse auctoritis and maters' is replaced with a substantial and carefully
worded string of prose. The first significant element in this new strand is a positive description of the way the book proceeds, 'specyfyenge & declarynge the
blyssed lyfe of our sauyour and redeemer'. 'Specyfyenge' is not only a matter
of relating in detail but also one of identifying and elucidating the individual
components of which the text is constructed, whilst 'declarynge' comprises
forthright description and is also a form of public announcement, and thus
of valorisation: for anything worthy of being declared is per se worthy in the
first place. This strategically chosen doublet, replacing and changing Love's
words about sources expanded and sources cut, sits well with the subsequent,

---

15   'Wherefore at the instance and the prayer of some devout souls is this translation of the
      foresaid book of Christ's life written in English for the edification of such men or women,
      with more added in certain parts and also with the excision of divers authorities and mat-
      ters as it seems to the writer of this work to be most successful and edifying for those who
      are of simple understanding'.
16   'Therefore at the instance and the prayer of some devout souls and for the edification of
      such men or women is this translated from the foresaid book, specifying and declaring
      the blessed life of our saviour and redeemer Jesus Christ written in our vulgar English
      tongue, and given such order and method as seems to its writer to be most fitting and
      edifying for those who are but of simple understanding and frail comprehension'.

second, significant change within this passage; for next it is to be noted that Love's 'wryten in englysche' becomes a judgemental-looking 'our English and vulgare tonge'. The negativity of the linguistic and cultural judgementalism that would otherwise be inflicted by such a statement has, however, already been neutralised by the previous change to the source, for 'specyfyenge & declarynge the blyssed lyfe of our sauyour and redemer Iesu Chryst' has already outflank-ingly proclaimed the value of what this text does, despite it being 'writen in our English and vulgare tonge'. This is a marker of, and testimony to, the blessed life and, by extension, to this text in its current adapted form.

The third significant feature of this replacement of Love's words concern-ing sources amplified and sources reduced consists of an acknowledgement that the work's mode of proceeding is congruous with, and beneficial for, its intended users, that is, 'put into such order and method as semeth to the wryter therof most meete & edifienge to them that be but of symple vnderstandynge and frayle entendement'. The work, seen again in terms of analytic structural terminology with a whiff of scholasticism, is declared to possess 'order and method': this is certainly true, because the *Mirror* functions typically by cycles of narration and imaginative extrapolation followed by moral or spiritual com-ment leading at times to prayerfulness. This sequence is identified by the early modern adaptor as not just edifying but as 'meete'—that is, as congruous and as proportionate to the specific needs, shortcomings and capabilities of the readers, who, in the original, as here, are those of simple understanding, and who are for the most part relatively uneducated or not mystically athletic. This category of readers is extended, in the Douai paratext, however, to those of 'frayle entendement', whose intellectual stamina or strength of purpose might in other circumstances (but not now of course in reading this 'meete' book) fail. Here, the early modern text advertises its own judgement—that it in par-ticular, rather than other books, will continue to be used by those who might otherwise be lost to Christocentric piety.

Cecile, Cecily and Reading

In a volume on religious reading it is particularly appropriate to pay due attention to a saint who was seen as a model reader of the life of Christ in the Middle Ages and afterwards. St Cecilia always bore the gospel of Christ hidden within the privity of her heart. She was the ultimate reader who never stopped reading and ingesting the ultimate text, even when she had no book with her. Her soul always faced heavenward in prayer—this being most famously so at her wedding feast, as narrated at the opening of the Latin *prohemium* of the

Meditationes vitae Christi, as translated by Nicholas Love, and as adapted fascinatingly in the Douai version of the work:

> unde in pompa nuptiarum existens, ubi tot vana geruntur, cantantibus organis, ipsa stabili corde soli Deo vacabat, dicens: 'Fiat, Domine, cor meum, et corpus meum immaculatum, ut non confundar'.[17] (Peltier 510)

> For in alle þe grete pompe of weddyngis, where so many vanytees bene usede, whene þe organes blewene & songene, she set hir herte stably in god, seying & praying, *Lord be my herte & my body clene, & not defiledeː so þat I be not confondet.*[18] (Love 12)

> For in all the greate pompe of weddinge where so many vanities be vsed, when the organs blewen and songe, she sette her heart stedfastly in God, praying & sayinge *Lord is my harte, and my body cleane and not defiled, so that I be not confounded.*[19] (Douai 12)

There are two subtle differences between the English texts. Whereas Love's Cecile sets her heart 'stably' in God, reflecting the Latin 'stabili', the Douai Cecily does so 'stedfastly', the later text being less interested in the idea of stabilisation and more in using an adjective which, although it services a sense of stability, also accommodates notions of fixity and loyalty. More intriguingly, 'stedfastly' is suitable because it is so commonly collocated with 'hope'—the key theological virtue dominating the paratext and indeed the whole conception of Love's *Mirror*.

The other small but transformative difference with Cecily, as opposed to Cecile, is an apparent new declarativeness and logical outcome to her prayer. Cecile beseeches God to protect her from defilement, so that she be not undone: 'seying & praying. *Lord be my herte & my body clene, & not defiledeː so þat I be not confondet*'. The Middle English saint is presented as 'seying &

17　'Thus, even as a guest amid the pomp of wedding celebrations where so much vanity was on display and the blaring music played on, she prayed with unshaken heart, and sang to her God alone, *"Keep my heart clean, O Lord, that I not be confounded"*'. John of Caulibus, *Meditations on the Life of Christ*, trans. F.X. Taney – A. Miller – C.M. Stallings-Taney (Asheville NC: 1999) 1–2.

18　'For amidst all the great pomp of the wedding, where so many vanities were used, when the organs blew and sang she set her heart stably in God, saying and praying, *Lord be my heart and my body clean, and not defiled; so that I be not confounded*'.

19　'For amidst all the great pomp of wedding, where so many vanities are used, when the organs blew and sang she set her heart steadfastly in God, praying and saying, *Lord, is my heart and my body clean, and not defiled, so that I be not confounded*'.

praying': Cecily, rather differently, is presented as praying and saying: 'praying & sayinge *Lord is my harte, and my body cleane and not defiled, so that I be not confounded*. It is more fitting that someone in a perpetual state of prayer should be depicted as praying before vocalising (even though the two activities are simultaneous): the voice is a merely physical external symptom of the interior spiritual motion of heavenward address and action.

Cecily's prayer itself is, rather challengingly, worded differently from Cecile's: the petitionary 'be' is replaced with the declarative 'is': Cecily thereby would seem to be announcing baldly that her heart and body are indeed clean—which has the effect of making her words, '*so that I be not confounded*', into a present logical consequence rather than the hoped-for future state besought by her Middle English predecessor. This reformulation of such a famous prayer is surprising. One would have to entertain the notion that there may be error somewhere in transmission, especially as, 'are' would be more grammatically correct than 'is'. On the other hand, the word 'is' is typographically, transcriptionally, grammatically and semantically so unlike 'be' that it does seem to suggest a deliberate decision to reword the source to some end.

Following on from this iconic re-representation of an idealised meditant of the life of Christ, it is fitting next to look at alterations to key instructions to the readership on how to read properly:

> ¶ Wherefore þou þat coueytest to fele treuly þe fruyt of þis boke⸱ þou most with all þi þought & alle þin entent, in þat manere make þe in þi soule present to þoo þinges þat bene here writen seyd or done of oure lord Jesu, & þat bisily, likyngly & abydyngly, as þei þou hardest hem with þi bodily eres, or sey þaim with þin eyen don.[20] (Love 12–13)

> ¶ wherfore thou that coueytest to feele truly, the fruyte of this present booke thou must with all thy thoughte & thyne entent procure thee in thy soule present to those thinges that be here written, said, or done of oure lorde Iesu, And that earnestly and respectively, as though thou heardest them with thy bodily eares, or sawest them done with thy bodily eyes.[21] (Douai 14)

---

20   'Wherefore you who yearn to feel truly the fruit of this book, you must with all your thought and all your intent, in like manner make yourself present in your soul to those things that here are written, said or done of Our Lord Jesus, and doing so busily, happily and abidingly, as though you heard them with your bodily ears, or saw them done with your own eyes'.

21   'Wherefore you who yearn to feel truly the fruit of this present book, you must with all your thought and all your intent procure yourself present in your soul to those things that

Whereas the Middle English reader is counselled to 'make' him/herself present to what happens, the later reader is given the words 'procure thee in thy soule present'. Procuring is a more complex and formal task than simple making: it involves an element of forethought, supplicatory effort and sought grace, and a process of interior and transcendent negotiation rather than the simple action of the will—as signalled perhaps by 'make'.

The Middle English trio of adverbs, 'bisily, likyngly & abydyngly', services a particular range of meanings and spiritual conditions. The first, 'bisily', requires the kind of attentiveness that in late medieval moral and spiritual literature is so often depicted as being threatened by the vice of *idelnesse*. The second, 'likyngly', means both 'cheerfully' or 'happily', but also 'pleasantly' or 'pleasingly', and thus allows and promotes a degree of pleasure in the devotional experience. The third, 'abydyngly', requires sustained engagement and routine habituation: a pious imagination should rightly stay on the scene and reap benefit from that scene even after the book is closed.

The early modern English adverbs perform significantly different, albeit related, work, and suggest somewhat different spiritual conditions and desiderata. The first, 'earnestly', responds with some proximity of meaning to 'bisily', but it carries a sense of zeal and passion going beyond the diligence expressed by the Middle English adverb. The second Middle English adverb, 'likyngly', has disappeared. By now, this word was dropping out of use, and, apart from probably now being unfamiliar, it may have had too many associations with the kind of meanings we associate with the word 'like' nowadays—senses to do with trivial and fleeting whim, pleasure and selfishly unreflective preference disengaged from morality and religious life. (Ironically enough, the last attested use of the form 'likingli' in medieval England in the *Oxford English Dictionary* is that of Nicholas Love himself.)

The third adverb, 'abydyngly', has some propinquity with 'respectively', which seems to have been chosen with a degree of semantic and psychological subtlety by the Douai adaptation for its opportune range of senses. At this time, 'respectively' could mean 'carefully' or 'attentively' (*OED* sense 2.a): this would give it overlap with 'abydyngly' and also with 'bisily'. *OED* sense 4, 'respectfully', is also helpfully in play here. More intriguing and fitting, however, especially given our adaptor's concern with 'order and method' and 'specyfyenge & declarynge', is *OED* sense 3, 'considered individually or in turn, and in the order mentioned ... separately'. It is also worth considering that, inasmuch as it is etymologically related to the latinate lexis of seeing (for example,

---

here are written, said or done of Our Lord Jesus – and that earnestly and respectfully/ attentively, as though you heard them with your bodily ears, or saw them done with your bodily eyes'.

spectare), the use of the term here might have been at least partly suggested or buttressed by this passage's emphasis on the reader being present to visual experience (as in 'procure thee in thy soule present to those thinges' and as in 'sawest them done with thy bodily eyes'). That the seventeenth-century adaptor of Love's *Mirror* could bring such variegated possibilities of meaning into action through a single word choice says much about his/her capabilities and also about the lively and attentive potential of the religious culture of the time for resourcefully taking minute care of texts and readers *en mouvance*.

The closures of the earlier *proheme* and later preface represent the final local moves of Love and his adaptor at coordinating source, source-author, translator/adaptor, hearers, readers, and even the Almighty in pious transactional mutuality:

> ¶ And amongis oþere who so rediþ or heriþ þis boke felyng any gostly swetnes or grace þereþorth: pray he for charite specialy for þe auctour, & þe drawere oute þereof, as it is writen here in english, to þe profite of symple & deuoute soules as it was seide before. And þus endiþ þe proheme, & after foloweþ þe contemplacion for Moneday in þe first partie, & þe first chapitre.[22] (Love 13)

> Finally who so readeth or heareth this booke, feelinge any ghostly sweetnesse of grace thereby, pray yee of charitie specially for the author, & the drawer out therof as is writen here in englishe to the profite of the simple and deuoute soules as it was saide before. And thus endeth the preface, & after foloweth the contemplacion of the life of Christ the first part, and the first chapter.[23] (Douai 16)

The most obvious change here is that Love's reader/hearer, appealed to as a third-person singular 'he', is now addressed as a polite second-person plural 'yee'. One advantage of this shift is that it is, at one and the same time, more intimate but also more accommodating than is the third-person singular to a

---

22   'And amongst other things, whoso reads or hears this book and feels any spiritual sweetness or grace through it, pray for charity's sake especially for the author and the translator of this, as it is written here in English for the profit of simple & devout souls, as it was said before. And thus ends the proem, and hereafter in the first chapter of the first part follows the contemplation for Monday'.

23   'Finally, whoso reads or hears this book and feels any spiritual sweetness of grace thereby, pray in charity especially for its author and the translator of what is written here in English to the profit of the simple and devout souls, as it was said before. And thus ends the preface, and hereafter follows the contemplation of the first part and the first chapter of the life of Christ'.

plurality (or community) of readers and hearers. It should also be noted that what Love called a 'proheme' is now redesignated a 'preface'. In the usage of the church, the Preface was 'the introduction to the central part of the Eucharist' (*OED* sense 1). The term 'preface' clearly, then, had important associations with the living body, blood, presence and divinity of Christ. What term could then be better, in an adaptation of a *vita Christi*, for introducing the Sacred Humanity narratively and imaginatively into the souls of Christian readers? The *Meditationes vitae Christi* (along with its translations) envisages that it may instigate in its readers real dialogue in the soul with Christ: it therefore shares the Eucharist's transcendental semiotics as a *signum efficiens*, bringing into being that which it signifies—with analogously great spiritual profit to the recipient.

John Heigham's *Dedicatory Epistle*

Now we turn to John Heigham's 1622 text. It is a thoroughgoing revision of Love's text (even when it reconfirms and recycles Love's words), occasionally resorting to the Latin original, sometimes going its own way, and sometimes using sources that have not yet been identified by modern scholarship. In particular, the 'Documents for Vs', a series of numbered points or short lessons at the end of each chapter, regulate and interpret the meaning and application of the life of Christ for its community of readers, be they the immediate audience of Poor Clares at Gravelines, or a wider public of recusants at home or abroad. The paratextual features of Heigham's revision are rich in design and programmatic subtlety. The renovated and reworked title, for a start, signals much about the nature and the ambition of his project:

> The life of our blessed Lord and Sauiour Iesus Gathered, out of the venerable and famous doctor, Saint Bonauenture, and out of diuers other rare, renowned and Catholique doctors. Augmented, with twentie fiue whole chapters: each one enriched with manie most excellent and diuine documents. The second edition. [Newly coposed [sic]] by Iohn Heigham, and by him also published.

The first thing to note is that the *Mirror* title has gone. The work has been made by being 'Gathered, out of the venerable and famous doctor, Saint Bonauenture, and out of diuers other rare, renowned and Catholique doctors', in other words extracted and collected from the main Bonaventuran source and others. It might seem odd, however, that 'renowned' doctors should be also be 'rare', an intriguing word choice. However, 'rare' could at this time mean 'excellent' and 'refined', as well as expressing the property of seldom being found. If this last sense is in fact present, it could be referring to the difficulty of access that an exiled, impoverished, de-institutionalised and sparse recusant community might have to repositories of learned theological works.

Heigham's *Life* presents itself as something more than the *Meditationes vitae Christi*, and also something more than Love's *Mirror*, for it is 'Augmented, with twentie fiue whole chapters', and each chapter has something extra: points or lessons of instruction to be taken from each chapter of the book—'manie most excellent and diuine documents'. A 'document' is a lesson, admonition or piece of evidence: in this work 'the documents for vs' (as they are always enti-tled throughout the text) play all these roles. No wonder, then, that Heigham, claiming a degree of initiative and agency, labelled his work as being 'Newly co[m]posed'—a term that can indicate making in general and also the par-ticular kind of excerption and arrangement of materials in which a compiler engages.

Heigham's *Dedicatory Epistle* is a new, self-penned composition, completely replacing Love's *proheme*. It is startlingly different from its predecessor, and is in its own right an illuminating measure of the changed circumstances and directives now governing the work. Whereas Love's *proheme* was addressed to a national public, Heigham's epistle personally and individually addresses Mother Clara Mariana and by extension the Poor Clares of Gravelines in their house in the Francophone Spanish Netherlands. He starts by telling this 'REuerend and Religious Mother' (3) that, without the encouragement of her gracious nuns, he would have consigned his efforts to the flames shortly after beginning his enterprise. It is only right, therefore, that, having been supported so charitably in his venture by the Poor Clares, he should dedicate his work to 'their worthy Mother' (4). This is particularly fitting because Mother Clara Mariana, unlike the unworthy Heigham, leads a worthy spiritual life remark-ably in keeping with the very life of Christ that this unworthy 'Orator' (3) wishes to compose. Heigham accordingly would fly to the Abbess and her daughters (who have already profited from the *vita* Christi) and seek protection and an assured reception for his work. He closes his epistle by offering not only his work for her to harbour, love and look into often as her 'spouses picture' (6), but also his prayers that she and her daughters might thrive and live happily in this world and the next.

Throughout his remarkable epistle, Heigham, for all his florid formality and decorum, is subtle and particular in fine-tuning his paratext for specific pur-poses. He re-performs his own version of a conventional mini-drama in which a topically unworthy would-be devotional author is dissuaded from abandon-ing his project by the spiritual worthiness, encouragement and prayers of a pious commissioning audience:

REuerend and Religious Mother, I haue now at last brought to an end, the Treatise of the life of Christ; Which as is well knowen to some of your Religious daughters, when I had but newly begun the same, and imparting to their view, the suruey of some few imperfect sheets, albeit they greatly besought me to goe forward therin, yet the feare that I had of myne owne insufficiencie, to touche or handle any further that sacred historie, moued me with all sinceritie to beseech them, to take and burne them, to the end I neuer more might ether see them, or thinke vpon them: fearing euen from that first abord, to spot or blemishe the praises of that worthie life, with my prophane and vnworthie pen; yea iudging that such humble ashes would far more honor it, then so far vnworthie an Orator could worthily extoll it: whose venerable sanctitie indeed is such, as nether Cherubin nor Seraphin, nor any sufficiencie ether of man or Angell, is able to extoll as it deserueth.

Notwithstanding, so far did their most pious desires preuayle with me, depending much (next after God) vpon the assistance of their holy prayers, that I promised them to employ therein, all the litle talent which God had lent me. Confessing my selfe, therfore, both encouraged, & assisted, by these your deuout and religious daughters, I could in dutie doe no lesse, then dedicate the same vnto your selfe, their worthy Mother. (Heigham 3–4)

Heigham's fleeting tantrum is decorous, for it signals the humility of humiliation. His resumption of the task is defensible by being defined as a 'dutie' rather than as a matter of personal achievement. With Christocentric fittingness, he casts himself as the good servant of Jesus's parable, who did not bury his talent, but employed it productively in accordance with the wishes of his master (allegorically, God). The Poor Clares' prayers thus have an agency in the production and use of the work, and bestow spiritual authority on its transcendent textual economy.

Heigham portrays himself as an 'Orator', that is, as a petitioner, advocate, someone who prays, someone who deals in rhetorical discourse. All these roles overlap and interact in the moralised persona voicing and acting in his paratext. This moralised persona is developed further when Heigham applies to himself the role of confession: 'Confessing my selfe, therfore, both encouraged, & assisted, by these your deuout and religious daughters...'. Note here, however, that Heigham is playing with the term and giving it an empowering new sense *in bono*. Normally, confession applies to bad deeds and sins, but here what is confessed is good and transformative. Here Heigham is preserving his humility by applying an otherwise fault-inventorying discourse to himself, whilst at the same time benefiting from a remedial transformation of attitude assisted by the nuns. In the same operation and at the same time he valorises his textual behaviour as a function of his own free will and inalienable responsibility (as any good Catholic must).

Heigham's self-presentation as an unworthy confessing subject is not, however, the only example of how he deploys theologically conceitful narrativisation in his paratext to advance his ends. In the next stage of his dedicatory epistle he casts the actants involved in the production of his text in terms of a theologised plot informed by the processes and problematics of congruous grace—which was very much a concern of the Jesuits and the wider Catholic learned culture of the time that shaped Heigham, who was influenced by the likes of 'Bellarmine and other Jesuit authors'.[24] Put briefly, for a free-willed act of grace to be fully salutary, it was thought desirable not only for there to be a sufficiency of grace (routinely designated 'sufficient grace') on the part of the free-willed Christian committing any given act or motion of the will, but also that God would freely and graciously, through His 'congruous grace', dispose circumstances conducing to the efficacy and completion of such a salutary act. This external grace is 'congruous' because it homologously fits the interior disposition and exterior situation of the soul endeavouring to commit a salutary act of grace. Heigham adopts the terms and logistics of congruous grace in order to justify and valorise the production and authority of his work.

We saw above how Heigham, initially 'insufficient' to his task, was stirred into a measure of sufficiency by the encouragement and prayers of the Poor Clares. Next, he takes pointed care to exploit further the conceit of sufficiency and congruity in order to bring his work into complete and fruitful being for its own befitting sake:

> But this reason alone, although at the first it may seeme sufficient, yet did I feele my selfe moued hereto by another reason, of greater force and more important. For considering, that to dedicate so inestimable a pearle as the life of Christ, it seemeth congruous, that ether in the dedicator, or else in them to whom the same is to be dedicated, there should be some conformitie with the same life: which finding to be wholie wanting in my selfe, I iudged it to be my securest course, humbly to fly to you and to those of yours, as vnto those who haue profited so well, & who approache so nere to that blessed life, as is hardly possible for human frailtie to approach more nere, leading, as I may trulie say, in earthely bodies, the liues of Angells. (Heigham 4–5)

---

24   Scheck, "The Polemics of John Heigham" 13.

The final grace guaranteeing completion is, of course, the Religious Mother: she is the agent of gracious congruity, and this congruity is all the stronger by being twofold. Firstly, the congruity of her life with the life which is the matter and meaning of Heigham's work licenses the Religious Mother as the force of teleologically apt congruous grace simultaneously embodied in her being the work's ideal reader—as its dedicatee—a reader who has already 'profited so well' from the *vita Christi* that Heigham's work is already justifiable in terms of its bestowable benefits. Note here, that for all Heigham's inferior petitionary pose and alleged unworthiness, he never loses clear sight of his own free will and responsibility, for he judges his own course: 'I iudged it to be my securest course, humbly to fly to you and to those of yours'.

Heigham decides to flie/flee to the Religious Mother and her daughters as would a religious exile seeking shelter, or a pilgrim seeking hospitality. In addition to this, he continues to assert the congruity of his enterprise with those who inspired and are best fitted to receive it—simply because they are already shaped by it anyway:

> For this reason therfore, although all shall iudge me most vnworthie, to dedicate the same vnto you and yours, as indeed I am, yet all will iudge you most worthie to protect the same, as indeed you are; For to whom could I better dedicate it, then to those who first induced me to compile it? Who could I deeme would more gladly receiue it, then those whose [*sic*] so nerely imitate it? Who more carefully foster it, then those who so nerely follow it? Or who more willingly protect it, then those who in their owne liues, so strictly obserue it, that to behould the same, sensuall Libertines stand amazed, lazie Heretiques are quite confounded virtuous Catholiques are maruellously edified, and God him selfe is greatly glorified.[25] (Heigham 5)

These nuns would 'gladly receiue it': the verb of receiving invokes not only the idiom of hospitality but also the receiving of the Eucharist, and the loving receiving of the divine spouse, which this new 'mirror of Christ' contains and envisions. In accordance with this, the Religious Mother, at the climax of the *Dedicatory Epistle*, is eloquently petitioned by her orator to lodge, love and look often at his unworthy present to her:

---

25   The words 'lazie Heretiques are quite confounded virtuous Catholiques are maruellously edified' echo Love's *Mirror* 7, 152, 221, which thrice advertises a policy of confounding false Lollards and heretics and edifying the faithful.

> Receiue then (Right virtuous and Religious Mother) this my poore and
> vnworthie present, under the winges of your protection, to whom my pen,
> my hande, and hart, hath wholie deuouted this diuine treatise. Lodge it,
> loue it, and looke often into it. Lodge it nere vnto you: loue it as deare
> vnto you: looke often into it as delighting you. Lodge it, because it cometh
> to you for harbour; loue it, because it is your spouses picture: looke often
> into it, because it is a most perfect mirour. (Heigham 6)

The new wings of protection remind one of the Virgin Mary conventionally
sheltering Franciscans under her cloak. This book, however, is to be lodged
with hospitality and harboured in loyallest recusant style. The Religious
Mother will indubitably be able to 'lodge it nere vnto' her because her life, as
we have heard so assertively, is near to that holy life already. She will love the
book, because it is her spouse's picture. She will 'looke often into it, because
it is a most perfect mirour' (a notion prompted perhaps by Love's words in
his *proheme*: 'as þe ymage of mans face is shewed in þe mirroure' (p. 11). This
connexion with Love's *Mirror*, whether it is an allusion or not, is nevertheless
a salutary reminder that this text, for all its changes, new audience and new
circumstances of production, is still, in one sense, the *Mirror*, even though, in
another sense, it is not.

Heigham signs off with a closure in which the words 'blesse' and 'life' echo
his new title, blessing the Abbess and her daughters with all that the text means:

> And I your humble orator shall euer pray, that God would daylie prosper
> your religious designes, make you Mother of many religious couents, day-
> lie multiplye your religious daughters. And finally, blesse both you and
> them, with long life and happines in this world, and with euerlasting life
> and happines in the other.
>
> Your Reuerences euer humble seruant in our Sauiour Iesus.
> IOHN HEIGHAM.
> (Heigham 3–4)

There is more here than Heigham's expression of a general desire for the
increase and the flourishing of the kinds of convents and pious daughters
overseen by the Religious Mother. By signing his own name into this desidera-
tum, Heigham definitively signs himself into the service of his readers and his
God, and also takes full public confessional responsibility and potential credit
for his devout labour. His opening paratext has done its work well.

Conclusion

Paratextual changes in the tradition of this text are often eloquent and revealing. We have seen how the 1606 reprint modified the *Mirror*: these modifications were not always consistent but they frequently seem to be the result of
someone thinking purposefully about the import of such details for the good
of the text and the reader. Frequently, such modifications suggest a mode of
understanding as to how Love's text does or should work, as with the scholastic-
looking choices of rewording that describe the nature and procedure of the
work. Sometimes, the modifications may be a matter of emphasis—as with
the seeming concern to highlight Christ as a pattern of moral exemplarity and
to downplay the nature of the Incarnation. They provide evidence of what the
adaptor found to be of most value him/herself or what s/he believed to be
most needful to know and follow for his intended readers (or hearers).

In the 1606 Douai edition of Nicholas Love's text, a fascinatingly amended
proheme repeats old work and makes new work, endeavouring to assure the
Mirror of a fruitful reception whilst keeping faith with its original intent and
devotional character. And even though it is so very different, Heigham's total
replacement of Love's public *proheme* with a (more ostensibly private and personally addressed) dedicatory epistle in the 1622 St Omer revision performs
a similar range of old and new work in fitting this monument of devotional
tradition to new and straitened circumstances. 1606 shows how fine-tuneable
paratexts could be; 1622 shows that total paratextual replacement, far from
being a gesture only of rejection, can more importantly be a tool in the pres-
ervation and continued advancement of the mighty *Meditationes vitae Christi*
and Love's *Mirror*, which would in the following centuries would undergo
further transformations, as, for example, with the Reverend Edward Yates's
politely accessible Anglican version of 1739. In later re-adaptations, the work
would enjoy new readerships, as it did amongst the Irish Catholic diaspora of
the nineteenth-century United States—and the story does not stop here.

Modern scholars and critics of translation have been known to favour the
idea of displacement for understanding the relations between, on the one
hand, source-texts and cultures and, on the other, target texts and cultures.[26]
As far as the history of the *Mirror* is concerned, it is the readers who, most
palpably and most often, were displaced. Its translators and translations had to
accommodate this, and from the various (in)congruities and (in)sufficiencies

---

26   For extensive and influential discussion of translation and displacement, see Copeland R.,
     *Rhetoric, Hermeneutics, and Translation in the Middle Ages. Academic Traditions and
     Vernacular Texts* (Cambridge: 1991).

with which translators and adaptors went about their work in their paratexts, we can only learn.

Bibliography

Allison A.F., "John Heigham of S. Omer (c. 1568–c. 1632)", *Recusant History* 4,6 (1957–1958) 226–240.

Caulibus John of, *Meditations on the Life of Christ*, trans. F.X. Taney – A. Miller – C.M. Stallings-Taney (Asheville NC: 1999).

———, *Geographies of Orthodoxy*. Queen's University Belfast-St Andrews Arts and Humanities Research Council project web site at: http://www.qub.ac.uk/geographies-of-orthodoxy/.

Copeland R., *Rhetoric, Hermeneutics, and Translation in the Middle Ages. Academic Traditions and Vernacular Texts* (Cambridge: 1991).

Doyle A.I., "Recusant Versions of the *Meditationes Vitae Christi*", *Bodleian Library Record* 15 (1994–1996) 411–413.

Ghosh K., "Nicholas Love", in Edwards A.S.G. (ed), *A Companion to Middle English Prose* (Cambridge: 2004) 53–66.

Gillespie V., "From the Twelfth Century to *c.* 1450", in Minnis A. – Johnson I. (eds), *The Cambridge History of Literary Criticism*, vol. II, *The Middle Ages* (Cambridge: 2005) 145–235.

Heigham J., *The life of our blessed Lord and Sauiour Iesus Gathered, out of the venerable and famous doctor, Saint Bonauenture, and out of diuers other rare, renowned and Catholique doctors* (St Omer, C. Boscard: 1622) STC 13034, accessed as EEBO TCP02A.00015594.

Johnson I. – Westphall A. (eds), *The Pseudo-Bonaventuran Lives of Christ. Exploring the Middle English Tradition* (Turnhout: 2013).

Love N., *Nicholas Love's Mirror of the Blessed Life of Jesus Christ. A Critical Edition Based on Cambridge University Library Additional MSS 6578 and 6686*, ed. M.G. Sargent (Exeter: 2005).

McNamer S., "The Origins of the *Meditationes vitae Christi*", *Speculum* 84 (2009) 905–955.

Meditationes vitae Christi, in Peltier A.C. (ed), *Opera omnia sancti Bonaventurae*, 15 vols. (Paris: 1864–1871), vol. XII (1868) 509–630.

The Miroure of the Blessed Life of our Lorde and Savioure Iesus Christe (Douai, C. Boscard: 1606) STC 3269, accessed as EEBO TCP02A.00014580.

Rogers D.M., *The Contemporary Printed Literature of the English Counter-Reformation between 1558 and 1640. An Annotated Catalogue*, 2 vols. (Aldershot: 1989–1994).

Salter E., *Nicholas Love's 'Myrrour of the Blessed Lyf of Jesu Christ'*, Analecta Cartusiana 10 (Salzburg: 1974).

Scheck T., "The Polemics of John Heigham and Richard Montagu and the Rise of English Arminianism", *Recusant History* 29,2 (2008) 22–29.

Tóth P. – Falvay D., "From the Apostle Peter to Bonaventure the Cardinal: Rethinking the Date and Authorship of the *Meditationes Vitae Christi*", in Kelly S. – Perry R. (eds.), *Devotional Culture in Late Medieval England and Europe. Diverse Imaginations of Christ's Life* (Turnhout: forthcoming, 2015).

CHAPTER 9

Vernacular Biblical Literature in Sixteenth-Century Italy: Universal Reading and Specific Readers

Élise Boillet

The sixteenth century saw a vast production of printed biblical literature in Italian, a significant part of which was devoted to the Psalms. In Christian tradition the Psalter, either in whole or in part, was always one of the major aids for exegesis, liturgy and devotion. In sixteenth-century Europe, the Psalms were central to the revival of biblical literature, which was connected with the climate of religious turmoil, the expansion of the printing industry and the rise of the vernacular tongues. In Italy, the decades of the 1520s and 1530s saw the dissemination of Erasmian and Lutheran ideas and the development of 'evangelical' thinking. They were also marked by the *questione della lingua*, which opposed two conceptions of the vernacular: one as an instrument of wide cultural transmission and the other as a medium of rhetorical and literary expression. This contribution, which will focus on printed Italian books on the Psalms in the sixteenth century, will therefore consider the issue of vernacular language and intended readership in connection with Italian history, religion and linguistics.

Italian Psalm Books in the Sixteenth Century: An Overview

The Psalms generated a remarkable quantity and variety of texts in sixteenth-century Italy.[1] From the early days of printing, the Psalter was available in the translation by Nicolò Malerbi, a Camaldolese monk from Venice. Malerbi

---

1   Anne Jacobson Schutte provides a list of translations, commentaries, sermons, rewrites in verse and prose in *Printed Italian Vernacular Religious Books 1465–1550: a finding list* (Geneva: 1983) 86–90. As we will see, this production consisted of both old and new books. It was in any case part of a tradition of vernacular Bible translations which began long before the age of the printing industry (cfr. Corbellini S., "Looking in the Mirror of the Scriptures: Reading the Bible in Medieval Italy", in François W. – Den Hollander A.A. (eds.), *Wading Lambs and Swimming Elephants: The Bible for the Laity and Theologians in Late Medieval and Early Modern Era* (Leuven: 2012). See also below, n. 58.

entered the orders a year before the Venice publication in 1471 of his translation of the Bible from the Latin Vulgate, the first complete printed vernacular translation of the Bible, appearing even before the German and English versions.[2] The Psalter was published separately in 1476, the oldest partial edition of the Bible in Italian.[3] In the early 1530s, the Bible from Greek and Hebrew sources was published in a translation by the layman Antonio Brucioli, a Florentine exile who spent time in France and Germany before settling in Venice. There, he published a series of biblical works, translations and commentaries.[4] Brucioli's translation, based on Erasmus's Latin translation of the New Testament and Pagnini's of the Old Testament, clearly reflects the advances of biblical philology.[5] In terms of biblical disclosure and access, the decision, new in Italy, to publish the New Testament in 1530 and the Psalms in 1531, before the entire Bible in 1532, was inspired by Lefèvre d'Étaples and Luther.[6] It highlights, in a Christocentric religious perspective focused on the question of salvation, the joint importance of evangelical revelation and the prophecies of David. The publication of the Psalms, the translation in 1531 and the commentary in 1534,

---

2   On Malerbi and his translation, see especially Barbieri E., *Le Bibbie italiane del Quattrocento e del Cinquecento* 1 (Milano: 1992) 15–106; Fragnito G., *La Bibbia al rogo. La censura ecclesiastica e i volgarizzamenti della Scrittura (1471–1605)* (Bologna: 1997) 40–43; Barbieri E., "Malerbi (Malermi, Manerbi), Nicolò" in *Dizionario biografico degli italiani* 68 (2007) 149–151; Pierno F., "Pregiudizi e canone letterario. La Bibbia in volgare di Niccolò Malerbi (Venezia, 1471)", *Rassegna europea di letteratura italiana* 36 (2011) 143–157. See the description of the 1471 edition in Barbieri, *Le Bibbie italiane*, 187–190.

3   See the description of the Psalter of 1476 in Barbieri, *Le Bibbie italiane* 197–198. On this edition, see also Trovato P., *Il primo Cinquecento*, in Bruni F. (ed.), *Storia della lingua italiana* (Bologna: 1994) 171–176.

4   On Brucioli, see Spini G., *Tra Rinascimento e Riforma. Antonio Brucioli* (Firenze: 1940); Dionisotti C., "La testimonianza del Brucioli" [1979], in Dionisotti C., *Machiavellerie* (Turin: 1980) 193–226; Boillet É. (ed.), *Antonio Brucioli. Humanisme et évangélisme entre Réforme et Contre-Réforme* (Paris: 2008). On his translation of the Bible, see Paccagnella I., *Il fasto delle lingue. Plurilinguismo letterario nel Cinquecento* (Rome: 1984) 146–151; Barbieri, *Le Bibbie italiane* 107–127; Paccagnella, "La 'Bibbia Brucioli'. Note linguistiche sulla traduzione del 'Nuovo Testamento' del 1530", in *Omaggio a Gianfranco Folena* (Padua: 1993) 1075–1087; Fragnito, *La Bibbia al rogo* 29–32, 34–39, 63–65, 71–72.

5   Cfr. Fragnito, *La Bibbia al rogo* 29–31. But Brucioli's translation, which is also based on that of Malerbi, must not be set in opposition with the latter from the point of view of a modernity that characterizes each at the time of its publication. Cfr. Pierno, "Pregiudizi e canone letterario" 156–157.

6   Cfr. Pierno, "Pregiudizi e canone letterario" 64. See the description of the Psalms of 1531 in Barbieri, *Le Bibbie italiane* 244–245.

while reflecting a choice to 'neutrally' address all Christians,[7] guide the reader to an interpretation that tends to negate the meritorious value of human activity performed with a view to salvation.[8]

Between the translations by Malerbi and Brucioli, books such as *Psalterio abbreviato di sancto Hieronimo* and *Virtù di psalmi*[9] were more modest popularization works with reduced textual material and, in the case of the latter, a superstitious approach. In the early decades of the sixteenth century, new works primarily intended for the monastic milieu present the biblical text as an aid to meditation and mental prayer. This is especially true of the penitential psalms, translated with commentary by Girolamo Benivieni (Florence, 1505), and a collection of sermons on the Psalms by Lodovico Pittorio (first edition Bologna, 1524), two works to be discussed in greater detail below.[10]

In Venice, the 1530s, which opened with the publication of Brucioli's translation, was a particularly rich decade for biblical literature, an incentive for Christians to read, study and meditate on the biblical text.[11] This literature, much of it devoted to the Psalms, consisted of first editions and re-editions,[12] translations, commentaries and literary rewritings. In poetry, the penitential psalms by Luigi Alamanni, published in Florence, have to be mentioned as a discrete point of transition in the Florentine tradition prior to the wealth of Italian of poetic versions in the second half of the century.[13] In prose, the penitential psalms by Pietro Aretino, published in Venice in 1534, was reprinted several times in the 1530s and 1540s until 1551.[14]

---

7   Cfr. Fragnito, *La Bibbia al rogo* 72.

8   See below, n. 61–62.

9   Cfr. Jacobson Schutte, *Printed Italian Vernacular Religious Books* 87, 90.

10   See below, n. 24–25, 35–36.

11   Cfr. Boillet É., "L'Écriture traduite, commentée, réécrite: Antonio Brucioli, Teofilo Folengo, l'Arétin", in Boillet D. – Plaisance M. (eds.), *Les années Trente du XVI*e *siècle italien* (Paris: 2007) 163–181. The authors of the introduction of *Psalms in the Early Modern World* (Farnham – Burlington, VT: 2011) evoke this period and mention Brucioli, Alamanni and Aretino in connection with a European production.

12   After Brucioli's translation came that of Giovanni Francesco da Pozzo, *Novissima traslatione degli Psalmi davitici dall'hebreo nella nostra volgar lingua, con brieve & christianissima espositione* (Venice, Bartolomeo Zanetti: 1537), whose title also emphasizes the novelty of a translation from the Hebrew.

13   The Alamanni's paraphrase, published in his *Opere Toscane* (1532), came between the versions of Girolamo Benivieni (1505) and Laura Battiferri (1564). It was later included in a Venetian anthology of penitential psalms (Giolito: 1568), in which we see this penitential poetry travel from its birthplace in Florence to the rest of Italy (on this anthology, see below, n. 18).

14   See below, n. 63.

In the second half of the century, when ecclesiastical censure came to bear heavily on biblical translations, the success of the Psalms in Italian is noteworthy, both in verse and prose.[15] From the 1560s onwards, the fortune of the versified Psalms, especially the penitential corpus, fostered the rising popularity of the *lagrime penitentiali* genre into the 1590s.[16] In prose, especially in the last three decades of the century, books on the Psalms are notable for their use of multiple forms that may be described in specific terms elsewhere encountered: *traduzione, esposizione, dichiarazione*, and also generic terms such as *discorsi, ragionamenti* and *considerazioni*.[17] This is a far cry from the verse and prose texts of the late fifteenth century, typified by authorial anonymity and a vagueness about the intended audience. Books from the second half of the sixteenth century highlight the status of the author, who often addresses a dedicatee of important social rank, and their contents are obviously impacted by the climate of censorship, but also by higher and more specific cultural expectations.[18]

This brief overview of the Psalms' fortune in Italian in the sixteenth century demonstrates how the issue of genre affected the readership of texts. Edoardo Barbieri, author of a systematic study of Italian Bible translations in the fifteenth and sixteenth centuries,[19] also provides an overview of related genres (the sermon, the commentary, the sacred narrative, the biblical anthology),[20] in which certain works may be classified in several categories at once. This overlap

---

15   Cfr. Fragnito, *La Bibbia al rogo* 204–208 et 302–308; Fragnito G., *Proibito capire. La Chiesa e il volgare nella prima età moderna* (Bologna: 2005) 208–211; Leri C., *"La voce dello Spiro". Salmi in Italia tra Cinquecento e Settecento* (Alessandria: 2011).

16   Cfr. Quondam A., *Note sulla tradizione della poesia spirituale e religiosa (parte prima)*, in Quondam A. (ed.), *Paradigmi e tradizioni* (Rome: 2005) 189–192, here 191.

17   For example: Bonaventura Gonzaga da Reggio, *Ragionamenti sopra i sette peccati mortali & sopra i sette salmi penitentiali del Re David ridotti in sette canzoni, & parafrasticati dal medesimo* (Venice, Gabriel Giolito: 1566); Teofilo Fedini, *Discorsi spirituali, sopra il giardino de peccatori: nella espositione de sette salmi penitentiali* (Venice, Gabriel Giolito: 1567); Chiara Matraini, *Considerationi sopra i Sette Salmi penitentiali del gran re, e profeta Davit* (Lucca, Vincenzo Busdraghi: 1586).

18   Thus, the anthology published by Francesco Turchi at Giolito, Venice, in 1568 (with a second emission in 1569) and reprinted in 1572 before the 1574 ban from Rome against the poetic versions of the Bible (cfr. Fragnito, *La Bibbia al rogo* 131–132): *Salmi penitentiali di diversi eccellenti autori. Con alcune rime spirituali, di diversi illust. cardinali; di reverendissimi vescovi, & d'altre persone ecclesiastiche. Scelti dal reverendo p. Francesco da Trevigi carmelitano* (cfr. Fragnito, *La Bibbia al rogo* 304; Quondam, *Note sulla tradizione della poesia spirituale e religiosa* 189–190, n. 119). Similarly, the paraphrase by Flaminio de' Nobili published in Venice in 1583 (see below, n. 72).

19   Barbieri, *Le Bibbie italiane*.

20   Barbieri, "Panorama. Parte I"; Barbieri, "Panorama. Parte II".

results from the close link between translation, commentary and paraphrase; it is also attributable to lack of clear boundaries between these genres and others, such as literary rewriting or the devotional book. Added to the hybridism of genre is that of language. Works are often bilingual: they may include the Latin biblical text, and Latin quotes may be inserted in the Italian text. Gigliola Fragnito, who examines the complex history of the Catholic Church's ban on Bible translations, from the Index of 1559 to that of 1596, describes the ecclesiastical scrutiny of Italian biblical book production in its various forms, production milieu and reception.[21] The most suspect texts were the poeticized works. In the case of the Psalms, only the prose paraphrase works by Flaminio de' Nobili and Francesco Panigarola were approved by the Sacred Congregation of the Index.[22] In terms of the forms and the purpose of biblical books in Italian vis-à-vis their intended readership, the commentary and analysis of Danilo Zardin are worthy of note. Zardin emphasizes the Bible's significant presence in sixteenth- and seventeenth-century Italian culture, even when its translation was banned. Zardin's work also details the many ways in which the simple believer gained access to the Bible, and the permeability of the categories of documents whereby biblical knowledge was transmitted.[23]

On the basis of this brief historical and critical overview, I will proceed to a closer examination of several sixteenth-century editions of the Psalms in Italian. Although these are texts of different types, a parallel may be established in terms of the issue at hand: the link between the use of the vernacular and the intended readership, specific or universal.

Girolamo Benivieni

If the title *Psalmi penitentiali di David tradocti en lingua fiorentina et commentati per Hieronymo Benivieni* leads us to expect a translation and commentary,[24] the text is a product of a 'converted' poet who is rethinking a form of humanism, cultivated in the circle of Lorenzo de' Medici, from a spiritual perspective

---

21   Fragnito, *La Bibbia al rogo*; Fragnito, *Proibito capire*.

22   Cfr. Fragnito, *La Bibbia al rogo* 204, 303, 307. On these texts, see below, n. 72, 74.

23   Zardin D., "Bibbia e apparati biblici nei conventi italiani del Cinque-Seicento. Primi appunti", in Borraccini R. M. – Rusconi R. (eds.), *Libri, biblioteche e cultura degli ordini regolari nell'Italia moderna attraverso la documentazione della Congregazione dell'Indice* (Città del Vaticano: 2006) 63–103.

24   *Penitential Psalms of David translated in Florentine language and commented by Girolamo Benivieni* (Florence, Antonio Tubini and Andrea Ghirlandi: 1505).

influenced by Girolamo Savonarola.[25] After the death of the Dominican, Benivieni published several works in Italian combining poetic text with commentary: a revised version of his own poetic compositions (1500), his verse translation of the penitential psalms (1505), and *The Divine Comedy* of Dante (1506).[26] In his *Psalmi penitentiali*, the prose commentary not only pertains to the translation *in terzine* for which the author substitutes the biblical text, but is itself driven by poetic inspiration that enriches the text with figures and images and, indeed, intermittent passages of verse. The book's purpose, to assist the devotional practice of the sisters of the Florentine nunnery Le Murate, determines a form of writing which mimics the mystical fervour that Bible reading is meant to arouse in nuns.

Moreover, the words 'tradocti' ('translated') and 'commentati' ('commented'), appearing in the title and seeming to refer to well-defined categories, are found in the preface to be defined with less precision. Benivieni wrote that he wanted his translation to stay very close to the original biblical text, but had not hesitated to 'interpret' certain passages; in such cases, he saw fit to move away from the 'shadow of words' towards 'the truth of meaning.'[27] Similarly, rather than a commentary in the conventional sense of the word, he wanted what he called a 'simple narrative' to be a 'continuous prayer', like the Psalms themselves.[28] The meaning this narrative reveals is only 'that which concerns the soul of the penitent', the mystical and especially Christological meaning, consistent with an exegetical line of thinking that runs from Augustine to

---

25   On Benivieni, see Vasoli C., "Benivieni, Girolamo", in *Dizionario Biografico degli Italiani* VIII (1966) 550–554; Di Benedetto S., "L'edizione giuntina delle 'Opere' di Girolamo Benivieni", *ACME – Annali della Facoltà di Lettere e Filosofia dell'Università degli Studi di Milano* LXIII, I (2010) 165–203 with the bibliography included.

26   Cfr. Zorzi Pugliese O., "Il *Commento* di Girolamo Benivieni ai salmi penitenziali", *Vivens Homo* 5 (1994) 475–494, here 475.

27   'non ho dubitato di allargarmi in qualche luogo, maxime dove o la difficoltà del senso o la disparilità delle lingue m'ha in uno certo modo sforzato, non partendomi però mai dallo stipite et dal fondamento delle sentenie, benché qualche volta [...] habbi interpretando lasciata l'ombra delle parole et mi sia, doue m'è paruto più opportuno, accostato alla verità del senso di quello dico che principalmente riguarda alla anima del penitente'. Benivieni, *Psalmi penitentiali*, f. a2v.

28   'uno alquanto più che el proprio suo texto diffuso, et in similitudine di perpetua oratione continuato, non so se io mi dico commento o più presto semplice et enarrativo discorso referente e medesimi loro sensi et mysterii'. Benivieni, *Psalmi penitentiali*, f. a2v. On this type of comment derived from Augustine and Erasmus, see Zorzi Pugliese, "Il *Commento* di Girolamo Benivieni" 481–482.

Gregory the Great.[29] But if this commentary, based on the idea of a penitential journey over a series of seven psalms, is limited to a simple continuous statement useful to the penitent's soul,[30] it must be emphasized that it also articulates very well-constructed concepts pertaining to the question of salvation, and constitutes a veritable moral and doctrinal treatise of great subtlety.[31]

Though a nonscholarly work, Benivieni's translation and commentary lacks neither literary ambition nor intellectual integrity. The edification of the minds and hearts of the Florentine nuns was to occur through the 'Florentine language' and all its resources for the expression of feelings or the transmission of knowledge. The profile of the 'devout sisters' (so called in the preface) must have overlapped that of many lay devotees, for the nunnery Le Murate, opened to girls of diverse social status, had became one of the largest in Florence and a centre of book production with a *scriptorium* in which liturgical books and vernacular religious literature were reproduced.[32] Still Benivieni's book, in its single edition, preserved its specific readership and Florentine perspective.

Paolo Giustiniani, one of the authors of the famous *Libellus ad Leonem X*, in which the liturgical use of the Bible in Italian is encouraged, wrote to Benivieni in 1514 requesting a new translation of the Bible.[33] As noted by Gigliola Fragnito, such a project, which Benivieni did not undertake, presupposed imminent advances in the field of biblical philology.[34] But perhaps Benivieni was also not willing to lend his mastery of Latin, knowledge of Greek and Hebrew, and finesse in writing, inherited from the Trecento literary tradition, to this type of project. And indeed, in terms of both process and result, there is quite a distance between his *Psalmi penitentiali*—a successful example of spiritual poetry and devotional prose designed to foster reform in the convent world—and Brucioli's translation of the Psalms, which reply to the call for universal dissemination of the Bible, now reunited with its original sources.

---

29   Zorzi Pugliese, "Il *Commento* di Girolamo Benivieni" 482–486.

30   Zorzi Pugliese, "Il *Commento* di Girolamo Benivieni" 479–482, 489–490.

31   For example, the problematic relationship between divine justice and mercy, the various aspects of which are highlighted in the commentary, is resolved in the seventh psalm in the concept of fairness. The problem of human freedom is resolved in the idea of servitude freely chosen by the human will, none other than the filiation the penitent finds in Jesus Christ.

32   Strocchia S.T., *Nuns and Nunneries in Renaissance Florence* (Baltimore: 2009) 20, 144–147, 160.

33   Fragnito, *La Bibbia al rogo* 27–29; Barbieri, "Panorama. Parte I" 101, 172–173; Pierno, "Pregiudizi e canone letterario" 155.

34   Fragnito, *La Bibbia al rogo* 29.

Lodovico Pittorio

The humanist Lodovico Pittorio was a member of the Savanarola intellectual circle of Ferrara.[35] He is the author of a *Psalterio,* which belongs to the same line of popularization works as Benivieni's book. Its full title indicates that the biblical text has been popularized for reasons of moral edification, notably for the female convent community [Fig. 9.1].[36] However, unlike Benivieni's book, published in a single edition in Florence, Pittorio's, published in Bologna in 1524, was reprinted in Venice in 1526, and again three times (in Venice) in 1547, 1556 and 1573.[37] Here I will discuss the first edition, which already contained the reasons for the book's long good fortune, concerning which I have recently published a more detailed analysis.[38] Pittorio's book corresponds to a more extensive popularization initiative than that of Benivieni. Pittorio's encompasses the entire Psalter, and the intended readers are not only nuns,[39] but as the title indicates, 'other devout persons without knowledge of Latin'. The title's emphasis on a larger reading public probably reflects the printer's desire to boost the book's commercial success, but the idea of expansion turns up again in the conclusion of the dedicatory letter, when the author recommends

35   Fioravanti Baraldi A.M., "Ludovico Pittorio e la cultura figurativa a Ferrara nel primo Cinquecento", in Bertozzi M. (ed.), *Alla corte degli estensi: filosofia, arte e cultura a Ferrara nei secoli XV e XVI. Atti del convegno internazionale di studi di Ferrara (5–7 marzo 1992),* (Ferrara: 1994) 217–246, here 220–224; Fioravanti Baraldi A.M., "Vita artistica e dibattito religioso a Ferrara nella prima metà del Cinquecento", in Fortunati V. (ed.), *La pittura in Emilia e in Romagna, Il Cinquecento,* II, (Milan: 1996) 105–125, here 105, 109 (with 124, n. 31); Samaritani A., *Lucia da Narni ed Ercole I d'Este a Ferrara tra Caterina da Siena Girolamo Savonarola e i Piagnoni* (Ferrara: 2006) 65, 72.

36   *Psalterio Davitico per Lodovico Pittorio da Ferrara moralmente in forma di Omeliario con lo latino intertexto declarato & de sententia in sententia volgarezzato ad consolatione maximamente de le Spose de Iesù Christo Vergini Moniali & de altre persone devote & del latino ignare* (Bologna, Eredi di Benedetto Faelli: 1524). The letter of dedication is titled: 'Epistola a tutte le Reverende de Christo Iesu spose vergini Moniali el suo divoto Lodovico Pictorio da Ferrra Salute desidera sempiterna'.

37   Cfr. Barbieri, *Le Bibbie italiane* 136; Fragnito, *La Bibbia al rogo* 306, n. 95; Fragnito, *Proibito capire* 102, 209, 262–263, 307. An edition published in Fermo at Astolfo di Grandi in 1578 reduces Pittorio's book to the penitential corpus.

38   Boillet É., "La fortune du *Psalterio Davitico* de Lodovico Pittorio en Italie au XVIᵉ siècle", *La Bibliofilía,* 115,3 (2013) 563–570.

39   The *Psalterio* does not appear to target a religious convent or a particular order. On books dedicated by Pittorio to nuns, see Fioravanti Baraldi A.M., "Testo e immagini: le edizioni cinquecentesche dell'Omiliario quadragesimale di Ludovico Pittorio", in Fragnito G.– Miegge M., *Girolamo Savonarola: da Ferrara all'Europa* (Florence: 2001) 146–147 and n. 22.

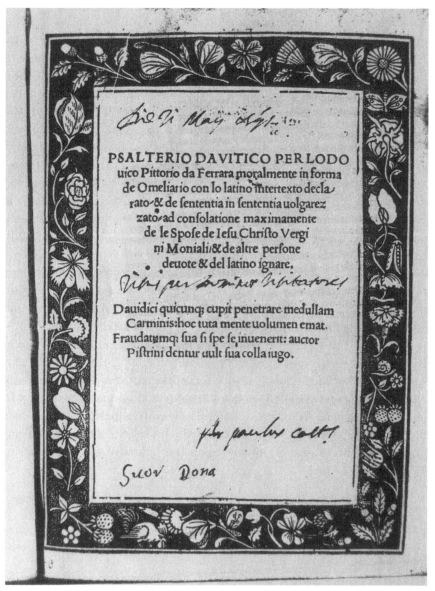

FIGURE 9.1 *Title page of* Psalterio Davitico per Lodovico Pittorio da Ferrara [...] (*Bologna, Eredi di Benedetto Faelli: 1524*). *London, British Library, 218 f 5. Image © British Library.*

himself to the prayers of the nuns and 'all others who will read' the book.[40] This
expansion arises from the very type of reading Pittorio prescribes to the nuns.
Whereas Benivieni, who at first, when inviting his readers to 'listen in silence' to
the penitential psalms, probably had a community reading in mind,[41] Pittorio
explicitly and exclusively refers to the reading of each individual nun in her
cell.[42] This incentive to individual and independent reading, something the
lay reader can easily do at home, was coupled with a guarantee of orthodoxy:
the book was published with the permission of the Vice-Inquisitor of Ferrara.[43]

Pittorio's Italian prose, with the Latin of the psalms and other Latin quotations, as well as the final prayers in Latin,[44] reflect the book's first intended
readership, that is, people familiar with Church Latin. But his prose displays the
rhetorical resources of a homily in Italian where exclamatory phrases, binary
and ternary constructions, anaphora, metaphors and simile are employed to
capture the reader's spirit and sensibility. It does not aim to provide a scholarly
explanation of the biblical text, but to shed light on issues that arise in the text
in an accessible and up-to-date way, especially when it comes to the question
of salvation. This prose, through its quality and its use, as recommended by the
author, was capable of satisfying the needs of a broader audience.

In fact, the title of the 1547 edition changes the book's intended audience.
It is no longer simply addressed to 'the virgin brides of Christ' or 'devout persons ignorant of Latin,' but to anyone from the 'non-literary' to the 'literary
and scholarly' population.[45] The book's new orientation, due to this change in
audience, is at once downwards (it is primarily written for those who are not
literary) and upwards (it is also for those who have the ability to read scholarly books). This change of orientation was the source of many revisions to

---

40   'a le orationi vostre & de tutte le altre persone che legerano detta opera di continuo &
      divotamente me racommando'. Pittorio, *Psalterio* f. IV.

41   'ascolteremo hora con silentio lo auctore di quelli [i.e. epsi septe hymni, o vero psalmi
      predecti], mentre che lui in ella patria nostra lingua e loro celesti mysterii resonando'.
      Benivieni, *Psalmi penitentiali* f. A3r.

42   'con speranza che tale lettione vi debba essere in la cella vostra in luogo di uno cesendello
      o di una candelletta continuamente accesa'. Pittorio, *Psalterio* f. IV.

43   'notificandovi che per ubidire alla apostolica laudabile determinatione con la examina-
      tione & con buona licentia del venerabile frate Domenico Reggio viceinquisitore nostro
      de Ferrara, mando fuora & in stampa l'opera nostra'. Pittorio, *Psalterio* f. IV.

44   The final prayers in Latin are addressed to the Virgin Mary and to the author's guardian
      angel and in the 1524 edition they are not translated in Italian.

45   *I Salmi di David* […] *I quali non solamente a persone illiterate, ma etiamdio a literati &
      dotti, saranno molto utili, & di grandissima consolatione* (Venice, Al Segno della Speranza:
      1547).

Pittorio's work in and after the 1547 edition, which I discuss elsewhere.[46] Here, suffice it to say that the title of the 1547 edition replaces the word 'consolatione' ('comfort') with the expression 'molto utili, & di grandissima consolatione' ('very useful and of great comfort'), an expression clarified in the dedicatory letter, giving the word 'consolatione' a more literary connotation, based on the dual purpose of a text whose pleasing qualities serve its utility.[47] On the other hand, starting with the 1547 edition, the link between the Latin text and its popularization, formerly closely intertwined, is evolving towards a clearer delineation between the text accepted by the Church and the Italian homily.

Silvio Fileto

In 1524, when Pittorio's *Psalterio* was published in Bologna, the Roman Silvio Fileto published an edition of Malerbi's translation of the Psalms in Venice (Fileto was known only for this work). The title makes explicit the edition's contents and intended readership, which, without naming the author, incorporates an existing translation ('formerly translated from Latin to the vernacular'), but boasts the added value of a new, quality work ('newly printed with all care and attention'). It includes reading aids: an easy commentary ('with a beautiful and easy declaration of the text as a commentary') and an alphabetical table ('and also with the usual table at the beginning of the book'). The table, which did not appear in Malerbi's Psalter, seems to respond to modern editorial criteria. These features make the book 'a work definitely useful, practical and necessary to all faithful Christians'.[48]

The common term 'faithful Christians' also appears in Malerbi's translation of the Bible.[49] As stated in the lengthy *Epistola a Laurentio* that serves as an introduction for the 1471 edition, Malerbi's work is intended for all Italian-speaking readers. He states that the Bible is addressed to 'everyone, universally,

---

46   Boillet, "La fortune du *Psalterio Davitico*".

47   The author of the letter revised in 1547 (called 'A i benigni lettori Lodovico Pittorio da Ferrara, in Christo Iesu salute') hopes that the book will be something 'useful and enjoyable', that it will 'give much delight and be useful' and that those who will meditate on it will find something 'very useful and of great comfort'.

48   *Il Psalterio di Dauitte: & di altri Propheti del testamento vecchio: per Siluio Phileto Romano gia di latino in volgare tradotto: & nouamente con ogni cura & diligentia stampato: con certa bella & facile declaration del testo in modo di co[m]mento: & etiamdio con la sua solita Tauola nel principio del libro: opera certamente vtile: commoda: & necessaria a tutti fideli christiani* (Venice, Stefano Nicolini da Sabio: 1524).

49   See above, n. 2–3.

regardless of sex or age' and that it has been translated so that 'faithful Christians' can 'understand while reading'.[50] Malerbi also states that the translation has stayed close to the Latin except when necessary to clarify the literal, that is to say, historical sense; and so the translator has used the comments of the doctors of the Church to 'enlarge' the titles of the Psalms, whose literal meaning could not otherwise have been understood by readers.[51]

The *Epistola a Laurentio* only appears in the 1478 edition of the Bible. It is not included in the separate edition of the Psalter of 1476, which does, however, contain the six introductory texts attached to the book of Psalms in the Malerbi Bible. In the spirit of practicality proclaimed by its title, the 1524 edition contains only three of these introductory texts. The first two have titles more explicit than those of the originals, and the layout emphasizes the individuality of each: *Prologo de santo Hieronymon el Psalterio, a Paula et Eustachio*; *Delli compositori de psalmi*; and *Titulo. Incomincia il libro del Hymni ouer soliloquy del propheta de Christo*.[52] The third and final text, which discusses the biblical title of the book of Psalms, unlike the others is not a translation but based on Pietro Lombardo's prologue to the commentary on the Psalms.[53] It suggests that the primary meaning of the Psalms is a prophetic revelation of the coming of Christ, whose various points are listed in a sort of credo, providing readers with an interpretative framework. It also explains the meaning of the first psalm, untitled in the Bible. The story of the blessed man who does not follow the counsel of the godless prompts 'faithful Christians' to flee the advice of 'heretics' and read and study the Psalms, which contain the true Christian doctrine.

It must be stressed here that the 1524 edition of the Psalter is part of the catalogue of the printer Stefano Nicolini da Sabio which counts many religious publications, including liturgical books and the vernacular devotional works written by Tullio Crispoldi to support the reforms of Bishop Gian Matteo

---

50   'A li fideli christiani daremo materia di legendo intendere, e *cum* sentimento gustare, e
        di appetendo desiderare de attingere al suo ultimo fine, che è vita eterna'; 'Ma noi [...]
        convochiamo tutti universalmente senza alcuna differentia de maschio o de femina o de
        età a tale celestial[e] et utilissime vivande'. Quoted after Barbieri, *Le Bibbie italiane* 42–43.

51   'se noi avessamo lassati li tituli come iaceno quanto alla littera, non foria stato concedente
        supplimento a satisfare a l'intellecto di lectori'. Quoted after Barbieri, *Le Bibbie italiane* 43.

52   I consulted the Malerbi edition of the Bible published in Venice at Elisabetta Rusconi in
        1525, which contains six introductory texts to the Psalms (f. CLXXII–CLXXIII). On this
        edition, see Barbieri, *Le Bibbie italiane* 238; Lumini, *La Bibbia. Edizioni del XVI secolo* 78–79.

53   Barbieri, *Le Bibbie italiane* 72.

Giberti in the diocese of Verona.[54] Continuing the reflection on access to the Bible in the vernacular, and the benefits but also the risks of such access for unprepared readers, the 1524 edition of the Psalter incorporates the Malerbi translation as an endorsement and also a framing of its universal destination. The title's indication of the book's content and purpose, the selection and development of introductory texts, and the addition of an alphabetical table all provide 'faithful Christians' of the 1520s with a book suited to their needs in a climate of ideological turmoil.

It should be noted that the title of the Psalter of 1524, again in the spirit of a book adapted to contemporary needs, praises its 'beautiful and simple' Italian prose. For Malerbi, as for Brucioli after him, a translation must first of all make the biblical text understandable for a non-literate readership. This prompts the choice of a 'medium' vernacular, which, as we may expect, did not always meet the literary standards associated with the grand tradition of the Trecento authors.[55] The positive reception of this language in 1524 demonstrates its importance in the history of biblical literature in Italian.[56] Like the literary connotation given to the word 'consolation' in the 1547 edition of the Psalter by Lodovico Pittorio, it also signals the growing importance of the literary dimension in sixteenth-century biblical book production, to which we will later return.

Antonio Brucioli

The religious turmoil of the 1520s, which prompted the reissue of the Psalter by Malerbi in 1524, was answered with an even more up-to-date reply with the publication, in 1531 and 1534, of Antonio Brucioli's translation and commentary of the Psalms.[57] In the dedicatory letter of 1531, Brucioli offers a translation

---

54   Cfr. Jacobson Schutte, *Printed italian vernacular religious books* 436; Sandal E., "Cronache di un mestiere", in Sandal E. (ed.), *Il mestier de le stamperie de i libri. Le vicende e i percorsi dei tipografi di Sabbio Chiese tra Cinque e Seicento e l'opera dei Nicolini* (Brescia: 2002) 28–30.

55   On the language chosen by Malerbi, according to the intended universal readership, see Pierno, "Pregiudizi e canone letterario", especially 152–153. On the linguistic corrections in later editions of the Psalter, in 1476 and 1524, see Trovato, *Il primo Cinquecento* 172–173; Barbieri, *Le Bibbie italiane* 237. On the language chosen by Brucioli, see Paccagnella, *Il fasto delle lingue* 146–151; Paccagnella, "La 'Bibbia Brucioli'" 1075–1087; Pierno, "Pregiudizi e canone letterario" 156–157.

56   Pierno, "Pregiudizi e canone letterario".

57   See above, n. 4–5.

'for the common good of pious Christian minds who do not know Greek or Latin,' concerned that everyone may have the opportunity to achieve salvation by receiving 'the light of Christian doctrine'.[58] Compared with Malerbi's translation, that of Brucioli marks a further step in the promotion of Bible reading for all Italian Christians. It is indeed the work of a layman who speaks directly to Christians without the intermediary of the Church and without seeking its approval. In addressing the dedicatee, Count Guido Rangone, Brucioli exposes the context that made the translation possible. Expelled from Florence by Dominicans hostile to a layman's involvement in biblical studies, he found asylum in Venice, where he was introduced to Hebrew by a Jewish grammarian.[59] Here, Brucioli's remarks echo those of Jerome in the preface to one of his translations of the Psalter ('Eusebius Hieronymus Sofronio suo salutem'), in which he alludes to a desire to return to the Hebrew sources and the hostility of his critics. Similar to Malerbi in his own translation of the Psalter, but in a different way, Brucioli positions himself as 'another Jerome'.[60] Malerbi constantly refers to the authority of Jerome, whose Latin translation, the Vulgate, he reproduces in the vernacular.[61] Brucioli completely replaces Jerome by adapting his approach and discourse to the context of sixteenth-century Italy. He justifies his work by referring to Paul: just as the apostle advises the Corinthians, we must not merely read or hear the Bible but also understand the meaning so the mind and heart may turn to God.[62] Not unlike Silvio Fileto in his edition of the Malerbi Psalter, though with an entirely different doctrinal perspective, summarized in a sentence, Brucioli provides the key for interpreting the Psalms, namely the inadequacy of human strength compared with the power of the

---

58   'Havendo [...] alla commune utilità delle pie menti christiane, che la lingua Greca o Latina non sanno, tradotto nel nostro vulgare toscano il nuovo testamento [...] Et veggiendo questo santissimo cibo evangelico [...] portare questa tanto divinissima luce non piccola utilità alle christiane menti che altre lingue non sanno, et che sono desiderose del lume della christiana dottrina'. *Psalmi di David nvovamente dalla Hebraica verita, tradotti in lingua Toscana per Antonio Brucioli* (Venice, Lucantonio Giunta: 1531) f. iir–v.

59   *Psalmi di David* f. iiir.

60   The reference to Jerome is constant in Italian Bible translations since the late Middle Ages (cfr. Corbellini S., " 'Se le scienze e la scrittura sacra fussino in volgare, tu le intenderesti': traduzioni bibliche tra medioevo e rinascimento in manoscritti e testi a stampa", in Bossier P. – Hendrix H. – Procaccioli P. (eds.), *Dynamic Translations in the European Renaissance. Traduzione del moderno nel Cinquecento europeo* (Manziana: 2011) 5–6.

61   Barbieri, *Le Bibbie italiane* 58 and n. 84.

62   Brucioli, *Psalmi* (1531) f. iiiir.

Almighty God.[63] He incorporated the same idea even more explicitly in the dedicatory letter for the commentary that accompanies in the 1534 edition the 1531 translation, slightly revised [Fig. 9.2].[64]

Pietro Aretino

Taking advantage of the way opened up by Brucioli's translations, but with different intentions, Pietro Aretino published *I sette salmi della penitenzia di David* in 1534.[65] Aretino, a Tuscan settled in Venice, was also in large part an autodidact layman. His book, dedicated to a secular personality, Antonio de Leyva, head of the imperial army in Milan, is also addressed to an ecclesiastical personality, Bishop Gian Pietro Carafa, the author voicing his support for the reforming action of the new pope Paul III.[66] The book is a literary paraphrase,[67] in which the biblical text remains perfectly identifiable, viewed through a moral and doctrinal lens that is not scholarly but well constructed, articulate and arranged in a progression resembling that of Benivieni's commentary.[68] In his paraphrase Aretino, like Benivieni in his commentary, chooses continuity; that is, he proceeds from the literal, historical meaning of the penitential psalms (a meaning that Benivieni had abandoned).[69] He makes David a full-

---

63   'In questo divino prophetico poeta si leggerà l'alto giudicio, et la misericordia, o giustitia d'Iddio, et la ingiustitia delle humane forze, la omnipotentia di quello, et la imbecillità degli huomini'. Brucioli, *Psalmi*, f. [v]v.

64   'acciochè si vegga Iddio, come omnipotente, così anchora operante tutte le cose, et vana essere ogni salute che viene dall'huomo'. *I sacri psalmi di David, distinti in cinque Libri, Tradotti dalla Ebraica uerita in lingua toscana, & con nuouo co[m]mento dichiarati. Per Antonio Brucioli*, Venice, Francesco Brucioli et i frategli: 1534, f. iiiv–iiiir.

65   *I sette salmi della penitentia di David. Il divino Pietro Aretino* (Venice, Giovan'Antonio Nicolini da Sabio for Francesco Marcolini, 1534). It was republished by the author in 1536, in 1539 and in the anthology of his biblical works in 1551; it was published in various other editions, with or without a printer's name, between 1535 and 1545 (two editions are not dated). On Aretino and his biblical works, see Boillet É., *L'Arétin et la Bible*, "Travaux d'Humanisme et Renaissance" CDXXV (Geneva: 2007) with the bibliography included.

66   On the dedicatory strategy in this work, see Boillet É., "L'adaptation des ambitions romaines de l'Arétin aux événements de 1533–1534: du *Pronostic de l'année 1534* aux lettres de dédicace des *Psaumes*", in Civil P. – Boillet D. (eds.), *L'actualité et sa mise en écriture aux XVe–XVI et XVIIe siècles (Espagne, France, Italie et Portugal)* (Paris: 2005) 169–189.

67   Boillet, *L'Arétin et la Bible* 240–241, 244, 319–373.

68   Boillet, *L'Arétin et la Bible* 297–319. The contents of Benivieni's commentary described above (n. 31) are found in Aretino's paraphrase.

69   Zorzi Pugliese, "Il *commento* di Girolamo Benivieni" 480.

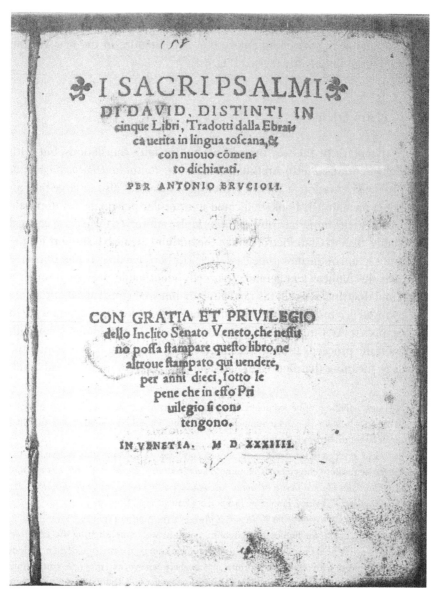

FIGURE 9.2 *Title page of* I sacri psalmi di David [...] (*Venice, Francesco Brucioli et i frategli: 1534*). *London, British Library, 1408 k 14. Image © British Library.*

fledged character and inserts in the account of his penitence seven penitential prayers.[70] This continuity is achieved through the choice of a very elaborate poetic prose that aims to convey the penitent's thoughts and feelings in the throes of anxiety or the joy of mystical ecstasy.[71]

The paraphrase by Aretino is intended for the heterogeneous readership of cities and the Italian courts, combining a secular and ecclesiastical audience, and further, for Italian readers thirsting for works both pious and pleasing. To some degree, its form foreshadows developments in the production of books on the Psalms in Italian in the second half of the sixteenth century. The latter period was the heyday of poetic versions of penitential psalms written by and for an urban community in which the interests of devout laity converge with those of outward-looking clergy. *Salmi penitentiali di diuersi eccellenti autori* is a prime example, published in Venice in 1568 at Giolito and reprinted in 1572.[72] But the ecclesiastical censors, mistrusting poetry, which they accused of casting a veil over biblical truth, authorized only two Italian texts on the Psalms: the Flaminio de' Nobili prose paraphrase and that of Francesco Panigarola, published in the 1580s, well after the Tridentine reformation of Catholic dogma.[73] The paraphrase of the penitential psalms by de' Nobili is presented as a 'brief and clear exposition' adapted to the needs of the penitent.[74] De' Nobili was a member of a Tuscan literary academy and wrote in literary Italian, which was becoming increasingly standardized and mandatory. In the dedicatory letter that introduces the book, printed in Venice in 1583, Fabio Biondo explains that the author writes for the community of noble ladies of Lucca and knows that the dedicatee, the mother of a cardinal, will derive 'spiritual enjoyment' from her reading, an idea evoked earlier in relation to Pittorio's Psalter and the evolution of its readership.[75] The letter to readers that opens the Psalms by Panigarola, an illustrious Franciscan preacher, does not promise a complex commentary identifying the various meanings of the biblical text, but a paraphrase that gives priority to the continuity and coherence of discourse while staying close to the biblical text and identifying its essential meaning in a

---

70   Boillet, *L'Arétin et la Bible* 246–255, 269–297.

71   Boillet, *L'Arétin et la Bible* 360–373.

72   See above, n. 18.

73   Cfr. Fragnito, *La Bibbia al rogo* 204, 303, 307; Fragnito, *Proibito capire* 98, 109, 227, 306.

74   *I sette salmi penitentiali con vna breue, et chiara spositione, secondo quel sentimento, che conuiene ad vn Penitente, senza allontanarsi dal letterale del signor Flaminio Nobili* (Venice, Domenico Nicolini: 1583) f. A2r.

75   *I sette salmi penitentiali* f. A2r.

devotional perspective.[76] Hence, different aspects of the Psalms by Aretino—the choice of a penitential corpus; the foundation and intent, both secular and ecclesiastical; the choice of poetic prose for a paraphrase intended as a literary aid to devotion as well as a manual of Christian doctrine—herald the multiple orientations, in terms of the religious and literary requirements of the circles that produce and consume these texts, of books on the Psalms in Italian in the second half of the sixteenth century. It is remarkable that Aretino, whose work was put on the Index in 1559, was able to anticipate these orientations through his authorial choices, combining ambition and caution.

Conclusion

Beyond the variety of definitions they gave the 'letter' of the biblical text and its 'literal meaning', authors of Italian printed Psalms in the sixteenth century wished to enable readers to penetrate the text, understand its richness and depth, rather than remain on the surface. The evolution from Malerbi's Psalms to its new edition by Fileto and the new translation by Brucioli, from the first edition of Pittorio's sermons (which already contained this possibility) to later ones, from Benivieni's poetry and 'narrative' to Aretino's literary paraphrase, lies in the will to extend the readership from 'specific' to 'universal', with great attention from authors, editors or printers to new needs in terms of religious knowledge ('true' sources and doctrine) and linguistic accessibility or literary quality (an up-to-date vernacular). Towards the second half of the century, such a will had to take into account restrictions connected with the assertion of a strong norm, religious as well as linguistic and literary.

Bibliography

Aretino Pietro, *I sette salmi della penitentia di David. Il divino Pietro Aretino* (Venice, Giovan'Antonio Nicolini da Sabio for Francesco Marcolini: 1534).

Austern L. – Boyd McBride K. – Orvis D. (eds.), *Psalms in the Early Modern World* (Farnham – Burlington, VT: 20102011).

Barbieri E., *Le Bibbie italiane del Quattrocento e del Cinquecento* (Milan: 1992).

---

76   Cfr. Zardin D., "Tra latino e volgare: la 'dichiarazione dei salmi' del Panigarola e i filtri di accesso alla materia biblica nell'editoria della Controriforma", *Sincronie* IV, 7 (2000) 125–165.

————, "Panorama delle traduzioni bibliche in volgare prima del Concilio di Trento. Parte I", *Folia Theologica* 8 (1997).

————, "Panorama delle traduzioni bibliche in volgare prima del Concilio di Trento. Parte II", *Folia Theologica* 9 (1998).

————, "Malerbi (Malermi, Manerbi), Nicolò" in *Dizionario biografico degli italiani* 68 (2007) 149–151.

Benivieni Girolamo, *Psalmi penitentiali di David tradocti en lingua fiorentina et commentati per Hieronymo Benivieni* (Florence, Antonio Tubini and Andrea Ghirlandi: 1505).

Boillet É. (ed.), *Antonio Brucioli. Humanisme et évangélisme entre Réforme et Contre-Réforme* (Paris: 2008).

————, "L'Écriture traduite, commentée, réécrite: Antonio Brucioli, Teofilo Folengo, l'Arétin", in Boillet D. – Plaisance M. (eds.), *Les années Trente du XVIᵉ siècle italien* (Paris: 2007) 163–181.

————, "L'adaptation des ambitions romaines de l'Arétin aux événements de 1533–1534: du *Pronostic de l'année 1534* aux lettres de dédicace des *Psaumes*", in Civil P. – Boillet D. (eds.), *L'actualité et sa mise en écriture aux XVᵉ–XVI et XVIIᵉ siècles (Espagne, France, Italie et Portugal)* (Paris: 2005) 169–189.

————, *L'Arétin et la Bible*, Droz "Travaux d'Humanisme et Renaissance" CDXXV (Geneva: 2007).

Brucioli Antonio, *Psalmi di David nvovamente dalla Hebraica verita, tradotti in lingua Toscana per Antonio Brucioli* (Venice, Lucantonio Giunta: 1531).

————, *I sacri psalmi di David, distinti in cinque Libri, Tradotti dalla Ebraica uerita in lingua toscana, & con nuouo co[m]mento dichiarati. Per Antonio Brucioli* (Venice, Francesco Brucioli et i frategli: 1534).

Corbellini S., " 'Se le scienze e la scrittura sacra fussino in volgare, tu le intenderesti': traduzioni bibliche tra medioevo e rinascimento in manoscritti e testi a stampa", in Bossier P. – Hendrix H. – Procaccioli P. (eds.), *Dynamic Translations in the European Renaissance. Traduzione del moderno nel Cinquecento europeo* (Manziana: 2011) 1–21.

————, "Looking in the Mirror of the Scriptures: Reading the Bible in Medieval Italy", in W. François – A.A. den Hollander (eds.), *Wading Lambs and Swimming Elephants: The Bible for the Laity and Theologians in Late Medieval and Early Modern Era* (Leuven: 2012) 21–40.

Di Benedetto S., "L'edizione giuntina delle 'Opere' di Girolamo Benivieni", ACME – *Annali della Facoltà di Lettere e Filosofia dell'Università degli Studi di Milano* LXIII, I (2010) 165–203.

Dionisotti C., "La testimonianza del Brucioli" [1979], in id., *Machiavellerie* (Turin: 1980) 193–226.

Fileto Silvio [Malerbi Nicolò], *Il Psalterio di Dauitte: & di altri Propheti del testamento vecchio: per Siluio Phileto Romano gia di latino in volgare tradotto: & nouamente con ogni cura & diligentia stampato: con certa bella & facile declaration del testo in modo di co*[*m*]*mento: & etiamdio con la sua solita Tauola nel principio del libro: opera certamente vtile: commoda: & necessaria a tutti fideli christiani* (Venice, Stefano Nicolini da Sabio: 1524).

Fioravanti Baraldi A.M., "Ludovico Pittorio e la cultura figurativa a Ferrara nel primo Cinquecento", in Bertozzi M. (ed.), *Alla corte degli Estensi. Filosofia, arte e cultura a Ferrara nei secoli XV e XVI* (Ferrara: 1994) 217–246.

———, "Vita artistica e dibattito religioso a Ferrara nella prima metà del Cinquecento", in Fortunati V. (ed.), *La pittura in Emilia e in Romagna, Il Cinquecento*, II, (Milan: 1996) 105–125.

———, "Testo e immagini: le edizioni cinquecentesche dell'Omiliario quadragesimale di Ludovico Pittorio", in Fragnito G. – Miegge M., *Girolamo Savonarola: da Ferrara all'Europa* (Florence: 2001) 139–154.

Fragnito G., *La Bibbia al rogo. La censura ecclesiastica e i volgarizzamenti della Scrittura (1471–1605)* (Bologna: 1997).

———, *Proibito capire. La Chiesa e il volgare nella prima età moderna* (Bologna: 2005).

Jacobson Schutte A., *Printed Italian Vernacular Religious Books 1465–1550: a finding list* (Geneva: 1983).

Leri C., *"La voce dello Spiro". Salmi in Italia tra Cinquecento e Settecento* (Alessandria: 2011).

Paccagnella I., *Il fasto delle lingue. Plurilinguismo letterario nel Cinquecento* (Rome: 1984).

———, "La 'Bibbia Brucioli'. Note linguistiche sulla traduzione del 'Nuovo Testamento' del 1530", in *Omaggio a Gianfranco Folena* (Padua: 1993) 1075–1087.

Pierno F., "Pregiudizi e canone letterario. La Bibbia in volgare di Niccolò Malerbi (Venezia, 1471)", *Rassegna europea di letteratura italiana* 36 (2011) 143–157.

Pittorio Lodovico, *Psalterio Davitico per Lodovico Pittorio da Ferrara moralmente in forma di Omeliario con lo latino intertexto declarato & de sententia in sententia volgarezzato ad consolatione maximamente de le Spose de Iesù Christo Vergini Moniali & de altre persone devote & del latino ignare* (Bologna, Eredi di Benedetto Faelli: 1524).

Quondam A., *Note sulla tradizione della poesia spirituale e religiosa (parte prima)*, in Quondam A., (ed.), *Paradigmi e tradizioni* (Rome: 2005) 189–192.

Samaritani A., *Lucia da Narni ed Ercole I d'Este a Ferrara tra Caterina da Siena Girolamo Savonarola e i Piagnoni* (Ferrara: 2006).

Sandal E. (ed.), *Il mestier de le stamperie de i libri. Le vicende e i percorsi dei tipografi di Sabbio Chiese tra Cinque e Seicento e l'opera dei Nicolini* (Brescia: 2002).

Spini G., *Tra Rinascimento e Riforma. Antonio Brucioli* (Florence: 1940).

Strocchia S.T., *Nuns and Nunneries in Renaissance Florence* (Baltimore: 2009).

Trovato P., *Il primo Cinquecento*, in Bruni F. (ed.), *Storia della lingua italiana* (Bologna: 1994).

Vasoli C., "Benivieni, Girolamo", in *Dizionario Biografico degli Italiani* VIII (1966) 550–554.

Zardin Z., "Tra latino e volgare: la 'dichiarazione dei salmi' del Panigarola e i filtri di accesso alla materia biblica nell'editoria della Controriforma", *Sincronie* IV, 7 (2000) 125–165.

———, "Bibbia e apparati biblici nei conventi italiani del Cinque-Seicento. Primi appunti", in Borraccini R.M. – Rusconi R. (eds.), *Libri, biblioteche e cultura degli ordini regolari nell'Italia moderna attraverso la documentazione della Congregazione dell'Indice* (Città del Vaticano: 2006) 63–103.

Zorzi Pugliese O., "Il *Commento* di Girolamo Benivieni ai salmi penitenziali", *Vivens Homo* 5 (1994) 475–494.

CHAPTER 10

The Catholic Church and the Vernacular Bible in the Low Countries: A Paradigm Shift in the 1550s?

Wim François

Confronted with the increased biblical fervour of the 1520s, the authorities in the Low Countries did not respond with a severe and general prohibition of Bible reading in the vernacular, as sometimes has been argued. Since the late Middle Ages, the Low Countries had become familiar with semi-religious women and even laypeople in the world who nourished their spiritual life through reading the Scriptures, and this was not considered flirtation with heresy. After the spread of humanism and the Reformation, and the Bible versions that originated in their wake, the religious authorities in the Low Countries continued to tolerate Bible reading in the vernacular; nevertheless, from an early stage—in the mid 1520s—a strict ban was proclaimed on versions that contained dubious paratextual elements such as prologues, summaries above the chapters, and marginal glosses. It was also forbidden to read and comment on the Bible in all kinds of clandestine 'conventicles' that had come into existence at the time and in which heterodox ideas were nurtured. Bible reading in the vernacular had always to be pursued in connection with the official liturgy of the Church.[1] In the midst of the century, however, both in the Low Countries and on a Roman level, a change became apparent in the Church's attitude. It is the aim of this essay to shed light upon what we may call a paradigm shift.

---

* I wish to thank Ms. Jennifer Besselsen-Dunachie and Dr. Paul Arblaster for their invaluable assistance in translating the text.

1 François W., "Vernacular Bible Reading and Censorship in Early Sixteenth Century: The Position of the Louvain Theologians", in Hollander A.A. den – Lamberigts M. (eds.), *Lay Bibles in Europe. 1450–1800*, Bibliotheca Ephemeridum Theologicarum Lovaniensium 198 (Leuven: 2006) 69–96.

Trent, the Louvain Index, and the Louvain Vulgate Bible(s)

1546 was an important year for the Church's biblical policy, in the Catholic world in general and in the Low Countries in particular. On 8 April 1546, during its fourth session, the Council of Trent had declared both the Scriptures and apostolic traditions to be the channels through which evangelical faith and morals were brought to the faithful. The fathers of the Council further proclaimed the Latin Vulgate to be the authentic version of the Church, as it was considered to be completely conform to sound evangelical doctrine. In addition, they expressed a desire that a critical edition be produced as soon as possible. The fathers of the Council, however, did not pronounce any judgment regarding the permissibility of Bible translations in the vernacular, despite the lobbying work of both proponents and adversaries of a prohibition. The Council fathers in this way tacitly confirmed the prevailing customs of local churches.[2]

About a month later, on 9 May 1546, the Louvain theologians issued an Index of Forbidden Books, in which 42 Dutch Bible editions that were considered to be unreliable were censured, in addition to six French Bibles.[3] In an

---

2 "Acta. 34. Sessio quarta: Decretum [...] Recipitur vulgata editio Bibliae", in *Concilium Tridentinum: Diariorum, actorum, epistularum, tractatuum nova collectio, vol. v. Actorum Pars* IIa, ed. S. Ehses (Freiburg i/Breisgau: 1911), 91–92 (henceforth abbreviated as CT 5-III). For a recent translation of the decree, see Béchard D.P. – Fitzmyer J.A. (eds.), *The Scripture Documents: An Anthology of Official Catholic Teachings* (Collegeville MN: 2002) 4–6. On this phase of the Council of Trent, see Jedin H., *Geschichte des Konzils von Trient, vol. II. Die erste Trienter Tagungsperiode 1545/47* (Freiburg i/Breisgau: 1957) 42–82, here 76–77. On the discussion regarding Bible reading in the vernacular, see, amongst others, Cavallera F., "La Bible en langue vulgaire au Concile de Trente (IVe Session)", in *Mélanges E. Podéchard. Études de sciences religieuses offertes pour son éméritat au doyen honoraire de la Faculté de Théologie de Lyon* (Lyons: 1945) 37–56; Lentner L., *Volkssprache und Sakralsprache. Geschichte einer Lebensfrage bis zum Ende des Konzils von Trient*, Wiener Beiträge zur Theologie 5 (Vienna: 1964) 226–264, here 237–264; McNally R.E., "The Council of Trent and Vernacular Bibles", *Theological Studies* 27 (1966) 204–227; Coletti V., *L'éloquence de la chaire. Victoires et défaites du latin entre Moyen Âge et Renaissance*, trans. S. Serventi (Paris: 1987) 199–219; Fernández López S., *Lectura y prohibición de la Biblia en lengua vulgar. Defensores y detractores* (León: 2003) 161–178.

3 *Edictum Caesareae Maiestatis promulgatum anno salutis M.D.XLVI. Praeterea Catalogus & declaratio librorum reprobatorum a Facultate sacrae Theologiae Lovaniensis Academiae, Iussu & ordinatione praenominatae Maiestatis Caesareae* (Leuven, Servatius a Sassen: 1546). For the Dutch version, see *Mandament der Keyserlijcker Maiesteit wytgegeven int Iaer xlvi. Met Dintitulatie ende declaratie vanden gereproobeerde boecken gheschiet bijden Doctoren inde faculteit van Theologie in Duniversiteit van Loeven: Duer dordonnantie ende bevel der selver*

explicatory note, the dean of the Faculty opposed those Bible editions that did not sufficiently respect the text of the Vulgate and the sense of faith endorsed in it, which is quite understandable given the decision of the Council of Trent. Furthermore, the dean forbade those Bible editions—even when they were faithful translations of the Latin Vulgate—that included prologues, marginal glosses, summaries above the chapters or registers that were either dubious or were obviously derived from the assertions of Luther and his followers. In addition, failure to give required information such as the name of the printer, the place and/or date of publication seems to have been an important criterion for the decision to ban an edition.[4] Although the Louvain theologians dismissed the examination of the Bibles in a rather superficial way, it is clear that they wanted to do away with the vernacular Bible editions that contravened the prohibitory rules as expounded by the dean[5] and were only prepared to continue to tolerate editions that contained the 'naked' text of the Vulgate, such as the 1527 New Testament of Michiel Hillen van Hoochstraten (and later editions by the same), as well as the 'good-Catholic' editions of the Vorsterman Bible, including the New Testament of 1529 and both editions of 1530, in addition to the complete Bible of 1531, and possibly even that of 1532.[6]

The imperial government and the Faculty of Theology of Louvain, however, did not wish to only respond in a negative way, by forbidding the 'unreliable' Bible translations, but they had also the aim of bringing a new 'reliable' Vulgate translation onto the market. To that purpose, only a few weeks after the publication of the Index, they made arrangements with the Louvain publisher Bartholomeus van Grave for the publication of an authorized Latin, French and Dutch Bible. The Latin Vulgate revision made by the Louvain theologian Jean Henten was finished in late October or early November 1547. In the course of 1548, Van Grave published the Dutch Louvain Bible, a Vulgate

---

K.M. (Leuven, Servaes van Sassen: 1546). For an analysis: Bujanda J.M. De et al., *Index de l'Université de Louvain, 1546, 1550, 1558*, Index des livres interdits 2 (Sherbrooke – Geneva: 1986). Regarding the Bible editions that were put on the Index, see particularly: Hollander A.A. den, *Verboden bijbels. Bijbelcensuur in de Nederlanden in de eerste helft van de zestiende eeuw* (Amsterdam: 2003) 11–21.

4 Comp. François, "Vernacular Bible Reading" 89–90. The preface as given by the dean has also been published in *Recueil des ordonnances des Pays-Bas. Deuxième série: 1506–1700. Règne de Charles-Quint, vol. V. Contenant les ordonnances du 1er janvier 1543 (1544, N. ST.) au 28 décembre 1549*, ed. J. Lameere – H. Simont (Brussels: 1910) 255–257.

5 For the list of Bibles included on the Index, see Den Hollander, *Verboden bijbels* 13.

6 For these editions, see Hollander A.A. den, *De Nederlandse bijbelvertalingen. Dutch Translations of the Bible 1522–1545*, Bibliotheca Bibliographica Neerlandica 33 (Nieuwkoop: 1997), as well as the online database http://www.bibliasacra.nl.

translation that was made by Nicholas van Winghe, Augustinian canon of the congregation of Windesheim in the monastery of Sint-Maartensdal in Louvain. Apart from Henten's Vulgate Bible, Van Winghe used as his sources the Delft Bible of 1477 for the Old Testament and the Vorsterman Bible for the New Testament. Furthermore, late medieval biblical language, as preserved in the numerous books providing the Epistle and Gospel lessons from Mass, resounded throughout the text. And although Van Winghe explicitly claimed to have based himself upon the German 'Korrekturbibeln'—Luther versions 'corrected' on the basis of the Vulgate—made by Johann Eck and Johannes Dietenberger, the extent to which he actually used these versions remains to be demonstrated. His claim should rather be considered as the expression of a more general wish to align himself with the well-tried German tradition of offering the Catholic faithful 'good' alternatives to the Protestant Bible editions. Van Winghe's Dutch Louvain Bible in a certain sense replaced the Bible of Willem Vorsterman, issued from 1528 onwards, as the semi-official Dutch-language Bible for the Low Countries.[7] In 1550, Van Grave also issued a French translation of the Vulgate, which was intended to replace the previously semi-official Bible of Jacques Lefèvre d'Étaples, edited by Martin Lempereur in 1530. It was this edition incidentally that was subject to a revision by Nicolas de Leuze, licentiate in theology, assisted by the prior at that time of the community of the Celestines in Heverlee, François de Larben.[8] The realization of both vernacular Louvain Bibles was supervised by the Louvain theologian Pieter de Corte and the Dominican friar Godevaert Strijrode.

In his extensive prologue to the Dutch Louvain Bible,[9] Van Winghe offers a good summary of the Louvain theologians' position regarding the relation

7   Regarding the Dutch Louvain Bible, see especially Herreweghen P. Van, "De Leuvense bijbelvertaler Nicolaus van Winghe. Zijn leven en zijn werk", *Ons Geestelijk Erf* 23 (1949) 5–38, 150–167, 268–314, 357–395. See also: Bruin C.C. de, *De Statenbijbel en zijn voorgangers. Nederlandse bijbelvertalingen vanaf de Reformatie tot 1637*, rev. F.G.M. Broeyer (Haarlem – Brussels:1993) 141–147; Gilmont J.-F., "La concurrence entre deux Bibles flamandes", in Gilmont J.-F., *Le livre et ses secrèts*, Cahiers d'humanisme et renaissance 65; Temps et espaces 2 (Geneva – Louvain-la-Neuve, 2003) 151–162, here 152–155. For the Bible edition itself: *Den gheheelen Bybel* [...] *met grooter naersticheyt ende arbeyt nu corts in duytsche van nyews overghestelt wt den Latijnschen ouden text*, trans. Nicholas van Winghe (Leuven, Bartholomeus van Grave: 1548).

8   On the French Louvain Bible see, amongst others, Bogaert P.-M. – Gilmont J.-F., "La première Bible française de Louvain (1550)", *Revue Théologique de Louvain* 11 (1980) 275–309; Bogaert P.-M. – Gilmont J.-F., "De Lefèvre d'Étaples à la fin du XVIe siècle", in Bogaert P.-M. (ed.), *Les Bibles en français: Histoire illustrée du Moyen Âge à nos jours* (Turnhout: 1991) 47–106, here 89–91.

9   Winghe Nicholaus van, "Onderwijs van der Heylegher Scriftueren", in *Den gheheelen Bybel* f. A1r–C2v. For an elaborate analysis, see François W., "Het voorwoord bij de 'Leuvense bijbel'

between Bible and Tradition—systematized especially by Johannes Driedo (and consecrated at the Council of Trent)—as well as concerning the legitimacy of Bible reading in the vernacular. Using the metaphor of the light and the lamp, Van Winghe stated in the first part of his prologue that the light of God's Word reached the people by way of the lamp that was the Scripture.[10] Without the Scriptures and before their having been written down, God had instilled the pure light and the pure Word in the hearts of patriarchs, prophets and apostles. They had in turn handed down to later generations what God had revealed to them. And, argued Van Winghe, the Lord continued to inspire popes, bishops, pastors and doctors of the Church to teach many salutary things that are not explicitly written down in the Scriptures. Consistent with Louvain thinking with regard to this matter, he suggested that, since the Church already existed before a single letter of the Scriptures had been written, it was only through the ecclesiastical Tradition that it had become clear to the faithful which Bible books were sacred and canonical. Moreover, in the Tradition of the Church, several customs, and even teachings, that are not explicitly testified by the Scriptures, were passed down via an unbroken line of succession. Finally, the Tradition had the role of discerning the proper interpretation of obscure and difficult passages, a frequent enough occurrence in the Bible. To understand the Scriptures, especially their more obscure passages, an astute mind, acquired knowledge and God's grace were necessary requisites. People not fulfilling these requirements would do better to become acquainted with the text through the aid of the commentaries of the sacred doctors, or by listening to the sermons of competent preachers. These people were, after all, able to explain the Scriptures in the light of the traditional doctrine(s) and customs of the Church that were not explicitly mentioned in the Bible, but that had been handed down from the apostolic times via an unbroken line of succession. Van Winghe was thus very reticent to grant the illiterate masses direct access to the 'naked' text of the Bible. The danger was, after all, that they might interpret it according to their own particular opinions and inevitably fall into error and heresy.[11]

---

van Nicholaus van Winghe (1548). Over Schrift, Traditie en volkstalige Bijbellezing", *Ons Geestelijk Erf* 79 (2005–2008) 7–50. See also Van Herreweghen, "De Leuvense bijbelvertaler Nicolaus van Winghe" 311–314 and De Bruin, *De Statenbijbel*, rev. Broeyer 143–144.

10   Van Winghe, "Onderwijs" f. A1v–B5v. Comp. François, "Het voorwoord bij de 'Leuvense bijbel' " 17–38.

11   Van Winghe, "Onderwijs" f. B4v–B5r, amongst others: 'maer hebben willen haer selfs meesters sijn ende die heyleghe scrifuere selver lesen ende nae haer verstant uutlegghen [...] Ghelijck hier voortijts ende noch meer in onsen tijden veel dolinghen ende ketterien

Van Winghe expressed similar ideas in the second part of his prologue, where the Bible was compared to a garden full of (spiritual) food and vigorous herbs.[12] The Louvain Bible translator, however, underlined that the crucial point was to prepare, serve and consume this spiritual nourishment in the right way. In spite of the rather restrictive position he defended in his prologue, it should be remembered that it was actually Van Winghe who was responsible for the redaction of the new official Dutch Vulgate translation, and that he placed himself in line with a tradition in the Low Countries that had continued for decades, if not for centuries. In the last part of his prologue Van Winghe then contrasted his own translation with a large number of 'falsified' Bibles that were circulating at the time.[13] He recalled that the errors of the texts resided in the fact that the Latin Vulgate was insufficiently well rendered and that mistakes had crept into the translations. In the marginal notes and the summaries above the chapters erroneous propositions were also put forward. Furthermore, Van Winghe insisted that a new 'orthodox' Bible translation, such as his, always had to function in a strict ecclesiastical setting: common people were allowed to engage in personal Bible reading as part of the spiritual process of preparing and ruminating on the sermons they would hear in church. In short, the *Lovanienses* opted for a restrictive position—since they were in no way proponents of an indiscriminate reading of the Scriptures in the vernacular (as some Reformers were)—and emphasized the ecclesiastical context and the role of priests and preachers as the mediators between God's Word and their flock [Fig. 10.1].

---

opghestaen sijn door dese vermetelijcheyt dat ongheleerde ende simpel menschen hen te zeer hebben willen onderwinden die scriftuere te verstaen sonder meesters ia oock teghen den ghemeynen sin der meesters ende leeraers der heylegher kercken latende hen duncken dat sij die heylighe scriftuere beter verstaen' ('but they wanted to be their own masters and to read the Holy Scripture by themselves and explain it according to their own understanding [...] Just as in former times and even more today many errors and heresies have arisen by the temerity of uneducated and simple people who aimed at understanding the Scripture without masters, even more, against the common sense of the masters and doctors of the Holy Church, being under the illusion that they understand the Holy Scripture better'; translation ours).

12   Van Winghe, "Onderwijs" f. B5v–C2r. Comp. François, "Het voorwoord bij de 'Leuvense bijbel'" 38–44.

13   Van Winghe, "Onderwijs" f. C2r–C2v. Comp. François, "Het voorwoord bij de 'Leuvense bijbel'" 44–48.

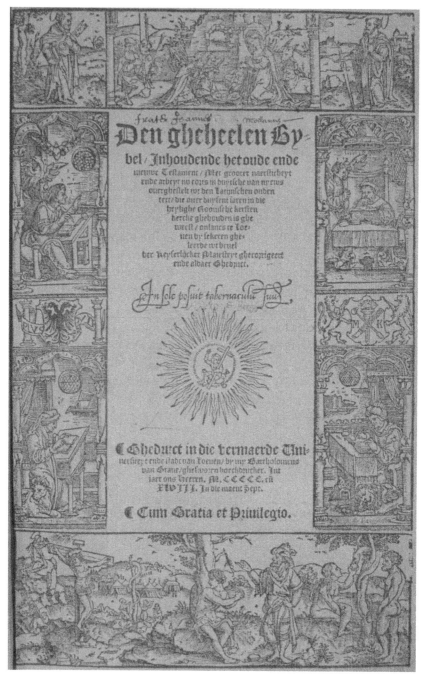

FIGURE 10.1   *Title page of the Dutch 'Louvain Bible':* Den gheheelen Bybel, Inhoudende
het oude ende nieuwe Testament (*Leuven, Bartholomeus van Grave: 1548*).
KU Leuven, Maurits Sabbe Library, P 22.055.1/F°/Bijb 1548.

A Louvain Censure of Erasmus's Plea for Vernacular
Bible Reading (1552)

Nevertheless, there are indications that in the 1550s the Louvain theologians grew even more reticent. This becomes clear in the first place from the project, drafted at the Louvain Faculty, to censure Erasmus's works, with the intention of it being taken by the Louvain representatives in 1552 to the Council of Trent.[14] This censure campaign had to be carried out discretely because Erasmus and his writings continued to enjoy the Emperor's protection (although sixteen years had already passed since the humanist's death). In the Royal Library in Brussels, a manuscript is preserved in which the aforementioned Louvain theologian Jean Henten jotted down his own statements censuring Erasmus's works, likely accompanied by remarks made by one or more of his colleagues.[15]

The censured statements there are carefully given in the order in which they appear in the edition of Erasmus's *Opera Omnia*, published in Basel in 1540. According to Henten, four passages, in which Erasmus pleaded candidly for all people to have access to the Scriptures and for their translation into the vernacular, needed to be censured. The reference is to a statement from the *Paraclesis* of 1516 (one of the introductory writings to the New Testament),[16] one from the writing *De Vidua Christiana* (*On the Christian Widow*) from 1529,[17] a large passage from Erasmus's *Apologia adversus debacchationes Petri Sutoris* (*Apology against Petrus Sutor's Furies*) from 1525,[18] and, fourth, a few sentences from his *Declarationes ad censuras Facultatis Theologiae Parisiensis* (*Declarations against the Censures of the Parisian Faculty of Theology*) from 1532.[19] Henten's reference concerns statements that he considered unorthodox, but which he

---

14   These Louvain representatives were Ruard Tapper, Francis Sonnius, John-Leonard van der Eycken (or Hasselius) and Josse Ravesteyn (or Tiletanus). See Ram P.F.X. De, *Mémoire sur la part que le clergé de Belgique et spécialement les docteurs de l'Université de Louvain, ont prise au Concile de Trente* (Brussels: 1841) 31.

15   *Collectaneum eorum in quibus Erasmus Roterodamus videtur erronee aut scandalose scripsisse* [...], Brussels, KBR, Ms. II 194, f. 1–52. See also François W., "De Leuvense theologen over de bijbel in de volkstaal. De discussie tussen 1546 en 1564", *Tijdschrift voor Theologie* 47 (2007) 340–362, here 348–350, and Crahay R., "Les censeurs louvanistes d'Érasme", in Coppens J. (ed.), *Scrinium Erasmianum. Historische opstellen gepubliceerd onder de auspiciën van de Universiteit te Leuven naar aanleiding van het vijfde eeuwfeest van Erasmus' geboorte*, 2 vols. (Leiden: 1969) I 221–249, here 233–237.

16   *Collectaneum* f. 23 k.

17   *Collectaneum* f. 26 c.

18   *Collectaneum* f. 45.

19   *Collectaneum* f. 46 b.

did not necessarily classify within the weighty category of openly heretical. Remarkable then is the fact that Henten did not quote any statements from Erasmus's preface to his *Paraphrases* of Matthew, the writing *par excellence* in which the humanist pleaded for vernacular Bible reading. This, however, can be easily explained: Henten did not note a single censuring statement of his own in reference to the seventh part of the *Opera Omnia*, in which Erasmus's *Paraphrases* are included, but did refer explicitly to the Parisian censure of the work dating from the year 1527 (published in 1531).[20] And from the preface to the *Paraphrases* of Matthew, the Parisian theologians had taken five statements concerning Bible reading that were considered highly reprehensible. We can thus assume that Jean Henten intended to join the Parisian censure.[21] Moreover, it should be added that certain propositions expressed by Erasmus in his preface to the *Paraphrases* of Matthew were, in some way or another, again taken up by him in his 1532 reply to the Parisian censure, and this work is actually discussed by Henten, as has already been mentioned.

A second part of the manuscript from the Royal Library in Brussels is filled with censured statements excerpted from Erasmus's works by another writer.[22] This author is identified as Tilman Clercx, Louvain theologian and president of the Pope's college from 1527 until 1550. In contrast to Henten, he had actually read Erasmus's *Paraphrases* and had undoubtedly also consulted the Parisian censure of the work. When Tilman Clercx addressed the issue of Bible reading and Bible translation in the vernacular, he opened his own censure with five passages taken from Erasmus's preface to the *Paraphrases* of Matthew that had already been condemned by the Parisian theologians. Clercx even augmented the Parisian censure systematically by quoting longer passages. Furthermore, he also quoted extensively from the plea that Erasmus made in the *Paraclesis* in favour of vernacular Bible reading, in addition to other passages from the humanist's works.

In any event, the Council of Trent did not accept the Louvain censures. But the dossier was possibly used again in the years of 1570–1571, when the *Index*

20   *Collectaneum* f. 41r.

21   *Collectio judiciorum de novis erroribus* [. . .] *Censoria etiam judicia insignium academiarum* [. . .], *vol. II. In quo exquisita monumenta ab anno 1521 usque ad annum 1632 continentur*, ed. C. du Plessis d'Argentré (Paris, Andreas Cailleau: 1728) 60–62. For a discussion of the Parisian censure, see François W., "La condamnation par les théologiens parisiens du plaidoyer d'Érasme pour la traduction de la Bible dans la langue vulgaire (1527–1532)", *Augustiniana* 55 (2005) 357–405, here 377–387.

22   *Collectaneum* f. 53r–100r. Comp. Crahay, "Les censeurs louvanistes d'Érasme" 241–248.

Expurgatorius was drafted, although its influence on the Index's stance towards Bible translation in the vernacular remains to be investigated.

A Louvain Recommendation for an Imperial Prohibition of Vernacular Bibles (1552–1553)

Another significant event proves that the position of the Louvain theologians became more constrained in the 1550s. In the second half of 1552, or perhaps in the course of 1553, a dramatic meeting took place at the Faculty of Theology with the vernacular translation of the Bible at stake. The first and foremost source for this event can be found in the Louvain Faculty of Theology's Book of Letters (the *Liber <Literarum> Facultatis sacrae theologiae in Universitate Lovaniensi*).[23] From this source we learn that the Emperor (or his administration) asked the Faculty for its advice concerning the question of whether or not an edict should be issued in the Low Countries to completely prohibit the reading of the Bible in vernacular. The consultation came about as a result of the Magistrate of (the Flemish town of) Kortrijk (English: Courtray) having called the Emperor's attention to the fact that reading the Scriptures in the vernacular had encouraged the resurgence of the Anabaptist movement in the town.[24] The town's Magistrate was convinced that the more the people read the Bible in vernacular, the more they became alienated from the doctrine of the Church and its holy ceremonies, and the more they became enmeshed in errors and heresies (such as those of the Anabaptists). The Magistrate's opinion was said to be supported by several pastors, who had come to the same conclusion as a result of their confessional experiences.[25]

In its answer to the Emperor, which takes up six pages, the Faculty aligned itself with the request of the Courtray city Magistrate, and showed itself to be an advocate of a general prohibition of Bible translations in the vernacular. To underpin this prohibition, the Louvain theologians first appealed to several

---

23   *Liber Literarum Facultatis sacrae theologiae in Universitate Lovaniensi* (*Book of Letters of the Louvain Faculty of Theology*), Leuven, State Archives in Belgium, Collection Old University of Louvain, 443, f. 21r–23v. See also François, "De Leuvense theologen over de bijbel" 350–354, and Bogaert – Gilmont, "La première bible française de Louvain" 291–297.

24   On the resurgence of the Anabaptist movement in Courtray in that period, and the activity of the inquisitor Pieter Titelmans, see Decavele J., *De dageraad van de Reformatie in Vlaanderen*, Verhandelingen van de Koninklijke Academie voor Wetenschappen, Letteren en Schone Kunsten van België: Klasse der Letteren 76, 2 vols. (Brussels: 1975) I 469–472.

25   *Book of Letters of the Louvain Faculty of Theology* f. 23v.

passages, taken from the Epistles of Paul, which were invoked to corroborate that the Scriptures were good, sacred and salutary, and by their very nature in no way obscure. The reading of the Scriptures did not, however, automatically bring salvation; moreover, such reading could even be a source of perdition for those who did not properly interpret their words. By way of comparison, the *Lovanienses* referred to the people of Israel who, although familiar with the Scriptures, did not recognize its Lord and Saviour.[26] In the same vein, the theologians called attention to the testimony of Peter, who in his second Letter[27] had stated that in Paul's Epistles a number of difficult passages were included, which ran the risk of being distorted by ignorant and unstable people, to their own perdition.[28]

From these basic insights, the Louvain theologians subsequently went on to the testimony of the Church fathers. The Fathers had argued that the Scriptures could only be read (and interpreted) in a salutary way if two conditions were fulfilled. Firstly, the readers of the Scriptures should be sufficiently instructed in the 'sententiae et regulae fidei', by which are meant the teachings of the Church as they had been handed down by the fathers and authoritatively established by the *magisterium*. Secondly, according to the Fathers, the reader had to give proof of piety, which the theologians interpreted as the spiritual preparedness to subject one's own interpretation to the 'regulae fidei'. Those who did not observe both conditions ran the risk of distorting the meaning of the Scriptures to their own perdition, a warning the Louvain theologians repeated time and time again, undoubtedly with the Protestants in mind.[29] It would lead us too far astray to enumerate all the patristic references included in this part of the Letter, but we find references to the *Recognitiones*—which were still uncritically ascribed to the 'apostolic father' Clement Romanus or Pope Clement I—as well as to Gregory of Nazianzus, Basil the Great, and of course to Augustine, Jerome and Chrysostom.

The Louvain theologians subsequently also referred to the testimony of Erasmus.[30] From their perspective, this may appear surprising, but they realized all too well that the Rotterdam' humanist was held in high esteem by the Emperor. In this regard, they drew, in a rather selective way, from a few passages taken from Erasmus's *Declarations against the Censure of the Parisian*

---

26   *Romans* 15:4; 11:7–10; 2 *Corinthians* 2:15–16; 1 *Corinthians* 11:29.

27   2 *Peter* 3:16.

28   *Book of Letters of the Louvain Faculty of Theology* f. 21r.

29   *Book of Letters of the Louvain Faculty of Theology* f. 21r–v.

30   *Book of Letters of the Louvain Faculty of Theology* f. 21v–22r.

Faculty of Theology (1532).[31] The *Lovanienses* had to recognize that Erasmus, 'before having experienced the audacity and brutality of the uninstructed people',[32] had defended the statement that nobody was to be withheld from the reading of the Scriptures.[33] But at the same time they underlined that the humanist regarded the reading of the Scriptures only as salutary if the people were prepared beforehand, through the instruction of a number of rules and statements ('regulis et sententiis'). Furthermore, Erasmus had stated that the people had to withhold themselves from more daring interpretations.[34]

The *Lovanienses* were convinced that the requirements set forth by the said authorities were no longer being met in their own time. The illiterate populace did not see any problem in ignoring the ancient rules of the faith ('regulae fidei') or in despising the preaching and teaching of pastors or doctors. On the contrary, the people arrogated to themselves the right and competence of understanding the Scriptures according to their own insights; yes, even of being able to explain it to others. In their recklessness they even ventured to explain the Epistles of Paul to the Romans, Galatians and Ephesians, which eminent doctors of the Church, in the wake of Peter himself, deemed as extremely difficult to understand.[35]

In conclusion of the aforementioned considerations, the Louvain theologians solemnly advised the Emperor Charles, given the circumstances of the times, to issue a general edict prohibiting the reading of the Bible, both the Old and the New Testament, by uneducated and unstable people.[36]

---

31   Erasmus Desiderius, *Ad censuras Lutetiae vulgatas sub nomine Facultatis Theologiae Parisiensis*, in *Desiderii Erasmi Roterodami Opera Omnia* [...], *vol. IX. Qui apologiarum partem primam complectitur*, ed. I. Clericus (Leiden, Petrus Vander Aa: 1706; anast., London: 1962), c. 813–928 (henceforth abbreviated as LB IX).

32   *Book of Letters of the Louvain Faculty of Theology* f. 21v.

33   See, amongst others, Erasmus, *Ad Censuras Facultatis Theologiae Parisiensis*, LB IX, c. 873B.

34   Clear reference to Erasmus, *Ad Censuras Facultatis Theologiae Parisiensis*, LB IX, c. 871C.

35   *Book of Letters of the Louvain Faculty of Theology* f. 22r: 'indocta et imperita multitudo abiectis antiquis fidei regulis et contempta petulanter pastorum et doctorum viva voce et enarratione presumat sacras literas suo mente suoque ingenio intelligere, interpretari, ire demum aliis tradere et exponere, secundum sensum quemdam etiam antiquis fidei regulis prorsus contrarium' ('the uneducated and inexperienced multitude, having thrown off the ancient rules of the faith, and in impudent contempt of the public speech and exposition by pastors and teachers, arrogates to itself to understand the Sacred Scriptures through its own intellect and insights, to interpret them and even to go passing them on and explaining them to others, even according to a sense that is completely contrary to the ancient rules of faith'; translation ours).

36   *Book of Letters of the Louvain Faculty of Theology* f. 22r: 'postulare sane nobis ratio horum temporum imo et rogare clementissimum et religiosissimum principem caesarem semper

The *Lovanienses* declared that they aimed to go further than the measures of 1546, when the Emperor had put those vernacular Bibles on the Index that were judged to be corrupted and contaminated by heresy, but at the same time had allowed a number of orthodox editions (that had been translated and approved by scholarly men). According to the theologians, this leniency did not have the desired effect: instead of reading these 'good' Bibles with due reverence, religiousness and piety, laypeople had taken advantage of their lecture to aggravate the situation negatively. There was then no other solution than to deny the Christian people the reading of the Scriptures and the divine Word, which was said to be their most precious possession.[37] In light of this position, it must be taken for granted that the Louvain professors who, from 1546 on, had collaborated with the publication of the vernacular Bibles, had willingly or unwillingly sided with this more severe viewpoint. In this regard Pieter de Corte in particular comes to mind.

The Louvain theologians were prepared to admit that the reading of the Scriptures was indeed salutary for certain people. But the possible benefits that some could draw from reading the Scriptures did not make allowance for the dangers it constituted to the masses. Those who remained strong in their faith, had, like members of the same body, to undergo the same prohibition, 'until the time when it would please the Lord to restore the tranquility in his Church'.[38] In other words, notwithstanding the fundamental objections that they had formulated against Bible reading in the vernacular, the Louvain theologians did contemplate the possibility of a relaxation of the proposed measures, if the circumstances 'on the field' should change for the better.

The *Lovanienses* voiced the opinion that was to increasingly win adherence in the Catholic Church, according to which common people would not have

---

Augustum videtur ut ad extremum remedium confugiat et publico edicto imperite et indocte ac instabili multitudini [...] lectionem tam veteris quam novi testamenti prorsus interdicat' ('the way the times are now seems to us reason enough to beg, even to ask the most clement and pious prince, the ever August Emperor, that he may resort to the last remedy and through a public edict may forbid completely the reading of both the Old and the New Testament to the inexperienced, uneducated and instable multitude'; translation ours).

37 *Book of Letters of the Louvain Faculty of Theology* f. 22r: 'Vehementer sane dolendum est eo malitie prolapsam esse christianam plebem ut quod optimum habet christianus populus sacrorum voluminum et divini verbi lectionem necesse sit ei subtrahere' ('Intensive regret is justified since Christian folk have lapsed into such maliciousness that it became necessary to take away from them the best thing the Christian people has, viz. the reading of the Sacred Scriptures and the Word of God'; translation ours).

38 *Book of Letters of the Louvain Faculty of Theology* f. 22v–23r.

immediate access to the Scriptures in the vernacular, but would have to be content with a simple and clear instruction of the faith, which they could receive through the preaching given by their parish priests and preachers.[39] More and more, the role of the clergy as the necessary mediators between God's Word and the flock was emphasized. Biblical passages from both the Old and the New Testament were even invoked to underpin the belief that the Scriptures were not meant for immediate reading by laypeople, but had to be mediated via the preaching by prophets and priests.[40] The Louvain theologians were indeed concerned with the quality of the preaching in the churches. In order to guarantee this quality, they also requested that the Emperor urge the bishops to make a thorough visitation of their diocese.[41] Regarding this point, the Louvain theologians asked for exactly that which the Council of Trent had stated during its fifth session of 17 June 1546. The Council had entrusted the bishops with the mission of organizing the preaching in a convenient manner, and had threatened those ministers who refused to preach with canonical punishments.[42] With regard to the sermons, the Council specified that they had to be 'short and simple', and should restrict themselves to proclaiming 'what is necessary for salvation'.[43]

To sustain its proposal to promulgate a general prohibition on reading the Bible in the vernacular, the Louvain Faculty further referred, amongst other prohibitions, to a similar ban that had been proclaimed twenty years earlier

---

39   *Book of Letters of the Louvain Faculty of Theology* f. 22v.

40   *Deuteronomy* 31,9; *Nehemiah* 8:7; *Ephesians* 4:11–14.

41   *Book of Letters of the Louvain Faculty of Theology* f. 23r.

42   For the text of the decree see: "Sessio quinta: Decretum de lectione et praedicatione", CT 5-III 241–243. For a recent translation see Béchard – Fitzmyer (eds.), *The Scripture Documents* 6–10. On the origin of the Tridentine decree on Bible study and preaching, and particularly the influence of Erasmus's *Ecclesiastes sive de ratione concionandi* (1535) see especially McGinness F.J., "An Erasmian Legacy: Ecclesiastes and the Reform of Preaching at Trent", in Delph R.K. – Fontaine M.M. – Martin J.J. (eds.), *Heresy, Culture, and Religion in Early Modern Italy: Contexts and Contestations*, Sixteenth century essays and studies 76 (Kirksville MO: 2006) 93–112. See also: Rainer J.E., "Entstehungsgeschichte des Trienter Predigtreformdekretes", *Zeitschrift für katholische Theologie* 39 (1915) 255–317 and 465–523; Allgeier A., "Das Konzil von Trient und das theologische Studium", *Historisches Jahrbuch im Auftrage der Görres-Gesellschaft* 52 (1932) 313–339; Jedin, *Geschichte des Konzils von Trient* II 83–103; Lentner, *Volkssprache und Sakralsprache* 264–274; Larios A., "La reforma de la predicación en Trento (Historia y contenido de un decreto)", *Communio* 6 (1973) 22–83; Byrne A., *El ministerio de la palabra en el concilio de Trento*, Diss. Doct. (Pamplona: 1975) 58–92.

43   "Sessio quinta: Decretum de lectione et praedicatione", CT 5-III 241–243.

by the Parisian Faculty of Theology.[44] They also referred to the work of the famous Spanish Franciscan theologian Alphonso de Castro who, in his work *Adversus omnes haereses* (*Against all Heresies*) of 1534, had called the reading of the Bible in the vernacular a breeding ground for heresies. In the same book he had also recalled how King Ferdinand of Spain had once proclaimed a ban on Bible reading in the vernacular for his empire.[45] Several studies, however, have proven that this prohibition was not as absolute as De Castro has insinuated in his book.[46]

It is important to note that the Emperor and his administration in the Low Countries did not implement the prohibition on vernacular Bible translations as recommended by the *Lovanienses*, and that the latter should, for the time being, be perceived as a testimony of the growing reticence in theological milieus concerning vernacular Bible reading.

Giovanni a Bononia and the Rejection of Vernacular Bible Reading

In the context of a growing rejection of vernacular Bible reading in Louvain theological circles, the name Giovanni a Bononia emerges, a Sicilian aristocrat and theologian whose brief, but not unimportant, role at the Faculty

---

44   *Book of Letters of the Louvain Faculty of Theology* f. 23r. With regard to the Parisian theologians' condemnation of Bible reading in the vernacular, see François W., "The Condemnation of Vernacular Bible Reading by the Parisian Theologians (1523–31)", in François W. – Hollander A.A. den (eds.), *Infant Milk or Hardy Nourishment? The Bible for Lay People and Theologians in the Early Modern Period*, Bibliotheca Ephemeridum Theologicarum Lovaniensium 221 (Leuven: 2009) 111–139. See there for further literature.

45   *Book of Letters of the Louvain Faculty of Theology* f. 23v.

46   The prohibition obviously was aimed at the Jews and especially at the *conversos*, the newly converted Christians of Jewish origin. The risk was that they would interpret the translations in the vernacular in an uncontrolled way, on the basis of their own religious backgrounds, in which a Christological reading of the Scriptures would be absent. It was feared that they might clandestinely initiate their children in the Mosaic Law and the doctrines of their forefathers. In the same vein, Spanish translations had been targeted that went directly back to the Hebrew Bible and thus disregarded the doctrines of the faith that found expression in the Vulgate. It is clear, however, that tolerated biblical material, such as Epistle and Gospel books, continued to be translated and read. See amongst others: Fernández López, *Lectura y prohibición de la Biblia* 96–111; Bujanda J.M. De et al., *Index de l'Inquisition espagnole 1551, 1554, 1559*, Index des livres interdits 5 (Sherbrooke – Geneva: 1984) 33–34; Enciso J., "Prohibiciones españolas de las versiones bíblicas en romance antes del Tridentino", *Estudios bíblicos* 3 (1944) 523–554, here 537–541.

has almost completely disappeared from historical consciousness.[47] Bononia was present at the aforementioned meeting of the Faculty, and apparently he stood out as one of the most vehement opponents of Bible translation in the vernacular in Louvain during the years under consideration.[48] Bononia was elected rector of the University of Louvain on 31 August 1554, in those days a largely administrative function. The very same year, his most important work was published by the Louvain publisher Anthonis-Maria Bergaigne: *De aeterna Dei praedestinatione et reprobatione* (*On God's Eternal Predestination and Reprobation*, 1554).[49] In a short appendix to his book, however, Giovanni a Bononia devotes ten octavo pages to the question of whether the Scriptures should be translated into the vernacular and whether they should be made available for all and sundry to read.[50] In this way, he returned to the discussion that had preoccupied him and the other members of the Faculty of Theology only a few years earlier [Fig. 10.2].

---

47   Scarce information on the life and the work of Bononia is to be found in, amongst others, Paquot J.N., *Mémoires pour servir à l'histoire littéraire des dix-sept provinces des Pays-Bas, de la principauté de Liège, et de quelques contrées voisines*, 18 vols. (Leuven: 1763–1770) XVIII 37–41; Mazzuchelli G., *Gli scrittori d'Italia cioe' notizie storiche, e critiche intorno alle vite, e agli scritti dei letterati italiani*, 6 parts in 2 vols. (Brescia: 1762), II/III 1486–1487; Bayle P., *Dictionaire historique et critique*, rev. and augm. P. Des Maizeaux, 4 vols. (Amsterdam – Leiden: 1730) I 607; Pirri R., *Sicilia sacra disquisitionibus, et notitiis illustrata* [...], rev. and augm. A. Mongitore and V.M. Amico, 2 vols. (Palermo: 1733), I c. 280 and 287; II c. 892B and 1023AB.

48   Bononia's presence is attested by, amongst others, the second important source giving testimony to the Louvain meeting, namely Furió Ceriol Fadrique, *Bononia*, in *Obra completa, vol. I. El Concejo y consejeros del Príncipe! Bononia*, ed. H. Méchoulan – J. Peréz Durà (Valencia: 1996) 245–621, here 344–345: 'Nam cum literas a Carolo quinto Caesare accepissemus (eram enim et ego una) quibus significabat gratissimum sibi futurum si diligenter examinaremus utrum esset rationi consentaneum sacras literas in natiuam certae cuiusdam prouinciae, quam honoris causa nominatim non appello, ad eius nationis usus quae iam erant uersae, retineri necne' ('Because we had received a letter from the Emperor Charles V (I was actually one of them) through which he expressed that he would be immensely greatful if we would diligently examine whether it makes sense to the reason that the Sacred Scriptures translated in the vernacular of a certain province— which for reasons of honour I will not mention—for use of this nation can be kept or not'; translation ours). Comp. Bayle, *Dictionaire historique et critique*, rev. and augm. Des Maizeaux I 607: 'Bononia étoit des plus échauffez contre les Versions de l'Ecriture en Langue vulgaire'.

49   We use the second edition: Bononia Joannes a, *De aeterna Dei praedestinatione, et reprobatione ex scripturis, & Patrum authoritatibus deprompta sententia* (Leuven, Antonis-Maria Bergaigne: 1555).

50   Bononia Joannes a, "Brevis appendix de Bibliorum versione", in Bononia Joannes a, *De aeterna Dei praedestinatione* 528–541, here 528–538.

FIGURE 10.2   *Title page of Giovanni a Bononia,* De aeterna Dei praedestinatione et
reprobatione (*Leuven, Anthonis-Maria Bergaigne: 1555*). *KU Leuven,*
Maurits Sabbe Library, *P 234.9 BONO.*

While Bononia insisted that he intended to respond to the question in an unbiased fashion, he nevertheless began by reacting against those who, inspired by a spirit of dissent, wanted to force the reading of the Bible on everyone ('obtrudere volunt'), even the unlettered and vineyard keepers. Such individuals give the impression that the reading of the Scriptures is a divine right ('iuri divino') and that they are free to counteract every positive decree that prohibited the reading of the Scriptures by the ordinary people, even if it came from the bishops or indeed the pope. Bononia's response clearly did not intend to imply that the Bible in the vernacular was wrong in itself, but, just as no right-minded person would argue that wine was bad *in se*, he declared, it could be considered damaging nonetheless for those suffering from fever. He emphasized, by analogy, that the temporal circumstances were so unfortunate and corrupt that the Church authorities were completely justified in forbidding the private reading of the Scriptures by whatever nation. The primary problem for Bononia was that the ordinary people of his day were strongly inclined to error, an observation that he claimed had the support of a considerable number of pastors. People who were receptive to such flawed ideas, he insisted, would also be inclined to interpret the Scriptures in an entirely erroneous manner, especially since the Scriptures are obscure, and complicated on account of their many metaphors, figurative language and enigmas.[51] Such people consciously ignored the interpretations of the Church and the explanations of the Fathers, the doctors and the pastors and threw themselves with unclean hands ('illotis manibus'—irreverently and without due preparation) upon the Scriptures. Because of such reading Bononia argued, profane people should be kept away from the Scriptures.[52] He quoted the often-read verse *Matthew* 7:6

---

51   Bononia, "Brevis appendix" 529–530: 'quae [scripturae] perobscurae sunt, et multis figuris, tropis, et enigmatibus involutae [...] Unde modus iste discendae fidei [=privata lectio] hoc pernicioso tempore alicui populo, aut provinciae iure optimo per Ecclesiae praefectos interdicitur, quum eos experientia doceat, ex plebe quosdamnimis arroganter evolvere scripturas, qui vel receperunt nova haec quorundam haereticorum perversa dogmata, vel eis faveat' ('and these [Scriptures] are thoroughly obscure, and packed in figurative language of all kind, tropes and enigmas [...] Therefore the authorities of the Church rightly forbid in these dangerous times this way of being instructed in the faith [= private reading of the Scriptures] to one or another people or province, since experience has taught them that several members of the populace arrogantly explain the Scriptures, viz. those who have embraced the new perverse dogmas or at least have a favourable attitude towards them'; translation ours).

52   Bononia, "Brevis appendix" 531–532: 'Simili modo rude et indoctum vulgus magna et intoleranda superbia, reiectis Ecclesiae interpretamentis, contemptis Patribus, Doctoribus, et Pastoribus ad Bibliorum lectionem illotis (quod aiunt) manibus

in this regard: 'Give not that which is holy to dogs; neither cast ye your pearls before swine, lest perhaps they trample them under their feet, and turning upon you, they tear you' [Douay-Rheims Version]. This New Testament verse was indeed a standard reference among the adversaries of free Bible reading.

Having expounded from the very beginning his fundamental objections to the unrestricted reading of the Bible by all, Bononia insisted that it was of course important for everyone to be well informed about the Catholic faith and the mysteries of religion, including those (explicitly) described in the Scriptures. Bononia stressed, however, that the faith should not be gleaned directly from the biblical books, but rather acquired through the teaching of the Church. The Church, he reminded his readers, enjoyed the same infallibility in matters of faith and morals ('fide et moribus') as the Scriptures themselves. He aligned himself with the abovementioned conviction of the theologians of his day, arguing that, since the Church already existed before a single letter of the Scriptures had been written, it was she that had been responsible for determining which books were to be included in the biblical canon and which were to be rejected. Furthermore, it was also the Church that determined and preached matters that could not be explicitly deduced from the Scriptures, since the Church was, after all, inspired in the same way by the Holy Spirit.[53]

Following on from this, Bononia also developed another interesting line of thought, asking himself whether the Church was permitted to include 4 *Esdras* (the authority of which Ambrose had also employed) among the canonical books. 4 *Esdras* was usually printed in the appendix to the editions of the Vulgate. Bononia was clearly inclined to give a positive answer to this question since he considered 4 *Esdras* 14:45–46 to be a fitting passage in which God prescribed to Ezra the names of the biblical books that are open to all, both the unschooled and schooled, and the names of those restricted to scholars only.[54] He juxtaposed these words with *Joshua* 1:8: 'Let not the book of this law

---

impudenter, et perquam temere convolant [...] Atque ideo fit, ut tales frequenter inveniantur in scripturam sacram blasphemi ac propterea ab eius lectione, tanquam profani homines, sunt arcendi' ('In the same way the rude and uneducated populace who, with immense and intolerable pride, rejecting the interpretations of the Church, and disdaining Fathers, Doctors, and Pastors, launch themselves shamelessly with unclean hands and in a temerarious way upon the reading of the books of the Bible [...] And thus it happens that such blasphemers are frequently to be found in the Scriptures, and therefore they should, as profane men, be kept from reading it'; translation ours).

53   Bononia, "Brevis appendix" 532–533.

54   4 *Esdras* 14:45–46 [VUL]: 'priora quae scripsisti in palam pone, et legant digni et indigni. novissimos autem septuaginta conservabis, ut tradas eos sapientibus de populo tuo'; [Douay Rheims Version]: 'The former thinges which thou hast written, set abrode, and let

depart from thy mouth: but thou shalt meditate on it day and night, that thou mayst observe and do all things that are written in it: then shalt thou direct thy way, and understand it'. This Bible verse was often to be found on the title page of vernacular Bible editions, encouraging people to read and meditate on the Scriptures. According to Bononia, however, Joshua did not insist on the reading of the Scriptures in the strict sense. In his view, Joshua required only that the Law of the Lord be observed, but this can and ought to be done in a more effective manner, namely through the doctors who pass on what they read to the people and teach them what is fitting and what is not.[55]

In short, while Bononia considered the Scriptures to be good and holy in themselves, he was convinced that the chaotic times in which he lived made it inopportune for laypeople to read the Bible in the vernacular, aware as he was of the danger that the Scriptures would then be subject to an idiosyncratic, or even erroneous, interpretation. He also emphasized the intermediary role of the Church and its doctors and pastors in transmitting the true faith. For further support of his argument, Bononia referred his readers to the book *Adversus omnes haereses*, first published by Alfonso de Castro in 1534. Reference to the book is also to be found in the abovementioned recommendation issued by the Louvain theologians to the Emperor. De Castro's book would, incidentally, be reprinted in Antwerp in 1556, giving testimony to the relevance of the topic in the Low Countries.

Furió Ceriol versus Bononia on Vernacular Bible Reading

Bononia had undoubtedly become the face of those within the Faculty of Theology who advocated an utter prohibition of vernacular Bible reading. Not only was he manifestly present at the famous meeting where the Faculty

---

the worthie and vnworthie reade: but the last seuentie bookes thou shalt keepe, that thou mayest deliuer them to the wyse of thy people'; [RSV]: 'Make public the twenty-four books that you wrote first, and let the worthy and the unworthy read them; but keep the seventy that were written last, in order to give them to the wise among your people'.

55   Bononia, "Brevis appendix" 534: 'Non autem video, quibus verbis scripturae lectio mandetur; iubetur quidem meditari in lege domini, sed hoc interdum commodius fieri et potest et debet, cum doctores ea, quae ipsi legunt, populis tradunt; docentes eos, quid dextrum sit, quidve sinistrum' ('For I do not see by which words the reading of the Scriptures is ordered: what is actually commanded is to meditate upon the Law of the Lord, but this can and should happen in a more proper way, viz. when the doctors the things they read by themselves, hand down to the people, and teach them what is right and what is wrong'; translation ours).

issued its advice to the Emperor to promulgate a general ban on Bible reading in the vernacular, and had written down his ideas in an appendix to his book *De aeterna Dei praedestinatione et reprobatione*, but he had clearly also entered into a debate with the propagators of such reading resident in Louvain. Among them was the Spanish biblical humanist Fadrique Furió Ceriol, who published in 1556 in Basel, with the publisher Johannes Oporinus, a book that was given the revealing title *Bononia*, with as a subtitle *Two Books on the Translation of the Bible into the Vernacular*.[56] In the dedication of the book to Don Francisco Mendoza de Bobadilla, Cardinal and Bishop of Burgos, Furió Ceriol presents his work as the report of a more or less organized debate that had taken place between himself and rector Giovanni a Bononia in the presence of a considerable audience consisting mainly of Spanish students, apparently during the winter months of 1554–1555.[57] In the epilogue of the book, also dedicated to Don Francisco Mendoza de Bobadilla, Furió again alludes to 'the much attended meeting', although he concedes that its written reflection also has to be considered as a literary construction, a 'literaria disputatio'[58] [Fig. 10.3].

Focusing on the content of the work, we see how its first book offers a detailed explanation of Bononia's arguments against vernacular Bible reading, while in the second book, Fadrique Furió Ceriol assumes the position of defender of vernacular Bible reading. While it would be impossible to

---

56   See Furius Caeriolanus valentini Fridericus, *Bononia, sive de Libris sacris in vernaculam linguam convertendis, Libri duo* (Basel, Johannes Oporinus [In colophon: Basel, Michael Martin Stella]: 1556–1557). We refer to the aforementioned edition of Furió Ceriol, *Bononia*, in *Obra completa*, ed. Méchoulan – Peréz Durà 245–621. For a discussion of the content, see especially Agten E., "Fadrique Furió Ceriol, Giovanni di Bononia et la traduction de la Bible en langue vernaculaire: Analyse du *Bononia* (1556)", in François W. – Hollander A.A. den (eds.), *'Wading Lambs and Swimming Elephants': The Bible for the Laity and Theologians in Late Medieval and Early Modern Era*, Bibliotheca Ephemeridum Theologicarum Lovaniensium 257 (Leuven: 2012) 219–252. Also Bedouelle G., "Le débat catholique sur la traduction de la Bible en langue vulgaire", in Backus I. – Higman F. (eds.), *Théorie et pratique de l'exégèse*, Etudes de philologie et d'histoire 43 (Geneva: 1990) 39–59, here 48–59; Fernández López, *Lectura y prohibición de la Biblia* 203–210; Bleznick D.W., "Furió Ceriol y la controversia sobre la traducción de la Biblia", *Revista Hispánica Moderna* 34 (1968) 195–205.

57   See, amongst others, the dedication of the book to Don Francisco de Bobadilla: Furió Ceriol, *Bononia* 260–262. In the transition from the first to the second of the two parts of the disputation, Furió obviously aims at dissolving the meeting, since it is four hours into the afternoon and plainly wintertime ('bruma est'), but the audience present wishes to continue, since they have nothing special to do. See Furió Ceriol, *Bononia* 362–364.

58   'In frequenti illo consessu'. See Furió Ceriol, *Bononia* 618. Comp. Wilke C.L., "*Bononia* en su contexto histórico", in *Obra completa*, ed. Méchoulan – Peréz Durà 145–214, here 199–200.

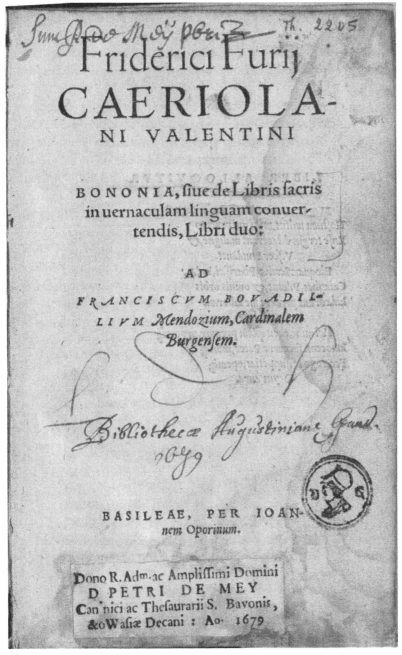

FIGURE 10.3   *Title page of Fadrique Furió Ceriol,* Bononia, sive de Libris sacris in
vernaculam linguam convertendis *(Basel, Johannes Oporinus
[In colofon: Basel, Michael Martin Stella]: 1556–1557). UGent,* University
Library, BIB. TH.002205.

summarize the contents of a 365-page book in a few short paragraphs—in spite of its octavo format—an outline of the main standpoints of both protagonists will be offered here, focusing a little more attention on the responses formulated by Fadrique Furió Ceriol to Bononia's reservations with respect to vernacular Bible reading.

Bononia underlines the role of 'praeceptores' or instructors—in other words, theologically trained preachers—as necessary mediators between God's Word and the unlettered masses, the same mediated access to the Scriptures also having constituted one of the main arguments of his appendix on vernacular Bible translations.[59] Furió Ceriol argues in response that while it was indeed necessary to appeal to human instructors on human affairs, it is necessary to turn directly to God, the instructor par excellence, in order to learn of God's Word and God's will. The Lord made his Word known through Moses, David and the prophets, in a language understood by the people of the time. Jesus likewise addressed the people of his time in the language with which they were familiar, namely Syriac. Furthermore, the evangelists and apostles wrote in Greek in order to introduce their readers to Christ. In like fashion, the Church—both Latin and Greek—had always tolerated the circulation of translations of the Scriptures because they helped people to understand them better. Furió Ceriol was thus fundamentally convinced that men, women, children, slaves and the free ought to be granted 'unmediated' access to God and his Word.[60]

---

59   This basic argument of Giovanni a Bononia is to be found in, among other places, Furió Ceriol, *Bononia* 264–272 and 282–284, o.a. 268: 'Quod si a magistris accipere nos Theologiam decet, parum profecto interest, imo nullo modo est opus, ut sacra scriptura in uulgarem linguam traducatur, nam semper tu ex magistri institutione intelliges ea, quae ad salutem fuerint necessaria, sicque superuacanea traductio uideretur' ('For, if we should hear about theology through the mediation of masters, it is of little interest, even more, there is no neccesity at all that Sacred Scripture be translated into the vernacular tongue, since you have always to understand through the instruction of a master that which is necessary for salvation, and in this sense a translation seems to be superfluous'; translation ours) (on 282 we find an exegesis of *Joshua* 1:8). In the second part of the first book, Bononia more or less resumes the argument on 308–324.

60   See amongst others Furió Ceriol, *Bononia* 366–390, e.g. 390: 'Scripsit autem Deus uernacula lingua, scripserunt Vates uernacula lingua, concionatus est Christus uernacula lingua, et Apostoli scripserunt et praedicauerunt uernacula lingua, Ecclesia Graeca scripsit uernacula lingua, D. Hieronymus Sacras Literas facit loquentes uernacula lingua, cur igitur nobis aut non liceat aut uitio dabitur, si Sacram Scripturam uernacula lingua loquentem in apertum demus?' ('God wrote in the vernacular language, the prophets wrote in the vernacular tongue, Christ spoke in the common language, and the apostles wrote and preached in the vulgar tongue; the Greek Church wrote in the vernacular language, St. Jerome made the Sacred Scriptures speak in the vernacular language:

According to Bononia, moreover, the need for 'mediated' access to the Scriptures was also intrinsically related to their obscure and difficult content, and not only with the complexity of their speech. Translations, in his opinion, did not make the biblical text any more accessible.[61] Furió Ceriol countered this argument by insisting that a good vernacular translation was already an important aid in making the content of the Scriptures clear, which was most required with respect to the points of faith necessary for salvation. He conceded, nevertheless, that the Bible did contain more difficult passages, particularly in the prophetic and apocalyptic books. Such difficulties were to be solved in the first instance with human assistance, including quality catechesis and good preaching, which, as Furió clearly admitted, continued to be of the utmost importance. In addition, however, Christians could rely on the help of the Holy Spirit and primarily of God himself. Every Christian was thus called to familiarize him- or herself as much as possible with God, Christ and the rule of faith. It was thus appropriate to refer to all Christians as 'theo-logians', in the literal sense of the word.[62]

---

why should we not be permitted or why should it even be counted to us as a vice, if we published the Sacred Scripture expressing itself in the vernacular'; translations ours). Furió resumes pieces of the argumentation in the second part of the second book, such as on 482–488, 494–496, 544 and in an interesting summary on 614.

61   Giovanni a Bononia's argument in Furió Ceriol, *Bononia* 272–278 and 308, such as 274–276: 'Sed difficultas non in uerbis sita est, sed in rebus ipsis. Quae fuerit ex se res difficilis, haec utcunque aliis uel aliis uerbis explicent, res eadem manet, eadem ergo difficultas' ('The difficulty is not situated in the words, but in the matters itself. If a matter is difficult in itself, whether it is explained in these or other words, this matter remains the same, and also thus the difficulty'; translation ours).

62   See Furió Ceriol, *Bononia* 432, 452–454, 518–526, among others 454: 'Itaque omnium rerum quae oratione explicantur, duplex difficultas esse solet: altera uerborum, altera ac praecipua rerum uerbis subiectarum. Quapropter si (ut alias dictum est, quod nemo negat) patrius sermo cuique est notissimus, diuinae literae in plebeium sermonum uersae, non in uerbis, sed in rebus facessent nobis negotium. Quid igitur facilius? quod una ne, an quod dabus difficultatibus teneatur? nimirum quod duabus. Ergo Scriptura Sacra in uernaculam linguam expressa, facilior erit intellectu' ('To all things that are explained by speech, a double difficulty used to be connected: the first has to do with the words, the second and most principal with the matters that underlie the words. Therefore, if (as is said elsewhere, which nobody denies) the paternal language is most familiar to everyone, the Sacred Scriptures translated into the vulgar tongue cause us difficulty not as regards the words, but as regards the matters. What is more easy? That someone is bound by one or by two problems? Undoubtedly that he is bound by two problems. Thus the Sacred Scripture translated into the vernacular tongue is much easier to understand'; translation ours).

According to Bononia, conversely, not everyone was a theo-logian and there was a genuine danger that everyone would attempt an arbitrary interpretation of the Bible in the light of his or her own preferences. Vernacular Scripture reading thus facilitated error and heretical interpretation. As Bononia points out by way of example, this is precisely what happened in Courtray: the people read the Bible in the vernacular and this rekindled their enthusiasm for Anabaptism. It was for this reason that the city Magistrate had asked the Emperor to forbid vernacular reading of the Bible.[63] According to Bononia, the pastors in Courtray had come to the same conclusions through what they had heard in private confession, but in order not to betray the secret of confession, they had confirmed 'per nutum', that is 'by nodding', what the magistrate had openly declared.[64] The danger of an idiosyncratic and thus erroneous reading of the Bible was one of the most commonly employed arguments against the publication of vernacular Bibles and Furió Ceriol was obliged to agree that it was indeed the most consistent argument. He nevertheless pointed out that it was not the vernacular Scriptures that had led to heresy, but the sinful and unsound attitude of the people who read them. Historically speaking, moreover, heretical movements tended for the most part to be generated by scholars and not so much by ordinary (Bible reading) folk. In a rather sarcastic way, Furió Ceriol also went into Bononia's point that the Courtray Magistrate's request was supported by what parish priests had heard in confession and that they had therefore nodded their assent. The implication was that, if they had used words, this would have been a betrayal of the secret of confession. For Furió, however, the content of this wordless communication could only be a conjecture ('coniectura') and was insufficient to require the imposition of such drastic measures.[65]

---

63   Giovanni a Bononia's argument in Furió Ceriol, *Bononia* 308–310 and 340–350, among others 346: 'Quare dubitare nemo potest quin ex uernacula Bibliorum traductione ingentes in Republica errores procreentur. Ventum est ad grauissimum omnium argumentorum locum, Caeriolane: non est quo fugias, hic te teneo; quandoquidem concedis ex Sacrorum Librorum lectione uernacula haereses tum esse ortas tum etiam posse oriri' ('Therefore, nobody can doubt that from the vernacular translation of the Scriptures gross errors may be produced in society. Here we have arrived at the most serious element of all the arguments, Ceriol. This is not something that you can escape from—I hold you to that; for you cannot but admit that from the reading of the Sacred Scriptures in the vernacular heresies both have originated and also can originate; translation ours').

64   Furió Ceriol, *Bononia* 344.

65   Furió Ceriol, *Bononia* 594–606, e.g. 594: 'Sunt loci qui facile possunt decipere, praesertim illiteratam plebem; perge. Fefellerunt multos, non solum illiteratos, sed etiam doctos' ('There are passages that may easily deceive, especially the uneducated populace; but go

The value of the biblical languages enjoyed a significant place in the discussion between Bononia and Furió. Bononia drew attention to the divine, elevated and refined character of Hebrew, Greek and Latin, arguing that the three biblical languages were particularly appropriate for rendering the Word of God. A knowledge of these biblical languages required considerable effort and only professional theologians had the time and dedication to acquire it. He argued furthermore that Hebrew, Greek and Latin could not be adequately translated into the vernacular. The languages of the peoples were coarse and barbaric, subject to degeneration into a multitude of dialects, and were thus unfit to render the Word of God.[66] Furió Ceriol sought to counter this by insisting that biblical Hebrew had a rough accent ('horridus') and was full of borrowed words, that the Greek of the apostles was unrefined and full of mistakes, and that Jerome's translation of the Bible had been written in barbaric Latin. Many of the Church fathers and doctors, he continued, were unfamiliar with Greek or Hebrew, but this did not prevent them from being expert theologians and Bible commentators. In his opinion, the vernacular languages were perfectly suitable to faithfully render the Word of God and were even capable of improving the style in which God's message was communicated.[67]

---

also a step further. They brought many into error, not only uneducated, but even learned; translation ours).

66   Giovanni a Bononia's argument in Furió Ceriol, *Bononia* 278–282, 318–320, 326–340, e.g. 278: 'Sed fac inania esse, quae a me nunc disputantur, fac uana esse, fac omnes linguas esse inter se aequales et pares, nec quicquam his tribus prae caeteris tribuatur; hoc abs te peto: quid ornamenti, quae elegantia, qui cultus magis ornabit Sacram Scripturam, in uulgares linguas interpretatam, quam ex Hebraeca, Graeca, Latina? Nullum profecto ornamentum, nulla elegantia, nullus cultus. Ergo, neque uertenda est sacra scriptura in uulgares linguas, ut sit ornatior et cultior' ('But suppose that it is nonsensical, what I have discussed, suppose that it is inconsistent, suppose that all languages are equal and the same among each other, and that nobody may rank these three [sacred languages] before the other languages; I beg you: what kind of ornament, which elegance, which stilistic refinement will decorate Sacred Scripture translated into the vernacular tongues more than Scripture in Hebrew, Greek and Latin? Not a single ornament, elegance or stylistic refinement! Therefore, Sacred Scripture should not be translated in the vulgar tongues, to become more ornate and stylistically refined'; translation ours).

67   Furió Ceriol, *Bononia* 454–458, 548–552, 578–590, among others 552: 'Tresne istas linguas iudicas necessarias esse ad theologiam, quod eius tanquam thesauro quodam diuinae literae contineantur, an non? uertantur igitur in uernaculas linguas, nec illarum usu indigebimus quoniam quod illae ad humanam intelligentiam faciunt, idem uernaculae linguae praestabunt' ('Are you judging these three languages necessary to theology, since the divine letters are contained in them as in a kind of treasure-chest, or not? Let them [the divine letters] be translated into the vernacular tongues, and we will not need to use

The use of the argument of language remains unusual in itself. At the beginning of the sixteenth century, there is evidence that it was precisely the more 'conservative' theologians who fulminated against the use of Hebrew and Greek in biblical studies, while Giovanni a Bononia clearly underlined the unique value of the biblical languages in his argumentation in order to condemn vernacular Bible translations. At the same time, we can read how a biblical humanist such as Furió Ceriol was capable of relativizing the significance of Hebrew and Greek in order to stress the equal merits of the vernacular languages. This illustrates how arguments could be manipulated 'pour le besoin de la cause' in the context of such discussions.

One aspect should certainly draw our attention: in his praise of possibilities of 'the vernacular languages', Furió insisted that the Church had always implicitly recognized the principle of translation, reminding his readers in this context that the universities of Paris and Louvain had permitted translations of the Sacred Scriptures into the language of the French- and the German-speaking people. And it was not as if the Louvain (and Parisian—dixit Furió) Faculty turned a blind eye and tolerated the practice. No, the theologians had explicitly given their consent to those vernacular Bible versions, on the condition that they be faithfully rendered. What troubled the Louvain theologians—as was evident from their famous negative recommendation—was that the common folk, in this case in Courtray, had, on the basis of these translations, pursued errors of every kind. Such circumstances of place or time might even have induced the said theologians to the promulgation of a (limited) prohibition.[68] Already in the first pages of the first book, Furió had stressed the 'intermediary' position of the mentioned universities in relation to Bible translations in the

---

these [languages] anymore, since what they mean for the human intellect, can also be supplied by the vernacular languages'; translation ours).

68 Furió Ceriol, *Bononia* 588: 'An non et Schola Sorbonia et tua Louaniensis, uidet diuinos libros in uulgares linguas Gallorum et Germanorum esse translatos? Quid istae duae scholae? Reprobantne huismodi translationes? Minime; uerum non solum conniuent, sed etiam ipsimet approbant tales translationes fideliter esse expressas, in quibus hoc unum ipsis displicet, quod sumat infinita multitudo per eas occasionem errandi, et non quod male ac infideliter uersae sint' ('And do not both the Faculty of the Sorbonne and your Faculty, that of Louvain, see the divine books translated into the languages of the French and the Germans? And what about these two faculties? Do they condemn translations of this kind? Not at all; and it is not that they merely tolerate [these translations], they even approve such versions that are truthfully translated. There is only one thing that displeases them, viz. that the undefinable masses draw from them the occasion to err, and not that they may badly or not truthfully be translated'; translation ours).

vernacular,[69] a position that was thus more nuanced than could be deduced from the one drastic proposition, which had co-inspired Bononia's rejection of such translations. Furió's representation could indeed be substantiated to a certain degree with regard to the University of Louvain, but it was a misrepresentation in the case of Paris, since the latter is known to have had a very restrictive tradition on the question of the new vernacular Bible translations that were published from the 1520s onwards. Furió added to his argument that if one recognizes the principle of oral explanation of the Scriptures, one could not do otherwise than also accept the principle of vernacular translations.[70]

This selection of the main arguments of Furió's book makes it immediately obvious that the author could not have expected the applause of the orthodox Catholic circles in Louvain. If we are to believe the dossier put together a few years later by Baltasar Pérez—Dominican and informant to the Spanish Inquisition—on Furió Ceriol and his contacts, the latter even spent a period in the city's jail in 1556, a penalty that was largely due to the publication of his *Bononia*.[71] Furió's *Bononia* was prohibited by the third edition of the Index of Louvain (1558), and by other European indices in its wake. He even spent a second period in Louvain's prison in 1559, from which he is said to have been released in 1560. He was rehabilitated after an investigation by the rector of the University, a process followed closely by Margaret of Parma, the governess of the Low Countries.[72]

It is further striking that Giovanni a Bononia, some months after the publication of the book carrying his name, returned to Sicily for good, after a little more than ten years in Louvain. The man did not return to Sicily empty-handed, however. Charles V appointed him abbot of the Sicilian monastery of Sant' Angelo di Brolo on his return, a position that also entitled him to an annual emolument from the incomes of the dioceses of Patti and Mazara del

---

69   Furió Ceriol, *Bononia* 259–260.

70   See e.g. Furió Ceriol, *Bononia* 588.

71   For the complete text of the Spanish report of Pérez, see Tellechea J.I., "Españoles en Lovaina en 1551–8: primeras noticias sobre el bayanismo", *Revista Española de Teología* 23 (1963) 21–45, here 38, copied in "Información de Fray Baltasar Pérez, O.P. Sevilla, 26 de mayo de 1558", in Méchoulan H. (ed.), *Raison et altérité chez Fadrique Furió Ceriol philosophe politique espagnol du XVIᵉ siècle* (Paris – The Hague: 1973) 220–221; comp. Méchoulan H. – Almenara M., "Elementos históricos y cronológicos para una biografía", in Furió Ceriol, *Obra completa*, ed. Méchoulan – Peréz Durà 15–43, here 21–23.

72   Brussels, KBR, Ms. II. 187, vol. I, f. 30, 32, 34–37, 41–45, 47, 67, 68, 188. These documents are reproduced in Méchoulan (ed.), *Raison et altérité chez Fadrique Furió* 259–271. For a discussion, see Méchoulan (ed.), *Raison et altérité chez Fadrique Furió* 32–36 and Méchoulan – Almenara, "Elementos históricos y cronológicos" 27–30.

Vallo, both located in Sicily. This appointment does raise the question whether Bononia was not simply kicked upstairs: having manifested himself on the public forum as an opponent of vernacular Bible reading, he publicly ran counter to the official policy of tolerance the Emperor had confirmed, notwithstanding the contrary advice of the Faculty. Whatever the case may be, in the course of 1556, both fierce antagonists in the Louvain controversy on vernacular Bible reading of the preceding years were neutralized.

A Parallel Evolution in Rome

We cannot ignore that a paradigm shift occurred during the years of 1552–1553, when the position of the Louvain theologians altered from toleration to an outspokenly unfavourable attitude to Bible reading in the vernacular. It was a response to the specific evolutions 'on the field', exemplified by what happened in Courtray, where the toleration of vernacular Bibles had not taken the wind out of the Protestants' sails, as the theologians had hoped, but, in contrast, had contributed to the resurgence of dissident religious movements. The intellectual evolution evident among theologians in the Low Countries cannot, however, be isolated from what was going on in Rome, where the adherents of a restrictive approach had likewise gained an increasing influence.[73] Among them was Gian Pietro Carafa, former head of the Holy Office of the Roman Inquisition, who, as Pope Paul IV, had ascended to the throne of Peter in 1555.[74] In 1559, during the 'unfortunate recess' of the Council that lasted for ten years,[75] he had published, through the intermediary of the Inquisition, an Index of Forbidden Books that was applicable to the entire Church.[76] In this

---

73   On the evolution of the Roman standpoint after the Council of Trent, see also François, "De Leuvense theologen over de bijbel" 356–357. For a more elaborate discussion of the matter, see Fragnito G., *La Bibbia al rogo. La censura ecclesiastica e i volgarizzamenti della Scrittura (1471–1605)*, Saggi 460 (Bologna: 1997) 75–109; Fragnito G., "Il ritorno al Latino, ovvero la fine dei volgarizzamenti", in Leonardi L. (ed.), *La Bibbia in Italiano tra Medioevo e Rinascimento* (Firenze: 1998) 395–407, here 396–398; also Prosperi A., "Bibbia", in Prosperi A., *Dizionario storico dell'Inquisizione*, 4 vols. (Pisa: 2010) I 185–187, and Frajese V., "La politica dell'Indice dal Tridentino al Clementino (1571–1596)", *Archivio italiano per la storia della pietà* 11 (1998) 269–345.

74   Santarelli D., "Paolo IV, papa (Gian Pietro Carafa)", in Prosperi (ed.), *Dizionario storico dell'Inquisizione* III 1164–1166.

75   McNally, "Trent and Vernacular Bibles" 226.

76   Bujanda J.M. De et al., *Index de Rome 1557, 1559, 1564: Les premiers index romains et l'index du Concile de Trente*, Index des livres interdits 8 (Sherbrooke – Geneva: 1990) 37–39, 128–131,

document, we read the general stipulation that no edition of the Bible in the vernacular, nor any edition of the New Testament, should in any way whatsoever be printed, purchased, read or possessed without the written permission of the Holy Office of the Roman Inquisition.[77] It is clear that the Roman Inquisition sought to reserve judgment for itself. The aforementioned general stipulations were preceded by what was considered a 'non-exhaustive' list, containing specific forbidden editions of the Bible and the New Testament. The list even includes a reference to the Dutch New Testaments printed by the Antwerp printers Adriaen van Berghen, Christoffel van Ruremund and 'Zeel'— the latter having been accepted as a reference to Jan van Ghelen—as well as to the French Bible of Martin Lempereur, amongst other editions.

The extremely severe Index gave rise to great concern and received no application whatsoever in the Church (let alone in the Church of the Low Countries). Therefore, the Holy Office felt obliged to issue, as early as February 1559, a so-called *Instructio circa indicem librorum prohibitorum*. In the document, the stipulations with regard to Bible reading were, to a certain degree, moderated. An absolute prohibition was maintained on Bibles provided with heretical commentaries and marginal glosses. Religious men, non-priests, and even pious and devout laypeople (but in no case women, not even sisters of female monastic orders) could obtain permission to read so-called 'good' Catholic Bibles in the vernacular. Priests, deacons and sub-deacons should only appeal to the Latin Bible and should by no means read Bibles in the vernacular. Permission to read books containing the Epistles and Gospels from Mass could easily be gained by those requesting such permission. It is important to note that these authorizations could be given by the inquisitors and their deputies, but in addition, 'in places where these were absent' ('ubi ipsi non sunt'), also by the local bishops, and this was a significant opening in comparison to the centralizing dispositions anticipated by Paul IV.[78]

Confronted with the opposition Paul IV's Index evoked, Pope Pius IV, his successor from the end of 1559, created a commission that would draft a

---

137, 307–331, here 325 and 331. Also Caravale G., *Forbidden Prayer: Church Censorship and Devotional Literature in Renaissance Italy*, trans. P. Dawson (Farnham: 2011) 71–73.

77   Amongst others: 'Biblia omnia vulgari idiomate, Germanico, Gallico, Hispanico, Italico, Anglico sive Flandrico, etc. conscripta nullatenus vel imprimi vel legi vel teneri possint absque licentia sacri Officii S. Ro. Inquisitionis' ('All Bibles, translated into the vulgar tongue, be it German, French, Spanish, Italian, English or Flemish, etc. may by no means be printed, read or held in possession without the permission of the Holy Office of the Roman Inquisition'; translation ours). See De Bujanda et al., *Index de Rome* 325 and 331, comp. 785.

78   De Bujanda et al., *Index de Rome* 46–49, 100–104, 138–140.

new, more lenient index. As early as 1561, the commission issued a so-called *Moderatio indicis librorum prohibitorum*. As far as Bibles in the vernacular were concerned, the *Moderatio* referred to the conditions that were included in the *Instructio* of 1559. The only difference was that even more authority was granted to the local bishops in making decisions regarding the printing, reading and possession of Bibles.[79] The drafting of a new index was eventually delegated to the Council fathers at Trent.

The Index of Trent, which was ultimately promulgated by Pius IV in 1564, has to be considered as a landmark in the Catholic Church's position with regard to vernacular Bible reading.[80] The fourth of the famous ten *Regulae* or *Rules* that were included in the Index, put forward, amongst other statements, that the unrestricted authorization to read the Bible in the vernacular had more disadvantages than advantages. When, however, no detriment but only an increase in faith and devotion was to be expected from Bible reading, an individual dispensation could be granted by the bishop or the inquisitor, who had to seek the prior advice of the parish priest or the father confessor. The translation had to be made by a Catholic author. The authorization, furthermore, had to be in writing.[81] Booksellers who sold Bibles to people who were not in possession of the requested permission had to forfeit the received payment to the bishop and exposed themselves to additional punishments. Members of religious orders and congregations could, however, purchase and read Bibles, after having received a simple authorization from their superiors.

---

79 De Bujanda et al., *Index de Rome* 51–54, 105–106, 141–142. Also Caravale, *Forbidden Prayer* 73–74.

80 De Bujanda et al., *Index de Rome* 91–99, 143–153, 814–815. Also Caravale, *Forbidden Prayer* 75.

81 'Cum experimento manifestum sit, si sacra Biblia vulgari lingua *passim* sine discrimine permittantur, plus inde, ob hominum temeritatem, detrimenti, quam utilitatis oriri; hac in parte iudicio Episcopi, aut Inquisitoris stetur; ut cum consilio Parochi, vel Confessarii Bibliorum, a Catholicis auctoribus versorum, lectionem in vulgari lingua eis concedere possint, quos intellexerint ex huiusmodi lectione non damnun, sed fidei, atque pietatis augmentum capere posse: quam facultatem in scriptis habeant' ('We have learned by experience that if the sacred books, translated into the vernacular, are indiscriminantly circulated, there follows because of the weakness of man more harm than good. In this matter the judgment of the bishop or the inquisitor must be sought, who on the advice of the pastor or the confessor may permit the reading of a Bible translated into the vernacular by Catholic authors. This may be done with the understanding that from this reading no harm, but an increase of faith and piety, results. The permission must be in writing'). See De Bujanda et al., *Index de Rome* 814–815; for the English translation, see McNally, "Trent and Vernacular Bibles" 226–227.

The list containing forbidden Bibles and New Testaments that was to appear in the Index of 1559 had been removed from this new Index of 1564.

Only seven years after the promulgation of the Tridentine Index, the new pope, Pius V, formerly a member of the inquisitorial apparatus, was already considering a revision of the Index. To that aim, he appointed, on 5 March 1571, a committee of cardinals, which a year later (13 September 1572) was converted into a genuine Roman congregation by Gregory XIII. During the first fifteen years of its existence, the Congregation of the Index collaborated with the powerful Congregation of the Holy Office of the Roman Inquisition in order to implement a blunt prohibition of Bible reading in the vernacular. From 1587 onwards, however, a tussle arose between the Congregation of the Inquisition and the Congregation of the Index, whereby the former defended a Rome-centred restrictive approach (the '1559 model') and the latter—in its new composition—was prepared to grant the right of discretion to the local bishops (the '1564 model'), whereas subsequent popes tended to the one or the other side, depending on their personal convictions. After a quarter of a century of debates, Pope Clement VIII was able to promulgate a new Index on May 1596, as we will see further on.[82]

Decreasing Bible Production in the Low Countries

Returning to the Low Countries, we must conclude that the Emperor, faithful to his longstanding biblical humanist principles and as a Bible reader himself,[83] did not implement the prohibition on vernacular Bible translations recommended by the *Lovanienses*, either in person or through his government. It is, furthermore, highly debatable whether the increasing reticence on the part of the Roman authorities had any impact at all on the production

---

82   For the evolution from the Tridentine (1564) until the Clementine Index (1596), see Fragnito, *La Bibbia al rogo* 111–198, among others 119; comp. Frajese, "La politica dell'Indice" 272–276, 284–288, 300–301, 316–320, 329, 339–341. A survey also in François W., "La Iglesia Católica y la lectura de la Biblia en lengua vernácula, antes y después del Concilio de Trento", *Mayéutica* 39 (2013) 245–273, here 262–268.

83   See e.g. Brandi K., *The Emperor Charles V: The Growth and Destiny of a Man and of a World-Empire*, trans. C.V. Wedgwood, Jonathan Cape Paperback 34 (London: 1965) 639: Dealing with Charles V's last years of life, in San Jeronimo de Yuste, Brandi writes that he 'had persuaded the Inquisition to give him permission to read a French translation of the Bible, as its study in the vernacular was otherwise not allowed'.

of Bibles in the Low Countries.[84] The Louvain theologians were nevertheless able to push through their standpoint in their own backyard. It must be said that in 1553, in the period of the aforementioned notorious meeting of the Louvain theologians, the sworn University printer Anthonis-Maria Bergaigne, one of the earliest partners of Bartholomeus van Grave, was able to re-edit the Dutch Louvain Bible, as it had been revised by the Dominican friar Jan van der Haghen and provided, by the same, with biblical cross-references and chapter-headings. But this edition was the very last that was published in the University town itself.

Given the fact that neither under the administration of the Emperor Charles, nor under that of his successor from 1555 onwards, Philip II, had any general prohibition on vernacular Bible translations been promulgated, and that the Index of 1558 continued the imperial Bible policy as it had been implemented since 1546, the production of vernacular Vulgate Bibles simply continued for some years.[85] This was at least the case in Antwerp, where five more editions of the Dutch Louvain Bible were published in the 1550s and 1560s, with as its apogee the prestigious Plantin Bible of 1566 [Fig. 10.4].[86] In Cologne, Arnold Birckmann published two attractively illustrated versions of the Louvain Bible in 1565 and 1566. And although the intensive publication activity in the years 1565–1566 may have been inspired by a renewed optimism, created by the Fourth Rule of Trent, the production of vernacular Bibles in Antwerp came to an end not soon thereafter: for more than thirty years to come, no more complete Dutch Bibles were published in the Catholic part of the Low Countries (until the publication of the Moerentorf Bible in 1599). No legal measure seems to explain this sudden standstill, but it was most likely due to the turbulent

---

84   For these editions, see the online databases: http://www.bibliasacra.nl; *Short Title Catalogue Netherlands* (http://picarta.pica.nl/DB=3.11); *Short Title Catalogus Vlaanderen* (http://www.database.stcv.be). Further Cockx-Indestege E. – Glorieux G. – Op de Beeck B., *Belgica Typographica 1541–1600. Catalogus librorum impressorum ab anno MDXLI ad annum MDC in regionibus quae nunc Regni Belgarum partes sunt*, Collection du Centre national de l'archéologie et de l'histoire du livre 2, 4 vols. (Nieuwkoop: 1968–1994); Valkema Blouw P. – Schuytvlot A.C., *Typographia Batava 1541–1600. A Repertorium of Books Printed in the Northern Netherlands between 1541 and 1600*, 2 vols. (Nieuwkoop: 1998); Pettegree A. – Walsby M., *Netherlandish Books: Books Published in the Low Countries and Dutch Books Published Abroad Before 1601* (Leiden – Boston: 2011).

85   De Bujanda et al., *Index de l'Université de Louvain* 55, 334–335, 345–346, 475–478.

86   With regard to the Bible editions of Plantin, see Voet L., *The Plantin Press (1555–1589): A Bibliography of the Works Printed and Published by Christopher Plantin at Antwerp and Leiden*, 6 vols. (Amsterdam: 1980–1983) I 381–391; also Clercq C. de, "Les Éditions bibliques, liturgiques et canoniques de Plantin", *De Gulden Passer* 34 (1956) 157–192, here 158–170.

events of the so-called 'Wonder Year', which saw the emergence of Calvinist preachers, the iconoclastic riots, and the start of the revolt against the Spanish Catholic monarch, as well as the staunch reaction of the Duke of Alba, who was sent to the Low Countries to restore order and sustained, without wavering, the attempts to re-Catholicize the country according to strict lines.[87] Silent testimony to the climate of fear and self-censorship is a New Testament in folio format that the daring Antwerp printer Johann Gymnich printed in 1567: since this is a highly unusual format for a single New Testament, it should be considered as the first part of what was to become a complete Bible edition. The printer, however, did not manage to continue the project, obviously because of the changed politico-religious circumstances.

The production of Catholic Dutch New Testaments, however, continued. Near to fifty editions containing the text of the Louvain New Testament are known to have been published from the 1550s until the 1570s, the large majority of them in Antwerp. This clearly testifies to the continuous demand for such literature in the Low Countries. These editions were made in a more popular octavo, duodecimo or sexto-decimo format. As had been the case for several decades already with New Testaments destined for the Catholic market, the Vulgate translation included a liturgical calendar that preceded the text, and it was followed by the text of the Epistle readings taken from the Old Testament that were read during Mass; it concluded with a table indicating which Epistles and Gospels were to be read on each Sunday or feast-day, as well as the most important saints' days. This arrangement of the material made the New Testaments suitable for following the Scripture readings at Mass, a link with the official liturgy of the Church that had always been considered a prerequisite for allowing Catholics to read the Bible in the vernacular. This series of Catholic New Testament editions was, however, concluded by Plantin's New Testament of 1577, which was, with the exception of two anonymous reprints based on it (one of them having been obviously printed in Delft, in the northern part of the Low Countries), the last Dutch Catholic edition of the sixteenth century [Fig. 10.5].

---

87   Pollmann J., *Catholic Identity and the Revolt of the Netherlands 1520–1635* (Oxford: 2011) 92–121; Benedict Ph. et al., *Reformation, Revolt and Civil War in France and the Netherlands 1555–1585*, Koninklijke Nederlandse Akademie van Wetenschappen, Verhandelingen, Afd. Letterkunde, Nieuwe Reeks 176 (Amsterdam: 1999), among others the contribution of González de León F. – Parker G., "The Grand Strategy of Philip II and the Revolt of the Netherlands 1559–1584" 215–232; Goosens A., *Les inquisitions modernes dans les Pays-Bas méridionaux 1520–1633, vol. I. La legislation* (Brussels: 1997) 92–121; Parker G., *The Dutch Revolt* (rev. and repr. London: 1990) 68–117.

FIGURE 10.5   Het nieuwe testament ons Heeren Jesu Christi (*Antwerp, M. van Roye for H. Wouters: 1576*). KU Leuven, Maurits Sabbe Library, P225.055.1 BIJB 1576.

As regards the French New Testament, the situation is even more remarkable.[88] The French Louvain Bible of 1550 was not reprinted, but in the decade between 1552 and 1561 some four editions of the New Testament were issued in Antwerp, all of which provided a more or less independent, albeit largely Catholic, revision of Lefèvre d'Étaples' version (three of them even included elements from the 'Protestantizing' version of Pierre-Robert Olivetan). The first of this series, Johann Gymnich's New Testament of 1552, would eventually end up on the Index of 1570.[89] Between 1563 and 1567 three editions of the New Testament that were based upon the text of the Calvinist Geneva Bible were published in Antwerp. While the usual delicate passages were adapted to the Vulgate, the editions nevertheless preserved the 'Protestant' summaries above the chapters and marginal notes in a similar vein.[90] Guillaume Sylvius—the king's typographer since 1560—who was responsible for printing one of the editions (during the turbulent year of 1566) was, for these reasons, jailed from March to May of 1568 during the regime of the Duke of Alba, and his New Testament would also be put on the Index of 1570.[91]

In 1567 Plantin eventually published the New Testament version translated by the Parisian theologian René Benoist—the openings that the Tridentine Index had still left for Bible reading in the vernacular may have also been a decisive impetus in this case.[92] Benoist had based his version of the Bible on

88   For bibliographical data, specifically for French Bible editions, see: Chambers B.T., *Bibliography of French Bibles, vol. 1. Fifteenth- and Sixteenth-Century French-Language Editions of the Scriptures*, Travaux d'humanisme et renaissance 192 (Geneva: 1983); Pettegree A. – Walsby M. – Wilkinson A., *French Vernacular Books: Books Published in the French Language Before 1601*, 2 vols. (Leiden – Boston: 2007).

89   It concerns a Lefèvre version, but obviously revised on the basis of the version made by Pierre-Robert Olivetan (?) and printed by Pierre de Wingle in Neuchâtel 1534—a 'Protestantizing version'—as well as containing elements of the version made by Nicolas de Leuze included in the Louvain Bible of 1550 (Chambers, *Bibliography* n° 166).

90   Comp. Goosens, *Les Inquisitions modernes* I 96–106.

91   Voet L., *The Golden Compasses: A History and Evaluation of the Printing and Publishing Activities of the Officina Plantiniana at Antwerp in two volumes, vol. 1. Christophe Plantin and the Moretuses: Their Lives and their World* (Amsterdam: 1969) 59; comp. Rouzet A., *Dictionnaire des imprimeurs, libraires et éditeurs des XVᵉ et XVIᵉ siècles dans les limites géographiques de la Belgique actuelle*, Collection du Centre national de l'archéologie et de l'histoire du livre 3 (Nieuwkoop: 1975) 201.

92   For an account of the publication history of Benoist's Bible in Louvain, see especially Clercq C. de, "La Bible française de René Benoist", *Gutenberg Jahrbuch* 32 (1957) 168–174; Bogaert – Gilmont, "De Lefèvre d'Étaples à la fin du XVIᵉ siècle" 91–101; Ingram E.M., "Dressed in Borrowed Robes: The Making and Marketing of the Louvain Bible (1578)", in Swanson R.N. (ed.), *The Church and the Book. Papers Read at the 2000 Summer Meeting and*

the Geneva Bible, but had 'corrected' suspect words and phrases on the basis of the Vulgate, while at the same time adding explicatory annotations to corroborate a Catholic, rather than a Calvinist, reading. Benoist's work, which was published for the first time in Paris at the end of 1566, was condemned by the Faculty of Theology there on 15 July 1567. This condemnation was connected in particular to several annotations to the Old Testament, in which Protestant theology was considered to still be all too evident. In the meantime, however, the Bible had been reviewed and approved in Louvain by no less than Jean Henten, the theologian who in 1547 had edited a revision of the Vulgate (but who had also had the intention of censuring some of Erasmus's over-enthusiastic declarations in favour of the vernacular Bible), together with three more members of the Louvain Faculty.[93] And although Plantin had the privilege of publishing the entire Bible, the severe judgment of the Paris theologians with regard to the Old Testament obviously induced him to put only the New Testament onto the market; the colophon has as its date 20 July 1567.

In 1573, Plantin published a second edition of Benoist's French New Testament, three years after printing had actually been completed. On the title page it was mentioned that the edition had been 'translated by the theologians of Louvain', without further mentioning the name of René Benoist, as a precaution. All marginal glosses were removed. In 1578 Plantin finally brought the complete French Bible onto the market, once again three years after its having left the Antwerp presses. The edition bore no name on the title page, but included a foreword from the hand of the Louvain theologian Jacques de Bay, thus providing the assurance that the edition was issued with the blessing of the very same corps that, a quarter of a century earlier, had expressed serious reservations with regard to vernacular Bibles. Marginal glosses had evidently also been removed from the Bible edition. Plantin's circumspection was dictated by a renewed condemnation of Benoist's biblical editions in both Paris and Rome [Fig. 10.6].[94]

A year later than the last Dutch New Testament had been printed, Plantin's French Bible was the very last Catholic Bible edition printed in Antwerp for more than two decades to come. In the following two decades, no vernacular

the 2001 *Winter Meeting of the Ecclesiastical History Society*, Studies in Church History 38 (Woodbridge: 2004) 212–221; Carter A., "René Benoist: Scripture for the Catholic Masses", in Racaut L. – Ryrie A. (eds.), *Moderate Voices in the European Reformation*, St. Andrews Studies in Reformation History (Aldershot: 2005) 162–177.

93   Comp. Ingram, "The Making of the Louvain Bible" 218.

94   De Clercq, "Les Éditions bibliques, liturgiques et canoniques" 169–170; Ingram, "The Making of the Louvain Bible" 219–220.

𝒜ijs.&.L.W.:1702

LA SAINCTE

BIBLE,

CONTENANT LE VIEIL

ET NOVVEAV TESTAMENT,

traduicte de Latin en François.

Auec les ARGVMENS *ſur chacun liure, declarans
ſommairement tout ce que y eſt contenu.*

A ANVERS,

De l'Imprimerie de Chriſtophle Plantin,

Architypographe de ſa Maieſté.

M. D. LXXVIII.

1578

FIGURE 10.6   *Title page of Plantin's edition of the French 'Bible des Théologiens de
Louvain':* La saincte bible, contenant le vieil et nouveau testament
(Antwerp, Christopher Plantin: 1578). KU Leuven, *Maurits Sabbe Library,
P 22.056.1/F°/Bijb 1578.*

Bible editions were printed in the southern part of the Low Countries. At the close of 1577, Antwerp had experienced the establishment of a Calvinist republic,[95] and after the re-conquest of Antwerp by the Spaniards in 1585, the printing of Catholic vernacular Bibles was not resumed. It is evident that an even more Counter-Reformational reflex inspired the re-Catholicization of the Spanish part of the Low Countries[96] than had been the case subsequent to the Wonder Year 1566, with the implication that the laity ought to be withheld from reading the Bible in the vernacular. Bible reading in the vernacular was increasingly frowned upon, so that no market remained for additional Bible editions.

The above-sketched dramatic decrease in vernacular Bible production has, until now, not been explained by any general prohibitive intervention of the authorities. The indices of 1569 and 1570, as well as the *Index Expurgatorius* of 1571, which were edited in the Low Countries in the wake of the Council of Trent by Benito Arias Montano with the help of the Louvain theologians, sustained the Bible policy as it had been developed since the last quarter of the century. The very same Bibles were explicitly forbidden as those prohibited since the Index of Louvain of 1546, with a few additions in the Index of 1570, comprising Protestant Dutch Bibles printed in Emden, as well as the French Bibles of Sebastien Castellion (1555), the Geneva Bibles (from 1540 onwards), the Bibles published by Sebastien Honoré (1558) and by Jean de Tournes (from 1551 onwards), and French New Testaments published by Gymnich (perhaps a reference to his editions of 1552, 1554 and/or 1567) and Silvius (undoubtedly his edition of 1566 is meant).[97] The Index of Antwerp of 1570, as well as that of Liège from of 1569 did include the Tridentine Rules, whereas respect for these

---

95   During the Calvinistic Republic in Antwerp, Dutch Calvinist *Deux Aes* Bibles were sold in the town by Jasper Troyens. From a *Deux Aes* Bible edited in 1583–1584, the printer-publisher had most likely even printed the first part of the Old Testament in Antwerp (*Biblia, dat is De gantsche Heylighe Schrift, grondelijck ende trouwelijck verduytschet*, Antwerp, J. Troyen [=seller]—Dordrecht, Jan Canin and Peter Verhaghen [=printers]: 1583–1584). The same Jasper Troyens also published, in a co-edition with Arnout Conincx, in 1582, a French edition of the New Testament in the Geneva version (*Le Nouveau Testament*, Antwerp, Jasper Troyen: 1582, and *Le Nouveau Testament*, Antwerp, Arnout Coninx: 1582).

96   Pollmann, *Catholic Identity and the Revolt* 125–158; Goosens, *Les Inquisitions modernes* I 125–130; Parker, *The Dutch Revolt* 199–224.

97   Bujanda J.M. De et al., *Index d'Anvers. 1569, 1570, 1571*, Index des livres interdits 7 (Sherbrooke – Geneva 1988) 74–77, 251–256, 259–268, 567, 672–673. Some of these editions had already been prohibited by earlier edicts, such as the Bible of Sébastien Honorat through an edict of 22 October 1561 (*Recueil des ordonnances des Pays-Bas. Deuxième série:*

INDEX
LIBRORVM
PROHIBITORVM,

CVM REGVLIS CONFECTIS
PER PATRES A TRIDENTINA SYNODO
delectos , Auctoritate Sanctiss. D. N. Iij IIII.
Pont. Max.comprobatus.

CVM Appendice in Belgio , ex mandato Regiæ
Cathol. Maiestatis confecta.

ANTVERPIÆ,
Ex officina Christophori Plantini.
M. D. LXX.

FIGURE 10.7   Index librorum prohibitorum (*Antwerp, Christopher Plantin:*
1570). *KU Leuven*, Maurits Sabbe Library, *P 348.416.4 EDIC*).

rules was also required by the important edict that Philip II had issued on 19 May 1570,[98] with the aim of regulating the book trade. Obedience to the *Regula Quarta* further appeared in the legislation of the provincial councils and synods of the Low Countries (first at the Provincial Council of Cambrai in 1586, and only from the seventeenth century onwards also at the diocesan synods of the Church province of Malines) [Fig. 10.7].

Concluding Remarks

The conclusion for the present is that the dramatic decline in Bible production in the last three decades of the sixteenth century seems in the first place to have been provoked by the politico-religious turbulence of these years, with the most important turning points being the restoration of the Catholic Spanish rule under the Duke of Alba after 1566 and the reconquering of the southern part of the Low Countries by the Duke of Parma in the 1580s. Catholicism in the Southern Low Countries increasingly developed along anti-Protestant lines and, in these turbulent years, Bible reading in the vernacular was, to put it mildly, not considered the most adequate means of spiritual edification. Another question that remains unresolved is who the owners and readers were of the Bibles that had been spread in the previous decades and continued to circulate in the second part of the sixteenth century. Is there reason to assume that, in this regard also, a paradigm shift occurred, in the sense that there was an alteration in the reading public, from laypeople in the world to religious men (and women) in monasteries, and especially to parish clergy looking for help in the preparation of their homilies? It is in any case certain that, in theoretical theological texts, a huge emphasis was put on the role of the clergy as necessary mediators between God's Word and his flock; they were in a position to explain the basic truths of the faith and to interpret the Epistle and Gospel readings of Mass in the light of the ecclesiastical Tradition. Whatever the case may be, the Catholic laity in the Low Countries were not deprived of spiritual literature, but were provided with other kinds of devotional, catechetical and otherwise edifying books, which were often attractively edited.

1506–1700. Règne de Philippe II, vol. II. Contenant les ordonnances du 7 septembre 1559 au 31 décembre 1562, ed. Ch. Terlinden – J. Bolsée [Brussels: 1978] 276–277).

98   Enno van Gelder H.A., *Vrijheid en onvrijheid in de Republiek: geschiedenis der vrijheid van drukpers en godsdienst van 1572–1798* (Haarlem: 1947) 17–19.

In 1599 a new version of the Dutch Louvain Bible appeared in Antwerp from the press of Jan Moerentorf (Moretus), 33 years after the publisher's father-in-law Chrisopher Plantin had published the previous Dutch Bible, and 22 years after the most recent Dutch New Testament. The so-called 'Moerentorf Bible' was revised on the basis of the Sixto-Clementine Vulgate that had been released in 1592 and, more importantly, its publisher felt unintimidated by the Clementine Index that had been promulgated in May 1596. At the instigation of the Inquisition, the Pope had included a so-called *Observatio circa quartam regulam* [*Tridentinam*] (*Observation Regarding the Fourth Rule* [*of Trent*]), which, amongst other measures, bluntly revoked the local bishops' and inquisitors' right to allow the purchasing, reading or possession of vernacular versions of the Bible or parts of it by individual laypeople requesting that favour.[99] That such a restrictive approach to vernacular Bible reading was inapplicable in the countries of Northern and Central Europe, where Catholics had to coexist with 'Bible-centred' Protestants, was also understood by the papal nuncios in the countries concerned. Bible translations continued to be published, with or without special Roman approval, and in the years 1603–1604 the Roman authorities recognized in principle that the Catholics of the countries under consideration were not subject to the *Observatio* but to Trent's Fourth Rule. It seems that even the Congregation of the Inquisition had accepted the *fait accompli*, since it decreed at a meeting on 25 April 1608 that the 'abuse' of Bible translations in the vernacular should also be tolerated in Flanders—probably the entire Low Countries are meant here—since it was stated that the 'abuse' was already widespread there and that the presence of heretics in the country demanded such toleration. Again, this should not be considered as an authorization of completely free reading of the Bible in the vernacular, but rather a return to the regime imposed by the Fourth Rule of the Tridentine Index, which left it up to the local bishop or the inquisitor to grant consent in individual cases. At the start of the seventeenth century, vernacular Bible reading among Catholics in the Low Countries entered into a new phase.[100]

---

99   Fragnito, *La Bibbia al rogo* 178–197; comp. Frajese, "La politica dell'Indice" 339–341; Caravale, *Forbidden Prayer* 211–214.

100   See Fragnito G., "Per una geografia delle traduzioni bibliche nell'Europa cattolica (sedicesimo e diciasettesimo secolo)", in Quantin J.-L. – Waquet J.-C. (eds.), *Papes, princes et savants dans l'Europe moderne: Mélanges à la mémoire de Bruno Neveu*, Ecole pratique des hautes études. 4e section: Sciences historiques et philologiques 5; Hautes études médiévales et modernes 90 (Geneva: 2007) 51–77, here 65–77 (for the Low Countries, see 71, no. 59).

Bibliography

Agten E., "Fadrique Furió Ceriol, Giovanni di Bononia et la traduction de la Bible en langue vernaculaire: Analyse du *Bononia* (1556)", in François W. – Hollander A.A. den (eds.), *'Wading Lambs and Swimming Elephants': The Bible for the Laity and Theologians in Late Medieval and Early Modern Era*, Bibliotheca Ephemeridum Theologicarum Lovaniensium 257 (Leuven: 2012) 219–252.

Allgeier A., "Das Konzil von Trient und das theologische Studium", *Historisches Jahrbuch im Auftrage der Görres-Gesellschaft* 52 (1932) 313–339.

Bedouelle G., "Le débat catholique sur la traduction de la Bible en langue vulgaire", in Backus I. – Higman F. (eds.), *Théorie et pratique de l'exégèse*, Etudes de philologie et d'histoire 43 (Geneva: 1990) 39–59.

Benedict Ph. et al., *Reformation, Revolt and Civil War in France and the Netherlands 1555–1585*, Koninklijke Nederlandse Akademie van Wetenschappen, Verhandelingen, Afd. Letterkunde, Nieuwe Reeks 176 (Amsterdam: 1999).

Bleznick D.W., "Furió Ceriol y la controversia sobre la traducción de la Biblia", *Revista Hispánica Moderna* 34 (1968) 195–205.

Bogaert P.-M. – Gilmont J.-F., "La première Bible française de Louvain (1550)", *Revue Théologique de Louvain* 11 (1980) 275–309.

———, "De Lefèvre d'Étaples à la fin du XVIᵉ siècle", in Bogaert P.-M. (ed.), *Les Bibles en français: Histoire illustrée du Moyen Âge à nos jours* (Turnhout: 1991) 47–106.

Bononia Johannes a, *De aeterna Dei praedestinatione, et reprobatione ex scripturis, & Patrum authoritatibus deprompta sententia* (Leuven, Anthonis-Maria Bergaigne: 1555).

Bruin C.C. de, *De Statenbijbel en zijn voorgangers. Nederlandse bijbelvertalingen vanaf de Reformatie tot 1637*, rev. F.G.M. Broeyer (Haarlem – Brussels: 1993).

Bujanda J.M. De et al., *Index de l'Université de Louvain, 1546, 1550, 1558*, Index des livres interdits 2 (Sherbrooke – Geneva: 1986).

——— et al., *Index de l'Inquisition espagnole 1551, 1554, 1559*, Index des livres interdits 5 (Sherbrooke – Geneva: 1984).

——— et al., *Index d'Anvers. 1569, 1570, 1571*, Index des livres interdits 7 (Sherbrooke – Geneva 1988).

——— et al., *Index de Rome 1557, 1559, 1564: Les premiers index romains et l'index du Concile de Trente*, Index des livres interdits 8 (Sherbrooke – Geneva: 1990).

Byrne A., *El ministerio de la palabra en el concilio de Trento*, Diss. Doct. (Pamplona: 1975).

Caravale G., *Forbidden Prayer: Church Censorship and Devotional Literature in Renaissance Italy*, trans. P. Dawson (Farnham: 2011).

Carter A., "René Benoist: Scripture for the Catholic Masses", in Racaut L. – Ryrie A. (eds.), *Moderate Voices in the European Reformation*, St. Andrews Studies in Reformation History (Aldershot: 2005) 162–177.

Cavallera F., "La Bible en langue vulgaire au Concile de Trente (IVe Session)", in *Mélanges E. Podéchard. Études de sciences religieuses offertes pour son éméritat au doyen honoraire de la Faculté de Théologie de Lyon* (Lyons: 1945) 37–56.

Chambers B.T., *Bibliography of French Bibles, vol. I. Fifteenth- and Sixteenth-Century French-Language Editions of the Scriptures*, Travaux d'humanisme et renaissance 192 (Geneva: 1983).

Clercq C. de, "Les Éditions bibliques, liturgiques et canoniques de Plantin", *De Gulden Passer* 34 (1956) 157–192.

———, "La Bible française de René Benoist", *Gutenberg Jahrbuch* 32 (1957) 168–174.

Cockx-Indestege E. – Glorieux G. – Op de Beeck B., *Belgica Typographica 1541–1600. Catalogus librorum impressorum ab anno MDXLI ad annum MDC in regionibus quae nunc Regni Belgarum partes sunt*, Collection du Centre national de l'archéologie et de l'histoire du livre 2, 4 vols. (Nieuwkoop: 1968–1994).

Coletti V., *L'éloquence de la chaire. Victoires et défaites du latin entre Moyen Âge et Renaissance*, trans. S. Serventi (Paris: 1987).

Collectaneum eorum in quibus Erasmus Roterodamus videtur erronee aut scandalose scripsisse [...], Brussels, KBR, Ms. II, 194, f. 1–52.

Concilium Tridentinum: Diariorum, actorum, epistularum, tractatuum nova collectio, 13 vols. in 20 (Freiburg i/Breisgau: 1901–2001).

Crahay R., "Les censeurs louvanistes d'Érasme", in Coppens J. (ed.), *Scrinium Erasmianum. Historische opstellen gepubliceerd onder de auspiciën van de Universiteit te Leuven naar aanleiding van het vijfde eeuwfeest van Erasmus' geboorte*, 2 vols. (Leiden: 1969) I 221–249.

Edictum Caesareae Maiestatis promulgatum anno salutis M.D.XLVI. Praeterea Catalogus & declaratio librorum reprobatorum a Facultate sacrae Theologiae Lovaniensis Academiae, Iussu & ordinatione praenominatae Maiestatis Caesareae (Leuven, Servatius a Sassen: 1546).

Enciso J., "Prohibiciones españolas de las versiones bíblicas en romance antes del Tridentino", *Estudios bíblicos* 3 (1944) 523–554.

Enno van Gelder H.A., *Vrijheid en onvrijheid in de Republiek. Geschiedenis der vrijheid van drukpers en godsdienst van 1572–1798* (Haarlem: 1947).

Fernández López S., *Lectura y prohibición de la Biblia en lengua vulgar. Defensores y detractores* (León: 2003).

Fragnito G., *La Bibbia al rogo. La censura ecclesiastica e i volgarizzamenti della Scrittura (1471–1605)*, Saggi 460 (Bologna: 1997).

———, "Il ritorno al Latino, ovvero la fine dei volgarizzamenti", in Leonardi L. (ed.), *La Bibbia in Italiano tra Medioevo e Rinascimento* (Firenze: 1998) 395–407.

———, "Per una geografia delle traduzioni bibliche nell'Europa cattolica (sedicesimo e diciasettesimo secolo)", in Quantin J.-L. – Waquet J.-C. (eds.), *Papes, princes et savants dans l'Europe moderne: Mélanges à la mémoire de Bruno Neveu*, Ecole pratique des hautes études. 4e section: Sciences historiques et philologiques 5; Hautes études médiévales et modernes 90 (Geneva: 2007) 51–77.

Frajese V., "La politica dell'Indice dal Tridentino al Clementino (1571–1596)", *Archivio italiano per la storia della pietà* 11 (1998) 269–345.

François W., "La condamnation par les théologiens parisiens du plaidoyer d'Érasme pour la traduction de la Bible dans la langue vulgaire (1527–1532)", *Augustiniana* 55 (2005) 357–405.

———, "Vernacular Bible Reading and Censorship in Early Sixteenth Century: The Position of the Louvain Theologians", in Hollander A.A. den – Lamberigts M. (eds.), *Lay Bibles in Europe. 1450–1800*, Bibliotheca Ephemeridum Theologicarum Lovaniensium 198 (Leuven: 2006) 69–96.

———, "De Leuvense theologen over de bijbel in de volkstaal. De discussie tussen 1546 en 1564", *Tijdschrift voor Theologie* 47 (2007) 340–362.

———, "Het voorwoord bij de 'Leuvense bijbel' van Nicholaus van Winghe (1548). Over Schrift, Traditie en volkstalige Bijbellezing", *Ons Geestelijk Erf* 79 (2005–2008) 7–50.

———, "The Condemnation of Vernacular Bible Reading by the Parisian Theologians (1523–31)", in François W. – Hollander A.A. den (eds.), *Infant Milk or Hardy Nourishment? The Bible for Lay People and Theologians in the Early Modern Period*, Bibliotheca Ephemeridum Theologicarum Lovaniensium 221 (Leuven: 2009) 111–139.

———, "La Iglesia Católica y la lectura de la Biblia en lengua vernácula, antes y después del Concilio de Trento", *Mayéutica* 39 (2013) 245–273.

Furió Ceriol Fadrique, *Bononia*, in *Obra completa, vol. 1. El Concejo y consejeros del Príncipe! Bononia*, ed. H. Méchoulan – J. Peréz Durà (Valencia: 1996) 245–621.

Furius Caeriolanus Valentini Fridericus, *Bononia, sive de Libris sacris in vernaculam linguam convertendis, Libri duo* (Basel, Johannes Oporinus [In colofon: Basel, Michael Martin Stella]: 1556–1557).

Gilmont J.-F., "La concurrence entre deux Bibles flamandes", in Gilmont J.-F., *Le livre et ses secrèts*, Cahiers d'humanisme et renaissance 65; Temps et espaces 2 (Geneva – Louvain-la-Neuve, 2003) 151–162.

Goosens A., *Les inquisitions modernes dans les Pays-Bas méridionaux 1520–1633*, 2 vols. (Brussels: 1997).

Herreweghen P. Van, "De Leuvense bijbelvertaler Nicolaus van Winghe. Zijn leven en zijn werk", *Ons Geestelijk Erf* 23 (1949) 5–38, 150–167, 268–314, 357–395.

Hollander A.A. den, *De Nederlandse bijbelvertalingen. Dutch Translations of the Bible 1522–1545*, Bibliotheca Bibliographica Neerlandica 33 (Nieuwkoop: 1997).

———, *Verboden bijbels. Bijbelcensuur in de Nederlanden in de eerste helft van de zestiende eeuw* (Amsterdam: 2003).

Ingram E.M., "Dressed in Borrowed Robes: The Making and Marketing of the Louvain Bible (1578)", in Swanson R.N. (ed.), *The Church and the Book. Papers Read at the 2000*

Summer Meeting and the 2001 Winter Meeting of the Ecclesiastical History Society, Studies in Church History 38 (Woodbridge: 2004) 212–221.

Jedin H., *Geschichte des Konzils von Trient*, 4 vols. in 5 (Freiburg i/Breisgau: 1949–1975).

Larios A., "La reforma de la predicación en Trento (Historia y contenido de un decreto)", *Communio* 6 (1973) 22–83.

Lentner L., *Volkssprache und Sakralsprache. Geschichte einer Lebensfrage bis zum Ende des Konzils von Trient*, Wiener Beiträge zur Theologie 5 (Vienna: 1964).

Liber Literarum Facultatis sacrae theologiae in Universitate Lovaniensi (*Book of Letters of the Louvain Faculty of Theology*), Leuven, State Archives in Belgium, Collection Old University of Louvain, 443.

Mandament der Keyserlijcker Maiesteit wytgegeven int Iaer xlvi. Met Dintitulatie ende declaratie vanden gereproobeerde boecken gheschiet bijden Doctoren inde faculteit van Theologie in Duniversiteit van Loeven: Duer dordonnantie ende bevel der selver K.M. (Leuven, Servaes van Sassen: 1546).

McGinness F.J., "An Erasmian Legacy: Ecclesiastes and the Reform of Preaching at Trent", in Delph R.K. – Fontaine M.M. – Martin J.J. (eds.), *Heresy, Culture, and Religion in Early Modern Italy: Contexts and Contestations*, Sixteenth century essays and studies 76 (Kirksville MO: 2006) 93–112.

McNally R.E., "The Council of Trent and Vernacular Bibles", *Theological Studies* 27 (1966) 204–227.

Méchoulan H. (ed.), *Raison et altérité chez Fadrique Furió Ceriol philosophe politique espagnol du XVIe siècle* (Paris – The Hague: 1973).

Parker G., *The Dutch Revolt* (rev. and repr. London: 1990).

Pettegree A. – Walsby M. – Wilkinson A., *French Vernacular Books: Books Published in the French Language Before 1601*, 2 vols. (Leiden – Boston: 2007).

———, *Netherlandish Books: Books Published in the Low Countries and Dutch Books Published Abroad Before 1601* (Leiden – Boston: 2011).

Pollmann J., *Catholic Identity and the Revolt of the Netherlands 1520–1635* (Oxford: 2011).

Prosperi A., "Bibbia", in Prosperi A. (ed.), *Dizionario storico dell'Inquisizione*, 4 vols. (Pisa: 2010) I 185–187.

Rainer J.E., "Entstehungsgeschichte des Trienter Predigtreformdekretes", *Zeitschrift für katholische Theologie* 39 (1915) 255–317 and 465–523.

Recueil des ordonnances des Pays-Bas. Deuxième série: 1506–1700. Règne de Charles-Quint, ed. Ch. Laurent – J.-P.-A. Lameere – H. Simont, 6 vols. (Brussels: 1893–1922).

———. *Deuxième série: 1506–1700. Règne de Philippe II.*, ed. Ch. Terlinden – J. Bolsée, 2 vols. (Brussels: 1957–1978).

Rouzet A., *Dictionnaire des imprimeurs, libraries et éditeurs des XVe et XVIe siècles dans les limites géographiques de la Belgique actuelle*, Collection du Centre national de l'archéologie et de l'histoire du livre 3 (Nieuwkoop: 1975).

Tellechea J.I., "Españoles en Lovaina en 1551–8: primeras noticias sobre el bayanismo", *Revista Española de Teología* 23 (1963) 21–45.

Valkema Blouw P. – Schuytvlot A.C., *Typographia Batava 1541–1600. A Repertorium of Books Printed in the Northern Netherlands between 1541 and 1600*, 2 vols. (Nieuwkoop: 1998).

Voet L., *The Golden Compasses: A History and Evaluation of the Printing and Publishing Activities of the Officina Plantiniana at Antwerp in two volumes, vol. 1. Christophe Plantin and the Moretuses: Their Lives and their World* (Amsterdam: 1969).

———, *The Plantin Press (1555–1589): A Bibliography of the Works Printed and Published by Christopher Plantin at Antwerp and Leiden*, 6 vols. (Amsterdam: 1980–1983).

CHAPTER 11

Reading the Crucifixion in Tudor England

Lucy Wooding

> Beholde me, I pray the,
> with all thyne hole reson,
> And be not hard-hertid,
> for this encheson,
> That I, for thi soule sake,
> was slayne in good seson.[1]

The idea that the Reformation replaced images with words is a seductive one, which 'seems so intuitively right' that it is often taken for granted.[2] Such a view argues that whatever the theological transformations at work in the six-teenth century, a more fundamental shift came in the ways people encoun-tered their religion. It suggests that a crudely symbolic language which spoke through pictures, statues and stained-glass windows was replaced with a more sophisticated conceptual language found in the printed word, or used to preach sermons. It implies that where late medieval believers had unthink-ingly worshipped, their early modern equivalents learned instead to read, and understand.

This idea is pervasive, and at first glance persuasive, but it is also deeply mis-leading. It both misunderstands the complex forms of communication within the pre-Reformation Church, and caricatures the workings of post-Reformation churches. Two fundamental misconceptions still need to be challenged, namely the assumptions concerning 'image-worship' in the pre-Reformation Church and those regarding the 'religion of the word' which succeeded it. First, we need to appreciate in more detail how pre-Reformation worship saw image, text, sermon and liturgy intertwined. Images were not worshipped in isolation, rather they were used as a conduit through which a range of religious meaning might be accessed. Second, a more careful appreciation of post-Reformation

---

1 Duncan T.G. (ed.), *Late Medieval English Lyrics and Carols 1400–1530* (Harmondsworth: 2000) 81–82.

2 Hunt A., *The Art of Hearing. English Preachers and Their Audiences, 1590–1640* (Cambridge: 2010) 21.

religious media suggests that much of the imaginative language of the late medieval period was not vanquished so much as recalibrated to fit the needs of a reformed religious understanding. The late medieval Church knew better than we sometimes realize how to read and understand, but it tended, for good reasons, to read images just as it read text. Once Reformation was underway the need for imagery remained, particularly among the illiterate, and aspects of the relationship between text and image endured, even though many material forms of imagery were destroyed or covered over. This was not a simple transition from visual media to word-based understanding. Religious meaning was conveyed in many different ways, in the context of an ongoing debate about how to 'read' religious messages accurately, a debate which was already well established in the pre-Reformation Church. The disputes of the Reformation added new elements to the discussion, but they did not invent it, nor did they resolve it.

The Medieval Crucifix

This essay will examine the responses to this question in Tudor England, using the image of the crucifixion as an example. The crucifixion stood at the heart of pre-Reformation faith in every sense. In material terms, the rood screen at the focal point of every parish church carried a depiction, sculpted or painted, of Christ on the cross. In liturgical terms, the central moment of the late medieval Mass was the re-enactment of Christ's sacrifice, and the elevation of the wafer and wine which evoked the lifting up of Christ's body on the cross.[3] At such a point in the Mass, the priest stood with his back to the congregation, frequently with a cross visible on the back of his chasuble. In theological terms, the central fact of the Christian faith was the redemption brought about by Christ's death, and in terms of the Church calendar, which in turn shaped the early modern understanding of time, Easter was the highest point of the ritual year. Weighted with all this meaning, the symbol of the crucifix came to have a profound significance, central to both private and public devotion. Images of the crucifixion were everywhere. Inside the church the central image on the rood screen was echoed elsewhere on screens, roof bosses, carved in chantry chapels or on pew-ends. Wall-paintings of the Passion cycle were probably intended to be viewed in conjunction with both liturgy and

---

3   Duffy E., *The Stripping of the Altars* (New Haven – London: 1992) 119–120.

FIGURE 11.1   *Fifteenth-century wall painting of the Passion, from the church of St Peter-ad-Vincula, South Newington, Oxfordshire, England. Image © Author.*

sermons [Fig. 11.1].[4] Outside the church there were palm Sunday crosses in the churchyard and wayside crosses marking sacred features of the landscape, whilst pilgrims wore badges of the crucifix.[5] Books contained many images of the crucifixion, from the missals which largely resided within the church building to the Books of Hours which travelled between church and home and the alabasters, woodcuts and treatises which belonged largely in a domestic setting [Figs. 11.2–3].[6] Crucifixes hanging from rosary beads also moved between public and private spheres.

4   Ross E.M., *The Grief of God. Images of the Suffering Jesus in Late Medieval England* (Oxford: 1997) 55; Gill M., 'Preaching and Image: Sermons and Wall Paintings in Later Medieval England', in Muessig C. (ed.), *Preacher, Sermon and Audience in the Middle Ages* (Leiden: 2002) 155; Gill M., "Reading Images: Church Murals and Collaboration between Media in Medieval England", in Bigliazzi S. – Wood S. (eds.), *Collaboration in the Arts from the Middle Ages to the Present* (Farnham: 2006) 17.

5   Walsham A., *Reformation of the Landscape. Religion, Identity and Memory in Early Modern Britain and Ireland* (Oxford: 2011) 60–61.

6   Driver M.W., *The Image in Print. Book Illustration in Late Medieval England and Its Sources* (2004) 9.

FIGURE 11.2   *Fifteenth-century alabaster of the crucifixion, made in England. London, Victoria and Albert Museum. Image © Victoria and Albert Museum.*

FIGURE 11.3   *Depiction of the crucifixion observed by the devout believer from the fifteenth-
century Abingdon Missal. Oxford, Bodleian Library, MS Digby 227, f. 113v.
Image © Bodleian Library.*

Images of the crucifix were routinely venerated but they were also read like a text in order to extract meaning. St Gregory's famous defence of images was central to the late medieval understanding of this: 'What Scripture is to the educated, images are to the ignorant, who see through them what they must accept... they read in them what they cannot read in books'.[7] In other words, the commonplace description of images as 'books for the laity' meant that such images were read to increase understanding as well as devotion. Images that were carved, painted, embroidered or pieced together out of coloured glass offered the viewer not just a beautiful object to inspire religious fervour, but the first step in a string of associations which elaborated the meaning behind the symbol. Medieval theories about memory and seeing make this clear, based on Augustine's notion of memory as a storehouse of images, and his tripartite division of corporal, spiritual and intellectual seeing, with each a step to a higher level of comprehension.[8] Images did far more than the modern imagination might grasp, cumbered as it is with assumptions about representational realism: they linked together seeing with understanding, and made of both a personal and emotional religious experience, akin to what Panofsky understood as 'iconology'.[9] It is appropriate that the words 'image' and 'imagery' can still to this day refer to something described in a text as much as carved in wood or stone, or reproduced in paint, embroidery or coloured glass.[10]

Only in recent years have historians and art historians begun to appreciate fully the importance of visual and material culture in the study of religion.[11] The understanding of how religion can be comprehended through imagery is at the forefront of much contemporary research, which is only now comprehending 'the visual construction of the sacred', in which symbols did not only

---

7   Davis-Weyer C. (ed.), *Early Medieval Art 300–1150. Sources and documents* (Toronto: 1986) 48, 'Epistle CV from St Gregory to Serenus, Bishop of Marseilles'.

8   Augustine St, *Confessions*, ed. R.S. Pine-Coffin (West Drayton: 1961) 214–215; O'Daly G., *Augustine's Philosophy of Mind* (Berkeley – Los Angeles: 1987) 106–130; Diebold W.J., *Word and Image. An Introduction to Early Medieval Art* (Michigan: 2000) 106. See also Carruthers M., *The Book of Memory. A Study of Memory in Medieval Culture* (Cambridge: 2008) 62–63, 65, 271, 275–276.

9   Panofsky E., "Iconography and Iconology. An Introduction to the Study of Renaissance Art", in Panofsky E., *Meaning in the Visual Arts* (Chicago: 1955) 51–81; as applied to the crucified Christ, 57–58.

10   Williams R., *Keywords. A Vocabulary of Culture and Society* (Oxford: 1976) 158.

11   Burke P., *Eyewitnessing. The Uses of Images as Historical Evidence* (2001) 48; see also Jordanova L., *The Look of the Past. Visual and Material Evidence in Historical Practice* (Cambridge: 2012); Sears E. – Thomas T.K. (eds.), *Reading Medieval Images. The Art Historian and the Object* (Michigan: 2002).

convey meaning, but constructed a relationship between the visual field and
the observer which was at once intellectual, transformative and emotional.[12]
Recent work on the history of the senses, and the history of the emotions, has
reinforced the multivalent properties of religious imagery, which stimulated
all the senses (with sight usually the most important) and was transformed
'into similitudes susceptible to processing by the five internal senses—
memory, imagination, fantasy, estimation and the common sense'.[13] It has also
been emphasized how much the use of late medieval and early modern texts
needs to be placed within an analogous series of responses, at a time when
books enjoined performative reading not just in a communal setting, but also
for the private reader.[14] It is clear that in 'reading' either image or text, just as in
watching a performance, imagining and understanding could become one and
the same thing.[15] Beholding an image could involve intense imaginative and
emotional processes aiding comprehension, and the act of seeing was widely
believed to be something which could shape the soul.[16]

Reading an image, however, was a complex process, and one which gave
rise to much debate at the time. Historians of the later medieval period have
often emphasized how images and books should be seen as 'parallel modes
of representation'.[17] More recently, however, we have also been reminded of

---

12   Morgan D., *The Embodied Eye. Religious Visual Culture and the Social Life of Feeling*
      (Berkeley – Los Angeles: 2012) xvii. See also Bynum C.W., *Christian Materiality. An Essay
      on Religion in Late Medieval Europe* (New York: 2011).

13   Melion W.S., 'Introduction: Meditative Images and the Psychology of Soul', in Falkenburg
      R.L. – Melion W.S. – Richardson T.M. (eds.), *Image and Imagination of the Religious Self
      in Late Medieval and Early Modern Europe*, Proteus: Studies in Early Modern Identity
      Formation 1 (Turnhout: 2007) 2. See also Milner M., *The Senses and the English Reformation*
      (Farnham: 2011), 25–26; Karant-Nunn S.C., *The Reformation of Feeling. Shaping the
      Religious Emotions in Early Modern Germany* (Oxford: 2010) 19–20.

14   Brantley J., *Reading in the Wilderness. Private Devotion and Public Performance in Late
      Medieval England* (Chicago: 2008) 2–3.

15   Ramakers B., "Eloquent Presence: Verbal and Visual Discourse in the Ghent Plays of 1539",
      in Brusati C. – Enenkel K.A.E. – Melion W.S., *The Authority of the Word: Reflecting on Image
      and Text in Northern Europe, 1400–1700*, Intersections: Interdisciplinary Studies in Early
      Modern Culture 20 (2011) (Leiden – Boston: 2012) 217–261, here 223.

16   Morgan D., *The Sacred Gaze: Religious Visual Theory in Theory and Practice* (Berkeley:
      2005) 96–110; Stronks E., *Negotiating Differences. Word, Image and Religion in the Dutch
      Republic* (Leiden: 2011) 34–41.

17   Scribner R.W., "Popular Piety and Modes of Visual Perception in Late Medieval and
      Reformation Germany", *Journal of Religious History* 15 (1989) 448–469; Laugerud H.,
      "Visuality and Devotion in the Middle Ages", in Laugerud H. – Skinnebach L.K. (eds.),
      Instruments of Devotion. The Practices and Objects of Religious Piety from the Late Middle

the tension between the two in the minds of fifteenth-century commentators.[18] The discussion about the correct use of images was not one begun by Protestants; it had begun long before, and had a particular intensity in England in the wake of the challenges posed by Wycliffe and the Lollards. *Dives and Pauper*, the treatise on the commandments written around 1410, identified three purposes for images. The first was simply to be put in mind of the thing represented, such as Christ's incarnation and Passion, or the lives of saints. After that,

> they be ordained to stir man's affection and his heart to devotion, for often man is more stirred by sight than by hearing or reading. Also they be ordained to be a token and a book to the lewd people, that they may read in imagery and painting that [which] clerks read in books (...).[19]

This conveyed how the 'reading' of images was intended to be a many-layered cognitive process embracing recognition, understanding and devotion all at once. In this popular tract the notion of the image as book was emphatically reinforced, alongside the important point that images, like books, could be read in different ways by different people. Yet the work also acknowledged some of the ambivalence and anxiety surrounding the use of images. 'How should I read in the book of painting and of imagery?', Dives asked, and the answer Pauper gave was a lengthy one, which explained how to both interpret, and then respond to the image. Interpretation required reading the image, here using a well-known passage attributed to St Bernard:

Ages to the 20th Century (Aarhus: 2007) 173–188; Bal M. – Bryson N., "Semiotics and Art History", *The Art Bulletin* 73 (1991) 174–208; Dikovitskaya M., *Visual Culture. The Study of the Visual Culture after the Cultural Turn* (Cambridge, MA: 2005) 17, 55–56; Mitchell W.J.B., *Iconology. Text, Image, Ideology* (Chicago: 1987) 53–74; Mitchel W.J.B., *What Do Pictures Want?* (Chicago: 2005) xvii, 7–8; Bynum, *Christian Materiality* 37–123.

18 Gayk S., *Image, Text and Religious Reform in Fifteenth century England* (Cambridge: 2010) 1, 4; Dimmick J. – Simpson J. – Zeeman N., *Images, Idolatry and Iconoclasm in Late Medieval England. Textuality and the Visual Image* (Oxford: 2002); Hamburger J.F., "Seeing and Believing: The Suspicion of Sight and the Authentication of Vision in Late Medieval Art", in Nova A. – Krüger K. (eds.), *Imagination und Wirklichkeit. Zum Verhältnis von mentalen und realen Bilder in der Kunst der frühen Neuzeit* (Mainz: 2000) 47–70.

19 'þey been ordeynyd to steryn mannys affeccioun and his herte to devocioun, for often man is more steryd be syghte þan be heryng or redynge. Also þey been ordeynyd to been a tokene and a book to þe lewyd peple, þat þey moun redyn in ymagerye and peynture þat clerkys redyn in boke (...)'. *Dives and Pauper*, vol. 1, part 1, ed. P.H. Barnum, *Early English Text Society* (Oxford: 1976) 82.

See how his side was opened and his heart cloven in two in token that his heart is always open to thee, ready to love thee (...). Take heed also how his feet were nailed very hard to the tree in token that he will not flee away from thee but abide with thee (...).[20]

The correct reading of the image then led on to the correct response, which was to worship God:

In this manner, I pray thee, read this book (...) and worship him above all things, not the image, not the stock, stone nor tree but he that died on the tree for thy sin and for thy sake (...).[21]

Dives and Pauper also addressed the question of the wrongful use of images with a passage where the identity of image and book again overlapped:

Oft thou seest that the priest in church hath his book afore hym on the desk. He kneels, he stares, he looks on his book, he holds up his hands and for devotion... he weeps and makes devout prayers. To whom, do you think, the priest doth all this worship?[22]

And Dives answered simply, 'to God and not to the book'.[23] The reading of an image was therefore a question which had been carefully considered, defended and explained in pre-Reformation debates, and when a priest or a treatise exhorted an audience to read either word or image devoutly it was not an unthinking admonition.

A vigorous and detailed debate about the place of images in religious worship and instruction produced a broad consensus which tightened the

---

20   'See how his syde was openyd and his herte clovyn on too in tokene þat his herte is alwey opyn to the, redy to lovyn the (...). Take heid also how hese feet weryn naylyd wol harde to þe tree in tokene þat he wyl nought flein awey from the but abydyn wyt the (...)'. *Dives and Pauper* 85.

21   'On þis maner, I preye the, rede þin book (...) and wurshepe hym abovyn alle thyngge, nought þe ymage, nought þe stok, stoon ne tree. but hym þat deyid on þe tree for þin synne and for þin sake (...)'. *Dives and Pauper* 85.

22   'Oft þu seeist þat þe preist in chirche hatз his book aforn hym on þe deske. He knelyзt, he staryзt, he lokyзt on his book, he heldyзt up hese hondys and for devocioun in caas he wepyзt and makyзt devowte preyerys. To qhom, wenyst þu, þe prest doth all þis wurshepe?'. *Dives et Pauper* 86.

23   *Dives and Pauper* 86.

fifteenth-century relationship between the visual image and the textual image.[24] Much reformist writing, from that of the Lollards to the more conventional work of authors like John Lydgate and Thomas Hoccleve, tried to clarify the correct use of images, and heighten religious devotion through the interaction of the painted image and the printed word. Lydgate's poems on the crucifixion used the common device whereby Christ himself addressed the beholder:

> The to restore, I hange upon this Croos,
> Crowned with thorn, woundid with a launce,
> Handis and ffeet, tencres of my grevaunce,
> With sharpe naylles my blood maad renne doun,
> Whan-ever thou felyst trouble or perturbaunce,
> Looke on my woundis, thynk on my passioun.[25]

This understanding was shared across the religious spectrum, and even some Lollards were capable of approving the use of images for the purpose of instruction, appropriating the metaphor of the *libri laicorum*, even whilst warning against the 'seduction of the sensory'.[26] In a Lollard sermon deploring the use of images and inveighing against the lavish use of gold, silver and jewels, it was acknowledged that 'sythen Crist was makid man, it is suffrid for lewid men to have a pore crusifix, by the cause to have mynde on the harde passioun and bitter death that Crist suffrid'.[27] Hoccleve, who himself wore spectacles, used them as a metaphor for writing which could 'bring images into clearer focus', so that word and image worked together to enhance spiritual perception.[28]

Mirk's *Festial* explained how images were intended to call forth a response which was at once intellectual, imaginative and devout:

> for this cause roodes and ymages ben set on hye in chyrches / for as soone as a man commeth in to the chyrche / he sholde se it and have it in his mynde and thynke on Chrystes passyon / Wherfore crosses and other ymages ben full necessary and nedefull / what so ever these lollers saye.

---

24 Gayk, *Image, Text and Religious Reform* 9.

25 *The Minor Poems of John Lydgate*, vol. 1, *Early English Text Society*, extra series cvii (Oxford: 1911) 216.

26 Gayk, *Image, Text and Religious Reform* 19–20.

27 Owst G.R., *Literature and Pulpit in Medieval England* (Oxford: 1961) 144.

28 Gayk, *Image, Text and Religious Reform* 45–47.

The object of popular veneration was also made clear with the use of a secular analogy:

> For ryght as the people do worshyp to the kynges seale / not for love of the seale / but for reverence of the kynge that it commeth fro. So roodes and ymages be set for the kynges seale of heven. And other sayntes in the same wyse / for ymages ben lewde peoples bookes.

The value of such imagery was clear to Mirk:.

> there be many thousaundes of people that can not ymagyn in theyr hertes how Chryst was done on the crosse / but as they se by ymages in chyrches and in other places there as they be.[29]

The experiences of Margery Kempe illustrate the way in which the sight of a religious image or ritual could instantly transport the beholder to the corresponding episode in the life of Christ. During meditations on the Passion in the Holy Land, she 'wept and sobbed as plenteously as though she had seen our Lord with her bodily eyes suffering his Passion at that time'. The process of 'reading' this ritual is described: 'Before her in her soul she saw him in truth by contemplation'.[30] Attending church on Good Friday, she described how her 'mind was drawn wholly into the Passion of our Lord Christ Jesus, whom she beheld with her spiritual eye in the sight of her soul as truly as if she had seen his precious body beaten, scourged and crucified with her bodily eye (…)'.[31] This illustrates how images were intended to work, connecting the material reality with the religious truth. Increasingly, however, the fifteenth century saw attempts to strengthen this connection with the use of text.[32] Margery Kempe combined her extremes of affective devotion with listening over the course of seven or eight years to many books which her priest read aloud to her: 'such

---

29   Mirk John, *The Festyvall* (London, Wynken de Worde: 1532); Sermon for Corpus Christi
      f. Llv.

30   *The Book of Margery Kempe*, ed. B.A. Windeatt (Woodbridge: 2004) 74.

31   *The Book of Margery Kempe* 148.

32   Gillespie V. "Medieval Hypertext: Image and Text from York Minster", in Robinson P.R. –
      Zim R. (eds.), *Of the Making of Books. Medieval Manuscripts, their Scribes and Readers*
      (Aldershot: 1997) 206–229; Hoogvliet, M. 'L'image légendée: théories modernes et
      cartes médiévales', in Heck C. (ed.), *Qu'est-ce que nommer. L'image légendée entre monde
      monastique et pensée scolastique* (Turnhout: 2010) 219–222; Giles K., "Seeing and Believing:
      Visuality and Space in Pre-Modern England", *World Archaeology* 39 (2007) 107.

as the Bible with doctors' commentaries on it, St Bride's book, Hilton's book, Bonaventura's *Stimulis Amoris*, *Incendium Amoris*, and others similar'.[33]

One particularly powerful evocation of the relationship between image and book was given by John Fisher's Good Friday sermon, printed in 1526, which developed an extended metaphor of the crucifix as the book of Scripture itself.[34] The sermon described how the two boards of the book equated to the two wooden beams of the cross; the pages were Christ's limbs; the lines the lines of scourging; the letters, great and small, in blue and red ink, were Christ's many wounds. Just as in the modern mind, the connection between reading and understanding is assumed, so Fisher took for granted that the act of seeing involved the comprehension of the religious message:

> Who then attentively doth beholde this Crucifix, and verely beleveth that on the Crosse was payd the raunsom of all sinners, how may he not fully trust that if he aske mercy for his sinnes, they shall be forgiven him.[35]

The image, the written and the spoken word, all worked together to transmit meaning, and Fisher used the same passage from St Bernard that had appeared in *Dives and Pauper*, describing Christ with

> his head bowing downe to offer a kisse, hys armes spreade to embrace us, hys handes bored thorow to make lyberall giftes, his side opened to shewe unto us the love of his harte, his feete fastened with nayles, that hee shall not starte away but abyde with us.[36]

Fisher's sermon also emphasized another important point about images, as being books which were available to all, much more widely available than printed books:

> A man may easily say and thinke with him selfe, beholding in his hart the Image of the Crucifixe, who arte thou, and who am I. Thus everie person

---

33 *Book of Margery Kempe* 182.

34 Rex R., *The Theology of John Fisher* (Cambridge: 1991) 46–48. This sermon was published as *A Sermon verie fruitfull, godly, and learned* (1526).

35 *The English Works of John Fisher*, ed. J.E.B. Mayor, *Early English Text Society*, extr. ser. 27 (Oxford: 1876) 412.

36 *The English Works of John Fisher* 411.

both ryche and poore, may thinke, not onely in the church here, but in
every other place.[37]

This confirmed the idea that images did not just have material form, but could
also be carried in the imagination. Since images were already seen as books,
the arrival of print was not the radical disjunction that some historians have
assumed; rather it served to supply an additional channel of explanation to the
rich array of religious media already in existence.[38]

Reformation Debates

The arrival of Reformation brought a new urgency to the debate about the
place of sacred images and objects, but this debate contained many of the
same concerns as the medieval debate. In particular, it was anxious to define
true beholding, and discover what kind of 'reading' could lead the believer to
God's truth. Within Protestantism as well as Catholicism there was a spectrum
of opinion as to what might truly convey a religious message. Some more radical Protestants deplored all forms of imagery, including that of the mind's eye,
but most did not.[39] Even Calvin, although he deplored the dead images created
by man, saw living images in the Word of God, which could be perceived with
the eyes of faith.[40]

At parish level, Protestants faced a different challenge, as a largely illiterate population still tended to conceptualize using images. Here the intercon-
nection between image and understanding was not easily severed, even if the
material images themselves were largely destroyed. Since the visual media of
the pre-Reformation Church embraced so much oral and literate culture in its
intrinsic meaning, then the shift to a literate culture which was also oral, and
which deployed so much that was imaginative, was not necessarily as radical a cultural transformation as reformers might have envisaged. Protestant

---

37   *The English Works of John Fisher* 391.

38   King J.N. (ed.), *Tudor Books and Readers. Materiality and the Construction of Meaning*
      (Cambridge: 2010); Crick J. – Walsham A. (eds.), *The Uses of Script and Print, 1300–1700*
      (Cambridge: 2004).

39   Watt T., *Cheap Print and Popular Piety, 1550–1640* (Cambridge: 1991) 211, 325–328;
      Hamling T. – Williams R.L. (eds.), *Art Re-formed? Re-assessing the Impact of the
      Reformation on the Visual Arts* (Newcastle: 2007); Hamling, T., *Decorating the Godly
      Household. Religious Art in Protestant Britain, c. 1560–c. 1660* (New Haven – London: 2010).

40   Zachman R.C., *Image and Word in the Theology of John Calvin* (Notre Dame: 2007) 437–
      440; Dyrness W.A., *Reformed Theology and Visual Culture* (Cambridge: 2004) 68–72.

iconoclasts emphasized the need for a clear break with the past, but as the new faith was gradually disseminated, it was compelled to adapt to popular needs and existing modes of religious communication. In some contexts it seemed to be less a rejection of the past than a more modest rearrangement of religious modes of expression.

Once the printing press was established in England, the image of the crucifix was given new expression, being both depicted and described in printed image and text. Early printed books enhanced, extended and repeated existing ideas about the crucifixion, as well as giving manuscript works a new lease of life in printed form. The debates about the correct use of images were rehearsed again: *Dives and Pauper*, for example, was published by Pynson in 1493, Wynkyn de Worde in 1496 and Berthelet in 1536. A disjunction came, not from the arrival of print, but from the arrival of political Reformation and unofficial Protestantism; under their combined influence, the debate about images intensified during the second half of Henry VIII's reign. Henry's self-representation of himself as an Old Testament king incorporated an emphasis upon ridding his realm of idolatry, often in a highly theatrical manner, and the early English Protestant debates often had an iconoclastic edge.[41] The burning of idols was not the same as the wholesale destruction of images, however. As the Ten Articles of 1536 insisted,

> touching images, truth it is that the same have been used in the Old Testament, and also for the great abuses of them sometimes destroyed and put down; and in the New Testament they have been also allowed, as good authors do declare.[42]

This ambivalence arguably had just as influential a role in shaping English attitudes as the more straightforward iconoclasm of the Edwardian regime of 1547 to 1553, which ordered the authorities to inquire whether the clergy had

> removed, taken away and utterly extincted and destroyed in their churches, chapels and houses, all images, all shrines, covering of shrines, all tables, candlesticks, trendals or rolls of wax, pictures, paintings, and all other monuments of feigned miracles, pilgrimages, idolatry, and

---

41   Rex R., *Henry VIII and the English Reformation* (Basingstoke: 1993) 17, 29, 103, 173–175; Ryrie A., *The Gospel and Henry VIII* (Cambridge: 2003) 227, 231–232.

42   *Formularies of Faith put forward by authority during the reign of Henry VIII*, ed. C. Lloyd (Oxford: 1856) 13.

superstition, so that there remain no memory of the same in walls, glass windows, or elsewhere.[43]

The emphasis on 'no memory of the same' is instructive, hinting at the link between the material and the mental image. Reformers were also conscious of the ways in which conservatives might insist on the proper use of images in order to avoid idolatry. George Joye mocked Gardiner's moderate views about the use of images, suggesting that Shadrach, Meshach and Abednego could have escaped being thrown into the fiery furnace for refusing to bow down to an idol; 'they myght have answerde the kynge with Winchesters worship / saying: We are content to knele downe to it with a certayne reverent behaviour / so that we geve it not any inwarde godly worship'.[44] Protestant rhetoric had continually to emphasize Catholic worship of images, precisely because in reality the Catholic attitude to images was far more cautious and defensible than their opponents would like.

Protestants who deplored or expressed anxiety about the use of images were of course alarmed at the risk of idolatry, but they had other concerns too. Some were merely doubtful about the ability of a material image to connect with an interior meaning, a connection which the pre-Reformation Church had viewed with more optimism. Hugh Latimer, in a Good Friday sermon of 1549, described Christ's meditation on death with some unflattering reflections on the skill of painters:

> There was offered unto him now the image of death; the image, the sense, the feeling of hell (. . .). As man's power is not able to bear it, so no man's tongue is able to express it. Painters paint death like a man without skin, and a body having nothing but bones. And hell they paint with horrible flames of burning fire: they bungle somewhat at it, they come nothing near it (. . .). No painter can paint hell, unless he could paint the torment and condemnation both of body and soul (. . .).[45]

Latimer's concern here was not that an image might provoke sin, merely that it could only prove inadequate, that 'reading' such an image could bring only partial understanding. Nicholas Ridley, in his treatise on images addressed to

43   Frere W.H. – Kennedy W.M. (eds.), *Visitation Articles and Injunctions of the Period of the Reformation*, vol. II (London: 1910) 177–178.

44   Joye George, *The exposicion of Daniel the prophete* (Antwerp, Catharine van Ruremund: 1545) f. 36v.

45   *Sermons by Hugh Latimer*, ed. G.E. Corrie, vol. 1, Parker Society (Cambridge: 1844) 219–220.

Edward VI, was emphatic that he wanted images kept out of the churches, but even so could not avoid some ambivalence in his account, concluding that the 'profit of images is uncertain; the peril, by experience of all ages and states of the Church, as afore, is most certain'.[46] Other reformers were more outspoken, and more antagonistic. John Hooper was concerned not just with material images, but with 'inward / and spirituall Idolatrie / of the mynd', and famously insisted that 'a man may lern / more of a live ape / then of a ded ymage if boothe shuld be browghte in to the scole / to teache'.[47] In the early seventeenth century, an English separatist would argue against the use of books in church, on the grounds that a book was in itself a kind of pictorial image. An opponent quite rightly pointed out that his conflation of books with images was precisely the justification used by Catholics to defend the use of images as books for laymen.[48] The boundary between visual image and printed text remained porous.

Protestant Images of the Crucifixion

Images of the crucifixion may have been taken down within the parish church, but Elizabethan parishioners were still urged by their preacher to behold Christ on the cross in their imagination. This extract comes from one of the Elizabethan homilies:

> Call to mind, O sinfull creature, and set before thine eyes Christ crucified. Thinke thou seest his Body stretched out in length upon the Crosse, his head crowned with sharpe thornes, and his handes and his feete pearced with nayles, his heart opened with a long speare, his flesh rent and torne with whippes, his browes sweating water and blood.[49]

This made the assumption, integral to pre-Reformation devotion, that the act of seeing, be it with the bodily eye or the spiritual eye, automatically involved comprehension of the religious truth embodied by the crucifixion. The printed word had not replaced imagery here so much as appropriated it. Passion narratives were to remain contentious for English Protestants, not least because the

---

46 *The Works of Nicholas Ridley*, ed. H. Christmas, Parker Society (Cambridge: 1841) 88.

47 Hooper John, *A declaration of the ten holy comaundementes* (Zürich, Augustin Fries: 1549) f. LXXVIII.

48 Hunt, *Art of Hearing* 28–30.

49 *The seconde tome of homelyes* (London, Richard Jugge and John Cawood: 1563) f. 199v–200r.

crucifixion scene so obviously seemed to demand a visual response, but they remained an essential focus of belief and devotion. In sermons and treatises on the Passion, Protestants strove to convey the meaning of this biblical scene with all the emotional force and spiritual intensity of pre-Reformation practice yet without what they saw as its risk of idolatry.[50]

The Elizabethan Homilies were designed to answer the needs of uneducated parishioners, and compensate for the lack of Protestant preachers. Protestant authors aiming at a more educated audience were more cautious about assuming a connection between sight and understanding, continuing the debate about the correct way to 'read' an image. For John Foxe, in *A sermon of Christ crucified* from 1577, the heart of papist error was the inability to connect sight with true meaning. Roman Catholics, in other words, did not know how to 'read' an image correctly:

> They make muche adoe about the Crosse of Christ (…) and yet they knowe not his Crosse, neither doe they see much more in the Passion of Christ, then (…) the sensible manne maie doe. They see him poore sweatyng, bleedyng, falsely accused, wrongfully oppressed, wounded, scourged, derided, crowned wyth Thorne, nailed, crucified, hangyng uppon the crosse naked, pearsed, deade, and buried (…) they magnifie and worshippe all the outwarde implementes that went to his blessed passion, the nailes, the crosse and timber, the speare the crowne and thornes (…). But this is not enough. To knowe Christ Jesus crucified, and to knowe him rightly, it is not sufficient to staie in these outward thinges: we muste goe further then the sensible man: we muste looke inwardly with a spirituall eye into spirituall thinges.[51]

Foxe was worried about a disjunction between bodily and spiritual sight; late medieval commentators had also been concerned with this, although they had taken steps to overcome the risk which had largely allayed that concern. Protestants were not so much dismissing imagery as displaying heightened anxiety about it, but they were still unable to function entirely without it.

Thomas Bilson, in a sermon of 1599, had similar anxieties to those of Foxe:

> if we beholde Christe crucified with carnall eies, as did the Iewes, wee shall see nothing in him but earthlie weakenesse, and deadlie woundes

---

50   Martin J., "English Reformed Responses to the Passion" in Ryrie A. – Martin J., *Private and Domestic Devotion in Early Modern Britain* (Aldershot: 2012) 115–134.

51   Foxe John, *A sermon of Christ crucified* (London, John Daye: 1577) sig. Aiiijr.

(...) but if we bende the eies of our faith to the truth of his person (...) we shall finde the power and wisedome, iustice and mercie of God so tempered in the crosse of Christ for our good; that by his paines we are eased, by his stripes we are healed.

Bilson also deplored the papist concentration on 'the matter and forme of the crosse' rather than 'the merite and fruit of Christ crucified'. Yet Bilson trusted his Protestant audience to be capable of the correct kind of seeing, as in language worthy of a pre-Reformation sermon, he described Christ's suffering:

from top to toe no part free from paine and griefe; but hoong on the wood, having his flesh torne with whippes, his cheekes swolne with buffets, his face defiled with spittle, his head stuckt full with thornes, his eies dejected for shame, his eares burning with taunts, his mouth sowred with vinegar, his hands and feete wounded with Iron spikes, his bones unjointed, his sinewes pricked and strained, his whole body hanging by the soreness of his hands and feet, and lastlie (...) his heart pierced with a Speare, whence issued bloud and water.[52]

This kind of imagery could still be used if the preacher could be sure that the imaginative response from his audience would be the correct one.

The way in which Protestants imagined the crucifixion preserved many elements from the pre-Reformation Church. The physicality of Passion meditations remained a feature of Good Friday sermons and Passion Week meditations. It is perhaps no surprise to find a Laudian such as Anthony Stafford writing of how Christ's 'guiltlesse hands (...) they binde so fast, that the Cord eates into his tender flesh. On that Head wherein Universall Wisedome was contained, they set a Crowne of Thornes so fast, that his purest Blood runnes in streames downe his sweetest Face'.[53] Yet the immediacy of the crucifixion experience, and the idea that the observer should participate in the scene, remained in more mainstream Protestant writing too. John Bradford's meditation on the Passion began with a prayer: 'grant me at this present to rehearse some of thy passions and sufferings'.[54] An intense preoccupation with the

---

52   Bilson Thomas, *The effect of certaine sermons touching the full redemption of mankind by the death and bloud of Christ Iesus* (London, Peter Short for Walter Burre: 1599) 2, 4, 5.

53   Stafford Anthony, *The day of salvation, or, A homily upon the bloody sacrifice of Christ* (London, N. and I. Okes: 1635) 105–106. See also McCullough P.E., 'Lancelot Andrewes's Transforming Passions", *Huntingdon Library Quarterly* 71 (2008) 573–589.

54   *The Writings of John Bradford*, ed. A. Townsend, Parker Society (Cambridge: 1848) 197.

spilling of Christ's blood emphasized the visceral nature of the encounter. The single line from the Gospels, how (in Tyndale's translation) Christ prayed in the garden of Gethsemane such that 'hys sweate was lyke droppes of bloud, tricklynge doune to the grounde', was elaborated in depth.[55] Bradford's meditation described the scene in lavish terms: 'here thou wast so discouraged and so comfortless, that even streams of blood came running from thine eyes and ears and other parts of thy body'.[56] The literal text of the Bible was overlooked, to insist that Christ had actually sweated blood. As Bartholomew Chamberlain, a writer noted for his Calvinism, still observed:

> It is an usual thing for a man in anguish to sweate; but to sweate bloud, and to sweate it in such abundance, that even drops like bloud should trickle from his Body upon the Ground, this is not an usuall thing: this was a strange thing: this was proper to Christ: this declared griefe unspeakable, paine intollerable.[57]

There was sometimes an awareness that this kind of meditation preserved the practices of the medieval past. A treatise of 1614 called *Christ his crosse*, by the Wiltshire minister and poet John Andrewes, began its preface by observing 'there is nothing new under the Sunne' and insisted on the usage of the past, although twice in the same paragraph reiterating that this must be 'without any superstition':

> We must use our selves to the olde and accustomed words for our instruction sake, seeing that wee have none other, the *Literall mediation* is the knowledge of the reading, the hearing, the thinking of, and the reciting of the Historie of the *Passion*, as it is preached or written, printed or painted, so it be without any superstition.[58]

Andrewes' description of the crucifixion echoed the affective devotion of the later Middle Ages:

---

55   *The New Testament 1526, Translated by William Tyndale*, ed. W.R. Cooper (London: 2000) 184.

56   *The Writings of John Bradford* 197.

57   Chamberlain Bartholomew, *The Passion of Christ and the benefits thereby* (London, printed for Thomas Pauier: 1612) sig. A3v–4r.

58   Andrewes John, *Christ his crosse* (Oxford, Ioseph Barnes: 1614) 51.

so wofull and dolefull a spectacle, which was forcible enough to have drawne streames of teares out of the driest eie that ever was in the head of man, and to have incited a multitude of heavie and sorrowfull groans, out of the hardest hart that ever God made. Oh! was there ever crueltie like unto this.[59]

Medieval prayers also survived in *A Booke of Christian Prayers* published in 1578, which went through three more editions, the last one in 1608. This volume contained the popular medieval prayers called 'The Fifteen Oes of St Bridget', accompanied by illustrations of the Fifteen Last Days and the Dance of Death, both common themes in pre-Reformation iconography. These prayers were not unthinkingly reproduced, but carefully pruned to suit a Protestant audience.[60] Yet the emphasis upon the beholding of the crucifixion remained: 'A Prayer upon the minding of Christes passion' began 'What man is this whom I behold all bloudy?' Others started with a similar emphasis upon the reader being able to see Christ's suffering: 'My minde beholdeth thy body crucified for my soul', began one; another, 'I see a wonderfull kinde of love'.[61]

Meditation on the sufferings of Christ lent itself particularly well to poetry, which often reinforced the idea of the onlooker beholding Christ in agony, tacitly echoing the language of the *improperia*, or reproaches from the cross, which had once been central to the Good Friday liturgy. A verse collection of 1601 described Christ in the garden of Gethsemane, and exhorted its audience:

All Christian soules, come see this agony!
Come count the drops, which trickles down his face.[62]

Christopher Lever's work of 1607, *A Crucifixe: Or a Meditation upon Repentaunce and The holie Passion*, relied on the connection between sight and understanding, and returned to the idea of the crucifix as a book:

Said I, a representment, and no more;
It is much more, then in my wordes can be.
My soule conceits, a verie Christ before;

59   Andrewes, *Christ his crosse* 54–55.

60   White H.C., *Tudor Books of Private Devotion* (Madison: 1951) 221–229; Duffy E., *Marking the Hours. English People and their Prayers 1240–1570* (New Haven – London: 2006) 171–174.

61   Day Richard, *A Booke of Christian Prayers* (London, John Daye: 1578) f. 76r, 77v, 78v.

62   *The song of Mary the mother of Christ containing the story of his life and passion* (London, E. Allde for William Ferbrand: 1601) sig. C2r–v.

> Spreading his sacred bodie on the *Tree*.
> Me thinkes, his verie torments I doe see.
> This *Crucifix*, is that most sacred booke,
> Wherein each happy Spirit needes must looke.[63]

Ballads developed the same theme, emphasizing the visual encounter with the crucifixion. 'Glad tydings from heaven' had Christ addressing the beholder on the subject of his sufferings. Another ballad called on onlookers to 'fix our eye / and thinke upon his precious death', and underlined how this was again a religious experience which depended on seeing:

> See him in the howre of parting
> hanging on his bloody Crosse;
> See his wounds, conceive his smarting,
> and our gaine, by his lives losse.[64]

The crucifixion was still, therefore, something which required the eye of the beholder. Andrewes wrote, 'thou shalt by looking up with the eies of thy minde, unto the Passion of Christ, be most ioyfully comforted and relieved'.[65] 'O fixe thine Eyes here for ever', echoed Anthony Stafford. Remarkably, in 1611 a translation was published, which went to at least three editions, of the meditations ascribed to St Bernard of Clairvaux; the author wrote in the preface of the effect he intended to produce with this work:

> I have much endevoured, so to expresse the grievous Passion of our gracious Redeemer, as if it were now in present action before our eyes, that I might the better stirre up fervent motions of Pietie in the minde, and kindle the sparkes of true devotion in the heart of the Reader.[66]

The author, 'W.P.', who described himself as 'Master of Arts in Cambridge', was clear that he wanted his readers to experience a profound and emotional encounter with the crucified Christ, to be 'neerely and deepely touched, and

---

63   Lever Christopher, *A Crucifixe. Or a Meditation upon Repentance and The holie Passion* (London, V.S. for Mathew Lownes: 1607) sig. D2v.

64   *Glad tydings from heaven* (London, printed for C. W[right]: c. 1630); *Two pleasant ditties, one of the birth, the other of the passion of Christ* (London [?]: 1628–1629), STC 14577.

65   Andrewes, *Christ his crosse* 14.

66   *Saint Bernard his Meditations: or Sighes, Sobbes and Teares, upon our Saviours Passion* (2nd ed., 1614) sig. A4r–v.

wounded with a feeling consideration of our Saviours death', and he argued that an intense appreciation was more valuable than a 'bare narration' of the fact of Christ's death:

> it cannot chuse; but more deeply wound the soule of every Christian, to heare, or read, the speciall and severall sufferings of Christ in his Passion, then if it were onely sayd thus, *Christ died for us*.[67]

And once again, the reader was admonished to look upon the crucifixion: 'But now (oh my sorrowful soule) turne thine eyes towards thy crucified *Iesus*'.[68]

The Crucifix and the Deathbed

In the pre-Reformation Church gazing upon the crucifix played a particularly vital part in the drama of the deathbed. Julian of Norwich described the moment of approaching death where the priest held the cross before her face, and said 'Daughter, I have brought you the image of your Saviour. Look upon it and be comforted, in reverence to him that died for you and me'.[69] In the *Ars Moriendi*, circulated in both manuscript and print, the use of the crucifix to comfort and strengthen the dying was a key part of the literary and visual tradition.[70] In *The boke of the craft of dying* this was described as follows:

> seynt Bernard seith thus: What man is it that schuld not be ravysshed and draw to hope and to have full confidence in god, and he take heed diligently of the disposicione of Cristis body in the crosse; take heed and see his heed enclyned to salve the, his mouth to kysee the, his armes I-spred to be-clyp the, his hondis I-thrilled to yeve the, his syde opened to love the (…).[71]

---

67   *Saint Bernard his Meditations* sig. A4v–A5r.

68   *Saint Bernard his Meditations* 294.

69   Julian of Norwich, *Revelations of Divine Love*, trans. E. Spearing, ed. A.C. Spearing (Harmondsworth: 1998) 5.

70   O'Connor M.C., *The Art of Dying Well. The Development of the* Ars Moriendi (New York: 1942); Beaty N.L., *The Craft of Dying. A Study in the Literary Tradition of the* Ars Moriendi *in England* (New York: 1970); Atkinson D.W., *The English* Ars Moriendi (New York: 1992).

71   Horstman C. (ed.), *Yorkshire Writers. Richard Rolle of Hampole and his Followers*, vol. 2 (London: 1896) 410.

The importance of beholding the crucifixion at the moment of death was not lost as a result of the Reformation. A work by Thomas Becon, sometime chaplain to Cranmer, called *The Sicke mannes Salve*, was essentially a Protestant version of the *Ars Moriendi*, cast in the form of a Platonic dialogue between a dying man and his godly neighbours come to support him. It was the most popular of Becon's works by far, and among the bestselling works of the Elizabethan period.[72] The encounter between the characters prompted a great deal of godly prayer, and much recitation of biblical passages, as well as a declaration of faith in impeccably Calvinist terms. Yet the idea of fixing one's dying gaze on the image of Christ crucified persisted, even though the image in question had become a mental one, rather than a material one.

> Whosoever is a true Christian, and fixeth the eyes of his mind, through true faith, on the death of Christ, he shall not greatly be afraid of death; but he shall rather triumph over death.

The theme of a deathbed struggle with Satan was also used:

> If Satan therefore hath either wounded you already, or else goeth about so to do, fear not, repair unto Christ, look on him with the eyes of your faith; so shall you be free from his venomous chaws.

In this struggle, the sight of Christ crucified was still deemed the best defence against dismay:

> Cast rather the eyes of your mind with strong faith on Christ and on his righteousness, on his merits, passion and death, on his blessed body-breaking, and his precious blood-shedding.

Alongside the biblical quotations, the dying man's comforters also recalled the words of Augustine exhorting them to 'behold Christ crucified', and the saying of St Bernard, 'When I am troubled and put in fear of my sins, then do I hide me in the bloody wounds of Jesus Christ'. Until the moment of death, the exhortations were reiterated, 'Only believe, only fix the eyes of your faith on Christ crucified'.[73] The imagery of the past had been internalized, but not lost.

This usage remained in the English Protestant tradition, even though the focus of the works in general shifted from emphasizing a good death to

---

72   Beaty, *Craft of Dying* 110.

73   *Prayers and other pieces of Thomas Becon*, ed. J. Ayre (Cambridge: 1844) 149, 157, 171, 172, 188.

exhorting a good life. The Elizabethan collection of prayers and meditations by Henry Bull, included a prayer to be said 'at the hower of death', which concluded, 'Graunt me mercifull Saviour, that when death hath shutte up the eyes of my body, yet the eyes of my soule may still beholde and loke upon thee'.[74] *The Anatomie of Mortalitie* by George Strode, published 1618, advised

> when any man feels his death to approach and draw neere with a fiery sting to pierce his heart, hee must then presently fixe his eyes of a true and lively faith upon Christ his Saviour exalted, lifted up, and crucified upon the crosse.[75]

The idea of the believer not only beholding Christ, but entering into dialogue with him, endured to be given expression by Jeremy Taylor in the 1650s. Taylor advised the dying man to 'have but very little conversation with the world', and instead 'antedate his conversation in heaven', and described the sick man on his deathbed, 'always having entercourse with God and still conversing with the holy Jesus, kissing his wounds, admiring his goodnesse, begging his mercy, feeding on him with faith, and drinking his blood', preferably whilst listening to the narrative of Christ's Passion read aloud.[76] The strong emotions of the deathbed were peculiarly appropriate to displays of this kind of affective devotion.[77]

Conclusion

If the debate about words and images in fifteenth- and sixteenth-century England was a complex one, it seems that the relationship between word and image was nevertheless an enduring one. This essay has suggested that we should see the developments of this time less as a straightforward transition from a visual to a verbal culture, than as an ongoing exploration of how best to read and understand different forms of religious media. Throughout the period, a range of different opinions on this were aired. Radicals both pre- and post-Reformation were suspicious of any form of material or even mental image, but arguably they remained in the minority. For most Reformation

---

74 Bull Henry, *Christian Prayers and holy meditations* (1574), STC 40295, f. 282r.

75 Atkinson, *English* ars moriendi 280. Atkinson describes Strode's work as one of several in which 'conditional salvation and predestination exist in paradoxical juxtaposition', xx.

76 Taylor Jeremy, *The rule and exercises of holy dying* (1651) 155.

77 Karant-Nunn, *The Reformation of Feeling* 189–214.

commentators, both Catholic and Protestant, the question was how best to use imagery in the service of the faith. As Luther wrote,

> Of this I am certain, that God desires to have his works heard and read, especially the passion of our Lord. But it is impossible for me to hear and bear it in mind without forming mental images of it in my heart. For whether I will or not, when I hear of Christ, an image of a man hanging on a cross takes form in my heart, just as the reflection of my face naturally appears in the water when I look into it (...).[78]

In England, St Gregory's words were quoted once more by the Elizabethan homilies:

> That thou dyddest forbyd Images to be worshipped, we praise altogether, but that thou dyddest breake them, we blame. For it is one thyng to worship the picture, and another thyng by the picture of the storye, to learne what is to be worshipped. For that whiche Scripture is to them that reade, the same doth picture perfourme vnto Idiotes or the vnlearned, beholdyng, and so foorth.[79]

If images ceased to instruct, or indeed came to blind, then they should be removed from the church, this homily went on to warn, but the possibility that they could still instruct the unlearned remained. The use of images in their role of layman's books was something which survived the Reformation in a recalibrated form. The printed word had served first to supplement, and later to absorb, pre-Reformation imagery, until the material images within the churches gave way to the mental images described in books and sermons. The continuities within these developments are underlined by the continuities in the debate about how images should be understood. The Reformation discussions of true and false understanding, and true and false worship, were in part a reaction against late medieval practice but also a continuation of a late medieval dialogue. This was, in essence, a conversation about how religious truth could be comprehended. Word did not replace image; rather words and images continued to be inextricably linked as they had been in the late

---

78   Luther Martin, *Against the Heavenly Prophets in the Matter of Images and Sacraments*, ed. B. Erling – C. Bergendorff, vol. 40 of *Luther's Works*, ed. H.T. Lehman (Philadelphia: 1958) 99–100.

79   *The seconde tome of homelyes* f. 31r.

medieval church. The Reformation reconfigured their relationship, but it could not break that connection.

Bibliography

Andrewes John, *Christ his crosse* (Oxford, Ioseph Barnes: 1614).

Aston M., *England's Iconoclasts: Laws against Images* (Oxford: 1988).

———, "Cross and Crucifix in the English Reformation", *Historische Zeitschrift* 33 (2002) 253–272.

Atkinson D.W., *The English Ars Moriendi* (New York: 1992).

Augustine St, *Confessions*, ed. R.S. Pine-Coffin (West Drayton: 1961).

Carruthers M., *The Book of Memory. A Study of Memory in Medieval Culture* (Cambridge: 2008).

Bal M. – Bryson N., "Semiotics and Art History", *The Art Bulletin* 73 (1991) 174–208.

Beatty N.L., *The Craft of Dying. A Study in the Literary Tradition of the* Ars Moriendi *in England* (New York: 1970).

Becon Thomas, *Prayers and other pieces of Thomas Becon*, ed. J. Ayre (Cambridge: 1844).

Bernard St, *Saint Bernard his Meditations. Or Sighes, Sobbes and Teares, upon our Saviours Passion* (2nd ed., 1614).

Brantley J., *Reading in the Wilderness. Private Devotion and Public Performance in Late Medieval England* (Chicago: 2008).

Bilson Thomas, *The effect of certaine sermons touching the full redemption of mankind by the death and bloud of Christ Iesus* (London, Peter Short for Walter Burre: 1599).

Bradford John, *The Writings of John Bradford*, ed. A. Townsend, Parker Society (Cambridge: 1848).

Bull Henry, *Christian Prayers and holy meditations* (1574).

Burke P., *Eyewitnessing. The Uses of Images as Historical Evidence* (London: 2001).

Bynum C.W., *Christian Materiality. An Essay on Religion in Late Medieval Europe* (New York: 2011).

Chamberlain Bartholomew, *The Passion of Christ and the benefits thereby* (London, printed for Thomas Pauier: 1612).

Crick J. – Walsham A. (eds.), *The Uses of Script and Print, 1300–1700* (Cambridge: 2004).

Davis-Weyer C., (ed.), *Early Medieval Art 300–1150. Sources and documents* (Toronto: 1986).

Day Richard, *A Booke of Christian Prayers* (London, John Daye: 1578).

Diebold W.J., *Word and Image. An Introduction to Early Medieval Art* (Michigan: 2000).

Dikovitskaya M., *Visual Culture. The Study of the Visual Culture after the Cultural Turn* (Cambridge, MA: 2005).

Dimmick J. – Simpson J. – Zeeman N., *Images, Idolatry and Iconoclasm in Late Medieval England: Textuality and the Visual Image* (Oxford: 2002).

Dives and Pauper, vol. 1, ed. P.H. Barnum, *Early English Text Society* (Oxford: 1976).

Driver M.W., *The Image in Print. Book Illustration in Late Medieval England and Its Sources* (2004).

Duffy E., *The Stripping of the Altars* (New Haven – London: 1992).

———, *Marking the Hours. English People and their Prayers 1240–1570* (New Haven – London: 2006).

Duncan T.G., *Late Medieval English Lyrics and Carols 1400–1530* (Harmondsworth: 2000).

Dyrness W.A., *Reformed Theology and Visual Culture* (Cambridge: 2004).

Falkenburg R.L. – Melion W.S. – Richardson T.M. (eds.), *Image and Imagination of the Religious Self in Late Medieval and Early Modern Europe*, Proteus: Studies in Early Modern Identity Formation 1 (Turnhout: 2007).

Fisher John, *The English Works of John Fisher*, ed. J.E.B. Mayor, *Early English Text Society*, extr. ser. 27 (Oxford: 1876).

Formularies of Faith put forward by authority during the reign of Henry VIII, ed. C. Lloyd (Oxford: 1856).

Foxe John, *A sermon of Christ crucified* (London, John Daye: 1577).

Frere W.H. – Kennedy W.M. (eds.), *Visitation Articles and Injunctions of the Period of the Reformation*, vol. II (London: 1910).

Gayk S., *Image, Text and Religious Reform in Fifteenth century England* (Cambridge: 2010).

Giles K., "Seeing and Believing: Visuality and Space in Pre-Modern England", *World Archaeology* 39 (2007) 105–121.

Gill M., "Reading Images: Church Murals and Collaboration between Media in Medieval England" in Bigliazzi S. – Wood S. (eds.), *Collaboration in the Arts from the Middle Ages to the Present* (Farnham: 2006) 17–32.

Gillespie V., "Medieval Hypertext: Image and Text from York Minster", in Robinson P.R. – Zim R. (eds.), *Of the Making of Books. Medieval Manuscripts, their Scribes and Readers* (Aldershot: 1997).

Glad tydings from heaven (London, printed for C. W[right]: c. 1630).

Hamburger J.F., "Seeing and Believing: The Suspicion of Sight and the Authentication of Vision in Late Medieval Art", in Nova A. – Krüger K. (eds.), *Imagination und Wirklichkeit. Zum Verhältnis von mentalen und realen Bilder in der Kunst der frühen Neuzeit* (Mainz: 2000) 47–70.

Hamling, T., *Decorating the Godly Household. Religious Art in Protestant Britain, c. 1560– c. 1660* (New Haven – London: 2010).

Hamling T. – Williams R.L. (eds.), *Art Re-formed? Re-assessing the Impact of the Reformation on the Visual Arts* (Newcastle: 2007).

Hoogvliet, M., 'L'image légendée: théories modernes et cartes médiévales', in Heck C. (ed.), *Qu'est-ce que nommer. L'image légendée entre monde monastique et pensée scolastique* (Turnhout: 2010).

Hooper John, *A declaration of the ten holy comaundementes* (Zürich, Augustin Fries: 1549).

Horstman C. (ed.), *Yorkshire Writers. Richard Rolle of Hampole and his Followers*, vol. 2 (London: 1896).

Hunt A., *The Art of Hearing. English Preachers and Their Audiences, 1590–1640* (Cambridge: 2010).

Jordanova L., *The Look of the Past. Visual and Material Evidence in Historical Practice* (Cambridge: 2012).

Joye George, *The exposicion of Daniel the prophete* (Antwerp, Catharine van Ruremund: 1545).

Julian of Norwich, *Revelations of Divine Love*, trans. E. Spearing, ed. A.C. Spearing (Harmondsworth: 1998).

Karant-Nunn S.C., *The Reformation of Feeling. Shaping the Religious Emotions in Early Modern Germany* (Oxford: 2010).

Kempe Margery, *The Book of Margery Kempe*, ed. B.A. Windeatt (Woodbridge: 2004).

King J.N. (ed.), *Tudor Books and Readers. Materiality and the Construction of Meaning* (Cambridge: 2010).

Latimer Hugh, *Sermons by Hugh Latimer*, ed. G.E. Corrie, vol. 1, Parker Society (Cambridge: 1844).

Laugerud H., "Visuality and Devotion in the Middle Ages", in Laugerud H. – Skinnebach L.K., (eds.), *Instruments of Devotion. The Practices and Objects of Religious Piety from the Late Middle Ages to the 20th Century* (Aarhus: 2007).

Lever Christopher, *A Crucifixe. Or a Meditation upon Repentance and The holie Passion* (London, V.S. for Mathew Lownes: 1607).

Luther Martin, *Against the Heavenly Prophets in the Matter of Images and Sacraments*, ed. B. Erling – C. Bergendorff, vol. 40 of *Luther's Works*, ed. H.T. Lehman (Philadelphia: 1958).

Lydgate John, *The Minor Poems of John Lydgate*, vol. 1, *Early English Text Society*, extra series cvii (Oxford: 1911).

Martin J., "English Reformed Responses to the Passion", in Ryrie A. – Martin J., *Private and Domestic Devotion in Early Modern Britain* (Aldershot, 2012) 115–134.

McCullough P.E., 'Lancelot Andrewes's Transforming Passions", *Huntingdon Library Quarterly* 71 (2008) 573–589.

Milner M., *The Senses and the English Reformation* (Farnham: 2011).

Mitchell W.J.B., *Iconology. Text, Image, Ideology* (Chicago: 1987).

———, *What Do Pictures Want?* (Chicago: 2005).

Mirk John, *The Festyvall* (London, Wynken de Worde: 1532).

Morgan D., *The Sacred Gaze. Religious Visual Theory in Theory and Practice* (Berkeley – Los Angeles: 2005).

———, *The Embodied Eye. Religious Visual Culture and the Social Life of Feeling* (Berkeley – Los Angeles: 2012).

Muessig C. (ed.), *Preacher, Sermon and Audience in the Middle Ages* (Leiden: 2002).

The New Testament 1526, Translated by William Tyndale, ed. W.R. Cooper (London: 2000).

O'Conner M.C., *The Art of Dying Well. The Development of the* Ars Moriendi (New York: 1942).

O'Daly G., *Augustine's Philosophy of Mind* (Berkeley – Los Angeles: 1987).

Owst, G.R., *Literature and Pulpit in Medieval England* (Oxford: 1961).

Panofsky E., "Iconography and Iconology: An Introduction to the Study of Renaissance Art", in Panofsky E., *Meaning in the Visual Arts* (Chicago: 1955) 51–81.

Ramakers B., "Eloquent Presence: Verbal and Visual Discourse in the Ghent Plays of 1539", in Brusati C. – Enenkel K.A.E. – Melion W.S., *The Authority of the Word. Reflecting on Image and Text in Northern Europe, 1400–1700*, Intersections: Interdisciplinary Studies in Early Modern Culture 20 (2011) (Leiden – Boston: 2012) 217–261.

Rex R., *The Theology of John Fisher* (Cambridge: 1991).

———, *Henry VIII and the English Reformation* (Basingstoke: 1993).

Ridley Nicholas, *The Works of Nicholas Ridley*, ed. H. Christmas, Parker Society (Cambridge: 1841).

Ross E.M., *The Grief of God. Images of the Suffering Jesus in Late Medieval England* (Oxford: 1997).

Ryrie A., *The Gospel and Henry VIII* (Cambridge: 2003).

Scribner R.W., "Popular Piety and Modes of Visual Perception in Late Medieval and Reformation Germany", *Journal of Religious History* 15 (1989).

Sears E. – Thomas T.K. (eds.), *Reading Medieval Images. The Art Historian and the Object* (Michigan: 2002).

The seconde tome of homelyes (London, Richard Jugge and John Cawood: 1563).

The song of Mary the mother of Christ containing the story of his life and passion (London, E. Allde for William Ferbrand: 1601).

Stafford Anthony, *The day of salvation, or, A homily upon the bloody sacrifice of Christ* (London, N. and I. Okes: 1635).

Stronks E., *Negotiating Differences. Word, Image and Religion in the Dutch Republic* (Leiden: 2011).

Taylor Jeremy, *The rule and exercises of holy dying* (London: 1651).

Two pleasant ditties, one of the birth, the other of the passion of Christ (London [?]: 1628–1629).

Walsham A., *Reformation of the Landscape. Religion, Identity and Memory in Early Modern Britain and Ireland* (Oxford: 2011).

Watt T., *Cheap Print and Popular Piety, 1550–1640* (Cambridge: 1991).

White H.C., *Tudor Books of Private Devotion* (Madison: 1951).

Williams R., *Keywords: A Vocabulary of Culture and Society* (Oxford: 1976).

Zachman R.C., *Image and Word in the Theology of John Calvin* (Notre Dame: 2007).

CHAPTER 12

The Other Nicodemus: Nicodemus in Italian Religious Writings Previous and Contemporary to Calvin's *Excuse à Messieurs les Nicodémites* (1544)

Federico Zuliani

The present article attempts to offer a first outline of the *fortuna* of the figure of Nicodemus in Italy at the time of the earliest reception of the *Excuse à Messieurs les Nicodémites* by John Calvin. First published in Geneva in 1544, and later translated into Latin and Italian, the *Excuse* belongs to the group of treatises written against sectarians,[1] and it is one of Calvin's most notorious and debated works. The term 'Nicodemites', chosen by Calvin, as well as the related abstract 'Nicodemism', coined by later historians, have a scriptural origin in the figure of Nicodemus, the Pharisee who believed in Jesus but visited him only by night out of fear (*John* 3:1–15) and did not dare to manifest his faith in public. We will deal more in detail below with Calvin's understanding of the term; for now we can summarise—however much a simplification—that Calvin used the word 'Nicodemites' to condemn and stigmatise those Christians who, following the example of Nicodemus, had embraced the true religion (i.e. the Reformed one) but were too scared to show it publicly and lived in secret, disguising their true beliefs. Calvin's polemic against such men was much older, however, and by this time entrenched: it had started already in 1537,[2]

---

* All quotations from Calvin's work have been taken from the editions in the Corpus Reformatorum: Calvin John., *Opera Quae Supersunt Omnia*, eds. W. Baum – E. Cunitz – E. Reuss (Brunswick: 1863–1880). Hereafter abbreviated as CO.

1 The other being those against Libertines and Anabaptists. For a general overview of the relationships between such treatises, see Firpo M., "Calvino e la riforma radicale: le opere contro nicodemiti, anabattisti e libertini (1544–1545)", *Studi Storici* 48 (2007) 97–105. For a reappraisal of Calvin's Libertines, see Zuliani F., "I *libertini* di Giovanni Calvino. Ricezione ed utilizzo polemico di un termine neotestamentario", *Archiv für Reformationsgeschichte* 104 (2013) 211–244.

2 With the publication of his *Epistolae duae de rebus hoc saeculo cognitu necessariis*.

was reiterated on several occasions (notably in 1541[3] and in 1543)[4] and it would continue after the publication of the *Excuse* as well, as we will see later in this article.[5] Calvin's works, moreover, were not isolated but inserted in a larger debate on religious dissimulation, especially strong in Central and in French-speaking Europe.[6] It is mainly to Italian historiography—to Carlo Ginzburg of course, but also to Delio Cantimori,[7] Antonio Rotondò,[8] Albano Biondi[9] and Massimo Firpo[10]—that we owe the use of the abstract term 'Nicodemism' to label not just the specific group of people against whom Calvin wrote in 1544

---

3   See White R., "Calvin and the Nicodemite Controversy: An Overlooked Text of 1541", *Calvin Theological Journal* 35 (2000) 282–296.

4   With the *Petit traicté monstrant que c'est que doit faire un homme fidele congnoissant la verité de l'Evangile*.

5   On Calvin's 'anti-Nicodemite' corpus of writings, see Droz E., *Chemins de l'hérésie. Textes et documents*, vol. 1 (Geneva: 1970) 131–171; Peter R. – Gilmont J.-F., *Bibliotheca Calviniana. Les oeuvres de Jean Calvin publiées au XVIᵉ siècle* vol 1 (Geneva: 1991) 40–43, 132–134, 164–166, 195–198, 303–307, 356–358, 427–429, 463–466 and 532–533 and White, "Calvin and the Nicodemite Controversy". The corpus has recently been translated into English by Seth Skolnitsky: Calvin J., *Come Out from Among Them: 'Anti-Nicodemite' Writings of John Calvin* (Dallas: 2001).

6   For such debate see Ginzburg C., *Il nicodemismo. Simulazione e dissimulazione religiosa nell'Europa del Cinquecento* (Turin: 1970); Fraenkel P., "Bucer's Memorandum of 1541 and a « Lettera nicodemitica » of Capito's", *Bibliothèque d'Humanisme et Renaissance* 36 (1974) 575–587; Higman F.M., "The Question of Nicodemism", in Neuser, W.H. (ed.), *Calvinus Ecclesiae Genevensis Custos. Die Referate des Congrès International des Recherches Calviniennes vom 6–9 September 1982 in Genf* (Frankfurt am Main: 1984) 165–170; Id., "Bucer et les Nicodemites", in Krieger C. – Lienhard M. (eds.), *Martin Bucer and Sixteenth Century Europe. Actes du colloque de Strasbourg (28–31 août 1991)*, vol. 2 (Leiden: 1993) 645–658 and White R., "Calvin, the Nicodemites and the Cost of Discipleship", *Reformed Theological Review* 56 (1997) 14–27. See also the two studies (especially focused on Calvin's positions) by Eire C.M.N.,"Calvin and Nicodemism: A Reappraisal", *The Sixteenth Century Journal* 10 (1979) 45–69 and the fundamental *War against the Idols: The Reformation of Worship from Erasmus to Calvin* (Cambridge: 1986).

7   Cantimori D., "Nicodemismo e speranze conciliari nel Cinquecento italiano", *Quaderni di Belfagor* 1 (1948) 12–23 and *Prospettive di storia ereticale italiana del Cinquecento* (Bari: 1960) 37–78.

8   Rotondò A., "Atteggiamenti della vita morale italiana del Cinquecento. La pratica nicodemitica", *Rivista Storica Italiana* 79 (1967) 991–1030.

9   Biondi A., "La giustificazione della simulazione nel Cinquecento", in *Eresia e Riforma nell'Italia del Cinquecento* (Florence – Chicago: 1974) 5–68.

10   Firpo M., *Tra alumbrados e « spirituali ». Studi su Juan de Valdés e il valdesismo nella crisi religiosa del '500 italiano* (Florence: 1990) 60–84.

but, much more generally, any minority religious group living in a hostile environment and opting for a practice of dissimulation.[11]

In this article I will leave aside the problem of religious dissimulation itself as well as the notion of 'Nicodemism' and its cognates, to concentrate instead on a specific chapter of the earliest reception of the *Excuse à Messieurs les Nicodémites* in Italy, in the light of the diffuse knowledge there of the figure of the scriptural Nicodemus. An interest in Calvin's position on dissimulation *religionis causa* arose among Italians due especially to the tragic end of several Reformed dissemblers—the most notable cases being Francesco Spiera and Fanino Fanini—and to the involvement of Calvin in the polemic that followed these events. However, despite the diffuse practice of dissimulation among Italian supporters of the Reformation, Calvin's text on the Nicodemites—I will argue—probably had a limited circulation, at least in its original French. I will also try to show that the scriptural figure of Nicodemus, on the contrary, was well known in Italy, and held in high esteem. An awareness of these facts may cast some light on a problem that has continued to puzzle historians: why Calvin's appeal for the Reformed and the philo-Reformed (the so-called Nicodemites) in Italy to change their way of life had, at least at an early stage, so little success. I would like to suggest, as a working hypothesis, that—since the immediate reference to Nicodemus was already present in the very title of Calvin's work—some may have tried to gather information from the only sources available to them, sources in which Nicodemus was presented as a very positive example of a true believer in Christ. Indeed, the significance of Nicodemus and his actions in the Gospels may have given a positive rather than a negative perception to those who took, or were accused of having taken, him as a role model.

To corroborate this I will turn to the rich, popular and widely used devotional and exegetical literature that circulated in Italy before and after the publication of Calvin's *Excuse*. I am not suggesting that such literature was solely responsible for the reception of the treatise, but rather that it may have *interfered* with the reception, especially among those who had no direct access to Calvin's works on dissimulation but were eager to know more on the subject. A final disclaimer is in order: my present study has no claim to be exhaustive on such a wide and complex topic. However, I hope that it might be a first

---

11   See George T., "Nicodemism", in Hillerbrand H.J. (ed.), *The Oxford Encyclopedia of the Reformation*, vol. 3 (New York – Oxford: 1996) 145. For examples of a broader use of the term, see, for instance, Pettegree A., "Nicodemism and the English Reformation", in *Marian Protestantism: Six Studies* (Aldershot: 1996) 86–117.

stage in further research and that it might help to stimulate academic debate, at least on what we actually know about the earliest reception of Calvin's treatise in Italy.

The Reception and the Circulation in Italy of Calvin's *Excuse à Messieurs les Nicodémites*

The *Excuse* was published by Calvin in French in 1544. The text was then translated into Latin two years later; however, the translation only appeared in print in 1549, in the *De vitandis superstitionibus*, together with several other treatises by Calvin dealing with the problem of religious dissimulation.[12] The circulation of the *Excuse* in Italy in the years following its publication, perhaps due to the great interest of Italian historiography on the theme, is often taken for granted despite the absence of proof. Actually, several pieces of information suggest the contrary. The Italian interest in both the *Insitutio* and the *Catechism* by Calvin, texts which were being read first in partial and later complete Italian translations already from the early 1540s, is well documented.[13] Nevertheless, in virtually none of these sources (the exemptions will be studied below)—written by both Italian Protestants and Catholic clergymen concerned about heresy and active in the persecution of dissenters—do we find open references to the *Excuse*.

Calvin's original work against the Nicodemites was directed, as his choice of language suggests, mainly to a French audience. Very soon afterwards, however, events forced Calvin to be involved with Italian matters to a far greater extent. Francesco Spiera was a respected lawyer from the Venetian city of Cittadella and a man of strong Reformed beliefs. Yet when he had to face an Inquisition trial in 1548, his fear was too great and he abjured his faith. Overwhelmed by shame, repentance and by the certainty of having doomed himself to eternal damnation since he had committed the unpardonable sin against the Holy Spirit (*Mark* 3:28–30; *Matthew* 12:30–32; *Luke* 12:8–10 and *Hebrews* 6:4–8), he died only few months later in Padua. Soon, a heated debate arose among

---

12   See Garavelli E., *Lodovico Domenichi e i « Nicodemiana » di Calvino. Storia di un libro perduto e ritrovato* (Manziana: 2004) 127.

13   See Higman F., "Calvin's works in translation", in *Lire et découvrir. La circulation des idées au temps de la Réforme* (Geneva: 1998) 547–548; Felici L., *Giovanni Calvino e l'Italia* (Turin: 2010) 14–31 and especially Rozzo U. – Seidel Menchi S., "Livre et Réforme en Italie", in Gilmont, J.-F. (ed.), *La Réforme et le livre. L'Europe de l'imprimé (1517–v. 1570)* (Paris: 1990) 327–374.

Italians of Reformed allegiance and sympathies on the lawfulness and the risks of hiding and dissimulating true beliefs. Giorgio Siculo, Matteo Gribaldi, Giulio della Rovere, Celio Secondo Curione and Pier Paolo Vergerio (who was on his deathbed) debated Spiera's case at length. Some, like Siculo, defended dissimulation, while those of a stricter Calvinist observance urged believers still in Italy to give up dissimulating and offer a public testimony of their faith, choosing martyrdom or exile.[14] Spiera's case became a paradigmatic example of the risks for the souls of those Protestant believers who kept living in 'Babylon'. Only a fragment of Calvin's correspondence with Italians survives, but it is probable that dissimulation was among the most discussed topics in this period.[15] This is also suggested by the fact that Calvin took a public position on Spiera's case: when the Scotsman Henry Scrimgeour published a Latin account of the events, Calvin added a harsh preface to the work with a clear condemnation of dissimulating practice.[16] With the Latin edition of several 'anti-Nicodemite' texts in the *De vitandis superstitionibus* (1549), we have another confirmation that, from the late 1540s, Calvin had realised that the debate about dissimulation could not be limited to the French-speaking world and was, on the contrary, very pertinent to Italy as well. The presence in the edition also of a *consilium* by Peter Martyr Vermigli,[17] who had escaped from Italy in 1542, is, of course, not enough to sustain the idea that the translation was meant as a response to the

---

14   For this case, its *fortuna*, and for the different positions in the debate, see Comba E., *Francesco Spiera. Episodio della riforma religiosa in Italia. Con aggiunta di documenti originali tratti dall'Archivio veneto del S. Ufficio* (Rome – Florence: 1872); Overell M.A., "The Exploitation of Francesco Spiera", *The Sixteenth Century Journal* 26 (1995) 619–637; Walker D., "Pier Paolo Vergerio (1498–1465) e il «Caso Spiera» (1548)", *Studi di teologia* 10 (1998) 3–83; Prosperi A., *L'eresia del Libro Grande. Storia di Giorgio Siculo e della sua setta* (Milan: 2000) 102–130 and Cavazza S., "Una vicenda europea. Vergerio e il caso Spiera, 1548–49", in Dall'Olio G. – Malena A. – Scaramella P. (eds.), *Per Adriano Prosperi. La fede degli italiani* (Pisa: 2011) 41–51.

15   Lelio Sozzini had already moved to Zurich; nevertheless, it is worth recalling here that the polemical epistolary exchange of 1549–1552 between Sozzini and Calvin had at its core religious dissimulation, and that Sozzini wrote to Calvin after the edition of the *De vitandis superstitionibus* had been published. See Sozzini L., *Opere*, ed. A. Rotondò (Florence: 1986).

16   Scrimgeour Henry, *Exemplum memorabile desperationis in Francisco Spiera, propter abiuratam fidei confessionem, cum praefatione D. Joannis Calvini* (Geneva, Jean Gerard: 1550).

17   Calvin John, *De vitandis superstitionibus, quae cum sincera fidei confessione pugnant, libellus Joannis Calvini. Eiusdem excusatio, ad pseudonicodemos. Philippi Melancthonis, Martini Buceri, Petri Martyris responsa de eadem re. Calvini ultimum responsum, cum appendicibus* (Geneva, Jean Gerard: 1549) 110–111.

debates which had arisen there after Spiera's death. Nevertheless, it does show that Calvin had Italy in mind as one of places where his voice now needed to be heard most clearly. A final confirmation comes from the fact that only few years later, in 1553, the *De vitandis superstitionibus* was also translated into Italian and printed, significantly, in Geneva. It was not the first time, however, that this text saw an Italian translation. Between 1550 and 1551—the actual date is disputed—a group of ardent Florentine Calvinists undertook an Italian translation of the text. This edition, however, was confiscated by Catholic authorities and the authors immediately faced trial.[18] Thus, thanks to Spiera, the Italian attempts at a translation, Calvin's letters, and, more generally, to the echoes of the European debate on dissimulation, we can affirm that the problems addressed by Calvin in the *Excuse* must have been perceived as especially relevant—and were possibly also well known—by his Italian supporters. However, owing to the sequestration of the translations and the stricter level of Catholic censorship from the early 1540s,[19] diffusion of the text would have been at the very least difficult; moreover, when it actually did circulate, it seems to have done so in Latin rather than in the original French.[20]

I have insisted on the differences between the two texts because Calvin's French work presented a kind of inner contradiction that was only later corrected by the Reformer himself. In the treatise, Calvin returns three times to the relationship between Nicodemus and the Nicodemites. The figure of Nicodemus is barely mentioned in Calvin's other works, but here the Reformer dedicates three long passages to him, all meant to defend him vigorously and to accuse the Nicodemites as usurpers of his good name:

> they borrow the name of Nicodemus to use as a shield, as if they were his imitators. I will call them this for the moment, until I have shown how they do great wrong to that holy man in putting him on their own level, and what is more, glorifying themselves by his example.[21]

---

18   I follow here Garavelli, *Lodovico Domenichi*.

19   See Rozzo – Seidel Menchi, "Livre et Réforme" 342–344.

20   We know for instance that in 1549 Baldassarre Altieri asked for 50 copies of the *De vitandis superstitionibus* to be sent from Geneva. See Garavelli *Lodovico Domenichi* 107–109. On Altieri see Cantimori D., "Baldassarre Altieri", in *Dizionario Biografico degli Italiani*, vol. 2 (Rome: 1960) 559 and Firpo M., *Vittore Soranzo vescovo ed eretico. Riforma della Chiesa e Inquisizione nell'Italia del Cinquecento* (Rome – Bari: 2006) 232–233.

21   'Pource qu'ilz empruntent le nom de Nicodeme, pour en faire un bouclier, comme s'ilz estoyent ses imitateurs: ie les nommeray ainsi pour ceste heure iusque à tant qui i'aye monstré combien ilz font grand tort à ce sainct personnage, en le mettant de leur ranc, et

What emerges from an attentive reading of the *Excuse* is that, for Calvin, the Scriptural Nicodemus is worthy of devotion, and those who attempt to imitate Nicodemus are wrong in doing so. Evidently, the initial ambiguity of Calvin's terminology soon became clear to him, for when he translated the text into Latin he gave it the title *Excusatio ad Pseudo-Nicodemos*; but in the subsequent years especially Calvin must have realised the true limits of his original choice, and also the inadequacy of his partial emendation. When Calvin would mention the 'Nicodemites' again, he always underlined their true nature as usurpers: we encounter 'falsi Nicodemitae' once more in the *Commentarius in Evangelium Ioannis* (1553),[22] as well as in the *Commentarius in Acta Apostolorum* (1554),[23] while in the *Commentarii in librum Psalmorum* (1556) on Psalm XVI, they even become the 'bewitched Nicodemites' ('larvati Nicodemitae').[24] And lastly, when the French text was finally reprinted by Beza in the *Recueil des Opuscules* in 1569, after Calvin's death, all the occurrences of the term 'Nicodémites' were replaced with the more precise 'faux Nicodémites'. However, it has been convincingly suggested that it was Calvin himself who later dropped the term, since when he wrote against the Dutchman Dirck Coornhert, accusing him of dissimulation, Calvin never called him 'Nicodemite'.[25] This point is relevant for two reasons. Firstly, it might help us to follow the actual readership of the treatise in Italy. Secondly, and probably more importantly, it suggests that the ambiguity was not irrelevant and that Calvin, in continuing to emend his terminology, realised that his original choice might be the cause of a certain degree of uncertainty and, therefore, had to be changed. But what about those who were interested in the topic, yet could not read Calvin's text and simply heard about those 'Nicodemites'—and not the 'pseudo' or 'false Nicodemites'—who acted following the example of Nicodemus?

---

qui plus est se glorifiant de son exemple'. CO, XXXIV, 596. I quote the translation as given in Cottret B., *Calvin: A Biography* (Grand Rapids: 2000) 274.

22 CO, XLVII, 424.

23 CO, XLVIII, 486.

24 CO, XXXI, 153. 'Nicodemiti' was also used in other occasions by Calvin. In the comment *In Hoseam* (1557) we read 'sed nebulonibus istis qui iactant se Nicodemitas' (CO, XLII 290) while in the *Praelectiones in Ieremiam Prophetam* (1563), 'Quid ergo dicent Nicodemitae, qui hodie sibi blanditias faciunt?'. (CO, XXXVIII 74). Since in both cases Calvin is discussing the sectarians' *self*-designation, the absence of prefix makes sense.

25 Eire, *War against the Idols* 243. The terminological problems may explain why in the very long introduction *Ai lettori* in the Italian translation of the *De vitandis superstitionibus* (Geneva, 1553), there is not a single reference to the Nicodemites, nor, even more remarkably, to Nicodemus or the relevant passages of John.

It is indicative then that the first secure references to Calvin's texts on the Nicodemites come from exiled Italians. Writing to the 'Italian brothers' on the 15 April 1551,[26] Pier Paolo Vergerio, without mentioning its title, suggested that they read the *De vitandis superstitionibus*.[27] However, Vergerio—once a Catholic bishop and a religious dissembler himself[28]—must have come to know Calvin's text only recently. In his pamphlet of November 1550, *Al serenissimo re d'Inghilterra*, he mentioned those prelates who, 'although they act as Nicodemus, they love the glory of the world more than the glory of God'.[29] Since he condemns here neither the example nor, much more importantly, the *sequela* of Nicodemus, it seems impossible that Vergerio had actually read Calvin's work; it is much more likely that he had simply heard of it. Vergerio's case is particularly relevant: he wrote his pamphlet when he had already escaped from Italy; he was, and had been, an avid reader of religious treatises; he had been in contact with almost all the most significant exponents of Italian 'evangelism';[30] he had taken a position on Spiera; and, last but not least, he had lived for several years as a 'Nicodemite' himself. It would be imprudent to draw general conclusions from a single occurrence. Nevertheless, due to Vergerio's prominent position, role and personal story, his case seems to at least present very good evidence that it was possible, and probably even quite common,

---

26   'Insieme con questo vorrei che leggessero un trattatello del Calvino, il quale mostra con quanta diligentia l'huom christano si de' guardare da falsi culti, & in quanto pericolo dell'anima stanno quei, che ad essi acconsentano'. [Vergerio Pier Paolo], *La historia di M. Francesco Spiera, il quale per havere in varij modi nagata la conosciuta verità dell'Evangelio, cascò in una misera desperatione* (s.l.t. [Poschiavo, Dolfin Landolfi]: 1551) f. 4r.

27   See Garavelli, *Lodovico Domenichi* 27–28.

28   See Jacobson Schutte A., *Pier Paolo Vergerio: The Making of an Italian Reformer* (Geneva: 1977): Pierce R.A., *Pier Paolo Vergerio: The Propagandist* (Rome: 2003) and Cavazza S., "Pier Paolo Vergerio", in M. Biagioni et al. (eds.), *Fratelli d'Italia. Riformatori italiani nel Cinquecento* (Turin: 2011) 145–152.

29   'benche fanno del Nicodemo, amano più la gloria del mondo, che la gloria di Dio'. [Vergerio Pier Paolo], *Al Serenissimo re d'Inghilterra Edoardo Sesto. De portamenti di Papa Giulio III. Et quale habbia ad essere il concilio che egli intende di fare* (s.l.t. [Poschiavo, Dolfin Landolfi]: 1550) f. 16r.

30   I use such terminology well aware of the intense scholarly debate on its use. See Fragnito F., "Gli «spirituali» e la fuga di Bernardino Ochino", *Rivista Storica Italiana* 84 (1972) 777–813; Del Col A., "Per una sistemazione critica dell'evangelismo italiano e di un'opera recente", *Critica storica* 17 (1980) 266–275; Peyronel Rambaldi S., "Ancora sull'evangelismo italiano: categoria o invenzione storiografica?", *Società e storia* 18 (1982) 935–967 and Jacobson Schutte A., "Periodization of Sixteenth-Century Italian Religious History: The Post-Cantimori Paradigm Shift", *Journal of Modern History* 61 (1989) 272–275.

to know about the Nicodemites and about Calvin's polemics on dissimulation without having any direct knowledge of the book. The supposition that Vergerio had not read Calvin's text appears even more convincing when his writings are compared to a letter sent from Geneva in 1554 to Angelo Castiglioni from Massimiliano Celso Martinengo. The latter accused those who 'falsely take the colour of Nicodemus' and hide under 'his mantle'[31]—almost a verbatim lifting from Calvin's work, which accuses them of trying 'to hide under the robe of Nicodemus'.[32] Those who had read the text carefully, like Martinengo (it has been suggested that he might be one of the Italian translators of the *De vitandis superstitionibus*),[33] could not avoid noticing that Calvin had in mind 'false Nicodemites', hiding themselves behind the name of Nicodemus, rather than genuine imitators of the scriptural figure.

The interest in Calvin's positions on dissimulation was strong in Italy and the topic—especially after the tragedy of Francesco Spiera—must have deeply touched several Italian dissemblers. But what were those who wished to know more, yet lacked access to Calvin's texts, likely to do? It seems most probable that they turned to the literature available to them, trying to gather as much information as possible.

Naming in the Sixteenth Century: A Few Remarks

Before turning to the reception of the figure of Nicodemus in Italy, it is necessary to offer a few reflections on the way that groups were named in sixteenth-century Europe. A proper philological study of this topic is, in my view, one of the most urgent *desiderata* in the field. It is a vast topic, far too complex to be dealt with properly here. Nevertheless, at least a few remarks must be made, as my working hypothesis is only plausible if we can demonstrate that

---

31   'forse un colore, ma falso, di Nicodemo, del cui mantello cotanti mal accortisi vergognansi di coprire'. Pascal A., "Una breve polemica tra il Riformatore Celso Martinengo e Fra Angelo Castiglioni da Genova (sec. XVI)", *Bulletin de la Société d'Histoire Vaudoise* 35 (1915) 83. For the emendation see Garavelli, *Lodovico Domenichi* 13. On Martinengo see also Ronchi De Michelis L., "Celso (Massimiliano) Martinengo", in *Dizionario Biografico degli Italiani* vol. 71 (Rome: 2008) 142–145 and Lorenzi R.A., "Per un profilo di Massimiliano Celso Martinengo, riformatore", in Lorenzi R.A. (ed.), *Riformatori bresciani del '500. Indagini* (Brescia: 2006) 105–168.

32   'ilz se peuvent cacher soubz la robbe de Nicodeme'. CO, XXXIV 608. Cf. also the Latin 'Verum adhuc sibi videntur honestum operculum habere, quamdiu sub pallio Nicodemi teguntur'. Calvin john, *De vitandis superstitionibus* (1549) 87.

33   Droz, *Chemins de l'hérésie* I 159–167. See, *contra*, Garavelli, *Lodovico Domenichi* 20–21.

the mere reference to 'Nicodemites' in the title of the *Excuse* could point its readers directly to the scriptural Nicodemus.

The general pattern seems to be that new groups were labelled after their real or alleged founders, for example Lutherani after Luther and Calviniani/ Calvinisti after Calvin, but also Quintinisti after Quintin of Hainaut and Hutteriti after Jakob Hutter. In practice, the scheme was neutral and the names were used by both supporters and detractors alike. Of course, naming might bring a negative or polemical pun, but that need not be the case. Examples like that of Jesuits after Jesus (with a reference to the followers of our Lord in the early church that has probably not yet been studied enough)[34] or of other religious orders (for instance Teatini or Orsolinae, not to mention older ones such as Franciscans or Dominicans) convey a proud statement of descent which was also shared by those who called themselves Lutherans, Calvinists and so forth. In both positive and negative cases, the pattern was clear: it referred either to a founder or to a model followed by the 'believers' (real as well as presumed). However, in order to be successful (i.e. to allow the reader to correctly identify the group), the reference given in the name had to be intelligible and immediate, otherwise the reference would be pointless.

Another issue should also be stressed here: even if the source for a given name was easily identifiable, naming does not bear any actual reference to the characteristics of the model himself, and this is probably the main reason why the same names kept being generally used by both detractors and supporters alike. Calvin—if we can attribute the 'Nicodemite' label as his invention[35]—was an acute polemicist, and highly effective when it came to labelling opponents. Though I believe that it was he who chose to call his opponents Nicodemites, the dedication of three long passages in his work to defending Nicodemus's good name confirms that, for Calvin, such a name still bore an immediate reference to Nicodemus, even if he was not the one who chose the label. In addition, the occasional use of similar expressions in the years previous to Calvin's *Excuse*, as studied by Carlos Eire, confirms that terms like 'Nicodemisch', 'Nycodemistes' or 'Nycodemysans', naturally pointed towards the scriptural Nicodemus.[36] Moreover, the aforementioned case of Vergerio proves that the connection must have been easy to make for Italians. In Italy, however, another fact must have made the association especially clear.

---

34   For the theme of the example of the early church as the ideal reference for the first Jesuits, see Mongini G., *«Ad Christi similitudinem». Ignazio di Loyola e i primi gesuiti tra eresia e ortodossia. Studi sulle origini della Compagnia di Gesù* (Alessandria: 2011).

35   Eire, *War against the Idols* 242.

36   Eire, *War against the Idols* 243.

The ill-fated Florentine translation of the *De vitandis superstitionibus* bore the title *Libro di Giovanni Calvino del fuggir le superstitioni le quali contrastano con la sincera confessione della Fede. Escusatione del medesimo a falsi Nicodemi*[37] following, correctly, the Latin original and mentioning Nicodemus rather than the Nicodemites. For those with access to this edition the connection was thus even easier. This might actually be the reason why the text came to be known, among the few that could read it, as 'Nicodemiana' ('about the *Nicodemi*') and not 'Nicodemitiana' ('about the *Nicodemiti*').[38]

Unlike other contemporary groups, however, the so-called Nicodemites were connected not with a heresiarch or with a charismatic leader, either still living or recently dead, but with a marginal scriptural figure. Nicodemus was, in fact, not an apostle nor a disciple who had followed Jesus during his human experience; absent in the synoptic Gospels, Nicodemus is mentioned only three times and by John alone. Once, at the beginning of the Gospel (3:1–15), Nicodemus is said to have been 'a Pharisee' and 'a leader of the Jews' who believed in Jesus but dared to visit him only by night. He appears a second time, briefly, at the end of an argument between the Pharisees and those who were sent to arrest Jesus, in which they disputed whether he was really the Christ (7:51). Finally, we see Nicodemus again after the Passion, when he is said to have been one of the two disciples—the other being Joseph of Arimathea—who deposed the corpse of the Saviour from the Cross (19:39). Unlike Lutherans, Calvinists or Hutterites, who could agree or disagree with their labelling, and who were associated with figures who were generally still alive or who were thought to be more or less easily accessible to them, the 'Nicodemites' who wanted to know more about the figure from which they took their name were directed to the Scriptures. Due to Nicodemus's marginal role, however, such readers were forced to turn especially to devotional works and exegetical commentaries that dealt in much greater detail with him and the value and the significance of his presence in

---

37   Garavelli, *Lodovico Domenichi* 115.

38   For the title *Nicodemiana* see Garavelli, *Lodovico Domenichi*. When Pietro Manelfi denounced his heterodox acquaintances to the Bolognese Inquisition in October 1551, speaking of the Florentine group, he twice mentioned the Italian translation of Calvin's work. See Ginzburg C., *I costituti di don Pietro Manelfi* (Florence – Chicago: 1970) 39. Both times Manelfi mentioned the text, however, he called it *Nicodominicana*. It is very likely that Manelfi never had access to the book (Garavelli, *Lodovico Domenichi* 102); nonetheless, it is surprising that in his testimony the name of the treatise presents a supernumerary syllable. Since it was a general pattern to label groups adding 'ni' to the name of their leaders or model (Lutherani, Calviniani, Domenicani, Franciscani etc.), why would Malefi not have referred here to *Nicodemini*, meaning in this way the supporters/followers of *Nicodemo*?

the Gospel. Though Calvin does not refer to these other authorities by name, it is clear that when he came to write the *Excuse*, he must have consulted these treatises at length. Nicodemus was scarcely mentioned by the Reformer in his previous works while, in the *Excuse*, Calvin engages in long considerations on his character and the value of his acts, demonstrating a knowledge which could only have been derived from the aforementioned sources.

Nicodemus in Italy before Calvin

In what space remains I will offer some examples—though my list is hardly exhaustive—of the portrayal of Nicodemus in Italian literature before the *Excuse*. I will deal first with the medieval sources that continued to be used and read in the sixteenth century, and will then move on to the new devotional and exegetical works published from the Reformation onwards. I intend to focus especially on those works that we know had a wide circulation, with particular attention to texts which were not placed on the *Index librorum prohibitorum* and which were thus easily available to Calvin's supporters and, more gener- ally, to those believers who supported Reform, and who most feared Roman censorship. Finally, I will also look at forbidden texts, though continuing to bear in mind the limited degree to which they circulated.[39] Although I shall not discuss the representation of Nicodemus in the visual arts, I hope that this will be studied on another occasion. However, it must be pointed out that the figure of Nicodemus in the Florentine *Pietà* has been regarded as Michelangelo's self-portrait.[40] As such, even if it is not actually a self-portrait, the prominence of the figure suggests that the scriptural Nicodemus was far from unknown in Italy in those days and that the connotation of the figure was far from negative.

Including medieval literature in this survey may seem slightly tangential, but it must be given proper consideration. In a devotional context, in fact, the

---

39 See, in general on all these issues, Fragnito G., *La censura ecclesiastica e i volgarizzamenti della Scrittura (1471–1605)* (Bologna: 1997); Barbieri E., "Fra tradizione e cambiamento: note sul libro spirituale italiano del XVI secolo", in Barbieri E. – Zardin D. (eds.), *Libri, biblioteche e cultura nell'Italia del Cinque e Seicento* (Milan: 2002) 3–61; Caravale G., *L'orazione proibita. Censura ecclesiastica e letteratura devozionale nella prima età moderna* (Florence: 2003) and Zardin D., "Bibbia e letteratura religiosa in volgare nell'Italia del Cinque-Seicento", *Annali di Storia moderna e contemporanea* 4 (1998) 593–616.

40 Shrimplin-Evangelidis V., "Michelangelo and Nicodemism: The Florentine Pietà", *Art Bulletin* 71 (1989) 58–66.

early sixteenth century showed no break in its readership and interests. These texts kept circulating and their popularity is proved also by their vernacular translations.[41] Moreover, especially as concerns the exegetical literature, we should keep in mind that several supporters of Reform were originally clergymen (both secular and, more importantly, monastic):[42] owing to their training, they would have often been exposed to this literature. Secondly, we have to remember that many of those who later showed interest in the Reformation had studied at Italian universities. Here, very often, the teaching of theology and Holy Scripture was still based mainly on medieval rather than humanist scholarship.[43]

Leaving aside older patristic sources,[44] we ought to underline that the figure of Nicodemus is mentioned often in the most influential medieval devotional works, especially in connection with the Passion of Christ and the deposition from the Cross. This is certainly the case in the *Meditationes* by the Pseudo-Bonaventura (a text which circulated both in Latin and in Italian translations),[45] in which the role of Nicodemus in the deposition is elaborated with great precision and at length.[46] Among many other references we might note that, when Joseph and Nicodemus depose the body, the Virgin exclaims: 'You do well in keeping the memory of your Master, because He loved you very much'.[47] Also in the *Vita Christi* by Ludolph of Saxony, a text widely known and read in

41   See, for instance, Jacobson Schutte A., *Printed Italian Vernacular Religious Books, 1465–1550: A Finding List.* (Geneva: 1983).

42   See Cantimori D., *Eretici italiani del Cinquecento. Ricerche storiche* (Florence: 1939) and Firpo M., *Riforma protestante ed eresie nell'Italia del Cinquecento. Un profilo storico* (Rome – Bari: 1993).

43   Especially relevant to this is the case of Sigismondo Arquer. See Cocco M.M., *Sigismondo Arquer dagli studi giovanili all'autodafé* (Cagliari: 1987) and Firpo M., "Alcune considerazioni sull'esperienza religiosa di Sigismondo Arquer", *Rivista Storica Italiana* 105 (1993) 411–475.

44   Such as, for instance, John Chrysostom, *In Joannem Homeliae*, and Cyril of Alexandria, *Commentarii in Joannem*.

45   Between the years 1520 and 1550, we know of eleven printed editions in Italy. See Zarri G., "Note su diffusione e circolazione di testi devoti (1520–1550)", in Biondi A. – Prosperi A. (eds.), *Libri, idee e sentimenti religiosi nel Cinquecento italiano* (Modena: 1987) 134. For the fortune of the text in Italy, see also Vaccari A., "Le *Meditazioni della vita di Cristo* in volgare", in *Scritti di erudizione e filologia*, vol. 1 (Rome: 1952) 341–378, and, especially for the sixteenth century, Barbieri, "Fra tradizione e cambiamento" 30.

46   John of Caulibus, *Meditaciones vite Christi, olim S. Bonaventuro attributae*, ed. M. Stallings-Taney (Turnhout: 1997) 279–281.

47   'Domina tandem dicit: Bene fecistis habentes memoriam Magistri uestri, quia multum uos dilexit'. John of Caulibus, *Meditaciones vite Christi* 279.

Italy (and later published in Italian translation as well),[48] Nicodemus is presented as a very positive figure, with the *crescendo* of his spiritual journey given special prominence. At first Ludolph points out that 'then by night he came to the light, because he wished to be enlightened'.[49] Nicodemus here stands as an example of humility,[50] a man whose faith is not yet perfect. Later in the work, however, he is remembered as having helped with the deposition of Jesus and his figure is presented in an extremely positive way: he is 'a man of knowledge and expert in the Law', but what matters most is that he is a 'disciple of Christ', even if, until that moment, a secret one.[51] A few lines below, quoting Anselm, Nicodemus is finally called 'beatissimus'.[52] In 1522, in Venice, too (the Italian and European capital of the book market but also, together with the nearby Veneto, one of the places most attentive to Protestant propaganda),[53] the apocryphal *Evangelium Nicodemi*—known in medieval Italy in vernacular translations as well[54]—was published by Antonio de Fantis in a collection of other texts under the title of *Opera nuper in lucem prodeuntia*.[55] Here, Nicodemus gains an even more prestigious status when, at the end of the fifth chapter, he

---

48 For this work's *fortuna* in Italy see my forthcoming article "Veronese's *Cena* for San Zanipolo and his Trial before the Inquisition", *Journal of the Warburg and Courtauld Institutes* 78 (2015).

49 'Et ideo nocte ad lucem venit, quia illuminari volebat', Ludolph of Saxony, *Vita Christi*, 5 vols. (Salzburg: 2006) vol. 2, 130.

50 'Per Nicodeum qui venit ad Jesum, ut de pertinentibus ad fidem plenius erudiretur, significatur discipulus humilis et diligens, qui venit ad doctorum, ut ab ipso instruatur: qui debet eum dulciter recipere, exemplo Christi, qui Nicodemum dulciter recepit, ac mansuete valde, et quiete ei loquebatur'. Ludolph of Saxony, *Vita Christi* II 130.

51 'Concesso autem sibi corpore, vocavit ad se quemdam virum sapientem, et Legisperitum, discipulum Christi similiter occultum, Nicodemum nomine'. Ludolph of Saxony, *Vita Christi* IV 678.

52 'beatissimus Nicodemus', Ludolph of Saxony, *Vita Christi* IV 678.

53 For these aspects, see di Filippo Bareggi C., *Il mestiere di scrivere. Lavoro intellettuale e mercato librario a Venezia nel Cinquecento* (Rome: 1988), Grendler P.F., *The Roman Inquisition and the Venetian Press, 1540–1605* (Princeton: 1977) and Martin J.J., *Venice's Hidden Enemies: Italian Heretics in a Renaissance City* (Baltimore: 1993).

54 See, for its reception and for its translations, Iannucci A.I., "The Gospel, of Nicodemus in Medieval Italian Literature: A Preliminary Assessment", in Izydorczyk Z. (ed.), *The Medieval Gospel of Nicodemus: Texts, Intertexts, and Contexts in Western Europe* (Tempe: 1997) 165–205.

55 For this text see Acerbi A., "Antonio de Fantis, editore della *Visio Isaiae*", *Aevum* 57 (1983) 396–415. The collection—which opens with the *Liber gratiae spiritualis* by Mechtilde of Hackeborn—was likely to have circulated among Padua's religious milieux given the great interest there for Central European mysticism. See Stella A., "Tradizione razionalistica

publicly admits that he has become a follower of Jesus and declares himself ready to accept his martyrdom.[56]

Medieval traditions concerning Nicodemus were also picked up and inserted into devotional texts written later in the century. Such is the case with the *Arte nuova del ben pensare e contemplare la passione del N.S. Jesu Christo* by Pietro Bernardo da' Lucca (with eight editions between 1525 and 1543)[57] and with the *Humanità di Cristo* by Pietro Aretino. Originally published in 1535, the latter text was one of Aretino's most criticised works, but also among those that enjoyed the longest *fortuna*: ten editions were published during his life and it continued to be printed, under the pseudonym of Partenio Etiro, even after its addition to the Roman *Index* in 1557. Here Aretino reported Nicodemus's role in the deposition of Christ (he called this act 'devoted and full of piety') and pointed out that Nicodemus had been a "secret disciple of Christ".[58]

A positive attitude towards Nicodemus was also shared in exegetical literature; this is the case in all of the most widely read medieval exegetical treatises and manuals. The current limits on space force me to offer here a very meagre selection, and I will confine myself to two of the most popular and well-read works; the *Postilla* by Nicholas of Lyra,[59] and the *Glossa ordinaria*, generally attributed to Anselm of Laon.[60] Both works deal at length with the figure of Nicodemus and explain his experience as a *crescendo*. Nicholas (commenting on *John* 3:1) points out that, at first, Nicodemus came to Jesus 'in secret' but

---

patavina e radicalismo spiritualistico nel XVI secolo", *Annali della Scuola normale superiore di Pisa* s.2 37 (1968) 288.

56   'Dixerunt Nichodemo. Tu discipulus eius es factus, & verbum pro ipso loquiris? Dixit ad eos Nichodemus, Nunquid & præses discipulis eius est? quia verbum pro ipso facit. Nunquid non constituit eum cesar super dignitatem istam? erant vero iudei frementes, & stridentes dentibus super Nicodemum, dicebant ei. Veritatem ipsisus accipias & portionem cum ipso, dixit Nichodemus. Amen, accipiam sicut dixistis'. *Opera nuper in lucem prodeuntia* [Venice, Giacomo da Leuco: 1522] f. Siiiir̄–Siiiiv.

57   See Jacobson Schutte, *Printed Italian Vernacular Religious Books* 75–76. I have checked the text in the edition: *Arte del ben pensare e contemplare la passione del N.S. Jesu Christo* (Venice, Alvise di Torti: 1535) f. 128r and f. 131r.

58   'un certo Nicodemo segreto discepolo di Cristo, andò a fare l'ufficio non men devoto che pietoso'. Aretino P., *L'umanità di Cristo* (s.l. [Rome]: 1945) 213.

59   For its popularity see Gosselin E.A., "A Listing of the Printed Editions of Nicolaus de Lyra", *Traditio* 26 (1970) 399–426.

60   Lobrichon G., "Latin Glosses on the Bible", in Vauchez A. (ed.), *Encyclopedia of the Middle Ages*, vol. 1 (Cambridge: 2000) 612–613 as well as Smalley B., *The Study of the Bible in the Middle Ages* (Notre Dame: 1964) 46–66.

'in order to be fully instructed'.[61] Then, after *John* 7:50, Nicodemus is somebody who 'secretly believed in him',[62] and finally, after the deposition, he is said to be an 'occult disciple' who has revealed himself.[63] Anselm then stresses that Nicodemus recognised Jesus as 'the son of God',[64] and presents him as a *figura* of all the Jews who believed in Jesus by faith, 'per fidem'.[65]

Due to the restrictions of space, I cannot offer a sustained analysis of humanist scholarship on the scriptural Nicodemus, although it does not greatly differ from the medieval work. In this case, too, I will limit the discussion to two examples from some of the most widely read authors: the Italian Dominican Tommaso de Vio, also known as Cajetan,[66] and Erasmus.[67] In the *Evangelia cum commentariis* (1530) by Cajetan, Nicodemus is depicted as somebody who was originally hindered by his fear of human judgment,[68] but who soon abandoned his hesitations and recognised Jesus as the Saviour. A similar position was shared by Erasmus. Accused of having acted as a Nicodemus,[69] Erasmus dealt with the figure in the *In evangelium Johannis paraphrasis*. Here Nicodemus is at first scared:

> He came to Jesus—we read—but at night. He showed in his action that he was still weak and wavering in love for Jesus, whom he did not admire enough to suffer a loss in his own position in society for Jesus' sake or on Jesus' account to be subjected to the malice of his own class. But it was fear rather than impiety, and a human kind of embarrassment rather than perversity.[70]

---

61   'Iste Nicodemus venit ad Iesum in secreto et extra tubam aliorum, ut ab ipso plenius instrueretur'. Nicholas of Lyra, *Postilla super totam Bibliam, Straßburg 1492*, vol. 4 (Frankfurt am Main: 1971) f. tij*v*.

62   'occulte credebat in eum'. Nicholas of Lyra, *Postilla* f. [Svii]v.

63   'erat Christi discipulus occultus. sed post passionem ex fervore se manifestavit'. Nicholas of Lyra, *Postilla*, f. riij*r*.

64   'Et quia dixerat de Filio hominis, ne hoc solum putet Nicodemus, subdit eumdem etiam essere Filium Dei'. Strabo W., *Opera Omnia*, ed. J.-P. Migne, vol. 2 (Paris: 1852) 368.

65   'Nicodemus, victoria populi, vel victor populi gestans figuram ominium qui ex Judaico populo in Christum credentes per fidem vincunt mundum'. Strabo, *Opera Omnia* 366.

66   See O' Connor M., "Cajetan on Paul", in Ward Holder R., (ed.) *A Companion to Paul in the Reformation* (Leiden: 2009) 337–362 and De Tanoüarn G., *Cajétan, le personnalisme intégral* (Paris: 2009).

67   See Seidel Menchi S., *Erasmo in Italia, 1520–1580* (Turin: 1987).

68   'Timor seu respectus humanus detinens Nicodemum a manifesto discepulatu Christi'. Cajetan Thomas., *Evangelia cum Commentariis* (Venice, Lucantonio Giunti: 1530) f. 147r.

69   Eire, *War against the Idols* 243.

70   'adijt Iesum, sed nocte, re declarans quod imbecillus ac uacillans adhuc esset in amore erga Iesum, quem hactenus admirabatur, ut tamen nollet eius causa suæ gloriæ iacturam

Then Erasmus depicts him as 'a secret disciple of Jesus',[71] up until Nicodemus's public manifestation at the moment at the deposition.

Until now I have only addressed those works which could have been easily accessed with no fear of persecution by Catholic authorities. Those interested in Calvin's positions, however, did not necessarily limit their readings to licit literature. It might be worthwhile then to make a brief survey of illicit works as well. Nicodemus is mentioned twice in the *Sommario della Sacra Scrittura*, a text of Protestant propaganda that circulated widely in Italy from the early 1530s, and that likely had five editions;[72] the *Sommario* does not pause over the figure of Nicodemus; however, he plays a role as Jesus's interlocutor at two significant points: one in a discussion about the value of the sacrament of baptism[73] (and these were the years of the Anabaptist crisis) and the other about the value of the faith in Jesus, since 'those who believe in him will not be condemned'.[74] Another text is much more striking. In 1543, Bernardo Ochino published a collection of sermons that enjoyed several reprints.[75] The fifteenth, *Del triompho della fede*, is highly remarkable. The sermon is constructed as a *climax* of Old and New Testament examples on the topic of faith and it ends with the very example of Joseph of Arimathea and Nicodemus: 'let us recognise in Joseph and Nicodemus the virtue of the faith, since in that time it was not without danger, or shame, that people might call themselves friends of Jesus. The two revealed themselves as loving disciples and asked Pilate for the body of Jesus'.[76] The sermon seems to rely on earlier sources on the figure of Nicodemus—hardly surprising, given that Ochino was a Capuchin friar who would have been imbued with this kind of reading. What is remarkable,

---

apud homines facere, nec eius gratia in sui ordinis inuidiam pertrahi. Metus autem erat potius, quam impietas, & pudor humanus uerius, quam peruersitas', Erasmus Desiderius, *Paraphrasis in evangelium secundum Johannem* (Basel, Johann Froben: 1523) f. 30r-v.

71   'clancularius Iesu discipulus'. Erasmus, *Paraphrasis in evangelium* f. 190r. The translations are taken from Erasmus D., *Paraphrase on John*, trans. and annot. J.E. Phillips (Toronto – Buffalo – London: 1991).

72   See Peyronel Rambaldi S., *Dai Paesi Bassi all'Italia. «Il Sommario della Sacra scrittura». Un libro proibito nella società italiana del Cinquecento* (Florence: 1997).

73   Peyronel Rambaldi, *Dai Paesi Bassi all'Italia* 285.

74   Peyronel Rambaldi, *Dai Paessi Bassi all'Italia* 305–306.

75   See Jacobson Schutte, *Printed Italian Vernacular Religious Books* 284–285. On Ochino, see Bainton R.H., *Bernardino Ochino esule e riformatore senese del Cinquecento, 1487–1563* (Florence 1940) and Williams G.G., *The Theology of Bernardino Ochino* (Tübingen 1959).

76   'si veda in Ioseph, & Nicodemo, la virtu della fede, da poi, che in quel medesimo tempo, nel quale non era chi senza suo gran pericolo, & vergogna, potesse demostrarsi amico di Christo, epsi scuprendosi per suoi amereuoli discipuli, domandorno a Pilato el corpo de Iesu'. Ochino Bernardino, *Sermones* (s.l.t. [Geneva, Jean Gerard]: 1543) f. lz2v.

however, is how Ochino—one of the most popular Italian religious writers of the early century, at the time a Calvinist himself, and having already escaped from Italy *religionis causa* by the time he published his work—presents Nicodemus as one of the most vivid examples (also due to the position of the quotation inside the sermon) of the 'virtue of the faith'. In this work, written before the publication of Calvin's *Excuse*, Nicodemus is also presented as an example of a disciple of Jesus who, despite the danger, has the courage to publicly show his faith.

It was only few years later, in 1547, that Antonio Brucioli published his *Commento in tutti i Sacrosanti libri del Vecchio, et Nuovo Testamento*. Together with other translations, vulgarisations and commentaries on the Scriptures, it enjoyed vast popularity.[77] It deserves special attention here, however, because its author—who had translated several passages of Calvin's *Institutio* into Italian[78]—was himself a crypto-Calvinist[79] and was avidly read by other supporters of the Reformer.[80] At first Nicodemus is represented as a man who believes that he might be saved by "his own works",[81] but, in commenting on

---

77   Fragnito, *La censura ecclesiastica*.

78   See Bozza T., *Calvino in Italia* (Rome: 1966) 3–10.

79   See Spini G., *Tra Rinascimento e Riforma, Antonio Brucioli* (Florence: s.d. [1940]). In
      1534 Brucioli translated into Italian the *Praecationes biblicae sanctorum patrum* by Otto
      Brunfels (Ginzburg, *Il nicodemismo* 101), however, it has been suggested that Brucioli was
      against a dissimulating practice. See Colangeli N., "L'antinicodemismo di Antonio Brucioli
      nell'interpretazione del *Libro di Iob*", *Dimensioni e Problemi della Ricerca Storica* 1 (1998)
      153–167. If this were the case then his positive remarks about Nicodemus would be even
      more significant.

80   Brucioli was also put under trial. See Del Col A., "Il controllo della stampa a Venezia e i
      processi di Antonio Brucioli", *Critica storica* 17 (1980) 457–510. We also find his name in the
      Costituti by Manelfi: 'Antonio Bruzzoli, Lutherano'. Ginzburg, *I costituti* 49.

81   'Questa disputa di Christo con Nicodemo è di sparere della sapientia, & giustitia della
      carne con la sapientia, & giustitia dello spirito, perche variano l'humana ragione, &
      Christo del modo della giustificatione. La ragione pensa di giustificarsi, se udendo la legge
      imita le opere sue. Tale è qui Nicodemo homo sapiente & inreprensibile al mondo. Esso
      per se si sforza di adempiere la legge, & simula le esteriori opere della legge, & pensasi per
      quelle essere giusto avanti a Iddio, perche non violo' la legge con alcuna opera esteriore.
      Et cosi questo Nicodemo venne primieramente a Giesu, accioche divenisse certo della
      dottrina della vita, perche era in qualche parte intento allo studio di Iddio. Questo
      Nicodemo, benche fusse fra pharisei gravissimi nimici di Christo, nondimeno il seme di
      Iddio, che era in questo Nicodemo vinceva tutto questo rispetto, & fece che da segni, che
      faceva il Signore, fussi gia persuaso che il Signore venissi da Iddio dottore, & maestro da
      doversi udire da tutti. Et cosi come è detto, questo luogo contiene egregia & notabile
      disputa fra la giustitia dello spirito & la giustitia della carne, Christo insegna, & defende

John 7:50–51, Brucioli returns to him. With the *Glossa ordinaria* presumably as his source, Brucioli lets Nicodemus serve as an example of 'how the seed of God bears fruit in his own people', since in turning away from his original position, Nicodemus has finally become a true believer of Christ. Nicodemus is even a model of how it is possible to become a true follower of Christ despite the original 'infirmity of his own faith'.[82]

Conclusion

I began this article by asking what sources Italians interested in Nicodemus and the Nicodemites would have used, since they could not have directly accessed Calvin's works—the *Excuse*, at least, is unlikely to have circulated widely in Italy. If they had turned to the devotional and exegetical literature more easily available at the time they would have gained a purely positive understanding of the scriptural character. The influence of this literature must still be studied in detail; however, we can state that for these contemporary readers Nicodemus would have been an example of someone initially weak in his faith but who, with time, reached a proper understanding of the true nature of Jesus and, finally, felt ready to follow him, despite the risks. This impression would not have been altered by consulting philo-Reformed works such as those of Ochino and Brucioli.

Since we are using an *argumentum e silentio*, it is hard to estimate the role played by this kind of literature in Calvin's reception; however, we may offer a

---

la giustitia dello spirito, & l'altra, cioè la carnale piglia a difendere Nicodemo, nondimeno non con quella pertinacia, che non voglia essere ammaestrato, & instrutto per la quale cosa [. . .]Et per questo vuole anchora Christo che quel vecchio Adam si mortifichi in noi, & divegnamo nuove creature, & di questa nuova regeneratione niente ne fa la carne, & la nostra natura, il che dichiara qui Nicodemo stando in su la giustitia delle proprie opere'. *Commento di Antonio Brucioli. In tutti i Sacrosanti libri del Vecchio, et Nuovo Testamento, dalla Hebraica verità et fonte greco per esso tradotti in lingua Toscana* 7 vols. (Venice, Alessandro and Francesco Brucioli: 1542–1546 [1547]), vol. 4, f. 198r-v.

82   '& cosi si vede anchora qui in Nicodemo come il seme di Iddio fruttifichi nel popolo suo, non voleva questo manifestarsi accostarsi a Christo, nondimeno non potette lasciarlo in tutto, credeva certamente in esso, benche infermamente, ma non havendo ardire oppose la legge la quale comanda che si faccia il giudicio giusto, & che nessuno si condanni se non convinto, & per questo tanto fece che non statuirno in quel concilio cosa alcuna contro al Signore. onde si vede questo Nicodemo havere operato alcuno frutto in questa pericolosa conditione di huomini, & nella infermita de la fede sua'. *Commento di Antonio Brucioli* IV 215r.

few considerations. As Ochino proves especially well, before Calvin had published his *Excuse*, Nicodemus was regarded also by staunch Italian Calvinists (clearly not having picked up the previous European debate)[83] as a positive figure. Whether Brucioli had read the *Excuse* when the time came to publish his commentary in 1547 cannot be stated with certainty; but since he does not spend any words defending Nicodemus against his detractors, it seems more plausible that he had not. Whether he had at least heard of it, the devotional and exegetical literature that he knew so well might have suggested a positive, rather than a negative, idea of Nicodemus. At least in one case, however, I suggest that these works certainly influenced one of their philo-Reformed readers. The aforementioned text by Vergerio, *Al serenissimo re d'Inghilterra*, (where we read that 'although [some prelates] act like Nicodemus, they love the glory of the world more than the glory of God") serves as confirmation that a positive interpretation of the figure of Nicodemus, and, most important, of his imitators, was easily reached.

Bibliography

Acerbi A., "Antonio de Fantis, editore della *Visio Isaiae*", *Aevum* 57 (1983) 396–415.

Aretino P., *L'umanità di Cristo* (s.l. [Rome]: 1945).

Bainton R.H., *Bernardino Ochino esule e riformatore senese del Cinquecento, 1487–1563* (Florence: 1940).

Barbieri E., "Fra tradizione e cambiamento: note sul libro spirituale italiano del XVI secolo", in Barbieri E – D. Zardin (eds.), *Libri, biblioteche e cultura nell'Italia del Cinque e Seicento* (Milan: 2002) 3–61.

Biondi A., "La giustificazione della simulazione nel Cinquecento", in *Eresia e Riforma nell'Italia del Cinquecento* (Florence – Chicago: 1974) 5–68.

Bozza T., *Calvino in Italia* (Rome: 1966).

Brucioli Antonio, *Commento di Antonio Brucioli. In tutti i Sacrosanti libri del Vecchio, et Nuovo Testamento, dalla Hebraica verità et fonte greco per esso tradotti in lingua Toscana* 7 vols. (Venice, Alessandro and Francesco Brucioli: 1542–1546 [1547]).

Cajetan Thomas, *Evangelia cum Commentariis* (Venice, Lucantonio Giunti: 1530).

Calvin John, *De vitandis superstitionibus, quae cum sincera fidei confessione pugnant, libellus Joannis Calvini. Eiusdem excusatio, ad pseudonicodemos. Philippi Melancthonis, Martini Buceri, Petri Martyris responsa de eadem re. Calvini ultimum responsum, cum appendicibus* (Geneva, Jean Gerard: 1549).

---

83   See Eire, *War against the Idols* 242–243.

————, *Opera Quae Supersunt Omnia*, eds. W. Baum – E. Cunitz – E. Reuss (Brunswick: 1863–1880).

————, *Come Out from Among Them: 'Anti-Nicodemite' Writings of John Calvin*, ed. S. Skolnitsky (Dallas: 2001).

Cantimori D., *Eretici italiani del Cinquecento. Ricerche storiche* (Florence: 1939).

————, "Nicodemismo e speranze conciliari nel Cinquecento italiano", *Quaderni di Belfagor* 1 (1948) 12–23.

————, *Prospettive di storia ereticale italiana del Cinquecento* (Bari: 1960).

Caravale G., *L'orazione proibita. Censura ecclesiastica e letteratura devozionale nella prima età moderna* (Florence: 2003).

Cavazza S., "Una vicenda europea. Vergerio e il caso Spiera, 1548–49", in Dall'Olio G. – Malena A. – Scaramella P. (eds.), *Per Adriano Prosperi. La fede degli italiani* (Pisa: 2011) 41–51.

————, "Pier Paolo Vergerio", in M. Biagioni et al. (eds.), Fratelli d'Italia. Riformatori italiani nel Cinquecento (Turin: 2011) 145–152.

Cocco M.M., *Sigismondo Arquer dagli studi giovanili all'autodafé* (Cagliari: 1987).

Colangeli N., "L'antinicodemismo di Antonio Brucioli nell'interpretazione del *Libro di Iob*", *Dimensioni e Problemi della Ricerca Storica* 1 (1998) 153–167.

Comba E., *Francesco Spiera. Episodio della riforma religiosa in Italia. Con aggiunta di documenti originali tratti dall'Archivio veneto del S. Ufficio* (Rome – Florence: 1872).

De Tanoüarn G., *Cajétan, le personnalisme intégral* (Paris: 2009).

Del Col A., "Per una sistemazione critica dell'evangelismo italiano e di un'opera recente", *Critica storica* 17 (1980) 266–275.

————, "Il controllo della stampa a Venezia e i processi di Antonio Brucioli", *Critica storica* 17 (1980) 457–510.

di Filippo Bareggi C., *Il mestiere di scrivere. Lavoro intellettuale e mercato librario a Venezia nel Cinquecento* (Rome: 1988).

Droz E., *Chemins de l'hérésie. Textes et documents*, vol. 1 (Geneva: 1970).

Eire C.M.N., "Calvin and Nicodemism: A Reappraisal", *The Sixteenth Century Journal* 10 (1979) 45–69.

————, *War against the Idols: The Reformation of Worship from Erasmus to Calvin* (Cambridge: 1986).

Erasmus Desiderius, *Paraphrasis in evangelium secundum Johannem* (Basel, Johann Froben: 1523).

Felici L., *Giovanni Calvino e l'Italia* (Turin: 2010).

Firpo M., *Tra alumbrados e «spirituali». Studi su Juan de Valdés e il valdesimo nella crisi religiosa del '500 italiano* (Florence: 1990).

————, "Alcune considerazioni sull'esperienza religiosa di Sigismondo Arquer", *Rivista Storica Italiana* 105 (1993) 411–475.

———, *Riforma protestante ed eresie nell'Italia del Cinquecento. Un profilo storico* (Rome – Bari: 1993).

———, *Vittore Soranzo vescovo ed eretico. Riforma della Chiesa e Inquisizione nell'Italia del Cinquecento* (Rome – Bari: 2006).

———, "Calvino e la riforma radicale: le opere contro nicodemiti, anabattisti e libertini (1544–1545)", *Studi Storici* 48 (2007) 97–105.

Fraenkel P., "Bucer's Memorandum of 1541 and a « Lettera nicodemitica » of Capito's", *Bibliothèque d'Humanisme et Renaissance* 36 (1974) 575–587.

Fragnito G., "Gli «spirituali» e la fuga di Bernardino Ochino", *Rivista Storica Italiana* 84 (1972) 777–813.

———, *La censura ecclesiastica e i volgarizzamenti della Scrittura (1471–1605)* (Bologna: 1997).

Garavelli E., *Lodovico Domenichi e i « Nicodemiana » di Calvino. Storia di un libro perduto e ritrovato* (Manziana: 2004).

George T., "Nicodemism", in Hillerbrand H.J. (ed.), The Oxford Encyclopedia of the Reformation, vol. 3 (New York – Oxford: 1996) 144–145.

Ginzburg C., *Il nicodemismo. Simulazione e dissimulazione religiosa nell'Europa del Cinquecento* (Turin: 1970).

———, *I costituti di don Pietro Manelfi* (Florence – Chicago: 1970).

Gosselin E.A., "A Listing of the Printed Editions of Nicolaus de Lyra", *Traditio* 26 (1970) 399–426.

Grendler P.F., *The Roman Inquisition and the Venetian Press, 1540–1605* (Princeton: 1977).

Higman F.M., "The Question of Nicodemism", in Neuser W.H. (ed.), *Calvinus Ecclesiae Genevensis Custos. Die Referate des Congrès International des Recherches Calviniennes vom 6–9 September 1982 in Genf* (Frankfurt am Main: 1984) 165–170.

———, "Calvin's works in translation", in *Lire et découvrir. La circulation des idées au temps de la Réforme* (Geneva: 1998) 545–562.

———, "Bucer et les Nicodemites", in Krieger C. – Lienhard, M. (eds.), *Martin Bucer and Sixteenth Century Europe. Actes du colloque de Strasbourg (28–31 août 1991)*, vol. 2 (Leiden: 1993) 645–658.

Iannucci A.I., "The Gospel, of Nicodemus in Medieval Italian Literature: A Preliminary Assessment", in Izydorczyk, Z. (ed.), *The Medieval Gospel of Nicodemus: Texts, Intertexts, and Contexts in Western Europe* (Tempe: 1997) 165–205.

Jacobson Schutte A., *Pier Paolo Vergerio: The Making of an Italian Reformer* (Geneva: 1977).

———, *Printed Italian Vernacular Religious Books, 1465–1550: A Finding List.* (Geneva: 1983).

———, "Periodization of Sixteenth-Century Italian Religious History: The Post-Cantimori Paradigm Shift", *Journal of Modern History* 61 (1989) 269–284.

John of Caulibus, *Meditaciones vite Christi, olim S. Bonaventuro attributae*, ed. M. Stallings-Taney (Turnhout: 1997).

Lobrichon G., "Latin Glosses on the Bible", in Vauchez, A. (ed.), *Encyclopedia of the Middle Ages*, vol. 1 (Cambridge: 2000) 612–613.

Lorenzi R.A., "Per un profilo di Massimiliano Celso Martinengo, riformatore", in Lorenzi R.A. (ed.), *Riformatori bresciani del '500. Indagini* (Brescia: 2006) 105–168.

Ludolph of Saxony, *Vita Christi*, 5 vols. (Salzburg: 2006).

Martin J.J., V*enice's Hidden Enemies: Italian Heretics in a Renaissance City* (Baltimore: 1993).

Mongini G., *«Ad Christi similitudinem». Ignazio di Loyola e i primi gesuiti tra eresia e ortodossia. Studi sulle origini della Compagnia di Gesù* (Alessandria: 2011).

Nicholas of Lyra, *Postilla super totam Bibliam, Straßburg 1492*, vol. 4 (Frankfurt am Main: 1971).

Ochino Bernardino, *Sermones* (s.l.t. [Geneva, Jean Gerard]: 1543).

O'Connor M., "Cajetan on Paul", in Ward Holder R. (ed.), *A Companion to Paul in the Reformation* (Leiden: 2009) 337–362.

Opera nuper in lucem prodeuntia (Venice, Giacomo da Leuco: 1522).

Overell M.A., "The Exploitation of Francesco Spiera", *The Sixteenth Century Journal* 26 (1995) 619–637.

Pascal A., "Una breve polemica tra il Riformatore Celso Martinengo e Fra Angelo Castiglioni da Genova (sec. XVI)", *Bulletin de la Société d'Histoire Vaudoise* 35 (1915) 77–89.

Peter R. – Gilmont J.-F., *Bibliotheca Calviniana. Les oeuvres de Jean Calvin publiées au XVIe siècle*, vol. 1 (Geneva: 1970).

Pettegree A., "Nicodemism and the English Reformation", in *Marian Protestantism: Six Studies* (Aldershot: 1996) 86–117.

Peyronel Rambaldi S., "Ancora sull'evangelismo italiano: categoria o invenzione storiografica?", *Società e storia* 18 (1982) 935–967.

———, *Dai Paesi Bassi all'Italia. «il Sommario della Sacra scrittura». Un libro proibito nella società italiana del Cinquecento* (Florence: 1997).

Pierce R.A., *Pier Paolo Vergerio: The Propagandist* (Rome: 2003).

Pietro Bernardo da' Lucca, *Arte del ben pensare e contemplare la passione del N.S. Jesu Christo* (Venice, Alvise di Torti: 1535).

Prosperi A., *L'eresia del Libro Grande. Storia di Giorgio Siculo e della sua setta* (Milan: 2000).

Rotondò A., "Atteggiamenti della vita morale italiana del Cinquecento. La pratica nicodemitica", *Rivista Storica Italiana* 79 (1967) 991–1030.

Rozzo U. – Seidel Menchi S., "Livre et Réforme en Italie", in Gilmont, J.-F. (ed.), *La Réforme et le livre. L'Europe de l'imprimé (1517–v. 1570)* (Paris: 1990) 327–374.

Scrimgeour Henry, *Exemplum memorabile desperationis in Francisco Spiera, propter abiuratam fidei confessionem, cum praefatione D. Joannis Calvini* (Geneva, Jean Girard: 1550).

Seidel Menchi S., *Erasmo in Italia, 1520–1580* (Turin: 1987).

Shrimplin-Evangelidis V., "Michelangelo and Nicodemism: The Florentine Pietà", *Art Bulletin* 71 (1989) 58–66.

Smalley B., *The Study of the Bible in the Middle Ages* (Notre Dame: 1964).

Sozzini L., *Opere*, ed. A. Rotondò (Florence: 1986).

Spini G., *Tra Rinascimento e Riforma, Antonio Brucioli* (Florence: s.d. [1940]).

Stella A., "Tradizione razionalistica patavina e radicalismo spiritualistico nel XVI secolo", *Annali della Scuola normale superiore di Pisa* s.2 37 (1968) 275–302.

Strabo W., *Opera Omnia*, ed. J.-P. Migne, vol. 2 (Paris: 1852).

Vaccari A., "Le *Meditazioni della vita di Cristo* in volgare", in *Scritti di erudizione e filologia*, vol. 1 (Rome: 1952) 341–378.

Vergerio Pier Paolo, *Al Serenissimo re d'Inghilterra Edoardo Sesto. De portamenti di Papa Giulio III. Et quale habbia ad essere il concilio che egli intende di fare* (s.l.t. [Poschiavo, Dolfin Landolfi]: 1550).

———, *La historia di M. Francesco Spiera, il quale per havere in varij modi nagata la conosciuta verità dell'Evangelio, cascò in una misera desperatione* (s.l.t. [Poschiavo, Dolfin Landolfi]: 1551).

Walker D., "Pier Paolo Vergerio (1498–1465) e il «Caso Spiera» (1548)", *Studi di teologia* 10 (1998) 3–83.

White R., "Calvin, the Nicodemites and the Cost of Discipleship", *Reformed Theological Review* 56 (1997) 14–27.

———, "Calvin and the Nicodemite Controversy: An Overlooked Text of 1541", *Calvin Theological Journal* 35 (2000) 282–296.

Williams G.G., *The Theology of Bernardino Ochino* (Tübingen 1959).

Zardin D., "Bibbia e letteratura religiosa in volgare nell'Italia del Cinque-Seicento", *Annali di Storia moderna e contemporanea* 4 (1998) 593–616.

Zarri G., "Note su diffusione e circolazione di testi devoti (1520–1550)", in Biondi A. – Prosperi A. (eds.), *Libri, idee e sentimenti religiosi nel Cinquecento italiano* (Modena: 1987) 131–154.

Zuliani F., "I *libertini* di Giovanni Calvino. Ricezione ed utilizzo polemico di un termine neotestamentario", *Archiv für Reformationsgeschichte* 104 (2013) 211–244.

CHAPTER 13

'What's Learnt in the Cradle Lasts till the Tomb': Counter-Reformation Strategies in the Southern Low Countries to Entice the Youth into Religious Reading

Hubert Meeus

From the moment the Catholic Church had to compete with Protestantism, it soon understood the importance of teaching children the principles of faith as early as possible. For this purpose Luther had developed a very efficient method, namely his Catechism.[1] Despite its Protestant origin this interactive learning system based on question and answer was soon adopted by the Roman Catholic Church. Youngsters between seven and twelve years of age were considered an optimal target group for learning. Religious education in primary schools up to about the age of fifteen consisted mainly in the memorization of Catechism questions.[2] As to the question whether it was also necessary that pupils actually understood what they studied by heart, the educators were not in agreement.[3] Sunday schools in particular adopted this memorization method which was, because of the emphasis on orality, very suitable for reaching illiterate children. They targeted children who mostly were too poor to attend ordinary schools, and their program almost exclusively consisted of learning the Catechism.[4]

---

1 Strauss G., *Luther's House of Learning. Indoctrination of the Young in the German Reformation* (Baltimore – London: 1978).

2 Henrivaux O., "Méthodes catéchistiques aux xvie–xviiie siècles dans les diocèses de Cambrai, Namur, Tournai et Liège", *Lumen vitae* 36 (1981) 57–97, here 64; Put E., *De cleijne schoolen. Het volksonderwijs in het hertogdom Brabant tussen Katholieke Reformatie en Verlichting (eind 16de eeuw–1795)* (Leuven: 1990) 208–211.

3 Henrivaux, "Méthodes catéchistiques" 62 ; Put, *De cleijne schoolen* 210.

4 Put, *De cleijne schoolen* 104–106; Van Roey E., "L'enseignement du catéchisme dans les anciens diocèses de Malines et d'Anvers", *La vie diocésaine* 5 (1911) 219–220.

Attractive Catechism Lessons

To attract pupils it was necessary to make and to keep Catechism lessons appealing. The Calvinist Philips van Marnix van Sint Aldegonde suggested adding an element of competition: 'Dans ces exercises, on les fera rivaliser entre eux, ou bien leurs maîtres les interrogeront, ou bien encore ils interrogeront eux-mêmes leurs maîtres'.[5] The Jesuit Philippe d'Outreman (1588–1652) advised illustrating the lessons with stories of miraculous events or warning examples of those who did not comply with the rules. These stories showed their audience a wonderful world full of improbabilities and supernatural forces. The virtually literary stories were sometimes a far cry from the message of the Gospel.[6] Antoine d' Averoult, rector of the college of the Falcon at Louvain until his entrance in the order of the Jesuits in 1600, offered several hundreds of short histories, which could serve as examples to all parts of the Catechism, in his collection *Fleurs des exemples, ou: Catéchisme historial, contenant plusieurs beaux miracles et excellents discours* [...] (Douai, Jean Bogart: 1603).[7]

Another way to make Catechism lessons attractive was the singing of religious songs set to popular melodies. Songs were very suitable for evoking feelings, refreshing memory and teaching. They made the students more enthusiastic to participate and helped in teaching the rules of faith.[8] As early as 1571 the Antwerp Bishop Franciscus Sonnius published *Een bequaem maniere om ionghers soetelyck by sanck te leeren 'tghene dat alle kersten menschen moeten weten* (A proper way to sweetly teach youngsters by singing what all Christian people have to know) (Antwerp: Widow of Ameet Tavernier). The booklet, counting only fourteen pages, contained a sung version of the Lord's Prayer, the Hail Mary, the Creed, and the Ten Commandments.[9]

In *Het prieel der gheestelijcke melodie* (The arbour of sacred melody) (Bruges, Pieter Soetaert: 1609) the Jesuit Bernardus Bauhusius introduced a new genre, the 'catechesatielied' ('catechizing song'). This kind of song expresses an almost literal interpretation of a Bible passage, a rhymed version of an existing

5   Marnix de Sainte Aldegonde, Philippe de, *Traité d'éducation de la jeunesse*, ed. J. Catrysse (Brussels: 1959) 52.

6   Henrivaux, "Méthodes catéchistiques" 76–78.

7   Backer A. de – Sommervogel C., *Bibliothèque de la Compagnie de Jésus* (Heverlee – Leuven: 1960) vol. I, 685–686.

8   Henrivaux, "Méthodes catéchistiques" 78–80.

9   *Synodicon Belgicum, sive: Acta omnium Ecclesiarum Belgii a Concilio Tridentino usque ad Concordantum anni 1801*, vol. III: *Nova et Absoluta collectio Synodorum episcopatus Antverpiensis*, ed. P.F.X. de Ram (Leuven: 1858) 87–88, 67–71.

prayer or one or more lessons from the Catechism. The song book was primarily intended as a pedagogical means to make catechizing more attractive and more efficient. Bauhusius assumed that the words of the song 'penetrate more profoundly in the heart and take root more easily, because of the rhymes and the sweet melody, than when the same words were heard or read without poetry or music'.[10]

On occasion, the practice of illustrating the Catechism by showing pictures was brought alive by having the pupils act out small scenes.[11] Once a year, as an extra incentive, pupils who knew their Catechism very well received a prize. On a more material level, attempts were made to lure children to the Sunday school by giving them coins, bread or eggs, and conversely, by withholding alms from those who remained absent.[12]

The Importance of Reading Good Books

As long as the pupils were attending the weekly Catechism lessons, there was little need for concern. The Church worried mainly about the pupils who had finished Sunday schools at the age of fifteen. As they grew older and as their sexual awareness increased, their pliability also diminished and they were harder to educate.[13] On this group, the Church had much less firm a hold since it could no longer regularly assemble them. In his *Onderwys der jeught in de christelyke godtvruchtigheyt* (Education of the youth in the Christian piety) the French theologian Charles Gobinet pointed to the fact that one could not always remain under the care of priests and pastors. However, it was important that their 'lessons, examples, exhortations and pieces of advice'[14] were

---

10   All translations from Dutch are my own. '[…] veel dieper in 't herte valt ende veel meer beclijft, door de wel ghedichte rijmen ende soete melodie, dan oft deselve dinghen sonder ghedicht oft musijcke werden ghehoort oft ghelesen'. Bauhusius Bernardus, *Het prieel der gheestelijcke melodie* (Bruges: Pieter Soetaert, 1609) +2r; Therry M., *De religieuze beleving bij de leken in het 17de-eeuwse bisdom Brugge* (Brussels: 1988) 20.

11   Henrivaux, "Méthodes catéchistiques" 81–83.

12   Henrivaux, "Méthodes catéchistiques" 83–88.

13   Moore C.N., *The Maidens's Mirror. Reading Material for German Girls in the Sixteenth and Seventeenth Centuries*, Wolfenbütteler Forschungen 36 (Wiesbaden: 1987) 24.

14   'lessen, betooningen aen-maningen en raden'. Gobinet Charles, *Onderwys der jeucht in de christelyke godtvruchtigheyt, ghetrocken uyt de H. Schriftuere en HH. Vaders* (Antwerp [=Amsterdam], Joannes Stichter: 1697) 120. The French original *Instruction de la jeunesse en la piété chrétienne, tirée de l'Ecriture sainte et des saints Pères* was published in 1655.

regularly recollected. This could be taken care of by reading good books offering the same lessons.[15]

Similarly the Flemish Jesuit Joannes David stated in his *Christeliicken Waersegghher* (1602):

> as regards the Catechism, or Christian doctrine, I usually summarized it: more to freshen up what one has heard before and has learned elsewhere than to fully repeat what has hitherto so often been posited and published by others.[16]

The *Ratio studiorum* with the guidelines for the Jesuit education also recommends encouraging pupils to read good books, but preferably only under supervision:

> He [the professor of the Lower classes] should enthusiastically recommend spiritual reading, especially about the lives of the saints. And on the other hand, he should not only for his own part refrain from teaching to the young those writers that are not wholesome and avoid altogether those in whom there is anything that can be damaging to good morals, but he should also discourage students as much as he possibly can from reading them even outside of class.[17]

Dodin A., "Charles Gobinet", in *Dictionnaire de spiritualité ascétique et mystique: doctrine et histoire* (Paris: 1967) vol. VI, 543–545.

15   Gobinet, *Onderwys der jeucht* 120.

16   'Dat den Catechismus, oft Christelijcke leeringe aengaet, dat hebb' ick meest al in t' corte ghestelt: als meer dienende tot een ververschen van t'ghene, dat men te veuren ghehoort ende elders gheleert heeft, dan tot een nieuw her-nemen van t'ghene, d'welck soo wel ende soo menighvuldelijck van andere tot noch toe ghestelt ende uyt-ghegeven is gheweest'. David Joannes, *Christeliicken waerseggher, de principale stucken en t'christen geloof en leven int cort begrijpende. Met een rolle der deugtsaemheyt daer op dienende. Ende een schildt-wacht teghen de valsche waersegghers, tooveraers, etc.* (Antwerp, Jan Moerentorf: 1603) **3r.

17   *The Ratio studiorum. The official plan for Jesuit education*, trans. and annot. C. Pavur, S.J., Jesuit primary sources in English translation, Series 1, no. 22 (Saint Louis, MO: 2005). 'Regulae Communes Professoribus Classium inferiorum, 8 Lectio spiritualis: Lectionem spiritualem, praesertim de sanctorum vitis, vehementer commendet; contra vero non solum ipse ab impuris scriptoribus omnino in quibus sit aliquid, quod bonis moribus nocere queat, iuventuti prealegendis abstineat, sed ab iisdem etiam extra scholam legendis discipulos, quam maxime potest, deterreat'. *Ratio studiorum: plan raisonné et*

The Church was well aware of the necessity of adolescents reading religious books. Reading aided in keeping girls and boys occupied and thereby preventing less acceptable activities. It was not considered to be a passive absorption of written material but rather a social activity that involved not only independent reading, but reading aloud, rereading, memorization, recitation and discussion. In this way, the reading material would continue to occupy their thoughts long after the book had been closed.[18]

Convincing Young People to Read Religious Books

The only problem here is the question of how to convince young people of the usefulness of reading religious books. There are, after all, so many other amusing activities. In a booklet which appeared around 1743 as a New Year's present, offered to the members of the sodality of married men, Joannes Delvigne treats this problem in the twentyfirst chapter: 'A means to promote education, by reading good books'.[19] Delvigne considers it important to instil in children already from an early age a tendency towards reading good books. Parents can encourage reading by pointing to its usefulness, by praising their children if they read and by promising them a reward.[20] Parents can be read to by their children and they should indicate that they enjoy this very much. In addition, they had to ensure that the books were 'fraey gebonden' ('nicely bound') so that they looked appealing.[21] Delvigne also indicates what is best for young people to read:

> some lives of Saints, or sacred histories; because they are more favourably disposed towards them, and this way they will easily be attracted to read other books that teach them a proper life. Give them some small

  institution des études dans la Compagnie de Jésus, eds. A. Demoustier – J. Dominique et al. (Paris: 1997) 153.

18   Moore, *The Maidens's Mirror* 34.

19   'Eenen middel om de onderwysingen te vervoorderen, in het lesen van goede boecken'. Delvigne Joannes, *Christelycke opvoedinge, dienende soo voor de ouders, meesters, meesterssen, etc. als voor de kinderen, op-gedragen voor een nieuw-jaer aen de Sodaliteyt der getrouwde, onder den tytel vande Boodtschap vande Alderheylighste Maghet Maria, in 't professie-huys der Sociëteyt Jesu* (Antwerp, Widow of Hieronymus Verdussen: [c. 1743]) 56.

20   Delvigne, *Christelycke opvoedinge* 56.

21   Delvigne, *Christelycke opvoedinge* 57.

booklets, or books which are divided into small chapters; because they are naturally inclined to something new, and to have it done quickly.[22]

Gobinet encourages the young people to seek wisdom because those who have done that during their youth will be blessed.[23] To be sure that the reading is useful Gobinet requires a special reading attitude of adolescents:

> Firstly, that you read the lessons with three attitudes: with desire to learn, with attention and with order, that is reading the chapters sequentially. Secondly, that you are aware, that it is not me, you are reading, but God [...] consequently read with all the reverence which you owe to this Master who is worthy of adoration.[24]

Gobinet also gives the young people seven directives they have to keep in mind for their reading to produce the desired result. These begin with understanding that pure curiosity must not be the motive for reading, for reading can only have the intention of learning lessons that can improve life, and therefore one should begin with reading a short prayer. As Gobinet explains:

> 1. Do not read out of curiosity, but with a desire to learn to live properly.[25] [...] 2. Read with much respect, because it is God who speaks to you. [...] 3. Do not read many books, but only one or two that are well suited to give rise to virtue: [such as *The Confessions* of St Augustine, the *Imitatio Christi* by Thomas a Kempis or *Den grooten leytsman der sondaren* ('The guide for sinners') by Ludovicus Granatensis.] 4. Read with order,

---

22 'eenige levens van Heyligen, oft Geestelijcke Historien; want hier toe zijn sy lichter genegen: en door het lesen van dese, sullen sy licht getrocken worden om ooc andere boecken, die hun tot een goet leven onderwysen, te lesen. Geeft hun eenige kleyne boecxkens, oft die in kleyne Capittelen verdeylt zijn; want natuerelijck zijn sy genegen tot iets nieuws, en om haest gedaen te hebben'. Delvigne, *Christelycke opvoedinge* 57.

23 Gobinet, *Onderwys der jeucht* *4r.

24 'i dat gy 't onderwijs leest met dry ghesteltenissen: met begeerte van te leeren, met op merckinge en met order, dat is de delen lesende achter malkander. Ten tweeden dat gy u in bemerkinge neemt, dat ik het niet en ben, die u leest, maer Godt [...] leest het by ghevolgh met al d'eerbiedigheyt, die gy ze schuldig sijt aen desen aenbiddelijcken meester'. Gobinet, *Onderwys der jeucht* *3v–*4r.

25 'i. Leest niet uyt nieuwsgierigheyt, en dat maar met begeerte van wel te leeren leven'. Gobinet, *Onderwys der jeucht* 120.

[i.e. from front to back.] [...] 5. Read every time little, but slowly and with attention. [...] 6. Read often, that is every day, or several times per week, mainly on Sundays and on feast days. 7. You should not be satisfied by having read a book once, but you should reread it several times.[26]

In reading this way, young people will understand the book better and it will be easier for them to remember.

Encouraging them to read is not without risk, however, because not all reading matter is suitable. Gobinet distinguishes four kinds of 'quade boecken' ('evil books') that must be avoided at all costs: all heretical books; all wicked books mocking religion, sacred objects and also priests and religious persons; unchaste wanton books; and books dealing with 'minneryen' ('love'), even if they use no indecent language, as there are many Latin, French and Dutch poets who write about love in this manner. These books are more dangerous than those in the third category, which by their explicitness often spontaneously provoke a distaste. Therefore Gobinet gives a further warning:

> but this kind of book seeming in principle not very dangerous, lures the intellect by its genteel wording and by the sweetness of the subjects which are treated. As the sense take delight in it, they inflame the fire of the impure love in the heart.[27]

Gobinet recommends that it is best to possess no such books because then you are not tempted to read them, and you also run no risk of committing a sin. He would not hear of the arguments that these books can also be read for their

---

26   '2. Leest met veel eerbiedigheydt; aenmerckende dat het Godt is, die in uwen boeck tot u sprekt [...] 3. Leest niet veel boecken, maer slechts een oft twee die goet gevonden en bequaem zijn om u tot de deugt te verwecken: [...] 4. Leest met order. [...] 5. Leest inder keer weynigh, maer langsaem en met aendacht. [...] 6. Leest dickwils, dat is alle dagen, of eenige reysen ter weke, voornamentlijk op Sondagen en Feest-daghen. 7. Hout u niet tevreden met eenen Boeck dickwils gelesen te hebben, maer her-leest het verscheyden mael'. Gobinet, *Onderwys der jeucht* 122.

27   'maer dit slagh in 't beginsel niet heel quaedt schijnende, lockt het verstant door sijne deftige reden-eeringe, en door de soetheyt der dingen, die in deselve verhandelt worden. De sinne hier in vermaeck scheppende, wort het vuyr der onsuyvere liefde in 't herte ontsteken'. Gobinet, *Onderwys der jeucht* 124.

beautiful style and that they promote eloquence, because eloquence can be learned elsewhere as well.[28]

The challenge for the religious authors consisted in offering a viable alternative. In order to entice the youth to read sacred books, religious authors especially had to compete with secular literature. They needed to instruct their readers how to spend their time free of 'sinful' pastimes in a playful manner, without any force and with great pleasure, while at the same time, as devotional literature, they were still intended to provide religious instruction.[29]

The Christian Fortune Teller

Much in line with his teaching, Joannes David published *Wijsheyt der simpel christenen* (Wisdom of ordinary Christians) (Brussels, Rutgerus Velpius: 1593).[30] The book contained questions and answers about the main truths of the Catholic faith in a hundred distiches. David expanded this work by adding detailed comments to each couplet, and brought it onto the market as a completely new work under the title *Christeliicken Waerseggher* (Christian Fortune Teller). At Moretus's behest he also made a Latin translation *Veridicus Christianus* [Fig. 13.1]. To make the work even more attractive, David took his inspiration from his Spanish colleague Hieronymus Natalis, who in 1593 had issued his *Evangelicae Historiae Imagines* at Martinus Nutius in Antwerp. In this work of meditational texts, written at Ignatius of Loyola's request, illustrations played an important role. Each of these *imagines* consisted of a title, an illustration and a caption, which referred to the details on the engraving with capital letters as reference points. Each engraving showed multiple scenes from one story, which were identified by a letter and explained in a caption that was engraved as well.[31]

David had the Antwerp engraver Theodoor Galle make a hundred similar copper engravings on separate sheets so that they could be inserted into the *Christeliicken waerseggher* [Fig. 13.2]. To some copies was added a 'concentus musicus', a polyphonic composition for four voices on which the distiches could be sung [Fig. 13.3]. By adding music, stories and illustrations, David

---

28   Gobinet, *Onderwys der jeucht* 125.

29   Moore, *The Maidens's Mirror* 33.

30   Andriessen J., "Joannes David", in *Nationaal Biografisch Woordenboek* vol. 1 (Brussels: 1964) 379.

31   Insolera M. – Salviucci Insolera L., *La spiritualité en images aux Pays-Bas Méridionaux dans les livres imprimés des XVIe et XVIIe siècles* (Leuven: 1996) 16–18, 135–144.

FIGURE 13.1   *Title page of Joannes David,* Veridicus Christianus (*Antwerp,
Jan Moretus: 1601*). *Antwerp, Museum Plantin-Moretus, R 56.1.
Image © Author.*

Peius letiferi vitem quid pefte veneni ?
Hærefin: hanc Stygiæ nidus confouit Echidnæ.

Wat moetmen van al die meer schouwen dan de peste?
Archeyt der Ketterie; ghebroeit in Duyuels neste?

Y at il de reste / Rien de plus funeste / Que peste, ou poison?
Ouy, c'est l'Hærese / Qui a prins sa vie / Au nid du demon.

FIGURE 13.2   *Engraving by Theodoor Galle, in* Christeliicken waersegghter, de
principale stucken en t'christen geloof en leven int cort
begrijpende (*Antwerp, Jan Moerentorf: 1603), picture 6. Antwerp,
Library of the Ruusbroecgenootschap, RG 3045 I 1. Image © Author.*

FIGURE 13.3   Concentus musicus *in Joannes David*, Veridicus Christianus (*Antwerp, Jan Moretus: 1601*). *Antwerp, Museum Plantin-Moretus, R 56.1. Image © Author.*

ultimately applied all traditional techniques to make the Catechism lessons more attractive, completely corresponding with Jesuit pedagogy.

By placing the couplet as a motto above a chapter with a long meditative comment [Fig. 13.4] and by using capital letters to highlight certain details or scenes in the illustration (*pictura*) with as a caption three distiches in Latin, Dutch and French [Fig. 13.5], David gave each chapter in his *Veridicus Christianus*, as well as in the *Christeliicken Waerseggher*, the format of an emblem. With both books David laid the foundation of a new genre in the Southern Netherlands, the Jesuit emblem book, which aimed at a very broad audience and which became very popular in the course of the seventeenth century.[32]

Because the captions also contain Latin distiches, David added a 'Vermaen tot den Leser' ('a warning to the reader'), printed in civilité type, a font that young people knew from their school books. He wanted to avoid at all costs that this Latin text would deter his readers and therefore he assured them

32   See Insolera – Salviucci Insolera, *La spiritualité en images*.

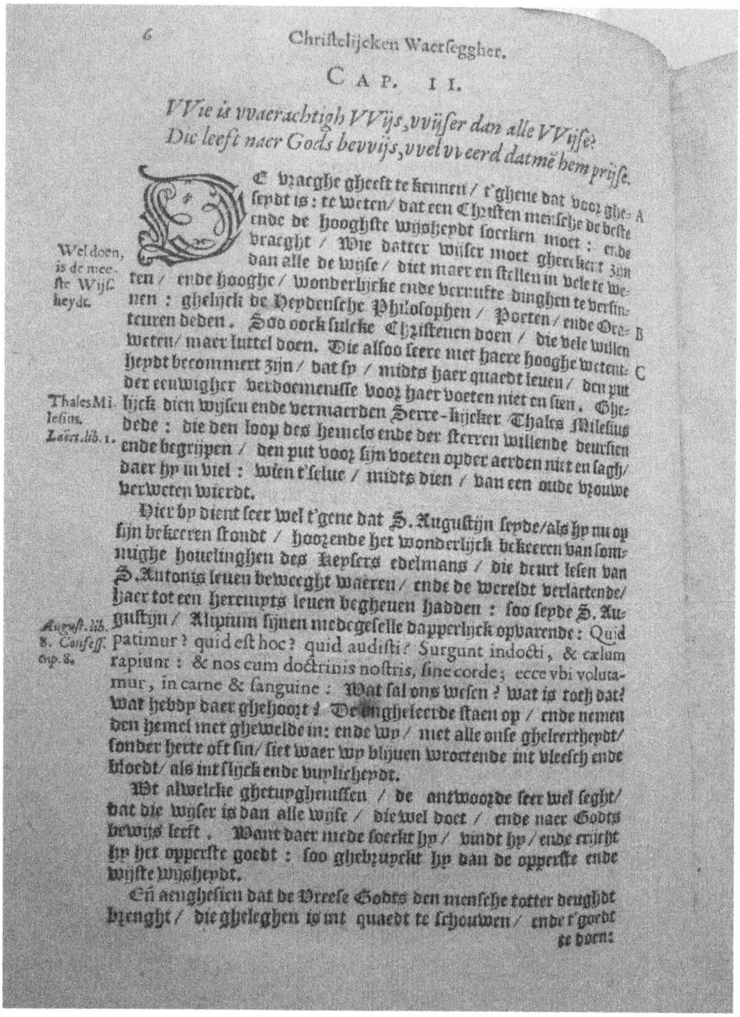
6 Christelijcken Waerseggher.

CAP. II.

VVie is vvaerachtigh VVijs, vvijser dan alle VVijse?
Die leeft naer Gods bevvijs, vvel vveerd datmẽ hem prijse.

DE vraeghe gheeft te kennen / t'ghene dat voor ghe-
seydt is: te weten / dat een Christen mensche de beste A
ende de hooghste wijsheydt soecken moet: ende
braeght / Wie datter wijser moet ghereckent zijn
Weldoen, is de meeste Wijsheyde. dan alle de wijse / dien maer en stellen in vele te weten / ende hooghe / wonderlijcke ende verrukte dinghen te versin-
nen: ghelijck de Heydensche Philosophen / Poeten / ende Ora-
teuren deden. Soo oock sulcke Christenen doen / die vele willen B
weten / maer luttel doen. Die alsoo seere met haere hooghe wetent-
heydt becommert zijn / dat sy / midts haer quaedt leuen / den put C
der eeuwigher verdoemenisse voor haer voeten niet en sien. Ghe-
Thales Milesius. Laert. lib. 1. lijck dien wijsen ende vermaerden Sterre-kijcker Thales Milesius
dede: die den loop des hemels ende der sterren willende deursien
ende begrijpen / den put voor sijn voeten opder aerden niet en sagh /
daer hy in viel: wien t'selue / midts dien / van een oude vrouwe
verweten wierdt.

Hier by dient seer wel t'gene dat S. Augustijn seyde / als hy nu op
sijn bekeeren stondt / hoorende het wonderlijck bekeeren van sommighe houelinghen des Keysers edelmans / die deurt lesen van
S. Antonis leuen beweeght waeren / ende de wereldt verlaetende /
haer tot een heremyts leuen begheuen hadden: soo seyde S. Au-
August. lib. 8. Confess. cap. 8. gustijn / Alypium sijnen medegeselle dapperlijck opvarende: Quid
patimur? quid est hoc? quid audisti? Surgunt indocti, & cælum
rapiunt: & nos cum doctrinis nostris, sine corde; ecce vbi voluta-
mur, in carne & sanguine: Wat sal ons wesen? wat is toch dat?
wat hebdy daer ghehoort? De ongheleerde staen op / ende nemen
den hemel met ghewelde in: ende wy / met alle onse gheleertheydt /
sonder herte oft sin / siet waer wy blijuen wroetende int vleesch ende
bloedt / als int slijck ende vuylicheydt.

Wt alwelcke ghetuyghenissen / de antwoorde seer wel seght /
dat die wijser is dan alle wijse / die wel doet / ende naer Godts
bewijs leeft. Want daer mede soeckt hy / vindt hy / ende crijght
hy het opperste goedt: soo ghebruyckt hy dan de opperste ende
wijste wijsheydt.

Eñ aenghesien dat de Vreese Godts den mensche totter deughdt
brenght / die gheleghen is int quaedt te schouwen / ende t'goedt
te doen:

FIGURE 13.4 *Joannes David*, Christeliicken waerseggher, de principale stucken en t'christen geloof en leven int cort begrijpende (*Antwerp, Jan Moerentorf: 1603*) *6. Antwerp, Library of the Ruusbroecgenootschap, RG 3045 I 1. Image © Author.*

FIGURE 13.5   *Engraving by Theodoor Galle*, Christeliicken waerseggher, de
principale stucken en t'christen geloof en leven int cort
begrijpende (*Antwerp, Jan Moerentorf: 1603*). *picture 2, Antwerp,
Library of the Ruusbroecgenootschap:* RG 3045 I I. *Image © Author.*

that they could use his book perfectly well without knowing Latin.[33] It was particularly important to prevent the reader from getting bored or appalling him with something so that he would not take the book in hand—or even worse—turn to secular literature. In direct competition with secular literature to win young people's attention, religious literature would almost certainly taste defeat. However, by presenting religious literature in the same format as secular literature, religious authors might be able to entice their audience to read their books.

Therefore David wanted more than just to offer Catechism lessons in printed form. The title of the *Christeliicken waerseggher* was deliberately chosen to be ambiguous, because it can refer to both a fortune-teller and to someone who speaks the truth. With this title David wanted to lure people who were

> inclined to seek advice of him, who is the vowed enemy of Christ and of the Christians: that is of the evil spirit in his wretched slavish servants and handmaids, magicians, fortune-tellers, astrologers, palmists and such demonic people.[34]

In order to preclude that the youth would not recognize the difference with pagan fortune-tellers and soothsayers, he added to the Dutch version *De schild-wacht tegen de valse waersegghers* (The sentry against the false fortune-tellers). With this book he wanted to counter some secular books which were apparently very popular, but due to their popularity, have left no preserved copies.

> Such is, among a thousand others, that unfortunate and unholy book of fortune called *T'huys der Fortuynen* [The house of fortune], which, on the one hand, offers with pleasure, to seek and find what has supposedly happened to man or has yet to happen: and on the other hand, from some precarious and deceptive signs at birth, seems to predict everyone's luck and misfortune, even boldly such events, which only God can know.[35]

---

33 David, *Christeliicken waerseggher* **2r.

34 'geneyght zijn om raedt en daedt te versoecken van hem, die de ghesworen vyandt Christi ende der Christenen is: dat is vanden boosen geest in sijn allendighe slaefsche dienaers en dienaeressen, Tooveraers, Waerseggers, Geborte-lesers, fortuyn-seggers, handbesienders, ende sulcke verduyvelde menschen'. David, *Christeliicken Waersegger* **3v.

35 'Sulck is, onder duysent andere, dien ongheluckighen ende onsalighen *Fortuyne-boeck*, die ghenaemt wordt, *T'huys der Fortuynen*. De welcke eens-deels met ghenoeghte te soecken ende te vinden geeft quantsuys wat den mensche moght over-comen zijn, oft noch te gheschieden staet: ende ten anderen, uyt eenighe onsekere ende bedrieghelijcke teeckenen der ghebuorte, elck een sijn gheluck ende ongheluck schijnt toe te segghen,

David concedes that the author of *T'huys der Fortuynen* himself warns that the predictions are unreliable, yet not convincingly enough to prevent the reader from being drawn 'to superstition, fortune-telling and such ungodly rashness'.[36] Many innocent people purchase such predictions and some people abuse these books to predict the future for curious and distraught people, under the guise of casting a horoscope:

> How could one convey dirtier, more wicked, and worse discourses than those, designated every time and everywhere in *T'huis der Fortuynen*? Presenting all villainy, flimsiness, roguery to make you ashamed and embarrassed when reading it, for all those present, since it is usually used in the company of young people.[37]

With his *Christeliicken Waerseggher* David wanted to compete with yet another 'schadelijck boecksken' ('harmful booklet'),

> that little farce booklet, called *Het spel van auonturen* [The game of adventures], which although it does not contain superstitions, or such dangers as the *Fortuyne-boeck*, and the astrology book, contains many indecent pieces, and more flimsiness, within its pages than it is great: making those who obtain it and who read or hear it, ashamed, and in their heart, name and fame damaged'.[38]

---

oock tot sulcke dinghen vermetelijck streckende, die gode alleenlijck kennelijck zijn'. David, *Christeliicken Waerseggher* 354.

36 'superstitien, valsche waerseggherije ende derghelijcke ongoddelijck vermeten'. David, *Christeliicken Waerseggher* 354.

37 'Wat moght-men vuylder, snooder, ende onghestichtigher redenen by brenghen, dan die u in t'huys der Fortuynen t'elcken keere en t'allen canten aen-ghewesen worden? Alle boeverije, alle dondeghelijckheydt, roffiaenschap, veur-houdende, oft emmers u beschaemt ende infaem maeckende in d' lesen, veur alle die daer teghenwoordigh zijn: ghelijck het ghebruyck van dien, meest onder gheselschappen, ende deur-gaens van ionghe lieden gheschiedt'. David, *Christeliicken Waerseggher* 355.

38 'dat cleyn cluchte-boecksken, ghenaemt *Het spel van auonturen*. Het welcke, al en heeft het geen superstitie, oft sulcken perijckel niet, als de Fortuyne-boeck, ende de gheboorte-boeck heeft: nochtans heeft het oock al veel oneerbaere stuckskens, ende meerder ondeghelijckheydt in d'lijf, dan t'selve groot is: den mensche die't in handen crijgt ende die 't leest, oft hoort, beschaemt maeckende, ende in sijn herte, naem en faem beschadigende'. David, *Christeliicken Waerseggher* 356.

David is likely referring to *Tboec vander auonturen ende van tijtcortinge, van versinnen* by Lorenzo Spirito Gualtieri, which was published in the last decade of the sixteenth century by Jan van Waesberghe in Rotterdam.[39]

To make his book even more attractive, David introduced a 'rolle oft keerspel' ('a wheel or game of chance').[40] This 'Rolle der Devgdsaemheydt [Wheel of Virtuousness], serving to imitate Christ in the *Christeliicken Waerseggher* with a rejection of all kinds of superstitious and ungodly attractions',[41] is actually a lottery game with a revolving disk. The wheel is attached with a piece of string through the centre point of the circle at the back of the page [Fig. 13.6]. Four small windows have been cut into the disk, each dedicated to one of the four Gospel writers. If one turns the wheel behind each of the four windows a different number appears [Fig. 13.7]. The reader picks a number at random and looks on the next pages, where he will find a numbered list with one hundred sayings. He chooses the motto with his number and that one in turn refers to one of the hundred chapters that can be studied. David states that he has tactically included this game element to counter the popular astrological work *T'huys der fortuynen*, which was equipped with a similar disk:

> Because the meaning and the intention of such a find is, to bring those who like it, by means of such a good and joyful device, to reading with pleasure a few chapters at random.[42]

Unlike the astrological works, David does not want

> to hint at any past, present, or future secret, luck or misfortune or something similar that might concern the reader or to predict something to him, in no way: but only, as a result of such a searching, finding and

---

39   *Short Title Catalogue Netherlands* (STCN). It was reprinted in Dutch in 1650, 1656 and 1661 (STCN). The first edition in Italy appeared in Perugia in 1482 under the title *Il libro delle sorte*. Arbizzoni G., 'Lorenzo Gualtieri', *Dizionario degli Italiani* vol. 60 (2003) (http://www .treccani.it/enciclopedia/lorenzo-gualtieri_(Dizionario-Biografico) [24/9/2012].

40   David, *Christeliicken Waerseggher* 353.

41   'Rolle der Devgdsaemheydt: Tot naer-volginghe Christi op den Christelijcken Waerseggher dienende Met een verworpinghe van alderley superstiteuse ende ongoddelijcke vermaeckelijcheydt'. David, *Christeliicken Waerseggher* 353.

42   'Want de meyninghe ende veur-nemen van dusdanighen vondt is, opdat de gene die 't belieft, deur sulcken goeden ende heughelijcken middel, tot het lesen van d'een Capittel oft d'ander soo 't vallen sal met ghenoeghte te brenghen'. David, *Christeliicken Waerseggher* 353.

FIGURE 13.6   *Joannes David*, Veridicus Christianus (*Antwerp, Jan Moretus: 1601*).
Antwerp, Museum Plantin-Moretus, R 56.1. Image © Author.

FIGURE 13.7   *Joannes David*, Veridicus Christianus (*Antwerp, Jan Moretus: 1601*).
              Antwerp, Museum Plantin-Moretus, R 56.1. Image © Author.

reading, to get any good sentiment, and to be touched in the experience of his name and calling, to become a better Christian and a more perfect follower of Christ.[43]

Tolle, Lege

The Jesuit Joannes David had to justify to his colleagues and superiors that a book playing with fortune still fitted in with religious lessons. He recommends to those who feel depressed or who need advice to take a good book and to open it to an indiscriminate page:

> Who could scorn that someone, being in moodiness, gloom or tempta-tion, or also having any profound feeling, for taking a good book, opening it at the first indiscriminate page, reading where his eye falls and finding therein a cause for good comfort, consideration, repentance, enlighten-ment, and an improvement of his virtues?[44]

David further illustrates this with the conversion of St Augustine, who heard a voice crying, ' "tolle, lege: tolle, lege": which was ordered by God, to make him open a book and read the first chapter he set his eyes on'.[45] David cites other examples where the text which is seen if the Bible is opened to a random page can be considered an indication from God. A first example David retrieves from *Luke* 4:16–21, where Jesus opens a scroll in the synagogue of Nazareth

---

43   'eenighe veur-ledene, teghenwoordighe, oft toecommende verholentheydt, gheluck, oft ongheluck oft iet des-ghelijcks dat hem oft ander aengaet, te kennen te gheven, oft uyt sulcks hem iet op te segghen: in gheender manieren: maer alleenlijck om, om uyt oorsaeck van sulcken soecken, vinden ende lesen, eenigh goedt beweghen te crijghen, ende gheroert te worden om in het beleven sijns naems ende roeps, als christen noch meer aen te nemen, ende volcomer naevolgher Christi te worden'. David, *Christeliicken Waerseggher* 357.

44   'Wie soude oock connen mis-prijsen, dat iemandt, oft in swaermoedigheydt, mistroostigheydt, ende tentatie: oft oock tot eenigh goedt innigh beweghen, eenighen goeden boeck name, end dien open doende, soo 't eerst valt, sagh wat hem daer eerst veur al vertoont: ende dat hy t'selfde lesende, een oorsaecke name, van goeden troost, beraedsaemheydt, inkeer, verlichtinghe, ende beter aen-nemen in deughden?'. David, *Christeliicken Waerseggher* 359.

45   'van Godts-weghe bevolen wierdt, dat hy den boek op doen soude, end het eerste capittel lesen, d'welck hem ter handt soude comen'. David, *Christeliicken Waerseggher* 360.

of the Prophet Isaiah and reads the words which confirm his divine mission.[46] In a second example he shows how the opposition against the appointment of St Martin as Bishop of Tours was silenced by an occasional preacher who happened to open the Bible to an appropriate passage of the eighth psalm, which indicated that God indeed wanted to see St Martin as bishop.[47] A third example comes from the life of the emperor Heraclius, who was in Albania with his army in 622 and decided to overwinter there. Opening the Bible, he came across the words of Paul in the first Epistle to the *Corinthians* 16:5–6, in which Paul says that he will spend the winter with them. From Gregory of Tours, David derived three more examples of 'considered decisions, inspired by opening Holy books'.[48]

To justify the wheel, David gives yet another example, this time of the Egyptian King Sesostris, to whom a prisoner pointed out the turning of the wheels of his chariot, which made him reminisce about the wheel of fortune and brought him to the insight that his power was very temporary.[49] David comes to the conclusion that:

> Now that all these arguments and examples have proven it, I will show with more grace that it is not only a permitted practice, but also useful and praiseworthy to bring man to reading an example that can help him. And to that end, also with honourable and pious entertainment, I intro- duce the use of such a wheel [...] which I with good reason have called the ROLLE DER DEVGHTSAEMHEYDT [wheel of virtuousness]: because it is an instrument to promote virtue.[50]

---

46   David, *Christeliicken Waerseggher* 366.

47   David, *Christeliicken Waerseggher* 367.

48   'van beraedsamigh onder-soeck, deur het open-doen der H. boecken'. David, *Christeliicken Waerseggher* 368.

49   David, *Christeliicken Waerseggher* 370.

50   'Alle dese redenen ende exemplen dus nu bewesen hebbent sal ick met meerder bevalligheydt toonen en goedt-doen, dattet niet alleen een gheoorloofde practijcke is, maer oock nuttelijck ende prijsbaer, met eenen sekeren goeden vondt den mensche tot het lesen te brenghen, van een saecke die hem helpen mogbt. Ende daer toe, oock met eerlijcke ende godtvruchtighe vermaeckelijckheydt, het ghebruyck van sulck een rolleken veur te houden [...] Twelck ick met reden de ROLLE DER DEVGHTSAEMHEYDT: heb willen noemen, om dattet een middel is tot s'deughds vermeerderen ghevonden'. David, *Christeliicken Waerseggher* 371.

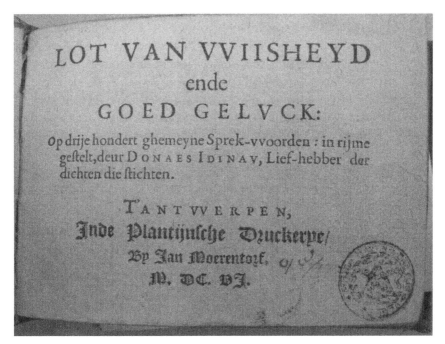

FIGURE 13.8   *Title page of Donaes Idinav, Lot van wiisheyd ende goed geluck, op drije hondert ghemeyne sprek-woorden (Antwerp, Jan Moerentorf: 1606). Antwerp, Museum Plantin-Moretus, R 6.30. Image © Author.*

Playing with Proverbs

In 1606 David went a step further to entice his readership. In that year, Jan Moerentorf, better known as Moretus, published *Lot van vviisheyd ende goed Gelvck: Op drije hondert ghemeyne Sprek-vvoorden* (Lot of Wisdom and good luck on three hundred common proverbs) by Donaes Idinav [Fig. 13.8].[51] Probably to prevent readers who already knew David's name from his *Christeliicken Waerseggher* and other religious works from identifying this work immediately as a religious booklet, he put 'Donaes Idinav', an anagram of his name, with the epithet 'liefhebber der dichten die stichten' ('lover of edifying poems') on the title page. But he did not mention that he was a Jesuit. The booklet contains three hundred common proverbs with moralizing explanations in verse. Every page contains one saying, each with a moralistic comment in a five-line poem. According to David, common knowledge of the proverbs

---

51   Meeus H., "Loterijen en literatuur in de Nederlanden (16e en 17e eeuw)", in *Geschiedenis van de loterijen in de Zuidelijke Nederlanden* (Brussels: 1994) 105–136, here 120–123.

had been lost so that they were often interpreted in a wrong and sometimes even indecent way. In this book, David not only wanted to give 'den rechten sin' ('the correct meaning') but 'oock eenighe morale of manierlijcke bediedinghen' ('also some moral and decent comments').[52] The small booklet in sextodecimo oblong format fitted in with the series of small books for lovers, which also included song books. The genre is based on the so-called 'lot- en steekboekjes' ('lot and stitch booklets'), which originally served as farce booklets for profane entertainment.

Just like the amorous stitch booklets, this booklet was intended for entertainment among company. With the amorous booklets, lovers had to stick in a pin to choose the page where to open the book. When it was opened one would see a poem for the man on one page, and one for the woman on the facing page. David's booklet also aims at couples, as David has

> put it in rhyme for the pleasure of the readers, alternately the first serving the men, and the second the women, however it may also be read jointly from whatever page may be opened.[53]

The verso pages were thus intended for the man, the rectos for the woman. In a preliminary poem David clearly explains how to use the book.[54] One can, however, use the booklet alone as well as among company, and just read the text on the open page. Each proverb puts forward a moral lesson, countering the verses in their secular counterparts which usually formulated an amorous or comical comment. The intention here is again to keep the readers away from the profane versions:

> All the more hoping that for this reason, some other old farce-booklets will be left aside, which with attractive entertainment of rhymes and farcical anecdotes, sometimes tend to stir up much indecency in the reader's heart.[55]

---

52   Idinav Donaes, *Lot van wiisheyd ende goed geluck, op drije hondert ghemeyne sprekwoorden* (Antwerp: Jan Moerentorf, [1606]) A2v.

53   'dit soo in rijme ghestelt, tot des lesers meerder verlustinghe, altijdts over handt, het eerste soo de mans dienende, ende het tweede de vrauwen, dattet nochtans al oock in t'ghemeyne magh ghenomen worden, so het vallen sal, in het open doen van het boecksken, waer het zy'. Idinav, *Lot van wiisheyd* A2v–A3r).

54   Idinav, *Lot van wiisheyd* A4r.

55   'Te meer hopende datmen deur dese oorsaeke, eenighe andere oude ghelijcke kluchtboecskens verlaten sal, die met een aenlockende vermaekelijckheydt van rijmen ende

Sing-along Songs

Pre-eminently suitable books to use in a group were religious song books. Some assume that the songs were more read than sung.[56] However, there are a number of songs that became very popular and remained so as sing-alongs.[57]

The Jesuit Delvigne also devoted a chapter to 'inappropriate songs, and evil books'.[58] Parents had to ensure that their children heard 'no impure or indecent songs, and even more, that they did not sing them'.[59] Just as was already the case with the *Souterliedekens* in the sixteenth century, the goal was replacing profane songs with religious ones. According to Petrus Maillart, the songs in *Den gheestelijcken Nachtegael* (The sacred nightingale) should serve as an

> antidote, particularly for the youth, who get to hear the loveliness of the secular songs (which are increasingly offered now, with so much diversity, hiding the venom that lurks under them) bewitching the senses, filling the heart with vanity, and often distracting the soul from the highest good.[60]

Het prieel der gheestelijcke melodie (The arbour of sacred melodies), compiled by some Jesuits led by Bernard Bauhuysen, also made this their aim:

> It is known, that just as the secular and indecent poems or songs are very annoying for the people, in the same way the pious and edifying songs are blessed, useful and beneficial. Not only because the pious keep away the useless for the most part, being a great advantage and invaluable,

---

kluchtighe kodden, den leser somtijdts veel oneerbaerheydts pleghen in t'herte te schieten'. Idinav, *Lot van wiisheyd* A3 r.

56   Porteman K. – Huybens G., "Het Zuidnederlands geestelijk lied in de 17de eeuw. Een vergeten bladzijde uit de Nederlandse literatuur en muziekgeschiedenis", *Belgisch Tijdschrift voor Muziekwetenschap* 32–33 (1978–1979) 21–142, here 122.

57   Therry, *De religieuze beleving* 19.

58   'ongeschickte Liedekens, en quade boecken'. Delvigne, *Christelycke opvoedinge* 69.

59   'geen onsuyvere oft lichtveerdige Liedekens en hooren, en noch meer, dat sy die niet en singen'. Delvigne, *Christelycke opvoedinge* 69).

60   'Antidotum, specialijc voor de Jonckheyt, wien de liefelijcheyt van de weerlijcke liedekens (die nu met soo veel verscheydentheyt, hoe langer hoe meer, haer wert aengeboden, bedeckende het fenijn datter onder schuylt) door 'tgehoor ontfangen, de zinnen betoovert, therte met ydelheyt vervult ende dickmael de siele afleydt van het hoochste goet'. Maillart Petrus, *Den Gheestelijcken nachtegael* (Antwerp, Ian Cnobbert: 1634) +5v–6r; Demarré I., *Het katholieke volksliedboek in Zuid-Nederland in de eerste helft van de 17de eeuw* (Leuven: 1962) 29.

because of their pernicious influence on the soul, which usually happens when singing such songs, [...] but also because of the good lessons which they contain.[61]

By singing sacred texts to the melodies of profane songs, the original secular words will soon be forgotten. Religious authors were very pragmatic and they realized that it would not be wise to also try to suppress the secular melodies.

And although some fit on melodies that were before used for secular songs, we have not found it wise to omit them, lest those who love such melodies very much (since they are sometimes very pleasant and charming) would not like to give them up: but one could also sing them with pious words: from which will follow that people will slowly abandon these indecent words, and that eventually they will be forgotten forever: something for which otherwise because of the loveliness of the melody could never have been hoped.[62]

The preface of *Het prieel der gheestelijcke melodie* indicates where and when the sacred songs can be used profitably:

This you may sing early in the morning, late in the evening, on the street and at home, at school, at your work, out in the fields, travelling, and walking. Yes even in church during the Catechism lessons, whereby you'll sing these sacred devotional hymns.[63]

---

61   'het is kennelick, dat ghelijck de wereltlicke ende oncuyssche ghedichten oft liedekens seer hinderlick zijn de menschen, alsoo de godtvruchtighe ende ghestichtighe zijn zeer salich, nut ende profijtelick. Niet alleen omdat de godtvruchtighe de onnutte groots deels pleghen te weiren, het welck een groote baete is, ende onweerdeerlick om den grooten Sielmoort, die ghemeynlick gheschiet int singen van dusdanighe Liedekens [...] maer oock om die goede leeringhe die sy zijn besluytende'. Bauhusius, *Het prieel* +2r.

62   'Ende hoe wel de sommighe gaen op thoonen die eertijts gheschict waren tot weerelicke liedekens, nochtans hebben wy goet ghevonden de selve niet achter te laten, op dat de ghene die op sulcken thoonen seer ghesint sijn (als, die somtijts seer playsant ende lieflijck zijn) ende over sulcx en souden de selve niet gheeren laten: oock goede godtvruchtighe woorden souden moghen singhen: waer wt volghen sal dat de menschen allenskens dese oneerlijcke woorden sullen laten varen, ende dat de selve in een eewige vergetenesse zullen comen: het welck anders om de lieflicheyt der voysen nimmermeer en waere te verhopen'. Bauhusius, *Het prieel* +2v–+3r.

63   'dese sult ghy moghen singhen smorgens vroech, s'avonts late, op strate, [...] Ja oock in de kercke, als den Catechismus gheschiet, onder den welcken ghylieden dese ende

Religious authors did not only want to replace the secular songs, they also presented their song books under titles which sounded very much like those of secular song books. In the beginning of the seventeenth century song books had a clear but pretty neutral designation, but later in the century their titles referred more to a *locus amoenus*, just like secular song books: *Gheestelijcke dreve* (The sacred alley; 1608), *Het prieel der gheestelijcke melodie* (The arbour of sacred melody; 1614), *Het paradijs der gheestelijcker vreughden* (The paradise of sacred pleasures; 1617), *Den berch der gheestelijcker vreughden* (The mountain of sacred pleasures; 1618), *Gheesteliick paradiisken der wellusticheden* (Sacred little paradise of good pleasures; 1619), *Den lusthof der christelijcke leeringhe* (The garden of pleasure of Christian learning; 1622), and *Het paradys der gheestelijcke ende kerckelijcke lofsangen* (The paradise of sacred and ecclesiastical hymns; 1631). From the 1630s onwards it is striking how many birds appear in the titles: *Den gheestelijcken Nachtegael* (The sacred nightingale; 1634), *Hemelsch nachtegaelken* (Heavenly little nightingale; 1639), *Den gheestelycken leeuwercker* (The sacred lark; 1645), *De gheestelijcke tortelduyve* (The sacred turtledove; 1648), *Den singhende Swaen* (The singing Swan; 1655), *Den lieffelycken paradysvogel* (1670) (The lovely bird of paradise; 1670), *Den seraphynschen nachtegael* (The seraphic nightingale; 1684), and *Het eensaem tortelduyfken* (The lonely little turtledove; 1694).[64]

The female author of *Triumphus Iesu oft godliicke lofsangen* (Antwerp, Geeraerdt van Wolsschaten: 1633) already mentions on the title page that she has the intention of wiping out all fabulous and indecent profane poems. In the dedication to Johannes Malderus, Bishop of Antwerp she states that 'by *Triumphus Iesu* all other fabulous triumphs, indecent songs, and secular poems will be darkened'.[65] And in doing so she very likely had in mind the *Triumphus Cupidinis* by Joan Ysermans, published in Antwerp in 1628.

Guilielmus Bolognino went a step further in practicing literature in the company of others. In 1641 he had the children of the parish of Saint George in Antwerp stage the life of Saint Dorothea, a play containing 'verscheyde Gheestelijcke Liedekens' [several sacred songs].[66] Already in 1640 he had

---

     dierghelijcke gheestelijcke, deuote lofsanghen sult singhen'. Bauhusius, *Het prieel* +5v.; Demarré, *Het katholieke volksliedboek* 27.

64   Huybens G., *Thesaurus canticorum Flandrensium. Het gedrukte Nederlandse liedboek in Vlaanderen (1508–1800)*, Miscellanea Neerlandica 30 (Leuven: 2004).

65   'dat door *Triumphus Iesu* alle andere fabuleuse, *Triumphen*, lichtveerdige liedekens, weirelijcke dichten moghen verduystert worden'. *Triumphus Iesu oft godliicke lofsangen* (Antwerp, Geeraerdt van Wolsschaten: 1633) A3v.

66   Bolognino G., *Dorothea Maeghet ende Marteleresse* (Antwerpen, Jacob Mesens: 1641) A1r.

written *De Ghenoechsaemheyt van Godt, ende de onghenoechsaemheyt vande Werelt, Speel-wijs verthoont in den H. Lavrentius Ivstinianus Patriarch van Venetien* (The satisfaction of God and the dissatisfaction of the world, shown by means of a play about St. Ivstinian Lavrentius Patriarch of Venice) and performed it with the children of the Catechism lessons. In the dedication to the Bishop of Antwerp Gaspar Nemius, he explains that he has written and performed this play

> to impress the lessons more explicitly and more profoundly upon the pupils' hearts. But because living voices, and the performance of the matter are easily forgotten, he therefore thought it well to publish this play performed by children so that the divine wisdom shown in Laurentius Iustinianus, would to everyone who reads it, reveal and offer the same lessons, even nowadays.[67]

In this way, Bolognino could teach his pupils with drama, songs and reading.

Conclusion

It is clear that reading good books to maintain the knowledge of religious truths was a priority in the Roman Catholic Church. One was equally aware of the difficult task of competing with profane literature, particularly for a specific target group like adolescents. A number of Catholic religious authors from the seventeenth century demonstrated creativity and willingness to adapt. When the English historian Geoffrey Parker came to the conclusion that the Catholic Church was quite successful compared with the Reformation, he attributed that to the willingness of the Catholics to compromise with traditional religious customs, to make full use of all available media and to simplify the Christian faith for the benefit of its congregation.[68] In the Southern Low

---

67   'om de voorghemelde leeringe te uytdruckelijcker en te dieper in de jonge herten te printen. Maer om dat de levende stemme, ende de uytbeldinge van de saecke, lichtelijck wederom vergeten wort, daerom heeft my goet ghedocht dat Kinder-Spel in druck uyt te gheven, op dat de Goddelijcke wysheyt, in Laurentius Iustinianus, soude aen een ieder, die het sal lesen, de selve leeringhe noch hedensdaeghs sal openbaeren ende aendienen'. Bolognino Guilielmus, *De Ghenoechsaemheyt van Godt, ende de onghenoechsaemheyt vande Werelt* (Antwerp, Jacob Mesens: 1640) A2v.

68   Parker G., "Success and Failure during the First Century of the Reformation", *Past and Present* 136 (1992) 43–82, here 73–75.

Countries the religious authors in the Catholic Church clearly adopted these attitudes. To entice young people to read religious books in order to continue repeating the lessons of the Catechism, they clearly made no bones about cloaking their sacred message in a profane dress.

Bibliography

Andriessen J., "Joannes David", in *Nationaal Biografisch Woordenboek* vol I (Brussels: 1964) 377–383.

Averoult Antoine d', *Fleurs des exemples, ou: Catéchisme historial, contenant plusieurs beaux miracles et excellents discours, tirez tant de l'Escriture Sainte, que les Saints Pères et anciens Docteurs de l'Église* (Rouen: Jean Osmont, 1616).

Backer A. de – Sommervogel C., *Bibliothèque de la Compagnie de Jésus* (Heverlee – Leuven: 1960; reprint of the edition Brussels: 1853–1861).

Bauhusius Bernardus, *Het prieel der gheestelijcke melodie* (Bruges, Pieter Soetaert: 1609).

Bibliotheca Belgica. Bibliographie générale des Pays-Bas, ed. M.-Th. Lenger (Brussels: 1979).

Bolognino Guilielmus, *De Ghenoechsaemheyt van Godt, ende de onghenoechsaemheyt vande Werelt* (Antwerp, Jacob Mesens: 1640).

———, *Dorothea Maeghet ende Marteleresse* (Antwerp, Jacob Mesens: 1641).

David Joannes, *Christeliicken waerseg’gher, de principale stucken en t’christen geloof en leven int cort begrijpende. Met een rolle der deugtsaemheyt daer op dienende. Ende een schildt-wacht teghen de valsche waersegghers, tooveraers, etc.* (Antwerp, Jan Moerentorf: 1603).

Delvigne Joannes, *Christelycke opvoedinge, dienende soo voor de ouders, meesters, meesterssen, etc. als voor de kinderen, op-gedragen voor een nieuw-jaer aen de Sodaliteyt der getrouwde, onder den tytel vande Boodtschap vande Alderheylighste Maghet Maria, in ’t professie-huys der Sociëteyt Jesu* (Antwerp, Widow of Hieronymus Verdussen: [c. 1743]).

Demarré I., *Het katholieke volksliedboek in Zuid-Nederland in de eerste helft van de 17de eeuw* (Leuven: 1962).

Dictionnaire de spiritualité ascétique et mystique: doctrine et histoire, ed. Viller M. et al. (Paris: 1933–1995).

Gobinet Carel, *Onderwys der jeucht in de christelyke godtvruchtigheyt, ghetrocken uyt de H. Schriftuere en HH. Vaders* (Antwerp [=Amsterdam], Joannes Stichter: 1697).

Henrivaux O., "Méthodes catéchistiques aux XVIe–XVIIIe siècles dans les diocèses de Cambrai, Namur, Tournai et Liège", *Lumen vitae* 36 (1981) 57–97.

Huybens G., *Thesaurus canticorum Flandrensium. Het gedrukte Nederlandse liedboek in Vlaanderen (1508–1800)*, Miscellanea Neerlandica 30 (Leuven: 2004).

Idinav Donaes, *Lot van wiisheyd ende goed geluck, op drije hondert ghemeyne sprek-woorden* (Antwerp, Jan Moerentorf: [1606]).

Insolera, M. – Salviucci Insolera, L. *La spiritualité en images aux Pays-Bas Méridionaux dans les livres imprimés des XVIᵉ et XVIIᵉ siècles* (Leuven: 1996).

Maillart Petrus, *Den Gheestelijcken nachtegael* (Antwerp, Ian Cnobbert: 1634).

Marnix de Sainte Aldegonde Philippe de, *Traité d'éducation de la jeunesse*, ed. J. Catrysse (Brussels: 1959).

Meeus H., "Loterijen en Literatuur in de Nederlanden (16de en 17de eeuw)", in *Geschiedenis van de loterijen in de Zuidelijke Nederlanden (15de eeuw tot 1934)* (Brussels: 1994) 105–136.

Moore C.N., *The Maidens's Mirror. Reading Material for German Girls in the Sixteenth and Seventeenth Centuries*, Wolfenbütteler Forschungen 36 (Wiesbaden: 1987).

Parker G., "Success and Failure during the First Century of the Reformation", *Past and Present* 136 (1992) 43–82.

Porteman K. – Huybens G., "Het Zuidnederlands geestelijk lied in de 17de eeuw. Een vergeten bladzijde uit de Nederlandse literatuur en muziekgeschiedenis", *Belgisch Tijdschrift voor Muziekwetenschap* 32–33 (1978–1979) 21–142.

Put E., *De cleijne schoolen. Het volksonderwijs in het hertogdom Brabant tussen Katholieke Reformatie en Verlichting (eind 16de eeuw–1795)* (Leuven: 1990).

The Ratio studiorum. The official plan for Jesuit education, trans. and annot. C. Pavur, S.J., Jesuit primary sources in English translation, Series 1, no 22 (Saint Louis, MO: 2005).

Ratio studiorum: plan raisonné et institution des études dans la Compagnie de Jésus, eds. A. Demoustier – J. Dominique et al. (Paris: 1997).

Roey E. van, "L'enseignement du catéchisme dans les anciens diocèses de Malines et d'Anvers", *La vie diocésaine* 5 (1911) 157–172, 217–232.

Strauss G., *Luther's House of Learning. Indoctrination of the Young in the German Reformation* (Baltimore – London: 1978).

Synodicon Belgicum, sive: Acta omnium Ecclesiarum Belgii a Concilio Tridentino usque ad Concordantum anni 1801, III: Nova et Absoluta collectio Synodorum episcopatus Antverpiensis, ed. P.F.X. de Ram (Leuven: 1858).

Therry M., *De religieuze beleving bij de leken in het 17de-eeuwse bisdom Brugge* (Brussels: 1988).

Triumphus Iesu oft godliicke lofsangen (Antwerp, Geeraerdt van Wolsschaten: 1633).

Index Nominum

Lightning Source UK Ltd.
Milton Keynes UK
UKOW06f0958021015

259676UK00001B/30/P